Austrian Economics in Transition

From Carl Menger to Friedrich Hayek

Edited by

Harald Hagemann

Tamotsu Nishizawa

and

Yukihiro Ikeda

palgrave
macmillan

First published 2010 by
PALGRAVE MACMILLAN

Palgrave Macmillan in the UK is an imprint of Macmillan Publishers Limited, registered in England, company number 785998, of Houndmills, Basingstoke, Hampshire RG21 6XS.

Palgrave Macmillan in the US is a division of St Martin's Press LLC, 175 Fifth Avenue, New York, NY 10010.

Palgrave Macmillan is the global academic imprint of the above companies and has companies and representatives throughout the world.

Palgrave® and Macmillan® are registered trademarks in the United States, the United Kingdom, Europe and other countries.

ISBN-13: 978–0–230–22226–7 hardback

This book is printed on paper suitable for recycling and made from fully managed and sustained forest sources. Logging, pulping and manufacturing processes are expected to conform to the environmental regulations of the country of origin.

A catalogue record for this book is available from the British Library.

Library of Congress Cataloging-in-Publication Data
Austrian economics in transition : from Carl Menger to Friedrich Hayek / edited by Harald Hagemann, Tamotsu Nishizawa, Yukihiro Ikeda.
p. cm.
ISBN 978–0–230–22226–7
1. Austrian school of economics. I. Hagemann, Harald, 1947– II. Nishizawa, Tamotsu, 1950– III. Ikeda, Yukihiro, 1959–
HB98.A973 2010
330.15′7—dc22 2010010803

10 9 8 7 6 5 4 3 2 1
19 18 17 16 15 14 13 12 11 10

Printed and bound in Great Britain by
CPI Antony Rowe, Chippenham and Eastbourne

Contents

List of Figures and Table

Figures

Table

Introduction

This book investigates both consistent and changing elements in the Austrian School of Economics since its foundation in the late nineteenth century up to the off-springs of this School at the end of World War II. The Austrian School of Economics has experienced various phases of transition when the flourishing place of this school, the city of Vienna and Austria in general, saw drastic changes in politics and in the economy, leading to the emigration of the leading members of the School in the 1930s. Representative examples are Friedrich August Hayek, Ludwig von Mises, Fritz Machlup, Gottfried Haberler and Oskar Morgenstern. We investigate the dynamic metamorphosis of the school, mainly with reference to its contact with other ideas and representatives of history of economic thought.

Part 1 begins with Carl Menger, the founder of the Austrian School of Economics. First, Yukihiro Ikeda investigates the economic liberalism of Carl Menger. Although later Austrians are known to be radical supporters of economic liberalism, it is an open question whether the founder of the School shared the same kind of radicalism. Using various materials, his published works as well as his unpublished papers now located at Duke University, Ikeda tries to tackle this riddle in the earlier phase of the development of the Austrian School of Economics. In the following paper, Kiichiro Yagi deals with Menger's methodological turn soon after the publication of the *Principles* (1871). The *Investigation* (1883), in which the 'principle of efficiency' determinates economic process in the idealized world, was only the middle point of his quest for the rational economic man. Menger was not content with the idealized world. He was interested in the economic action in the indeterminate world. Yagi also mentions Schmoller's review article and its influence on Menger in this context.

Part 2 deals with the German Historical School, which is often thought of as diametrically opposed to the Austrian School, particularly due to Schmoller's dispute on method with Menger. However, reality has been more diverse. In the first chapter of Part 2, Jun Kobayashi deals with 'substantial rationality' and 'formal rationality', two concepts playing important roles in Max Weber's methodological argument.

This is followed by Keith Tribe's contribution in which he shows that Weber was not only familiar with contemporary economic thinking in the 1890s, but that he had a special indebtedness to 'Austrian Economics'. According to Tribe, there was a lengthy process of reception reaching from the 1870s to the 1920s during which a 'new economics' became increasingly accepted, but without displacing historical or institutionalist economics. Finally, Tamotsu Nishizawa traces how German and Austrian ideas on economic theory and economic sociology exerted influence in Japan through the work of Ichiro Nakayama who had studied with Schumpeter at the University of Bonn in the late 1920s.

Part 3 consists of three contributions by Arena, Cangiani and Milford on the methodological problems of the Austrian School of Economics, with special attention to Menger. First, Richard Arena scrutinizes a transition of methodology from Menger to Wieser, the successor of the chair. In particular, Arena focuses on some aspects of Wieser's economic and social theory which are often ignored when his contributions on methodological individualism, power and institutions are discussed. Thus, Arena emphasizes that Wieser is more Wicksellian than Walrasian, and argues that in his analysis of money and credit Wieser in important aspects has anticipated Keynes's finance motive although no elaborated speculative motive exists in his theory. Next Michele Cangiani investigates the motives and results of Menger's revision of his 1871 book, by comparison with the posthumous edition of 1923. As the title indicates, a starting-point of the chapter is Polanyi's work and its relationship with Menger's new statements in the 1923 version of the *Principles*. Finally, Karl Milford, in analyzing Menger's problem situation, challenges the standard interpretation of Menger defending an Aristotelian essentialist position as counterintuitive, and instead emphasizes Menger's non- or even anti-essentialist approach to economics. Milford convincingly shows that Menger's methodological individualism conflicts with an essentialist approach to economics.

Due to the political developments of the 1930s most Austrian economists had to leave Austria and exerted a major influence in the hosting countries, particularly in the United States. Part 4 deals with this 'Dissemination of the Austrian School of Economics'. First, Harald Hagemann discusses the developments at the University of Vienna and the political developments which caused an enormous emigration of Austrian economists. He then gives a bird's eye view of important contributions of Austrian economists in the interwar period. Next, Arash Molavi Vasséi gives a thorough interpretation of Ludwig von Mises's approach with which the Austrian theory of business cycles takes its starting point. Then Hansjoerg Klausinger presents Hayek as a leading international researcher of business cycle theory, which had been the main economic issue in the interwar period. Klausinger also points at Hayek's odd position as the Director of an Institute mainly dedicated to the task of empirical research on business cycles, relevant to business people, to which he had severe reservations. Finally, Chikako Nakayama focuses on Oskar Morgenstern in her analysis of the impact and the experiences of emigrated Austrian economists in the United States. Morgenstern's discussions with Frank Knight can be seen as part of the dissemination of the Austrian School, but also as a new impact coming from outside.

The book is concluded by Part 5. First, Kurt Leube, deeply involved with the Austrian tradition, informs us about the concept of '*Verstehen*' and related methodological problems with special attention to Menger and Hayek. By examining Hayek's *Sensory Order*, Susumu Egashira links Hayek's psychological argument to modern economics. Egashira argues that the Hayekian perspective might lead to a new paradigm in microeconomics. In dealing with the so-called 'Transformation Problem' of Hayek, Makoto Nishibe claims that Hayek drastically transformed his vision of the market in the 1930s and that there should be another dividing line between 1945 and 1946. Lastly, Tsutomu Hashimoto tries to answer the following questions: How did Mises and Hayek succeed Menger's methodological principles? How did they transform or reform them?

All in all, the chapters shed some light on the new developments and find fruitful contributions of the Austrian School to the evolution of economics in an international perspective. At the same time, we try to answer the ambitious question of whether there can be a School of Economics in the definite sense of the word. Indeed this is a problem with which Schumpeter was seriously involved with when he wrote his *History of Economic Analysis*.

The volume originated from the conference 'Carl Menger and the Historical Aspects of Liberalism' held at Hitotsubashi University, 17–19 December, 2004, organized by the Center for Historical Social Science Literature at Hitotsubashi University.

Some of the chapters in the volume were papers read at the above conference, but have been revised in many ways considering responses from the participants. Furthermore, we have extended the scope of the volume by inviting other contributions by colleagues who are experts in the field. We are grateful to Hitotsubashi University for their generous financial support, without which the conference would not have been made possible. Particular thanks go to Professor Koichi Yamazaki, who organized the conference. Finally, we would like to thank Niels Geiger and Johannes Schwarzer for their support in adapting the manuscript to the publisher's guidelines and in preparing the index.

List of Contributors

Richard Arena, University of Nice-Sophia Antipolis and GREDEG-CNRS, France

Michele Cangiani, University of Venice, Italy

Susumu Egashira, Otaru University of Commerce, Sapporo, Japan

Harald Hagemann, University of Hohenheim, Stuttgart, Germany

Tsutomu Hashimoto, Hokkaido University, Sapporo, Japan

Yukihiro Ikeda, Keio University, Tokyo, Japan

Hansjoerg Klausinger, Vienna University of Economics and Business Administration, Austria

Jun Kobayashi, Rikkyo University, Tokyo, Japan

Kurt R. Leube, Hoover Institution, Stanford University, United States

Karl Milford, University of Vienna, Austria

Chikako Nakayama, Tokyo University of Foreign Studies, Japan

Makoto Nishibe, Hokkaido University, Sapporo, Japan

Tamotsu Nishizawa, Hitotsubashi University, Tokyo, Japan

Keith Tribe, Centre for Intellectual History University of Sussex, Brighton, United Kingdom

Arash Molavi Vasséi, University of Hohenheim, Stuttgart, Germany

Kiichiro Yagi, University of Kyoto, Japan

Part I

Carl Menger: Towards a New Image of the Founder

1
Carl Menger's Liberalism Revisited

Yukihiro Ikeda

1. Menger's liberalism: A myth?

Was Carl Menger a radical supporter of economic liberalism like the later members of the Austrian School of Economics? This is still an open question, even among scholars deeply involved with the study of the Austrian School in general and Menger in particular. There are good reasons for this: Menger's main works were in the fields of economic theory and methodology, published in 1871 and 1883 respectively. Although we have some other small pamphlets and papers dealing with specific topics, Menger did not have many opportunities to publish his works on economic policy while he was alive. Historians of economic thought are compelled to garner assorted comments that are scattered throughout the various papers and books that Menger did publish during his lifetime.

Fortunately, we are left with some hints that can help us to identify and interpret Menger's liberalism. After scrutinizing Menger's monetary theory, we are now inclined to answer this question in the following way: Menger was a moderate protagonist of economic liberalism, making him the odd man out among the later players of the Austrian School of Economics, such as Ludwig Mises and Friedrich Hayek (for details see Ikeda, 2008; see also Campagnolo, 2004, 2005). Our analysis is highly specific, in that it deals only with his monetary theories; yet, this chapter examines other aspects of Menger's liberalism as well, in an attempt to answer the aforementioned query.

In the next section, we examine Menger's lectures on Crown Prince Rudolf, who died tragically in Mayerling in 1889 (these shall hereafter be referred to as the Rudolf Lectures). Menger taught his pupils fundamental principles of economic policies. What are the agendas and non-agendas of government in a market economy? What is necessary to promote the well-being of the subjects of a monarchy? By reading the materials Menger taught to Rudolf, one can get a bird's eye view of Menger's economic policies. This examination is followed by Section 3, in which I address his lectures on public finance. The transcription of the lectures, now available, thanks to the efforts of Takeshi Mizobata, enables us to read the contents of the lectures that he gave at Vienna University. Since Menger did not offer a detailed account of the discipline in his published works, this offers us a good way to identify his position in the history of public finance. This section, together with the previous one, contributes to the basic understanding of Menger's economic policies. In Section 4, we turn to a newspaper article that was written by Menger to commemorate Adam Smith. Although it was addressed to general readers, it gives us a clue to his interpretation of Smith in comparison with those by other German scholars of that era, which is another way to identify Menger's liberalism. In Section 5, we demonstrate that there are important differences in opinion between Menger and Rudolf concerning the problem of how to deal with the Enlightenment. While Rudolf shared a basic political stance with his mentor, he was more optimistic in his belief in the further development of human beings. In the final section, some concluding remarks will be made. Although we have tried to extend the scope of this analysis to include aspects of Menger's ideas other than monetary theory, this is still a tentative answer to the abovementioned problem.

2. Economic liberalism in the Rudolf Lectures[1]

As is indicated by Erich Streissler, the Rudolf Lectures are heavily based on Heinrich Rau and Wilhelm Roscher, but another important source is Adam Smith (see Streissler, 1994, especially 6–22). In this section we will demonstrate that Menger had relied upon arguments in the English Classical School represented by Smith, as well as those traditional discourses of German economics beginning with *Cameralwissenschaften*, of which the dominant player in the first half of the nineteenth century was Rau. In fact, these lecture notes are good examples of the reception history of Smithian economics and of a still-surviving tradition of typically German economic discourse.

Menger used the following simple two-stage theory with respect to the necessity of governmental intervention:

> When a people is still uncivilized, the head of state may attempt to activate the sluggish economy on his own initiative; but where trade and commerce flourish because of a people's industry and education, the state can greatly harm the citizens' interests by interfering too much, while it will most definitely promote the interest of the national economy by allowing scope for individual action and lending support only in cases where an individual's strength is insufficient.
>
> (Streissler and Streissler, 1994: 109, 111)

In developing countries waiting for takeoff where 'a people is still uncivilized', one badly needs a kind of state intervention; however, after takeoff, governmental intervention is more or less a disturbing factor in a market economy. Thus, in developed countries, the state must stop playing a definitive role in order to orient the economy as a whole.[2]

Menger supports his arguments in a typically Smithian or Hayekian way. In his own words:

> However carefully designed and well-meant institutions may be, they will never suit everybody, since only the individual himself knows exactly his interests and the means to promote them. Innumerable influences, different for everyone, dominate man's activities, and only the individual knows the means for gaining his ends; from unhampered individual development there results a wide range of activities that permit an advanced stage of civilization to be reached. The individual citizen knows best what is of use to him and he will be most industrious when working for his own personal ends.
>
> (Ibid.: 113)

Each economic player knows his own interests and the surrounding situations better than anyone else, Menger argues (see Rosner, 2008: 138; Wilke, 2008: 155). Furthermore, he works harder when promoting his own interests than when serving others to promote theirs. Broadly speaking, this argument reminds us of the well-known explications in *The Wealth of Nations*, whose ideas Friedrich Hayek shares with the great thinkers of the Scottish Enlightenment. Menger's standing point can be neatly summarized as follows:

> Freedom (*Freiheit*) and self-reliance (*Selbstverantwortlichkeit*) in the economic efforts of citizens are the foundation of the overall

> development of a state; therefore the state has to realize and defend these fundamental principles.
>
> (Streissler and Streissler, 1994: 115)

As the above quotes show, Menger was supportive of economic liberalism, with some careful reservations. Let us look at government agendas from Menger's point of view.

> Important roads, railways and canals that improve the general well-being by improving traffic and communication are special examples of this kind of enterprise and lasting evidence of the concern of the state for the well-being of its parts and thereby its own power; at the same time, they are/constitute major prerequisites for the prosperity of a modern state. The building of schools, too, is a suitable field for government to prove its concern with the success of its citizens' economic efforts.
>
> (Ibid.: 121)

As is well known, roads and canals are included in government agendas in *The Wealth of Nations*. Smith did not mention railways, simply because they did not exist in England or in any other part of the world when he wrote his grand oeuvre. On the other hand, Menger did not refer to bridges and harbours either. It is difficult to determine whether he skipped them on purpose or if the omission has any substantial meaning.

Beyond these agendas, Menger goes so far as to say that the protection of forests must be provided by the government. He explains why this is necessary:

> Quite often a forest owner in the mountains who is temporarily short of money will want to clear his high-lying forests; this can easily cause irreparable damage, since the rainfall will then run off in torrents and wash out the humus layer; floods in springtime, droughts in summer, and other kinds of damage to agriculture in the plains result from such deforestation of the mountain sides and tend to worsen over time. The Southern Tyrol, Istria, Dalmatia are sad object lessons of the blind greed of individuals and thoughtless negligence of former governments.
>
> (Ibid.: 131)

This is an important proviso of economic liberalism. In general, Menger was of the opinion that the unconstrained behaviour of economic agents will lead to a socially desirable result; however, as is the case with forestry, this proposition is not always true. Greedy individuals tend to cut trees quite easily without any consideration of what will happen afterwards. Using the concrete examples of 'Tyrol, Istria, Dalmatia', Menger endeavours to show the exceptions to economic liberalism, where the government must step in:

> Protecting forests is among the major duties of the state which, by virtue of their importance, justify government intervention in individual economic activity.
>
> (Ibid.: 133)

While the case of forestry was not suggested in *The Wealth of Nations*, German scholars were eager to protect forests from various points of view. This leads to the conjecture that Menger took the above story from German textbooks, which are more or less concerned with the problem (see Rosner, 2008: 139–40). To demonstrate that this is indeed the case, we will briefly introduce the arguments of Rau, whose textbook Menger had studied eagerly in order to prepare for his *Habilitation*. Rau emphasizes the importance of governmental intervention in the field of forestry as follows:

> Private forestry is not only the target of purely police activities, which attempt to keep it away from various damages, but also of people who were careful enough to see it from the standpoint of the national economy [...] From early on it has been thought necessary to make private industries subject to state control [...] And there was no hesitation to limit the freedom of forest owners when it was justifiable to do so from the viewpoint of the national economy.
>
> (Rau, 1828: 154, author's translation)

The quote here is, in a sense, typically German. The idea has its origins in *Cameralwissenschaften*, and through Rau and others it became a tradition in German economics, later finding an echo in Menger's lectures to Rudolf.

Lastly, we examine Menger's understanding of the labour market at that time. Since the latter part of the nineteenth century, it has continued to be an issue; some people have seriously begun to think that the labour market must be seen as an exception to the *laissez-faire* principle.

Indeed it can be safely said that one of the urgent problems of Menger's time was the degraded working conditions of factory workers. Their condition was vividly described, for instance, in chapters of *Das Kapital* by Karl Marx. Workers in the midst of rapid industrialization were often forced to work for long hours under bad conditions, such as in hot and humid factories. Even small children and women were hired at low wages. Menger did not avoid mentioning the problem in his lectures, saying that workers must be protected by various measures not only to improve their conditions but also to prevent the arrival of communism:

> As mentioned above, we encounter this problem especially in factories; here the factory owner has the opportunity to further the intellectual and emotional development of many people by gentleness, benevolence, and good treatment and thus turn them into good citizens; by treating them roughly and overworking them, he can cause the workers, who are on a very low level any way, utterly to degenerate – to become the very scum of the population. Thus, the so-called proletarians and communists come into existence, as the result of the ill-treatment by the rich, who are now haunted by their spectre.
>
> (Streissler and Streissler, 1994: 127)

By working under good conditions, workers become good citizens, whereas if entrepreneurs force them to work under bad conditions for long hours, they turn to radicalism, thus opening a way to communism. In order to avoid this, daily working hours must be shortened. Menger continues:

> The factory owners may influence decisively even the physical development of the working class; and for this very reason, the state must pay close attention to life in the factories in order to prevent workers from degenerating physically as a result of their being overworked. Therefore, factory owners are not allowed to let their labourers more than a certain maximum [in the margin: 15 hours], even if workers were willing to submit to such disastrous treatment, pressed either by necessity or induced by a higher wage; the government prohibits, for example, a 15-hour day in factories since the worker's physical strength and health suffer if he spends that number of hours daily at hard labour, thereby having his mental faculties blunted completely and sinking to the state of a machine.
>
> (Ibid.: 127, 129)

Although Menger supported factory legislation, it is astonishing to find his suggestion of a modest governmental intervention in the labour market. If one works for 15 hours, as is indicated here, he or she will be left with only nine hours in the day, which is almost equivalent to total sleeping hours plus a short time for breakfast, lunch and dinner. Indeed, this concept must be acceptable for almost all capitalists, including those seeking to exploit their workers up to 15 hours a day. We can compare the above passage with the case of the United Kingdom, where the Ten Hour Act was passed as early as 1847. Certainly Menger did not go too far in promoting further governmental intervention in the labour market.[3]

3. Lectures on *Finanzwissenschaft* at Vienna University[4]

We now turn to Menger's lectures on public finance (*Finanzwissenschaft*), which were given at Vienna University. Thanks to the efforts of Takeshi Mizobata, a Japanese researcher, we are able to read transcriptions of the lectures without difficulty. According to Mizobata, it is highly probable that the lectures were given around 1888, considering various historical data that Menger included in them. Together with the Rudolf Lectures analysed in the previous section, the *Finanzwissenschaft* provides a good opportunity to examine Menger's economic policies in detail.

After mentioning Adam Smith, David Ricardo, John Stuart Mill and John Ramsay McCulloch, Menger refers to eminent German scholars who greatly contributed to the discipline of public finance; these were Julius von Soden, Johann Friedrich Eusebius Lotz, Ludwig Heinrich von Jakob, Carl August von Malchus, Karl Heinrich Rau, Karl Umpfenbach, Lorenz von Stein, Carl Julius Bergius, Johann Friedrich von Pfeiffer and Adolph Wagner. The way in which Menger lectured to the university students was different from the manner he used when lecturing to the future king; in the lecture room at Vienna University, he gave detailed information on the published works of the discipline, a routine procedure in university lectures, but a process that he totally skipped in the Rudolf Lectures.

Menger's basic understanding of the history of public finance can be aptly summarized as follows:

> In Germany, public finance was already well-developed even before Smith.
>
> (Mizobata, 1993: 33, author's translation)

It is true that public finance was not given an independent role in the treatises on British economic thought. Adam Smith, the founder of economics – and at the same time a representative player in the Scottish Enlightenment – dedicated only a part of the last book of *The Wealth of Nations* to the discipline. This makes an excellent contrast to the German way of dealing with the problem: Rau's third book exclusively deals with public finance. As Menger said, this tradition was deeply embedded in the tradition of *Cameralwissenschaften* in German-speaking areas, which continues to play an important role in the development of the discipline, even after the introduction of Smithian economics in Germany. On the whole, German influences were apparently dominant in these lecture notebooks.

Menger explains the differences between the private and state economies after engaging in historical descriptions of the discipline. Among the three points he indicated, the first deserves to be mentioned here:

> That the state has to have moral purposes. Not only the state economy but also revenue and expenditure must have this character. The state cannot concern itself with business that endangers morality. How stupid it is to receive revenue from, for instance, the lottery in order to promote moral purposes! The same can be said of expenditure. The state is not allowed to spend money for amoral agendas. If the expenditure is not adequately seen from this rule, it cannot be justified from an economic point of view.
>
> (Ibid.: 35, author's translation)

For Menger, the state is an ethical being; for this reason, it is neither allowed to collect state revenue through amoral methods, nor use that revenue for purposes that are problematic from an ethical point of view. The characterization of state as an ethical being cannot be found in British economic thought.

The arguments in *The Wealth of Nations* were a starting point of the taxation theory for the later generation. Menger also refers to the well-known passages of Adam Smith, before coming to the following conclusion:

> If one says that only those people who can pay the money can send their children to school, it is diametrically opposed to the essence

> of the state. There are many people in the country who cannot pay this tax.
>
> (Ibid.: 52, author's translation)

In the above quote, Menger criticized one of the taxation principles posed by Adam Smith: taxation based on the benefits that individuals enjoy under state control. Menger was against this principle, for there are many who cannot afford to pay certain taxes even if they are enjoying some of the benefits of state protection. Menger said that the principle was against the proper understanding of the state, implying that his is a community based on other values.

Furthermore, Menger advocated tax progression in a typical way:

> With increase in income, one feels less sacrifice, even if the loss is the same amount. For this reason, we must not tax with the same proportion; but with increase in income, the percent rate must be also increased. This means that the percent rate must be progressive as in income tax, and there must be a tobacco tax whose price increases progressively.
>
> (Ibid.: 52, author's translation)

The argument here is based on a well-known observation that for the rich, the marginal utility of a certain amount of money is much smaller than it is for the poor. In the history of economic thought, the foundation of this argument was severely criticized because it is based on an interpersonal comparison of utility; but Menger still stuck to the old-fashioned way of supporting the taxation progression.

4. Economic liberalism in *Socialtheorien*

In this section we examine Menger's homage to Adam Smith, which he extended in a newspaper article entitled 'The social theories of classical economics and modern economic policies' ('*Die Social-Theorien der classischen National-Oekonomie und die moderne Wirthschaftspolitik*'). In this article, intended to commemorate the founder of economics, Menger defended Smith's arguments against the criticism of German economists in general and of the German Historical School in particular.

Menger's arguments run as follows:

> In all cases of conflict of interest between the rich and the poor, A. Smith stands without exception on the side of the latter. I use the phrase 'without exception' very carefully. There are no places in *The Wealth of Nations* where A. Smith represents the interest of the rich and powerful against the poor and weak. While A. Smith quite positively recognizes the free initiative of individualism in economic matters, he supports in all the cases state intervention where the matter relates to the abolition of laws, and the application thereof, that suppress the poor and weak for the sake of the rich and powerful.
>
> (Menger, 1891: 223, author's translation)

This is clearly intended as a critique of the popular interpretation of Smith in German-speaking areas in the nineteenth century. Quite often, Smith was believed to be standing on the side of rich people, thus ignoring the interests of the poor. Menger argues that this is contrary to what Smith actually said.

Furthermore:

> When it comes to the protection of the poor and weak, the basic standpoint of A. Smith is in part more progressive than that of those modern politicians concerned with 'social policies'. His opinions, found in particular passages of his work, are similar to those of modern socialists. It is well-known that Louis Blanc, Ferdinand Lassalle and Karl Marx incessantly quote the theories of Smith and his pupils, but not those of his enemies.
>
> (Ibid.: 224–5, author's translation)

Here Menger's standpoint is clear: He defended Smith, saying that the latter's position in policy-making issues is more progressive than that of the economists who advocated social policies in Germany. Thus, Menger endeavours to distance himself from economists in the *Verein für Socialpolitik*. On the other hand, Menger went too far when he said that Smith's position on policy issues is close to those of socialists. This is a bold statement; as Menger emphasizes, Blanc, Lassalle and Marx continued to mention Smith, employing a part of his economic system in their theories. Yet, it is unclear whether or not they followed Smith in policy-making matters. In some way, they tried to go beyond Smith's position.

Menger goes on to show that Smith was not a *laissez-faire* economist.

> It is not true, indeed it is a forgery of history, to say that A. Smith was a dogmatic advocate of the 'laisser faire, laisser aller' principle and that he believed that the completely free play of individual interests would lead to the economic cure of society. In various parts of his work, he admits that the efforts and interests of individuals and entire social classes stand in direct opposition to public interests. Not only did he accept state intervention in most cases, but he believed it to be an order of humanity considering the public welfare.
>
> (Ibid.: 230, author's translation)

Menger claimed that Smith did not believe that the individual interests of economic agents necessarily led to the economic interests of society as a whole. In many parts of his 1776 book, Smith indicated cases in which the individual interests of players are diametrically opposed to public interests. In these cases, some form of state intervention is necessary. Indeed, the members of the German Historical School were not united in criticizing Smithian economics; Karl Knies emphasized by direct quotations from *The Wealth of Nations* that Smith was not a dogmatic supporter of the *laissez-faire* doctrine.[5] In this sense, Menger's interpretation in the above quote was not new in the context of German economics at that time.

Next, we proceed to Part II of the same article, which concerns itself with the problem of distribution between capitalists and workers and the possible means to improve workers' conditions. In Menger's opinion, members of the English Classical School understood the distribution mechanism better than German economists of the Social Policy School:

> While the economists of the Classical School are, in their sympathetic tendency toward workers, not inferior to the modern politicians concerned with social policies, it seems to me that the standpoint of classical economics is, when seen from another perspective, obviously better than that of the new politicians of social policies. What I mean is, their correct insight into the causes leading to the welfare of the working class.
>
> (Ibid.: 239, author's translation)

Menger continues:

> It is true that the distribution of income between capital and labour is a problem of the highest importance and that every measure to

> increase workers' distribution in the result of production must be welcomed as a delightful improvement of society, if it does not lead to the problem of the existence of industries. But it seems also certain that the considerable increase in wages is only a result of accumulation and the productive use of capital. The employment of more workers with the same or higher wages goes hand in hand with the prosperity of productive industries and capital accumulation.
>
> (Ibid.: 239–40, author's translation)

While Menger admits to the importance of the distribution between capital and labour, he emphasizes other factors determining the wage. One of them is an accumulation of capital and the productive use thereof, but the way in which to divide the cake between the two comes down to a distribution problem. Before dividing a cake, we must endeavour to have a bigger cake, thus making an absolute amount of each person's share larger. This is, in Menger's opinion, the crux of the matter. Whether or not the capitalist enjoys a lion's share in the relative sense is of secondary importance to Menger. It can be safely said that the above argument has one of its origins in Book 2, Chapter 3 of *The Wealth of Nations*.

Key terms in Part II of the article are *Kapital* (capital), *Unternehmungsgeist* (entrepreneurship), *individuelle Initiative* (individual initiative) and *Selbstverantwortlichkeit* (self-reliance). While Menger shares with most of the members of the Social Policy School the observation that the degradation of workers was an enormous social problem, he also realized that it can only be solved by relying upon further capital accumulation based on entrepreneurship. *Individuelle Initiative* and *Selbstverantwortlichkeit* are basic terms in the discourse of economic liberalism; Menger's belief that social problems can be relieved by policies based on classical liberalism is beyond doubt. It is also necessary to indicate that the above arguments are more or less a reproduction of what Menger taught to Rudolf in the 1870s. We encountered the same terminology of 'self-reliance' in the Rudolf Lectures. At the same time, the similarity suggests that the Rudolf Lectures are not just summaries of what was already known in the general scholarly circle, but really reflect what Menger thought to be valuable from his academic point of view.[6]

5. French enlightenment and beyond

Based on secondary literature, the political ideologies of Rudolf can be summarized as follows: (1) He was against anti-Semitism. (2) He was basically anti-clerical. (3) He was cosmopolitan and against nationalism in the narrow sense of the word. (4) He was deeply involved with enlightenment, especially French Enlightenment; and was confident that people continue to improve and in the end reach perfection, mainly due to the development of the sciences.

This section first examines a part of Rudolf's political standpoint, with special attention paid to the fourth point above. After dealing briefly with Menger's careful reservations about enlightenment, we will argue that there are some fundamental differences in opinions between Rudolf and his mentor.

First, we take a look at his descriptions of Joseph II, the son of the well-known empress Maria Theresia. Joseph II is known as an enlightened king who greatly contributed to the modernization of the monarchy through the emancipation of serfs and Jews, generous religious politics and so on.[7] The king was highly appreciated by Rudolf because he embodied the spirit of the French Revolution, a new spirit of the age. Before turning to the king himself, we examine Rudolf's interpretation of the Revolution, which can be neatly summarized as follows:

> These ideas were cherished and advocated by the prophets of the French Revolution. Against the amorality of the French court and the King who indifferently sees the fate of the people – sucking the country dry and paying too little attention to humanity – stood people like Montesquieu and the Encyclopedists. They constructed a philosophy of humanity that included human rights and the high position of human beings among God's creations.
>
> (Hamann, 1979: 244–5, author's translation)

After he had emphasized the importance of the French Revolution, Rudolf went on to mention writers of the French Enlightenment, such as Montesquieu and the Encyclopedists. In Rudolf's opinion, these writers contributed to the basic understanding and popularization of the ideas of humanity and human rights.

Rudolf also appreciated the efforts of Joseph II, as follows:

> Joseph II lived in this great age. We must see him as a supporter of the great ideas of his time, a supporter with a crown. The revolution that came from below against the establishment of society was realized by him, standing at the top of state power to promote the welfare of the whole.
>
> (Ibid.: 245, author's translation)

For the people in the monarchy, Joseph II endeavoured to accomplish from above what had been done in France from below. It is not unthinkable that Rudolf would have liked to complete the agendas of Joseph II if it had been possible for him. The king was certainly an icon for Rudolf; it is true that Joseph II was a great friend of French writers, a passion that Rudolf shared. Both of them were interested in Voltaire, Rousseau, Diderot and d'Alembert.

Among the personalities with whom Rudolf regularly corresponded was Moriz Szeps, a figure who deserves to be mentioned within the context of this chapter. Szeps, a well-known publicist and the editor of *Neues Wiener Tagblatt*, was introduced to Rudolf by Carl Menger himself in 1882 (Szeps, 1922: XV). Menger was very close to Szeps, and the founder of the Austrian School of Economics was seriously concerned with journalism before the publication of his 1871 book.[8]

Szeps continued to be an important informant for the lonely prince, not only in Austrian politics but also in international political relations. In his letter to Szeps dated 19 November 1882, Rudolf wrote the following passage:

> We owe France too much for all the liberal ideas and institutions of the continent. And in all the moments when great ideas come out, it serves us always as a model. Meanwhile Germany, which is nothing more than a huge Prussian military people, was a purely military state; only it has become bigger.
>
> (Ibid.: 17, author's translation)

Certainly Rudolf was a Francophile. The above quote shows that Rudolf was deeply involved with French ideas and institutions. Those French ideas and institutions are, in his understanding, models of other continental nations, while Germany was thought to represent a military state in the true sense of the word. Thus, Germany makes an excellent contrast to France in ideas and in its politico-economic system.

Now we turn to Rudolf's mentor, who had a different opinion. Menger thought that the main problem of Adam Smith and the French Enlightenment lay in:

> [...] the opinion appearing chiefly in their writings that the institutions of economy are always the intended product of the common will of society as such, results of expressed agreement of members of society or of positive legislation. In this one-sidedly pragmatic view of the nature of social institutions, the sphere of ideas of A. Smith and

> his closest followers comes into contact with that of the writers of the French Age of Enlightenment in general and of the French physiocrats in particular. Adam Smith, also, and his school predominantly strive for the *pragmatic* understanding of economy, even where such understanding is not adequate for the objective state of affairs.
> (Menger, 1985: 153)

Menger argues that both the writers of the French Enlightenment and Smith thought it possible to change society and its institutions as they wished. While it is difficult to believe in the basic similarity of the Scottish and French Enlightenment, this idea is definitely contrary to the Mengerian understanding of institutions as being developed without positive intervention from above. Those interested in the history of economic thought know that Menger's understanding of institutions has continued to play an important role in later Austrian thought, from Hayek to the modern members of the School in the United States.

The point here is that Menger, the mentor, had a different picture of the French Enlightenment from the one depicted by his pupil. Rudolf was not very far from the opinion that human beings can mould society as they like, and was firmly convinced that they continue to develop into better people largely by relying upon the further development of the natural sciences. Menger was less certain about the role of reason in interpreting and changing a human society.

6. Conclusions

Menger advocated liberalism in the Rudolf Lectures as well as in his public finance lectures at Vienna University. In the former, he supported economic liberalism by relying on two different tides of economic thought: Adam Smith and the German economics represented by Heinrich Rau and Wilhelm Roscher. As Streissler rightly summarized, the arguments there are far reaching: Menger was a market-oriented economist with some important reservations in his lectures. This standpoint goes hand in hand with his commemorative essay about Adam Smith that was published later on.

In his public finance lectures of the 1880s, Menger emphasized the importance of progressive taxation, denying the pay-to-benefit principle. In a manner slightly different from that of the Rudolf Lectures, Menger's arguments here are fundamentally based on German and Austrian sources. Moreover, his position in the Vienna lectures can be interpreted as opening a way to the welfare state. If this interpretation is justified, it means that the two sets of lectures are not insignificantly opposed to each other on the problem of state intervention; however, his arguments in the Vienna lectures are concerned almost exclusively with state revenue, which makes it difficult to hazard a good guess about his thoughts on the possible ways to use money for various purposes. Although Menger indicated the importance of examining state expenditure in the lectures, he was essentially silent on that subject. Thus, the final words on Menger's welfare state, if any exist, are still missing.

As a small *détour* from the main story, the last section is dedicated to the differences between Rudolf and his teacher, concerning the problem of how to interpret the Enlightenment. This is a necessary step not only in an interpretation of Menger's liberalism, but also in an examination of the relationship between the two in detail.

This chapter is still merely a halfway house on the journey towards a complete understanding of Menger's liberalism. Much more research must be done using both published and unpublished materials in the near future.

Notes

1. Sections 2 and 4 draw heavily on Streissler (1994), Rosner (2008) and Wilke (2008). Streissler's overall interpretation of the Rudolf Lectures, a starting point for all of the secondary literature, can be summarized as follows: 'The Rudolf Notebooks show Menger to have been a classical liberal of the purest water with a much smaller agenda for the state in mind than even Adam Smith' (Streissler, 1994: 14). Rosner follows Streissler by inclining to the view that Menger was more or less an advocate of economic liberalism: 'Although he was not as combative in favour of a market economy as Mises or Hayek in the twentieth century, it would be difficult to depict Menger having been a friend of intensive regulations of the economy' (Rosner, 2008: 127). See also Wilke (2008: 159) in the same volume, positively quoting Streissler's above-mentioned interpretation. The problem now is the exact extent and flavour of Menger's liberalism. A more detailed characterization of his politico-economic ideology is needed, with which the chapter is concerned. Sections 3 and 5 of the chapter are concerned with new material and a new way to look at Menger's liberalism, thus making it possible to draw a detailed picture of his economic policies.
2. Rosner emphasized the influences of Wilhelm Roscher on Menger's two-stage theory (2008: 138).
3. This point is already indicated by Streissler. In his words: 'The actual measures envisaged are, in contrast, extremely meager, e. g. limitation of hours of work to no more than 15 a day in the case of hard labour' (Streissler, 1994: 16). We share Streissler's scepticism and are strongly suspicious of the substantial meaning of the factory act proposed here by Menger. It obviously does not lead to an improvement in workers' conditions.

4. For an introductory account of Menger's lectures on public finance, see Part I of T. Mizobata (ed.) (1993), upon which the descriptions in this section are based. Unfortunately, Mizobata's introductory essay is available only in Japanese.
5. For details see Tribe (2008: 518).
6. This might support the view that the Rudolf Lectures are 'reflections of the mature judgment of Carl Menger' (Streissler, 1994: 23).
7. There is a huge secondary literature on Joseph II. See for instance Wangermann (1959). It is true that Joseph II contributed to the modernization of the monarchy, but the following cautious remark must be born in mind, as one is not allowed to overestimate the true standing point of the king: 'A policy of enlightened despotism thus appeared in Austria no less than elsewhere in response to certain practical and urgent necessities, and not as the fruit of philosophical persuasion. The statement is as valid for the reign of Joseph II as it is for that of his mother' (Wangermann, 1959: 2). A short but excellent introduction to Joseph II can be found in Mikoletzky (1979). For Rudolf, see Hamann (2006), Johnston (1972) and Kohn (1961).
8. For Menger as a journalist, see Ikeda (1997) and Yagi (1992).

References

Brusatti, A. (1965) *Österreichische Wirtschaftspolitik vom Josephinismus zum Ständestaat*, Vienna: Jupiter.

Campagnolo, G. (2004) *Critique de l'économie politique classique. Marx, Menger et l'École historique*, Paris: Presses Universitaire de France.

Campagnolo, G. (2005) 'Carl Menger's "Money as Measure of Value": An Introduction', *History of Political Economy*, 37(2): 233–43.

Campagnolo, G. (ed.) (2008) *Carl Menger: Discussed on the Basis of New Findings*, Frankfurt am Main: Peter Lang.

Hamann, B. (ed.) (1979) *Kronprinz Rudolf, Majestät, ich warne Sie... geheime und private Schriften*, Vienna: Amalthea.

Hamann, B. (2006) *Kronprinz Rudolf: Ein Leben*, Munich: Piper.

Ikeda, Y. (1997) *Die Entstehungsgeschichte der Grundsätze Carl Mengers*, St. Katharinen: Scripta Mercaturae.

Ikeda, Y. (2008) 'Carl Menger's Monetary Theory: A Revisionist View', *The European Journal of the History of Economic Thought*, 15(3): 453–73.

Johnston, W. (1972) *The Austrian Mind: An Intellectual and Social History 1848–1938*, Berkeley: University of California Press.

Kohn, H. (1961) *The Habsburg Empire 1804–1918*, New York: Van Nostrand Reinhold Co.

Menger, C. (1871) *Grundsätze der Volkswirthschaftslehre*, reprinted in Hayek, F. (ed.) (1968), *Gesammelte Werke*, 2nd edition, Tübingen: J. C. B. Mohr, Vol. 1.

Menger, C. (1883) *Untersuchungen über die Methode der Socialwissenschaften und der politischen Oekonomie insbesondere*, reprinted in Hayek, F. (ed.) (1969), *Gesammelte Werke*, 2nd edition, Tübingen: J. C. B. Mohr, Vol. 2.

Menger, C. (1891) 'Die Social-Theorien der classischen National-Oekonomie und die moderne Wirthschaftspolitik', *Neue Freie Presse* 6., 8., Jan. 1891, reprinted in

F. Hayek (ed.) (1970) *Gesammelte Werke*, 2nd edition, Tübingen: J. C. B. Mohr, Vol. 3.
Menger, C. (1985) *Investigations into the Method of the Social Sciences with Special Attention to Economics*, edited by L. Schneider, New York: New York University Press.
Mikoletzky, L. (1979) *Kaiser Joseph II. Herrscher zwischen den Zeiten*, Göttingen: Muster-Schmidt.
Mizobata, T. (ed.) (1993) *Transcript of Finanz-Wissenschaft von Prof. Carl Menger* (c. 1888), as Study Series, 28, Center for Historical Social Science Literature, Hitotsubashi University.
Rau, K. H. (1828) *Grundsätze der Volkswirtschaftspflege mit anhaltender Rücksicht auf bestehende Staatseinrichtungen*, Heidelberg: Universitätsbuchhandlung von F. Winter.
Rosner, P. (2008) 'Liberal Positions in Carl Menger's Writings', in G. Campagnolo (ed.), (2008).
Streissler, E. (1994) 'Menger's Treatment of Economics in the Rudolf Lectures', in E. Streissler and M. Streissler (eds), *Carl Menger's Lectures to Crown Prince Rudolf of Austria*, Aldershot: Edward Elgar.
Streissler, E. and Streissler, M. (eds) (1994) *Carl Menger's Lectures to Crown Prince Rudolf of Austria*, Aldershot: Edward Elgar.
Szeps, J. (ed.) (1922) *Kronprinz: politische Briefe an einen Freund 1882–1889*, Vienna: Rikola.
Tribe, K. (2008) 'Das Adam Smith Problem and the Origins of Modern Smith Scholarship', *History of European Ideas*, 34: 514–25.
Wangermann, E. (1959) *From Joseph II to the Jacobin Trials: Government Policy and Public Opinion in the Habsburg Dominions in the Period of the French Revolution*, London: Oxford University Press.
Wilke, W. (2008) 'Carl Menger in der Nachfolge von Adam Smith', in G. Campagnolo (ed.), (2008).
Yagi, K. (1992) 'Carl Menger as Editor: Significance of Journalistic Experience for his Economics and for his Later Life', *Revue Européenne des Sciences Sociales*, XXX (92).

2

Carl Menger after 1871: Quest for the Reality of 'Economic Man'

Kiichiro Yagi

1. Introduction: Posthumous edition of the *Grundsätze*

After nearly 20 years of retirement, Carl Menger died on 26 February 1921, leaving behind a considerable number of notes and manuscripts as well as over 20,000 books. In the turbulent and inflationary days after the war, the bereaved sold the main part of the library – one of the best collections of economic literature in the world – to a university in Japan. Some parts of Menger's manuscripts were edited by his son for inclusion in the second edition of the *Grundsätze der Volkswirtschaftslehre* (*Principles of Political Economy*) which was published two years later in 1923. Between two publications nearly half a century passed, during which period the author devoted time to reflecting on the nature of economic theory, to whose renovation he had contributed with the first edition of the *Grundsätze*.

This period of reflection began soon after 1871 and continued into his final years. The *Untersuchungen über die Methode der Socialwissenschaften und der politischen Oekonomie insbesondere (Investigations into the Methods of Social Sciences and of Political Economy in particular)* of 1883 was its interim product. However, the direction of the reflection showed subtle differences at each stage of those intervening years (see Hayek, 1934: xxxii–xxxiii). Hence, the posthumous edition of the *Grundsätze* incorporating Menger's reflections is like a geometrical stratification, ranging across many years.

The new edition was a disappointment for those who were interested in the refinement of the economic theory (Weiss, 1924; Wicksell, 1956). On the other hand, it provided inspiration on the economic anthropology to economists such as Karl Polanyi (1977).

2. Early stage of the revision of the *Grundsätze*

In the original plan, the *Grundsätze* of 1871 was to be 'the first, general part' of a systematic work with four parts (Menger, 1923: VII). However, there is no evidence that Menger made any serious attempt to fulfil this plan after the publication in 1871. In response to some reviews Menger did start to make some revisions; he ordered special author copies of the *Grundsätze*, bound together with blank sheets between each printed page, in order to annotate the reflections and corrections in them.

One of these special copies is found in the Menger Library of the Hitotsubashi University (Menger, 1961). The other two copies are in the Menger Papers, the personal papers of Carl Menger now housed in the Manuscript Department, William R. Perkins Library, Duke University.[1] Two of the Duke University copies have the marks of 'No. 1' and 'No. 2' on the title pages. The Hitotsubashi Copy is 'No. 3'. The title of these three numbered copies was changed to *Allgemeine theoretische Wirtschaftslehre* (*General Economic Theory*). Menger's entries in these special copies are without doubt precious texts from which we can know Menger's reflection on his theory as well as his attitude to the reviews his work received. Although we have only the transcription of entries in the Hitotsubashi copy by Emil Kauder (ibid.) in hand, still we can understand the situation in which Menger directed his research interest to the methodological problems of economic theory.

Although Menger dedicated the *Grundsätze* to Wilhelm Roscher, Menger's appreciation of Roscher was confined to the elaboration of basic concepts of economics, goods and value in particular, and Roscher's program of historicism was out of range. Along with Rau's *Grundsätze*, Roscher's *Grundlagen* was one of the key works which Menger studied during the formative years of his *Grundsätze*.[2] Roscher wrote in *Geschichte der Nationalökonomik in Deutschland* (*History of Political Economy in Germany*) the following:

> Lastly, we see an Austrian, C. Menger with his very abstract conceptual analysis that is mostly based on the detailed knowledge in the history of economics but always independent and considerably fruitful. It covers for example the price formation in the isolated exchange, then in the monopolistic trade, and lastly under the influence of competition on both sides.
>
> (1874: 1040)

This rather diplomatic reference was probably the best that an unknown author like Menger could have expected from an authority in German economics. However, we can assume that Menger must have been disappointed with Roscher's judgement of 'very abstract', particularly given that *Grundsätze* became a ground-breaking book in later years.

Of the reviews and publication notices that Menger's *Grundsätze* received, two came from reviewers of the Historical School. They introduced Menger's work satirically – as the debut of a schoolboy publishing a textbook – and admonished that young scholars have to work out a monograph first. One of the two reviews contained the reviewer's initial, G. Sch., no doubt that of Gustav Schmoller. This reviewer attacked Menger for being a follower of the fiction presented by egoistic economic man, à la Smith, and added as follows:

> Does the so-called psychological ground of the economic life change by each nation and by each age? Doesn't the author try to establish the wrong and obsolete fiction of the British by it that the economic life is exactly deduced on the assumption of the elementary propositions of the abstract and average man as the constant and evident entity? Scientists have made their exact research by using scales and microscopes. The corresponding direction in Economics is that of historical and statistical research.
>
> (Schmoller, 1873: 143)

It is clear that this reviewer misunderstood Menger's use of the word, 'exact science', and it is also true that he repeated his own view of the primacy of the specialized studies and paid no attention to the problem of theory construction. Apart from the question of how conscious of the issue Menger was at the time *Grundsätze* was published, the assumption of the dominance of self interest in economics is, according to Menger, not the approval of the materialistic view but a procedure in the isolation of an aspect of the human being, given his diverse dispositions. If another disposition should be observed in isolation, it should serve as the starting point for another species of social theory (moral theory, aesthetics and so on) (Menger, 1883: 44, 78–9).

The Hitotsubashi copy contains a clear rejection of the fundamental position of the Historical School:

> There is a historical method of description. Further, history can be the material for the research of laws. But, is there a historical method of research?
>
> (Menger, 1961: 26)

The attack Menger received from the reviewers of the Historical School and his rejection anticipated the future collision that divided the economists in the German speaking area. However, before entering into this collision, we have to notice that the critical remarks that a review by an author named Hack stimulated Menger's reconsideration of the causal relations in economic theory:

> We think, for example, that the so-called causal relation between wants and things should be interpreted not as the relation of cause and effect but as that of aims and means. We also think that the well-known question how the laws of economic actions can be concerted with the free will is not solved by saying that economic theory is concerned, not with practical rules for economic activity, but with the conditions under which men engage in provident activity directed to the satisfaction of their needs.
>
> (1872: 184)

In this short commentary, Hack suggested Menger should replace his causal view of economic action with a teleological view and urged him to take the problem of 'free will' in economic science more seriously. Hack's criticisms were not directed at the theoretical core of the *Grundsätze*, but at the ease of understanding the methodological questions Menger had posed in 1871.

From the Hitotsubashi and Duke University copies, one can see that Menger approved of the two issues raised by Hack. In the No. 1 Duke copy, Menger not only noted Hack's criticism in the margin of pages IX and 7 but also admitted the necessity to deepen the understanding of the causality in respect to the teleological relations between means and ends (p. 7). In the Hitotsubashi copy he altered the titles of sections and texts. Thus, the second section of the first chapter was changed from 'On the Causal Relations of Goods' to 'On the teleological relations of goods'. The following sentence was also added to the text: 'A relation can be dual; a mechanical relation and a teleological relation. The former must be the grounds for the latter.'[3] This change is similar to the revision in the third section of the second chapter, 'On the relations of goods in the end consciousness' as seen in the posthumous edition. As for the problem of free will, the part of the Preface in the *Grundsätze*, which Hack cited as being Menger's position, was deleted without any alternative.[4]

As Hack pointed out, Menger in 1871 saw (1) no difference between the relation of economic actions, which is originally a mental one, and the causal relations of the phenomena such as in the natural sciences, and (2) regarded the influential factors of the economic action only in the physical conditions outside the sphere of the free will – in particular, the scarcity of the available goods in relation to the quantities needed for want satisfaction. In other words, Menger in 1871 made no distinction of the tree: (a) the causal relation in the physical (external world) and the physiological (mind and body of man) process, (b) the recognition of the causal relation in (a), and further (c) the teleological relation in the action on the basis of (a) and (b). Presumably, Menger in 1871 might have thought that the end-means relation in human action should be nothing but the cause-effect relation reversed in the recognition (mind) (pp. 24–5).

However, from the point of view of methodology, this rather näive position presents two problems. First, the recognition of empirical regularity cannot in itself be seen as a causal relation (such as a rule), as it is in theoretical science. Second, the teleological relation which emerges in the mind of a man taking action is diverse and cannot be reduced to scientific knowledge of a causal relation in the external world – human mind and body.

Such weakness is related to the second point raised by Hack. In order to avoid Karl Knies's conclusion – denying the existence of any laws in social science because of free will recognition – Menger in 1871 tried to formulate the idea that economic theory does not deal with economic action itself (especially not with its purpose, that is, want) but deals only with the influence of objective conditions (scarcity of the goods) on the direction of economic action. But actions taken by real individuals, even if they could be regarded as an economic action, namely as oriented to the attainment of the want satisfaction, might alter their appearance under the influence of social norms and consideration of others, ignorance and misunderstandings, lack of capacities and so on. Therefore, Menger cannot avoid the problem of free will in the construction of his economic theory. In other words, the weakness of the methodological view of 1871 is based on the lack of distinction between real economic actions and 'ideal type' actions that are necessary to construct the rule in theory.

In the Preface of the first edition of *Grundsätze*, Menger presented his method of theoretical construction as follows:

> I have endeavoured to reduce the complex phenomena of human economic activity to the simplest elements that can still be subjected to accurate observation, to apply to these elements the measure

> corresponding to their nature, and constantly adhering to this measure, to investigate the manner in which the more complex economic phenomena evolve from their elements according to definite principles.
>
> (1950: 47)

Missing here is the distinction between theory and reality. Having interpreted Menger's reaction to the criticism by Hack, the review by Schmoller connotes a positive meaning for the start of Menger's methodological investigation.

Resentment may not have been Menger's only reaction to Schmoller's review. Though we cannot find a reference to Schmoller in the Hitotsubashi copy, it contains a remark on the 'dogma of private egoism' mentioning Knies (Menger, 1961: 2) and alludes to a plan to add a new article that discusses the influence of the ethical factor as a modification factor (ibid.: 59). Beyond the late 1880s, Menger's interest in the 'morphology' of economic phenomena, together with his reflections on the origins of the rationality of economic man seem to suggest some distant echo of Schmoller's proposition.

3. The 'subjective' turn

The second stage of the attempt at revision seems to have occurred in the mid-1880s, after the pause in the Debate on Method (*Methodenstreit*) enabled Menger to return to theoretical investigation. Throughout these years, owing much to the works of E. v. Böhm-Bawerk and F. Wieser, the 'Austrian School' was achieving a worldwide reputation. Menger encouraged younger generations in his seminars and published articles and reviews. This appears to have been Menger's golden age. Facing strong demand for the reprint of the *Grundsätze*, he promised the publication of the revised edition. However, the publication of this much awaited edition was not realized.

What, if any, effort was made at revision? I suppose it is rational to assume that the main part of the posthumous edition of the *Grundsätze* actually derived from this period. Since the first stage of an attempt at revision is seen in the Hitotsubashi copy, so the main body of the 1923 edition, with the exclusion of the additions after the 'new plan' in the mid-1890s, is representative of the second stage. If this guess is correct, the task for the second stage could be seen as how to introduce the dimension of economic action on the basis of methodological reflections from the first stage.

The following two changes in the 1923 edition, therefore, seem important:

(1) Adoption of the idea of 'disjunctive determination' in the theory of need of goods, and that of available quantity of goods.
(2) Introduction of the concept of the chance of economic activity (*Erwerbsgelegenheit*) as the proper object of economic action, as distinct from the technical-physiological concept of goods.

Each is discussed in turn.

3.1. 'Disjunctive determination'

As the text of the *Grundsätze* of 1871 began with the sentence 'All things are subject to the law of cause and effect', it maintained the framework of monistic determinism. The progress in the methodological reflection, as described above, naturally created a tension in the revision relative to the deterministic framework. If the free will of man is admitted, how can it be compatible with the deterministic view of economic phenomena?

First, his ideas developed towards two starting points: the situation of the need and the available goods, and also the goal, namely the most perfect satisfaction of the need given certain starting points, which are independent of the will of man (Menger, 1883: 45). In other words, he thought that the assumption of the given physical condition of the outer world, and the mind and body of a man at each given moment, automatically determines the quantity of the need for goods to satisfy given wants, as well as determines the quantity of available goods.

However, the Menger seen in the Hitotsubashi copy was already beginning to forsake this position. The need for higher-order goods and the quantity of goods available via the operation of production or exchange could not be considered as 'directly and exactly determined quantities' (Menger, 1961: 73). The posthumous edition pushes this indetermination forward to the 'direct needs' and 'quantity of the directly available goods'. It is only the physical quantities in the external world, and the objective wants of man, which are uniquely determined at each moment. But the needs and the available quantity of goods are, whilst objectively determined in the framework, dependent on selecting from alternative ways in order to satisfy wants and from alternative ways of production.

They are given only as a combination of the possible variants. Multiple determination instead of unique determination! This is the concept of 'disjunctive determination'. According to Menger, this is the reason why economics is more complicated than natural sciences. The concept 'disjunctive determination' states that the rational way to satisfy given wants or so called 'technical rationality' is the provision of a set of alternatives. On the basis of possibility of selection, in my interpretation, Menger wanted to establish the proper dimensions of economic action and economic rationality.

However, in the chapter on economy and economic goods (ch. 4) of the posthumous edition, this concept is not used, and in the next chapter on value we find the term 'law of economicity' used in many places without explanation, as if this concept should be already familiar to the readers. From this I assume that one of the core problems in the second stage of the attempted revision lay in finding a solution to in-determination, the concept of 'disjunctive determination' by the 'law of economicity', but the corresponding effort might not have been completed. It might be a reason behind the failure to deliver a much-promised revision in this period.

3.2. Chance of economic activity

Another change is also related to the distinction between technical rationality and economic rationality. In the 1871 edition of the *Grundsätze* the relations among goods were analyzed from the viewpoint of technical rationality or from the viewpoint of the 'physiological-technical sense'[5] which considers the provisions of goods as a natural process from production to the satisfaction of want. But Menger began to think this position too narrow to describe economic action. It is true that for an economic agent living in isolation there is no other way to use goods than the use appropriate to its physical nature. The use of goods cannot be separated from its possession. But in developed economic relations, the limitations as to the variety of uses is eliminated by the possibility of exchange. Even an object with no material existence (including physical service as well as material goods) must be considered an 'independent economic object', so far as it appears among men and is exchanged. Menger called this extended notion of 'economic object' a 'chance of economic activity'.

Menger tried to draw this distinction between the dimension of economic use and economic action and the dimension of the goods from a 'technical point of view'. This distinction is important to Menger particularly in the theory of use (or service) and capital. A good is considered to be capital in so far as it generates income for the owner, even if its material existence disappears as it is used in the production process or as it changes form by the operation of exchange. Therefore, the classification of possessions – the sum of goods under the possession of an individual – between capital and storage of consumption is based only on the way it is used and not on its physical property (Menger, 1923: 19–20, 87ff.). The concept of capital in the posthumous edition of the *Grundsätze* is similar to the proposal to revive the popular concept of capital in the monetary economy, namely 'the amount of money invested to the formation of income', in his 'Zur Theorie des Kapitals' ('Theory of Capital', 1888).[6]

At this point it is worth mentioning the correspondence between Menger and Böhm-Bawerk from 1884 to New Year's day of 1885,[7] because it illuminates the context of the emergence of these new concepts of 'chance of economic activity' and 'capital'. This discussion began with Böhm-Bawerk's criticism of Menger's interest theory in his *Geschichte und Kritik der Kapitalzinstheorien* of 1884. Böhm regarded Menger's theory as a variant of the use theory (*Nutzungstheorie*) and attacked it. In Böhm's opinion, in economics, goods are regarded as nothing other than the sum of their possible uses which are always limited in their time dimension; every use (service) forms part of this sum (goods), therefore, it is illogical to admit the 'value of capital use' beside the value of goods. The value of a good in itself is the sum of the value of all possible uses of it. Böhm tried to convert Menger to this concept of goods in his time preference theory of interest (*Zeitagiotheorie*) which seeks to rouse interest in the influence of time on the evaluation of goods. Menger answered Böhm, explaining his new theory in this field, that the 'use of capital' is not identical to capital goods or any part thereof but is the 'chance of economic activity' which supplies the control over capital goods. He explained that this recognition is an inevitable result of the daily experience of the trading of such a mere chance besides the trade of capital goods.

This difference between Menger and Böhm seems to stem from the vision of the economic world that the two masters of the Austrian School had in mind. In Böhm's view the present value of capital is obtained by discounting future income flows. Menger's main concern centred on both disequilibrium and uncertainty, where 'chance' plays its own role. To Menger, economic action is the action taken under such unstable circumstances; he rejected the objective concept of value and thought it more natural that some uncertainty would accompany the process of every price formation.

The above was the result of Menger's efforts to clarify the nature of economic action in the 1880s. It might have been an effort that hid the intention to extend 'passive' subjectivism of utility theory to 'active' subjectivism focused on expectation as was later proposed by Ludwig Lachmann (1986).

Owing to the reflections on economic theory for two decades, his subjectivism became a conscious one. But the results of the theory were not fruitful. Menger's reflection ended with the confinement of economic rationality to the inner world of the individual, a micro-cosmos leaving too much else in an indeterminate state.

4. Post-'New plan' reflections

Even after the frustrated attempt to revise the Grundsätze of 1871 in 1889, Menger maintained a strong desire to do it. According to the Introduction of the posthumous edition of the *Grundsätze*, it was 'a quarter century after' the publication of the first edition when Menger conceived a new plan to make a 'theory of want' to precede theories of goods and value. The Introduction tells us that 'in the end of the century' Menger once prepared for the publication of the non-revised edition of the *Grundsätze* having witnessed the slow progress made at the attempted revision (1923: viii–ix). Menger's reflections after the 'new plan' show a conspicuous difference with the direction before it. If it is right to characterize the reflections of the first and second stages as 'methodological', that of the third might be called 'ontological'.

While the reflections of the second stage had aimed at establishing the dimension for economic action, freed from the deterministic view or from the 'physiological-technical' viewpoint, Menger in the third stage endeavoured to locate the economy in reality. On the one hand, he was interested in the diversity of economic phenomena which were supplied by ethnographic works or reports of travellers and sought a concept for the economy that could embrace this diversity. On the other hand, he delved into the (once rejected) fields of biology, physiology and psychology in order to trace the origins of subjective rationality in relation to economic action.

Part of the results of this investigation can be read in the theory of wants and the theory of economy in the posthumous edition of the *Grundsätze*. However, they are still so fragmental that it is a sort of conjecture to sketch general features of the reflections in the third stage.

4.1. Morphology of economic phenomena

Though the reasons for the change in Menger's research direction are unknown, we can find several statements from Menger in his publications spanning the period from the late 1880s to the early 1890s. For example, in the 1889a article 'Grundzüge einer Klassifikation der Wirtschaftswissenschaften' ('Elements of the Classification of Economic Sciences') Menger suggested a 'morphology of economic phenomena' as a subdivision of economics which is classified beside the 'theory of economic phenomena' in the generalizing part of economic studies. As seen by its definition, 'the task of this subdivision lies in the classification (according to the family, species, and sub-species) of real economic phenomena and in the description of their general essence' (not verbatim), this idea of study came from morphology or taxonomy in the historical natural sciences. Today we would refer to it as a 'theory of (comparative) economic systems'. According to Menger, the morphological study cannot make an independent branch in such sciences as physics or chemistry, where the form appears only as a composition of simple elements. One might say Menger's description of the economic phenomena in the first edition of *Grundsätze* contains morphology subordinated to economic theory. But he now clearly admitted to the task of establishing a systematic morphology which should describe economic phenomena 'in its diversity affected by its complication and by non-economical factors', not trying to reduce them in simple elements and to reconstruct them.

A similar concept can be seen in several places in the posthumous edition. However, the meaning of morphology in 1889 is stated in a review that Menger wrote in *Wiener Zeitung* (7/8 March 1889b):[8]

> What we call 'national economy' is not the sum of economies of individuals, but an organization in which individual economies are combined in various forms and diversely stratified. Individual economies, family economies, and public economies of various forms and of diverse levels supply a number of examples of the different economic agents. Their aims and means show also no less diversity. Viewing all these equally, for example, from the view point of private economy is not only insufficient but also misleading.

4.2. Two directions of human economy

Even if the diversity of economic phenomena could be approved, one could not deal with such diverse and concrete ideas in a theoretical work such as the *Grundsätze*. What could be done would be to present a general framework, or to suggest the factors for diversification. So considering the reflections on human economy, which were adopted in the posthumous edition, the first and third sections of the fourth chapter could be seen as an attempt to supply the base for the 'morphology of economic phenomena'. In the first section Menger defined 'economy' as 'a specified area of dispositive activity over goods available to a person or circle of persons for the satisfaction of their wants' (1923: 19–20, 87–8) and picked up the 'dispositive activity' as its 'subjective aspect'. In the third section the 'two fundamental directions' of the 'dispositive activity' are discussed. It is suggestive that a variant for this text was titled 'On various Complexity of Economy' (Menger, 1923: 73, footnote).

The typical understanding of 'economy' relates to activity which aims to attain future satisfaction of wants and is mixed with the orientation towards efficiency. But, assuming the possibility that these two emerge rather independently, this text tries to describe their features separately.

First, the former, 'the technical-economical disposition' (*technisch-ökonomische Disposition*), consists of the following elements:

> A-1. Estimation of our future wants (recognition of their kinds, quantities, and time and location of their emergence)
>
> A-2. Recognition of consumable goods (their kinds, quantities, and time and location) which are directly available for the satisfaction of wants (A-1)
>
> A-3. Estimation of the scarce consumable goods for our need and technological recognition of the means of production for them
>
> A-4. Dispositive activities to give aims and direction to the available means of production (including labor services) so as to fulfill the needs in appropriate quantities, qualities, time and location.
>
> (Ibid.: 74–5)

On the other side, the latter, 'saving direction' (*sparende Richtung*):

> B-1. Added to A-1, effort to recognize the relative importance of each act of satisfaction of those wants
>
> B-2. Added to A-2, effort to recognize the quantities of those available goods as correctly as possible
>
> B-3. Effort to avoid the loss of scarce consumable goods
>
> B-4. Effort to minimize the consumption of scarce consumable goods in each act of want satisfaction

B-5. Efforts to maximize the want satisfaction in total on the basis of B-1, in the dispositive activities of the scarce goods among diverse acts of want satisfaction (distribution in time is also included).

(Ibid.: 76–7)

These two directions contrast in the way the issue of scarcity of directly available consumable goods is addressed. Direction A aims at the attainment of the wants satisfaction via production. Therefore, the correct coordination among means of production, consumable goods and wants satisfaction is the point of this direction. While B, takes given scarcity for granted and aims to attain maximum wants satisfaction with given available goods, on the basis of recognition of the relative importance of the diverse wants satisfaction. It is true that most economies are based on a combination of the two; namely dispositive activities towards an efficient distribution of higher-order goods. It is not necessarily implied that the two directions cannot appear separately. A situation where there is a scarcity of consumable goods should be relatively easy to overcome, and the direction B would be weak. Or, in the case of the passengers of a ship in distress, the beloved case by economists including Menger to explain marginal utility theory, direction A does not exist at that moment.

In the preceding stage of Menger's reflection, A was regarded as mere technical rationality preceding the proper economic rationality. The 'economicity' meant the principle of efficiency. But, if the direction A should also be called 'economic', then, what kind of economic theory would come from it? Here it might be justified to mention that Karl Polanyi (1977) regarded Menger as an antecedent for his economic anthropology based on this text. Polanyi discovered in Menger's fragment an open door for the economic theory which deals with heterogeneous dispositive activities in their own right, not from the reductionist viewpoint of the market economists. On the other hand, Karl Menger, Jr, the editor of the posthumous edition of *Grundsätze* made much of the direction B, saying that this should be the moment that transforms the 'disjunctive determination' to the 'economically absolute' determination (p. 77).

4.3. Reflection on wants in the last stage

Another theme in the last stage of Menger's reflection, wants (*Bedürfnisse*; see Bloch, 1937), also has some precedent history. Karl Menger, Jr, supplied information showing that the manuscript of the *Grundsätze* in 1871 originally had a one or two page description of want, which was later cut. The reason for the deletion could have been, I assume, related to the methodological utterance in the Preface, which we discussed before. However, the Lecture prints of National Economy (*Nationalökonomie*), presumably originated by Menger's courses in 1890s, allocated one or two pages, before the theory of goods, to the explanation of wants.[9] 'Theory of wants is the fundament of the economics' was its first sentence. Further, one might consider Menger's association with the philosopher-psychologists of the day, such as Alexius Mainong and Christian Ehrenfels, who showed interest in the value theory of economics in the years from 1892 to 1894. In particular, Oskar Klaus prepared his dissertation in close contact with Menger, it dealt with Menger's theory of goods and value and was itself a theory of wants.[10]

For a better understanding we must gather the location of wants in the economic theory of Menger. The problem lies in that, economic action is the action directed at the attainment of the wants satisfaction of an economic agent, economic theory cannot do without wants, but arguing the content of wants is beyond the domain of economics.

Further, wants in economic theory should not be arbitrary. So long as the economic action of man takes place in the real world, there should be no impact if objective requirements are not represented in wants. As the text adopted for the posthumous edition states:

> In correspondence with the complex psycho-physical organization and higher intellectual nature of man, the economy of human being can have its appropriate ground only in the recognition of human wants: necessaries for the maintenance and harmonic development of human nature in its totality.
>
> (Menger, 1923: 3)

By representing the objective requirements and serving as the rational starting point of economic action, wants as stated above combine the causal process of the external world (physiological conditions included) and the teleological relation within the mind of the actor. But, then, how can such rational wants (recognition of wants) come into being? If my explanation hitherto is correct, Menger's reflection would run in a Kantian direction. Wants, as the starting point of economic theory, must be taken as being in existence, because they are rationally required!?

However, such an *a priori* assumption of rational wants (wants recognition) seems to be meaningless. Even for the same individual wants will have enormous diversity and can change at any moment. Wants is not such an abstract form as the Kantian 'personality', but rather a substantial principle that influences the concrete appearance of human action. My conjecture is that Menger, in his reflections after the 1890s, might have hit upon a rather Aristotelian approach that supposes several stages of subjective recognition of human wants towards a rational one. The wants are distinct from the 'instinct' (*Trieb*) at the physiological or emotional level and also from 'desire' (*Begierde*) at the level of sentiment. In Menger's view, these remain imperfect or irrational representations of the lacking or disturbing state of the basis of the human mind and body. At this stage Menger supposes the process in which the recognition of wants proceeds from a lower level to a higher level:

> The recognition of our wants, too, has the ultimate origin in our feeling; in the process of the recognition, however, the moment of direct feeling retreats more and more; it becomes successively towards a rational want that is grounded by experience, forecast, and judgment. The more we make progress in the recognition of our physical and psychical nature, of the objective world, as well as the relation of the both, the more we reach towards the forecast of the necessities for the maintenance of our life and welfare particularly and learn to compare their significance each other. As more complete becomes the recognition of our wants, in so higher degree becomes the wants perceived in our consciousness towards the precise expression of the necessities of the all-round harmonic development of our nature.
>
> (Ibid.: 4–5)

This recognition of wants is nothing more than internalized economic action. The core of the argument on the 'two directions' of economy lies in the management of external scarcity, this argument on the 'rationalization' of wants absorbs the economic action totally (including factors in the external world) in the self-recognition of the subject as a microcosm.

However, the other side of the supposition of the rationalization process is the approval of the fact that real economic actions are not always guided by rational wants recognition.

> The practical economic life of human actors is not guided by the wants but by the temporary opinions on the necessaries for the maintenance of their life and welfare. Indeed, it is seldom determined directly by their emotions and drives.
>
> (Ibid.: 4)

We have seen before that in Menger's vision human economy is exposed to the uncertainty of the external world and to the possibility of misunderstandings. But, we must add that in the internal world it is also threatened by irrational factors.

Menger's reflection on economic theory has now reached the depth of subjective rationality (economic man).

As we have shown, after 1871 Menger's reflection on economic theory commenced with an effort to overcome the weakness of the methodological understanding of the first edition of the *Grundsätze*. The reflection finally reached the problem of the ontological foundation of rational wants. Judging this path, and the results of this all-too-long reflection, opinions will vary.

Notes

In this article, most of the original German texts are translated into English by the author.

1. On the origin and contents of the Menger Papers, see Barnett (1990).
2. See Yagi (1992, 1993) and Ikeda (1995, 1997). Menger's annotation to Rau's *Grundsätze* is provided by E. Kauder as Menger (1963).
3. Menger (1961: 45–6). Kauder apparently misread the correction of the title and transcribed it as 'Betrachtungen[?] über den Zusammenhang der Güter'.
4. Kauder's comment on this elimination was: 'Last sentence of first paragraph crossed out with red pencil or crayon, the words "Die [...] Volkswirtschaftslehre" have not been eliminated. Reason not clear' (Menger 1961: 25). Now, the reason is completely clear.
5. This term was used originally by Menger in correspondence with Böhm-Bawerk. See Menger (1884) in Yagi (ed.) (1983: 36).
6. In order to grasp the form and role of 'capital' in the process of development, Schumpeter (1911) rejected Böhm-Bawerk's substantial (or materialistic) concept of capital and praised Menger's proposal of the 'realistic' concept in the 1888 article. On the contrary, Wicksell regarded Menger's proposal as a retreat (Wicksell, 1956: 188).
7. Yagi (ed.) (1983) contains two of Menger's letters (13 November 1884 and 1 January 1885). See also Yagi's introduction, esp. pp. 8–9.
8. Menger (1889b). The book reviewed is Gross (1888). On the contents page of the complimentary copy of this book (now in the Menger Library), Menger left entries which dealt with the diversity of 'economic agents' and of 'economic purposes'.

9. This is one of the lithograph prints (*Skripten*) derived from Menger's lecture. I confirmed three copies of Menger's *Nationalökonomie* at university libraries in Vienna, Salzburg and Okayama.
10. For a glance at these philosopher-psychologists, see Fabian and Simons (1986).

References

Barnett, M. (1990) 'The Papers of Carl Menger in the Special Collection Department, William R. Perkins Library, Duke University', in B. Caldwell (ed.) (1990).

Bloch, H. S. (1937) *La théeorie des besoins de Carl Menger*, Paris: Pichon et Durand-Anzias.

Caldwell, B. (ed.) (1990) *Carl Menger and His Legacy in Economics*, Durham: Duke University Press.

Fabian, R. and Simons, P. M. (1986) 'The Second Austrian School of Value Theory', in W. Grassel and B. Smith (eds) (1986).

Grassel, W. and Smith, B. (eds) (1986) *Austrian Economics – Historical and Philosophical Background*, London: Croom Helm.

Gross, G. (1888) *Wirtschaftsformen und Wirtschaftsprinzipien: ein Beitrag zur Lehre von der Organisation der Volkswirtschaft*, Leipzig: Duncker & Humblot.

Hack, F. (1872) 'Carl Menger, Grundsätze der Volkswirtschaft', *Zeitschrift für die gesamte Staatswissenschaft*, XXVIII: 182–4.

Hayek, F. A. (1934) 'Carl Menger', bibliographical introduction to the *Collected Works of Carl Menger, Series of Reprints of Scarce Tracts in Economics and Political Science*, 17, London: The London School of Economics and Political Science.

Ikeda, Y. (1995) 'Carl Menger in 1860s: Menger on Roscher's *Grundlagen*', in G. Meijer (ed.), *New Perspective on Austrian Economics*, London and New York: Routledge.

Ikeda, Y. (1997) *Die Entstehungsgeschichte der 'Grundsätze' Carl Mengers*, St. Katharinen: Scripta Mercaturae.

Kauder, E. (1961) *Introduction* to C. Menger (196l).

Lachmann, L. M. (1986) *The Market as an Economic Process*, Oxford: Blackwell.

Menger, C. (1871) *Grundsätze der Volkswirthschaftslehre. Erster, Allgemeiner Teil*, Vienna: Braumüller.

Menger, C. (1883) *Untersuchungen über die Methode der Sozialwissenschaften und der Politischen Ökonomie insbesondere*. Leipzig: Duncker & Humblot.

Menger, C. (1884) Letter to Böhm-Bawerk, 13 November 1884, in K. Yagi (1983).

Menger, C. (1888) 'Zur Theorie des Kapitals', *Jahrbücher für Nationalökonomie und Statistik*, New Series 17.

Menger, C. (1889a) 'Grundzüge einer Klassification der Wirtschaftswissenschaften', *Jahrbücher für Nationalökonomie und Statistik*, New Series 19: 465–96.

Menger, C. (1889b) 'Nationalökonomische Literatur in Oesterreich', *Wiener Zeitung*, 7. u. 8. März, 1889.

Menger, C. (ca. 1890) *Nationalökonomie*. Vorlesungsskripten kept at University Libraries of Vienna, Salzburg and Okayama.

Menger, C. (1923) *Grundsätze der Volkswirthschaftslehre*, 2nd edition from the bequest, edited by Karl Menger, Vienna: Hoelder-Pichler-Tempsky.
Menger, C. (1950) *Principles of Economics: First General Part*, translated and edited by J. Dingwall and B. F. Hoselitz (translation of Menger 1871), New York: New York University Press.
Menger, C. (1961) *Carl Mengers Zusätze zu 'Grundsätze der Volkswirtschaftslehre'*, Tokyo: Library of Hitotsubashi University.
Menger, C. (1963) *Carl Mengers Erster Entwurf zu seinen Hauptwerk 'Grundsätze' geschrieben als Anmerkungen zu den 'Grundsätzen der Volkswirtschaftslehre' von Karl Heinrich Rau*, Tokyo: Library of Hitotsubashi University.
Menger, K. (1923) 'Einleitung des Herausgebers', to C. Menger (1923).
Polanyi, K. (1977) *The Livelihood of Man*, edited by H. W. Peason, New York: Academic Press.
Roscher, W. (1874) *Geschichte der Nationalökonomik in Deutschland*, Munich: Oldenbourg.
Schmoller, G. (1873) 'Carl Menger, Grundsätze der Volkswirtschaftslehre', *Literarisches Centralblatt*, 5(1): 142–3.
Schumpeter, J. A. (1911) *Theorie der wirtschaftlichen Entwicklung*. Leipzig: Duncker & Humblot.
Weiss, F. X. (1924) 'Zur zweiten Auflage von Carl Mengers "Grundsätzen"', *Zeitschrift für Volkswirtschaft und Sozialpolitik*, New Series 4.
Wicksell, K. (1956) *Selected Papers on Economic Theory*, edited by E. Lindahl, London: Routledge.
Yagi, K. (1983) 'Formation of Böhm-Bawerk's Capital and Interest Theory', in K. Yagi (ed.) (1983).
Yagi, K. (ed.) (1983) *Böhm-Bawerk's First Interest Theory with C. Menger – Böhm-Bawerk Correspondence 1884–85*, Study Series No. 3 of the Center for Historical Social Science Literature, Hitotsubashi University.
Yagi, K. (1992) 'Carl Menger as Editor: Significance of Journalistic Experience for his Economics and for his Later Life', *Revue Européenne des Sciences Sociales*, XXX(92).
Yagi, K. (1993) 'Carl Menger's *Grundsätze* in the Making', *History of Political Economy*, 25(4).

Part II

Liberal Aspects of the Historical School: Max Weber

3
Discoursing Freedom: Weber's Project

Jun Kobayashi

1. Prehistory of the theme

1.1. Methodenstreit and Weber

The new Historical School of German economics was created to find a new style of research to solve the social question. Pioneers began to revise academic practices through social research, statistics, the investigation of legislation and administration, and a 'Seminar'-system (Grimmer-Solem, 2003: 43–67). The old Historical School, which criticized the universal validity of economic theories, had interests in real society, and these interests were received by their successors as useful legacy. In the 'Methodenstreit' Carl Menger stresses the significance of theory in the academic episteme concerning economic phenomena, and insists on improving the status of theory. To Schmoller, the Austrian School was nothing but a new trend within the narrow theoretical interest and had nothing to do with resolving the social question. Schmoller could not accept their pretension. The two schools began a battle to seize a majority of professorships in German speaking areas.

When Max Weber obtained a professorship in economics at Freiburg, he first lacked theoretical training. In preparing lectures, he grappled with this new trend in economic theory. What attracted him was the hypothesis of 'homo oeconomicus'. He understood the theoretical significance of the new trend, but he recognized its inability to explain the uniqueness of events. Weber was also discontent that the Historical School could not draw a strict distinction between 'ought' and 'be', and so tended towards low esteem of the specific value of political decisions.

Weber himself felt an identity with the Historical School, referring to 'we disciples of German Historical School' (1971: 16). In the prefatory essay as the editor of a new journal he referred to the rivalry of the two schools, and made an effort to clarify the logical relationship of both schools (1969: 85–95). His effort resulted in the construction of 'ideal type', which would contribute to the understanding of the regularity, and so of the causality of individuality of the phenomena. He named this standpoint 'Realwissenschaft', and in this arena he located both schools logically. He edited *Grundriss der Sozialökonomik* (*GdS*) from this viewpoint and thought the conflict of the schools not fatal but converging, as shown in the Preface to *GdS* (1914: VIII).

1.2. Freedom: Criticism of Knies

When we look at Weber's conception of freedom, the first thing to be considered is his criticism of Karl Knies in 'Roscher and Knies'. Knies contrasts human action that is free, irrational and individual with the lawful determination of naturally given conditions for action. Weber criticized this and stated: free action is rational in the sense that its motive is comprehensive; susceptibility to a meaningful interpretation stands for calculability; the less susceptibility to interpretation is, the more the freedom of will is denied. 'Incalculability is the principle of the madman.' Purposeful action has a high level of susceptibility to rational interpretation and of calculability, and this would contribute to formulate regularity (Weber, 1975: 125–9). In the case of Knies's *Analogie*, one may at best acquire some similarity through widening the scope of comparison and observation. He saw economic phenomena as a mixture of the irrationality of human action and the rationality of natural conditions. In so far as irrationality intervenes, he could base regularity only on *Analogie* (Kobayashi, 2001: 56–61). In short, Weber changed Knies's conception of man; and of social science as well.

I will consider the task of Weber's interpretative sociology and the concept of free action. If we admit the occidental rationalization as his main theme, we may ask what he thinks about the relationship between the rational economic action required by modern capitalism as the most rationalized way of life, and the 'freedom of man'. This question seems to constitute one of the most important themes in Chapter 2 of *Economy and Society*, and that chapter will be my main focus.

2. Paradox of rationalization

2.1. Rational social relationship

Social actions form social relationships through their reciprocity. An actor enters into a variety of social relationships with others, and being restricted by these relationships he has to act socially. Weber's interpretative sociology deals with this dynamic process. I will follow the logic of Chapter 1 in *Economy and Society*.

> The meaningful content which remains relatively constant in a social relationship is capable of formulation in terms of maxims which the parties concerned expect to be adhered to by their partners.
>
> (Weber, 1964: 120)

The more rational action is, the more constant a social relationship. Such a maxim becomes the symbol of the norm of which an actor is subjectively conscious.

As the consciousness of an actor increases, the social relationship becomes further rationalized. In accordance with this process, the meaningful content of action becomes the explicit maxim. Furthermore, through mutual consent, this content may develop from a subjective and inner maxim to objective agreement (*Vereinbarung*). This can be seen as further rationalization.

Here the word 'rationalization' refers to an increase in consciousness of action. Alongside this concept of consciousness (and unconsciousness), we must also consider whether the actor understands his action as instrumental (end-oriented) or as consummatory (self-sufficient). These two viewpoints can be compiled into rectangular coordinates (see Figure 3.1) to better understand Weber's typology of action.[1] This is a very important framework applicable to Weber's sociological analysis as a whole.

Weber's theory constitutes two types of social relationships, namely, *Vergemeinschaftung* and *Vergesellschaftung*. The former is the case where 'the orientation of social action is based on a subjective feeling' of belonging together. The latter, 'if and in so far as the orientation of social action within it rests on a rationally motivated adjustment of interests or a similarly motivated agreement, whether the basis of rational judgment be absolute values or reasons of expediency' (Weber, 1964: 136).

In terms of the consciousness of an actor, rationality increases from the former to the latter. When *Vergemeinschaftung* continues, actors tend to hold the content of their feeling of belonging together as 'maxim', and social relationship is also rationalized accordingly. As actors, based on their own interests, orient themselves towards the maxim, the relationship develops into *Vergesellschaftung*. When rationality advances in this way, the maxim will be formulated into an explicitly consented agreement.

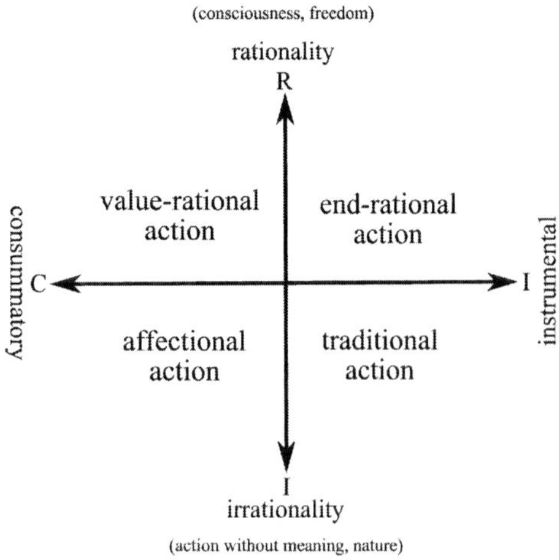

Figure 3.1 Typology of action

Weber cites three cases of pure *Vergesellschaftung*. First, temporal but rational, free market exchange; and second, *Zweckverein*, defined as 'a case of agreements as to a long-term course of action oriented purely to the promotion of economic or other (*sachlich*) interests of its members.' The third, purest case is a value-rationally motivated *Gesinnungsverein*, an example of which is 'the rational sect, in so far as it does not cultivate emotional and affective interests, but seeks only to serve a cause (*Sache*)' (ibid.: 136). Both *Vereine* (voluntary associations) are continuous and rational social relationships based on agreement. Whether an action as such is consummatory or instrumental does not matter. As rationality increases, a social relationship continuously pursues a cause.

2.2. Paradox of rationalization

Weber next considers corporate groups (*Verbände*). Concerning the order of a federation he says: 'the legally-established order of a *Vergesellschaftung* may originate in one of two ways: by voluntary agreement, or by being imposed and acquiesced in' (ibid.: 148). Here appears an odd reverse. *Vergesellschaftung*, a social relationship where rationalization of action has been advanced, becomes a group with an imposed and acquiesced order. Weber explains *oktroyiert* by saying that 'an order is always "imposed" to the extent that it does not originate from a voluntary personal agreement of all the individuals concerned' (ibid.: 149). Imposition (*Oktroyierung*) is a form that reduces the level of consciousness, and so the level of rationality (freedom). Corporate groups consist of *Verein* based on agreement and of *Anstalt* based on *Oktroyierung*, in both of which an action is subject to a rationally established order (ibid.: 151). From this, one may conclude the following: *Anstalt* is highly rational in terms of order, but brings about a lower level of rationality in terms of the consciousness of action. As the consciousness of action increases and a social relationship rationalizes, the order becomes established and rationalized. Conversely, there appears the possibility that the order may react to actors and reduce their consciousness.

This teaches us the paradoxical relationship between social action and social relationship, a version of the paradox of rationalization. If this primal problem embedded in the first chapter could be confirmed to be succeeding in the second, we could grasp one of the key problems of Weber's economic sociology.

Section 15 in Chapter 1 begins with a definition of *Betrieb*:

> An 'organization' (*Betrieb*) is a system of continuous purposive activity of a specific kind. A 'corporate organization' (*Betriebsverband*) is a Vergesellschaftung characterized by an administrative staff devoted to such continuous purposive activity.
>
> (Ibid.: 151)

First of all, the word '*Betrieb*' reminds us of business administration. Here we should not miss the fact that Weber has set modern corporations, the central agents of modern capitalism, as his main target. Weber began his academic career in commercial law. The most rational form of firm, corporation (*Aktiengesellschaft*), works today as 'going concern', typically representing the *Betriebsverband*.

2.3. Economic sphere: Formal and substantive rationality

Now I will consider the idea of rationality in the economic sphere. Weber contrasts formal and substantive[2] rationality. Formal rationality is best characterized as follows:

> A system of economic activity will be called 'formally' rational according to the degree in which the provision for needs, which is essential to every rational economy, is capable of being expressed in numerical, calculable terms, and is so expected.
>
> (Ibid.: 185)

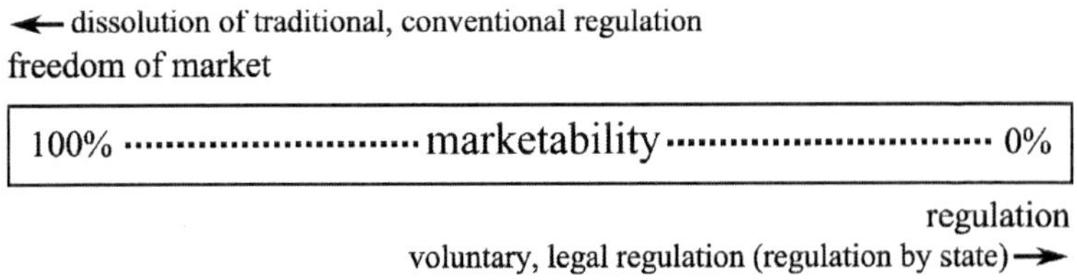

Figure 3.2 Marketability

Calculation is performed through money. Money is 'formally the most rational means of orienting economic activity' (ibid.: 186). Money calculation greatly increases calculability. As market exchange through money is repeated, the formal rationality of economic action increases. If people find their interests in trading according to their own calculation and in the increase of marketability (*Marktgängigkeit*: liquidity of goods and services), they seek to exclude various regulations of the market. Marketability and freedom of the market increase in this way (see Figure 3.2). We can speak here of the advancement of formal rationality in the economy.[3]

Weber explains with the phrase 'substantive rationality' 'the degree in which a given group of persons, no matter how it is delimited, is or could be adequately provided with goods by means of an economically oriented course of social action'. Weber continues: 'this course of social action will be interpreted under the viewpoint of certain evaluating postulates no matter what they may be. There is a variety of different possibilities' (1964: 184–5, 1972: 44). There can be a variety of postulates that evaluate the consequences of action. End-rational calculation through technically adequate means is not sufficient by itself. As Weber states:

> Substantive rationality cannot be measured in terms of formal calculation alone, but also involves a relation to the absolute values or to the content of the particular given ends to which it is oriented.
>
> (Ibid.: 158)

As examples, Weber listed such values as ethical, political, utilitarian, hedonic and egalitarian (1972: 45). The important fact is that there can be a number of rational postulates. We cannot easily speak of substantive rationalization of the economy.

Besides these substantive evaluations of the consequences of actions, there can also be the evaluation of economic action itself. Action adopted as the adequate means to achieve a goal is evaluated here from an ethical, aesthetic or other point of view. This suggests that the formally rational action of money calculation may have only secondary meaning.

In explaining substantive rationality, Weber uses the expression 'value-rational or substantively end-rational (evaluation)' (ibid.: 45). The point is not the contrast of 'consummatory – instrumental', but that this substantive rationality refers to the degree to which the original aim (value or end) was attained by the adopted means (action). We should keep in mind that the two pairs of concepts, 'value- and end-rational' and 'substantive and formal rationality', are constructed on logically different levels.[4]

2.4. Calculability

Weber stresses the importance of money accounting:

> From a purely technical point of view, money is the most 'efficient' means of economic accounting. That is, it is formally the most rational means of orienting economic activity.
>
> Accounting in terms of money, and not its actual use, is thus the specific means of end-rational economic production (Beschaffungswirtschaft).
>
> (Weber, 1964: 186, 1972: 45)

Capital calculation naturally includes the opportunity cost and depreciation of the means of production. The word '*Beschaffung*' here does not sound strange because the main target of his investigation is not profit-making in general, which is seen everywhere especially as trade, but the activity of modern industrial capital.

Weber's definitions go further:

> Capital accounting is the valuation and verification of opportunities for profit and of the success of profit-making activity. [...] 'Capital' is the sum of money in terms of which the means of profit-making which are available to the enterprise are valued.
>
> (Ibid.: 191–2)

Weber demands that the readers consult the textbook of accounting, saying 'the concept of capital has been defined strictly with reference to the individual enterprise and in accordance with accounting practice' (ibid.: 195). But in the midst of this description appears the heterogeneous expression: 'capital accounting has arisen as a basic form of economic calculation only in the Western World' (ibid.: 193). Concerning this point, he stresses that:

> By no means all profit-making enterprises with capital accounting are 'doubly' market-oriented in that they both purchase means of production on the market and sell their product there.
>
> (Ibid.: 201)

Tax farming is a good example where profit-making with capital accounting is not always market-oriented. Here we can identify Weber's thinking, that 'doubly' market-oriented profit-making represents one pole of his typology of profit-making activities. He also considers economic theory as having validity in the market economy, where production and consumption circulate via the market. In this sense economic theory is a kind of ideal type which treats the market economy.

Weber accepts from the Austrian School the modern-day conception of 'consumer sovereignty' and states:

> It goes without saying that in terms of economic theory the direction in which goods can be profitably produced by profit-making enterprises is determined by their marginal utilities for final consumers in conjunction with the latter's incomes.
>
> (Ibid.: 201)

Consumers' incomes are, of course, important. Capital calculation has also to account for such expenses as marketing organization and advertisement. It is bound with the social means of a disciplined organization, the appropriation of the means of production, and in this sense, with the condition of domination. In this context Weber points out that the formal rationality of money calculation is dependent on certain specific substantive conditions:

> It is not wants as such, but effective demand for utilities, which regulates the production of goods by profit-making enterprises oriented to capital accounting. What is to be produced is thus determined by the structure of marginal utilities in the income group which has both the inclination and the resources to purchase a given utility. This will depend on the distribution of wealth in the particular society.
>
> (Ibid.: 211–12)

Weber shows here the results of economic action in the market as the substantive conditions for the formal rationality of money calculation, such as the distribution of wealth or the structure of marginal utilities in certain income groups. Consumers' incomes matter. Formal-rational activity produces certain substantive consequences and they in turn form limitations on formal rationality.

As the income differential increases, for example, the ability of the poor to dispose of market freedom decreases. The changing desire of the rich may deprive certain goods of marketability. Money is a bearer of formal rationality, but never neutral in its function.

> [The price] results from the struggle of man against man. Money is rather, primarily, an instrument in the competitive struggle, and competitive price is a means of calculation in so far as it takes the form of quantitative evaluation of the opportunity (chance) of struggle for interest.
>
> (Weber, 1972: 58, 1964: 211)

Weber conceives money and money calculation in the manner outlined above. His original contrast of formal and substantive rationality might be this money calculation.

From this point of view, two elements in capitalism need attention: the possibility of crisis and the distribution of income. I will discuss the former. Expropriation of the means of production from producers brings about the domination on workers, and various relationships concerning ownership and management of the means of production. Here appear the interests who stand outside the enterprise.

> Interests are spoken of as 'outside the firm' (*betriebsfremd*) in so far as they are not primarily oriented to the long-run profitability of the enterprise. [They may have] control of the plant and capital goods of the enterprise or of a share in it as a means of making a speculative profit.
>
> (Weber, 1964: 249)

The separation of ownership and management and the increase of marketability (commercialization of bond and share) produced the rational capital market, which increased the rationality of business administration, and at the same time produced the germ of crisis. The advance of formal rationality produces specific elements, which disturb the economic order. This is named substantive irrationality.

We may pick up another part concerning this issue. Section 13 in Chapter 2 describes from the viewpoint of economic sociology the course well-known to the theoretical viewpoint.

> If the standard used is that of the provision of a certain minimum of subsistence for the maximum size of population, the experience of the last few decades would seem to show that formal and substantive rationality coincide to a relatively high degree. [...] Under all circumstances, it holds true that formal rationality can explain anything about the type of real want satisfaction only when it is combined with knowledge of the distribution of income.
>
> (Weber, 1964: 212)

In Chapter 1, we saw the contrast of end-rational and value-rational, where 'rational' is explained in terms of consciousness of action. In Chapter 2, the contrast of formal and substantive rationality is explained from the objective viewpoint. On the one hand, people have learnt to adopt more adequate means through empirical and theoretical knowledge. The high degree of formal rationality has been attained, and calculability has been increasing. On the other hand, substantive rationality reminds us of the difference between prior calculation and outcome. The original aim has not always been achieved.

Numerous kinds of arts have been developed to increase the rationality of instrumental action. The history of mankind seems to be a process of increasing formal rationality. In this process the pursuit of end-rationality may be transformed into the end itself, so that the action concerned may be oriented exclusively to the formal rationality with the help of other persons' objective viewpoint. However, it is not unusual that man feels alienated when unable to recognize whether he or she contributes substantively to the original end or not. This surely leads to the reduction of value-rationality, and thus of freedom. We cannot say simply that the increase of rationality brings more freedom.

Section 12 of Chapter 2 deals with calculation in kind and natural economy, and includes the famous phrases:

> The fundamental limitations of accounting in kind as the basis of calculation in enterprise [...] are found in the problem of imputation [...]
>
> The problem is fundamental to any kind of complete socialization. We cannot speak of any kind of a 'rational planned economy' so long

> as at this decisive point we have no way of working out a rational plan.
>
> (Weber, 1972: 55–6, 1964: 205)

Weber states here that the economic problems during World War I and the post-war period draw our attention to the possibility of accounting in kind, and that this point was taken up by Otto Neurath. Weber considers the war economy as a 'bankrupt economy' and thinks that calculation in kind remains at a primitive level in the face of alternative ends, and so is a type of 'household' (Weber, 1964: 209). The next quote is the last part of this section.

> Everywhere it is money that bears accounting, and this explains the fact that calculation in kind has remained on an even lower technical level than the actual nature of its problems might have necessitated (in this respect O. Neurath appears to be right). While the above was in press, the essay of L. Mises, dealing with these problems, appeared.
>
> (Weber, 1972: 58, 1964: 210–11)

Weber's position in the economic calculation controversy has been well described by Tribe (1995: 142–60). Weber's seat seems to be next to Mises, the originator of this controversy. I want to interpret Weber's words as follows: a planned economy (socialism) is irrationally possible. This expression might show the task of socialists of the day and expose the existence of other factors than economic rationality in the socialist movement. I will explain my opinion by looking at the history of economic discourse.

3. Dietzel the intermediary

3.1. Discussion of post-Methodenstreit period

Nau seeks to show how greatly the methodological self-consciousness of economics in German speaking areas changed during one generation by examining the methodologies of Schmoller, Menger, Dietzel and Weber (Nau, 1997: 25). He suggested that Dietzel presented self-interest and economic principle as two presuppositions of theoretical social economics, and that Weber's reception of these was ambivalent.

> Dietzel acknowledged, according to Weber, the heuristic and hypothetic value of economic teachings, but was not yet released perfectly

> from the conception that such teachings had psychological ground. Contrary to him, Weber would avoid every psychological foundation of economic teachings.
>
> (Nau, 1997: 234)

My research inspired by Nau's suggestion will show that Dietzel had a large influence on Weber's conception of *Wirtschaftsgesinnung*.

To understand Dietzel's statement, it is possible to summarize the Historical School's criticism against abstract theory as follows: economic theory should be induced from empirical facts; human nature is not composed only of egoism; the ethical improvement of mankind must also be taken into account.

Dietzel's criticism is, in short, as follows. It is a mistake to regard the motive of economic action as egoism. To gain maximum fruit from minimum cost is the *Erwerbstrieb* (acquisitive impulse) of economic principle (Dietzel, 1884a: 365, 1884b: 33ff.). Every action concerning scarcity, not limited to the economic, has in itself this psychic impulse (Dietzel, 1884b: 200). Social economics has the task as a theoretical science to describe socio-economic phenomena and give a causal explanation of them. Social economics presupposes 'homo oeconomicus' in order to construct theory. It considers the result of an event under the presupposition that the people concerned have been motivated exclusively economically. The task of theoretical social economics is to show what process the phenomena of wealth would take if the actions of individuals were motivated only by the desire for wealth. This is what J. S. Mill insisted; that not every action stems from the desire for wealth (Dietzel, 1895: 28–9, 57, 78–9).

The hypothesis of egoism is a mistake. Mill instead set the hypothesis of homo oeconomicus and so made theoretical progress. Mill has not yet been sufficiently assessed. Instead of taking Mill's approach, Adolph Wagner, Menger and others wanted to protect the hypothesis of egoism against the attack by the Historical School. They all insisted that the most general and strongest psychic impulse is egoism (Dietzel, 1895: 80–1).

Weber, the young professor of economics, must have seriously consulted Dietzel's opinion, which insisted on 'the separation of be from ought' and referred to Mill and 'homo oeconomicus'. Weber listed Dietzel's works in his 'reading guide', and stated in his 'lecture outline' that abstract theory presupposes a constructed 'economic subject' and does not deal with 'empirical men' (Weber, 1990: 5, 30; Tribe, 1995: 91).

We find sentences in the essay on 'Objectivity' (1904) that were obviously inspired by Dietzel:

> It has been believed that it [the naturalistic construction of economic theory] is a matter of the psychological isolation of a specific 'impulse', the acquisitive impulse, or of the isolated study of a specific maxim of human conduct, the so-called economic principle. Abstract theory purported to be based on psychological axioms and as a result historians have called for an empirical psychology in order to show the invalidity of those axioms and to derive the course of economic events from psychological principles. [...] Thus, the far-flung polemic, which centred on the question of the psychological justification of abstract theoretical propositions, on the scope of the 'acquisitive impulse' and the 'economic principle,' etc., turns out to have been fruitless.
>
> (Weber, 1969: 88–9)

Here appears the critic against Dietzel who stood for the possibility to isolate and grasp economic interests (Dietzel, 1884b: 241), and against assumptions based on psychological axioms. This was also the criticism against Schmoller's inclination to expect empirical psychology. Weber rejected such attitudes as to hypostatize some abstract ideal or psychological hypothesis and to derive from it empirical events.

Dietzel assumed the pure economic society and sought to construct social economics as a special discipline of a social economy differentiated from a national economy. Methodologically he stood clearly for the Austrian School.[5] Weber, by contrast, wanted to accept economic theory as the ideal type without a natural scientific foundation.

We should note the fact that Weber's 'ideal type' was first presented concerning economic theory. More important is that Dietzel saw socioeconomic phenomena as constructed by the economic interests of individuals, trusted to the economic theory for the abstract consideration of the causal relationship of events (Dietzel, 1884b: 228, 259). He regarded *Erwerbstrieb* as a self-evident principle of every reasonable action (Dietzel, 1884a: 365). Weber brought up the concept of 'spirit of capitalism' in his essay on 'Protestant ethic' also in 1904.

We cannot detect any single motive for writing 'Protestant ethic' in Weber, but this essay must be a product of his wrestling with the problematic discourse of '*Erwerbstrieb*' in both economic theory and economic history. The disseminating of this word has been investigated in detail by Takebayashi (2003). He described brilliantly the appearance of the concept of capitalism. Here we will not enter into the famous Weber thesis, but will focus on the usage of the word.

> [...] This was the case not because the acquisitive impulse [Erwerbstrieb] in pre-capitalist epochs was perhaps less well-known or developed, as is so often said, or because the auri sacra fames (craving for gold) was then, or is even today, smaller outside modern, middle-class capitalism, as is depicted in the illusions of modern-day romantic thinkers.
>
> (Weber, 2002: 20)

According to Takebayashi, Brentano and Schmoller named *Erwerbstrieb* or *Handelsgeist* what the former generation had called *Eigennutz, Egoismus* or *Individualismus*. The new generation derived it from self-interest, which was regarded as having validity in the classical school of political economy, and considered it to originate in the transitional period from the artisan to the putting-out system (Takebayashi, 2003: 86, 77, 335).

Weber's 'spirit of capitalism' was conceived as a critique of the explanation of the rise of capitalism with the help of *Erwerbstrieb*. First, concerning the usage, Weber was critical of both Dietzel and the Historical School. *Erwerbstrieb*, assumed by Dietzel to be valid in every socio-economic phenomena, cannot explain the professional ethic (*Berufsethik*) of the ascetic protestant that produced the spirit of capitalism. Likewise, the assumption by Brentano that the permeation of *Erwerbstrieb* or *Handelsgeist* brought about economic growth, cannot explain the appearance of modern rational capitalism in the West. Second, Weber proposed as his own solution the cooperation of non-economic factors as the motive of economic action. Nevertheless, Weber's introduction of religious factors does not mean a total denial of Dietzel, whose task was just one-sided explanation. In this sense, Weber might have supplemented Dietzel by showing how the introduction of factors other than economic can explain socio-economic phenomena.

The essays on 'Objectivity' and 'Protestant Ethic' were Weber's response to the *post-Methodenstreit* discussion of economics. Research into the methodological papers in this period of Dietzel or Hasbach[6] helps greatly to disclose the connotation of Weber's work. For all that, the fact that Weber sought to sophisticate the method to introduce the force of the ideal, for example, of 'hope for freedom' or 'religious motive to get certificate of salvation' into the explanation of economic action is especially important. He must have worked hard to find a method to explain the cooperation between the economic and other spheres.

> [...] the psychological motivation that arose out of the conception of work as a calling and as the means best suited (and in the end often as the sole means) for the devout to become certain of their state of salvation.
>
> (Weber, 2002: 121)

Here it is argued that the normative in economic action was produced in certain situations specific to religion, one cultural sphere, and that the religious element worked as psychological motivation for economic action. From here the task follows to clarify the *Eigengesetzlichkeit* (own law or logic) of each cultural sphere, to grasp how a certain content in a cultural sphere is to be accepted in the other cultural sphere as a factor of motivation, and to identify where and how elective affinity (*Wahlverwandtschaft*) functions in the midst of tension (repulsion and attraction) among various cultural spheres (Weber, 1969: 164–88). In this methodic investigation Weber's effort tended towards sociology of action. Weber himself, however, regarded these tasks as ones of 'social science', as seen in his statement that: 'the social science that we are striving for is a "*Wirklichkeitswissenschaft*"', or 'the qualitative aspect of phenomena concerns us in the social sciences' (1969: 72, 74, 1990: 170, 173).

3.2. Spirit of socialism

The preface of *Collected Essays on Sociology of Religion* stresses the specific character of rational capitalism in occident, saying:

> [...] a 'drive to acquire goods' has actually nothing whatsoever to do with capitalism, as little as has the 'pursuit of profit,' money and the greatest possible gain'.
>
> (Weber, 2002: 152)

Weber lists such spheres of life as economy, technology, scientific work, education, warfare, administration and the practice of law. After pointing out that each sphere has its own rationalization, he argues:

> Our concern is to identify this uniqueness [the characteristics of modern Western rationalism] and to explain its origin. Every attempt at explanation, recognizing the fundamental significance of economic

> factors, must above all take account of these factors. Nevertheless, the opposite line of causation should not be neglected.
>
> (Ibid.: 160)

He called capitalism the 'most fateful power of our modern life'. This seems to testify that the rationalization of the economy is one of the key motives in Weber's work. That the rationalization specific to the economic sphere is connected with the formal rationality of capital calculation is also pointed out here. 'The opposite line of causation' has been exemplified by the essay on 'Protestant ethic', which investigates the origin of a unique frame of mind named the 'spirit of capitalism'.[7]

Now we might ask whether we can set the frame of mind named the 'spirit of socialism.' It is not totally a reckless attempt because we read in Chapter 1 of *Economy and Society* the following:

> Even a socialist economy would have to be understood sociologically in exactly the same kind of 'individualistic' terms; that is, in terms of the action of individuals, the types of 'officials' found in it, as would be the case with a system of free exchange analyzed in terms of the theory of marginal utility. [...] The real empirical sociological investigation begins with the question: What motives determine and lead the individual members and participants in this socialistic community to behave in such a way that the community came into being in the first place and that it continues to exist?
>
> (Weber, 1964: 107)

The second half of section 14 in Chapter 2 is a response to this question. Section 14 contrasts the market economy with the planned economy, and points out those interests specific to the inhabitants in a planned economy. They would be obliged to conduct non-autonomous activity:

> Along with opportunities for special material rewards, a planned economy may have command over certain ideal motives of what is in the broadest sense an altruistic type, which can be used to stimulate a level of achievement in economic production comparable to that which autonomous orientation to opportunities for profit, by producing for the satisfaction of effective demand, has been able to achieve in a market economy. Where a planned economy is radically carried out, it must further accept the inevitable reduction in formal rationality of calculation which would result from the elimination of money and capital accounting. This is merely an example of

> the fact that substantive and formal rationality are inevitably largely opposed.
>
> (Weber, 1964: 214–15)

Weber knows clearly that every planned economy would demand substantive rationality, and therefore endure the inevitable reduction in formal rationality. But the fact that Weber refers here to the 'ideal motives of an altruistic type' attracts our attention. If a planned economy is to function, certain adequate motives are needed. We must answer rather negatively the question of whether there could be such a frame of mind. Nevertheless, this manner of discourse can be seen as Weber's response to Dietzel, who sought to explain every economic action by *Erwerbstrieb*. I have one reason for this interpretation.

Dietzel is regarded as one of the pioneers of comparative systems analysis. He contrasted decentralist and centralist organization (competitive and collective system) and insisted on the possibility of economic theory in both systems. He saw the real economic system as a mixture of both, one of which would come to the fore according to the circumstances of the time (Dietzel, 1895: 86–92, 118–20).

In contrast, Weber designed the typological casuistry of economic activity, which included marketability in terms of rationality, the contrast of money calculation and accounting in kind, a dichotomy of business administration and household, and his original discussion of 'Appropriation'.[8] This typology, covering almost all historical phenomena, constitutes a kind of spectrum, of which the market economy and the planned economy represent the opposite poles. Weber refers to the frame of mind in this context. He examined the significance of the economy as a fundamental factor and then went further along the reverse line of causation. Weber responded to Dietzel in this manner.

Weber's comment on ideal motive, in addition, came to be a critique against Neurath. Neurath became committed to the 'new humanity (*Neuer Mensch*)' of Austrian Marxism in the Vienna of the 1920s. This was an advocacy of a new ethos that should support Austrian socialization from within. Weber's comment can be seen as a critique against the spirit of socialism. Weber certainly did not use such a word. But we have traced Weber from the start where *Erwerbstrieb* had been regarded as a motive of action, via the period when he advocated the 'spirit of capitalism' resulting from the ethical selection of acquisitive impulse, to the stage where he analyzed the economic organization that would need 'ideal motives of an altruistic type' as an opposite of profit seeking. In this context, Weber might be justified in using the expression 'the spirit of socialism'.

4. Project of freedom as a task

Having examined Weber's use of plural rationalities, we cannot regard his so-called rationalization thesis as that various rationalities advance in parallel. We know from secondary sources that Weber saw the future pessimistically. Apart from Weber the pessimist, he empirically and soberly presents under what kind of rationality free action occurs, which rationalities would promote it and how it would contradict with its own end. His theory shows the motive and possible results of action, and so has utility for readers to provoke reflection. We should note the latent element, that is, the search for the possibility of 'freedom to value', exemplified in the 'Protestant Ethic' that Weber himself analyzed. The desire for the certificate of salvation was the symptom of a kind of religious freedom. Actions of ascetic Protestants amounted to a phenomenon that led to cultural creation. This importance must be realized clearly.

But do we have such a convenient possibility yet? We may set here the action with both value- and end-rational nature, consulting Figure 3.1. As an action not on the one-side of C-I axis we can imagine, for example, the one with the 'spirit of capitalism', which is regarded as contributing to the making of modern, middle-class capitalism. Actions oriented to natural law are evaluated to serve the making of modern legal systems. One might say, as after-wit, that these served only to let *Versachlichung* accelerate. It has little meaning. The point is, whether or not the creative phase in history can be clarified by Weber's analytical tools. According to this context, we may search for the room of freedom, where we feel normative to solve the accurate problem of the day, and at the same time feel content with our actions to resolve the problem.

Weber's ideal (pure) type has, in fact, almost no counterpart in reality. It is very unstable by itself, and has no guarantee for existence alone. This logical nature is valid for 'end- and value rational', and also for the three types of legitimate authority. Neither charismatic nor legal authority is stable by itself in reality. This holds for the pair of 'ethic of conviction and responsibility' in political sphere. Once this nature of Weberian concept formation is acknowledged, we can suppose the imagination of an action with two contradicting characters in Figure 3.1 as according to Weber's intention.

My last reference is to the unique discussion of O'Neil concerning the calculation controversy. According to O'Neil, Neurath and Hayek concur that 'the triumph of reason is "the clear recognition of the limits of actual insight".' Difference comes next. For Neurath, technical calculation is impossible in social choices because such choices have an ethical and political dimension that is incommensurable so that no algorithmic procedure could capture it. Hayek denies any end of market or of society. The coordination of competing values is to be solved by the 'Great Society'. Given the plurality of incommensurable values, Neurath has to rely on non-technical judgment, a kind of ethical judgment that Hayek would reject (O'Neil, 1996: 441–2).

Besides calculability, the focus of the controversy is set on the epistemological problem of how to understand social and economic phenomena as a basis of social choice. In this context Weber's introduction of plural rationalities presupposes the plurality of incommensurable values.[9] This evokes us of the significance of an element, namely 'freedom to value'. 'Socialism is irrationally possible' is not only a criticism against Neurath, but a representation of the project of searching for freedom on Weber's side as well. We arrive at the border of empirical scientific knowledge now. Weber's work continues to have applicability in the socio-philosophical field. This field is open beyond, to be ploughed now on.

Notes

1. Figure 3.1 is Nakano's simplified form (Nakano, 1983: 170). Nakano's work is full of originality and far-reaching insight.
2. Original is 'material' (Weber, 1972: 44).
3. Weber's argument here closely resembles some of Mises's ideas.
4. Weber might have created the idea of 'formal and substantive rationality' for the analysis of economic phenomena. He had contrasted subjective end-rationality and objective *Richtigkeitsrationalität* in 1913 (1988: 432–5). *Richtigkeitsrationalität* seems to be the prototype of this pair.
5. See also Dietzel (1890: 570).
6. Hasbach developed a discussion concerning the status of the controversy (1895: 480–2, 751–2, 772).
7. Kalberg's effort gave English readers access to Weber's potentiality concerning a sociological approach to economic history, half a century later than in Japan. See Schwentker (1998: 92–138, 220–39). Chapter 2 (especially typology of Appropriation) of *Economy and Society* remains generally untouched. See, for example, Scott (2000: 173–4, 179–81). In this sense (and surely by nature) Karl Polanyi, the author of *Livelihood of Man*, does not belong to 'English readers'. According to Cangiani (2007: 37–8), Polanyi's work is a succession of Weber's.

8. 'Appropriation' is a category specific to Weber's economic sociology. It would require another chapter to consider it fully.
9. Instead of capital accounting (on micro-level), Neurath suggests social utility accounting in socialist society (on macro-level). He presupposes the plurality of values and stands not for monetary profitability but for the increase of pleasure and the feeling of happiness (Neurath, 1925: 394–5). This is a version of Weber reception, and can be interpreted as Neurath's reaction to Weber's criticism.

References

Cangiani, M. (2007) 'The forgotten institutions', in M. Harvey, R. Ramlogan, and S. Randles (eds), *Karl Polanyi: New Perspectives on the Place of the Economy in Society*, Manchester and New York: Manchester University Press: 25–42.

Dietzel, H. (1884a) 'Literatur: C. Menger, Untersuchungen über die Methode der Sozialwissenschaften und der politischen Ökonomie insbesondere', *Jahrbücher für Nationalökonomie und Statistik*, N.S., 8: 107–34, 353–70.

Dietzel, H. (1884b) 'Beiträge zur Methodik der Wirtschaftswissenschaft', *Jahrbücher für Nationalökonomie und Statistik*, N.S., 9: 17–44, 193–259.

Dietzel, H. (1890) 'Die klassische Werttheorie und die Theorie vom Grenznutzen', *Jahrbücher für Nationalökonomie und Statistik*, N.S., 20: 561–606.

Dietzel, H. (1895) *Theoretische Sozialökonomik*, Leipzig: C. F. Winter'sche Verlagshandlung.

Grimmer-Solem, E. (2003) *The Rise of Historical Economics and Social Reform in Germany 1864–1894*, Oxford: Oxford University Press.

Hasbach, W. (1895) 'Zur Geschichte des Methodenstreites in der politischen Ökonomie', *Jahrbuch für Gesetzgebung, Verwaltung und Volkswirtschaft im Deutschen Reich*, 19(2): 465–90; 19(3): 751–808.

Kobayashi, J. (2001) 'Karl Knies's conception of political economy', in Y. Shionoya (ed.), *The German Historical School*, London: Routledge: 54–71.

Nakano, T. (1983) *Makkusu Weba to gendai: (<hikakubunkashi-teki siza> to <bussyouka tosite no gourika>)*, Tokyo: San'ichi shobo (in Japanese). (Max Weber and the Modern Age: <Comparative Cultural-historical Aspect> and <Versachlichung as Rationalization>)

Nau, H. H. (1997) *Eine Wissenschaft vom Menschen: Max Weber und die Begründung der Sozialökonomik in der deutschsprachigen Ökonomie 1871 bis 1914*, Berlin: Duncker & Humblot.

Neurath, O. (1925) 'Sozialistische Nützlichkeitsrechnung und kapitalistische Reingewinnrechnung', *Der Kampf*, 18(10): 391–5.

O'Neil, J. (1996) 'Who won the socialist calculation debate?', *History of Political Thought*, 17(3): 431–42.

Schwentker, W. (1998) *Max Weber in Japan: Eine Untersuchung zur Wirkungsgeschichte 1905–1995*, Tübingen: Mohr Siebeck.

Scott, A. (2000) 'The privatization of the state: The British experience', in K. McRobbie and K. P. Levitt (eds), *Karl Polanyi in Vienna: The Contemporary Significance of The Great Transformation*, New York: Black Rose Books: 173–90.

Takebayashi, S. (2003) *Die Entstehung der Kapitalismustheorie in der Gründungsphase der deutschen Soziologie: Von der historischen Nationalökonomie zur historischen Soziologie Werner Sombarts und Max Webers*, Berlin: Duncker & Humblot.

Tribe, K. (1995) *Strategies of Economic Order*, Cambridge: Cambridge University Press.

Weber, M. (1914) 'Vorwort', in *Grundriss der Sozialökonomik*, Vol. 1, Tübingen: Mohr: VII–IX.

Weber, M. (1964) *The Theory of Social and Economic Organization*, translated by A. M. Henderson and T. Parsons, New York: Free Press.

Weber, M. (1969) *The Methodology of the Social Sciences*, translated and edited by E. A. Shils and H. A. Finch, New York: Free Press.

Weber, M. (1971) *Gesammelte Politische Schriften*, 3rd edition, Tübingen: Mohr Siebeck.

Weber, M. (1972) *Wirtschaft und Gesellschaft*, 5th edition, Tübingen: Mohr Siebeck.

Weber, M. (1975) *Roscher and Knies*, translated by Guy Oakes, New York: Free Press.

Weber, M. (1988) *Gesammelte Aufsätze zur Wissenschaftslehre*, 7th edition, Tübingen: Mohr Siebeck.

Weber, M. (1990) *Grundriss zu den Vorlesungen über Allgemeine ('theoretische') Nationalökonomie*, Tübingen: Mohr Siebeck.

Weber, M. (2002) *The Protestant Ethic and the Spirit of Capitalism*, translated by Stephen Kalberg, Oxford: Blackwell.

4
Max Weber and the 'New Economics'

Keith Tribe

> Incidentally, you know just as well as I do that for years now he has directed his interests towards sociology and political science, and has almost completely given up economics as such (*daß er die eigentliche Nationalökonomie fast ganz an den Nagel angehängt hat*). However, with his enormous talent and ability to work, it would be easy for him to get used to it again.[1]

So wrote Ernst Troeltsch to Heinrich Dietzel on 22 October 1917, responding to a request that he assess the relative merits of Max and Alfred Weber regarding appointment to a University of Bonn chair in economics. His offhand remark noting a redirection of Weber's interests some years before serves to underline the fact that well into the new century Max Weber was indeed primarily thought of as an economist. His first permanent university appointment had been at Freiburg, as Professor of Economics and Financial Science;[2] he had then succeeded Karl Knies under the same title at Heidelberg in 1897, suffering a breakdown the following year and eventually resigning from the post in 1903.[3] When he formally resumed teaching in Vienna in 1918,[4] and when in 1919 he succeeded Brentano in Munich, the posts he occupied were also in economics. And as we shall see below, Weber would in fact return to his earlier work on economic theory in the second chapter of *Wirtschaft und Gesellschaft*, a dazzling achievement completed in the months before his death in June 1920.

Today there should no longer be any need to argue the point that Max Weber's intellectual orientation was primarily to law and economics, disciplines of thought as much as university faculties; and that his contribution to the new social sciences of the twentieth century originates in this specific nexus. The question is not therefore 'was Max Weber an economist?' but 'what kind of economist was Max Weber?' A preliminary response to this can only be that he was an economist trained in a German university in the 1880s and a teacher of economics in the 1890s at Freiburg and Heidelberg. He described himself in his Freiburg inaugural address as a representative of the 'Younger School' of German historical economics, apparently aligning himself with Schmoller, Brentano and of course Sombart. But just over two years later, presenting his lectures in Heidelberg as successor to the last representative[5] of the 'Older School', he was quickly identified as 'a proponent of the Austrian School who has taken on the task of importing the system of his teachers Böhm-Bawerk and Menger into Germany'.[6] In the conventional understanding of contemporary economic science it would seem that Weber had, since his 1895 inaugural, switched sides in the *Methodenstreit* – from historicism to the formal and abstract reasoning of the Austrians. But this contrast of historical to abstract method has always been based on a series of misunderstandings.

Or more precisely, the contrast is apparent from one perspective only, that of the German Historical School. As I have argued elsewhere (2006c: Ch. 4), whereas the 'Older' School sought to renew economic reasoning through a historical critique of existing theory, the 'Younger School' sought this renewal by induction from the history of economic organization. The ambitions of both Schools remained unfulfilled: the Older School never got beyond the historical critique, and the Younger School never got beyond the history of economic organization. The neat symmetry of this dual failure is however only superficial, for the Younger School was marked in its most extreme cases – Schmoller is the textbook example – by a complete disdain for economic theory of any kind, historical or otherwise. So far as Schmoller was concerned, 'economic science' had taken a wrong turn well before Adam Smith, and nothing that had been written since was of the slightest interest to him. It is this underlying hostility to economic analysis that underlies the *Methodenstreit*, not a contrast of theory and history, or of deductivism and inductivism. There is by contrast no such lack of interest in contemporary theory and history apparent in the work of the Older School. As we shall see, Knies's lecture room presentation of contemporary economics was based squarely in a Classical tradition established during the early nineteenth century and which was, by the 1880s, superseded; but by then Knies was well into his 60s and it would have been unusual for him to embrace the new subjectivist economics with any great enthusiasm.

1. The diffusion of the 'New Economics'

From the other end of the telescope things looked very different. Menger and his students Böhm-Bawerk, von Wieser, Sax and others certainly regarded classical theory as obsolete, and argued vehemently and at length for the basic principles of what, by the 1890s, they were calling 'modern economics', or the 'new economics'.[7] But they were not hostile to history in the way that Schmoller was hostile to theory. This impression is rather a very modern one, fostered to some extent by the existence today of a heterodox school of 'Austrian' economists which owes its 'Austrian' heritage more to the later Mises and Hayek than to the later Menger; and few, if any, of its adherents have any detailed or reliable historical knowledge of economics pre-dating the 1920s. Menger himself was in no respect a 'pure theorist' of the kind that Schmoller assumed. Hitotsubashi University convened a symposium on Menger in 2004, because the University had purchased Menger's library in the 1920s and maintains it as a separate special collection. Even the most cursory walk up and down the stacks[8] reveals a very large amount of travel and historical literature, confuting any suggestion that Carl Menger lacked interest in the variety of the economic world around him, and of the historical record of this world. As for Böhm-Bawerk, his major work on capital theory, *Kapital und Kapitalzins*, came in two parts: first a 'history and critique of theories of capital and interest'; and then a few years later a 'positive theory of capital' (Böhm-Bawerk: 1884, 1889). In 1892 the Society of Austrian Economists began to publish its own journal, and Böhm-Bawerk as the senior editor drafted its guidelines, printed in the first issue as 'Our Tasks'. Here the only economists explicitly named were Bastiat (approvingly) and Malthus, the prime task of the journal being: to reflect the problems of the day.[9] The first main article was devoted to social reform in Austria, in much the same way that the first main article ever published in the *Economic Journal* in March 1891 was devoted to the eight hour day in Australia.

In fact the foundation of the Vienna *Zeitschrift* was entirely in line with international developments in economics. In the later 1880s and the early 1890s a number of new academic economic and social science periodicals were founded that sought explicitly to inform their readers on international developments in the new discipline and in related areas of policy. Typically their contents were a mixture of social policy, theory, legislation, book reviews and, importantly, listings of the contents of other similar periodicals published in other countries and in other languages.[10] Some of the foregoing was true of Germany's pre-eminent social science publication, *Jahrbuch für Gesetzgebung, Verwaltung und Volkswirthschaft im Deutschen Reich,* from 1913 known as 'Schmollers Jahrbuch'[11] and in whose pages the *Methodenstreit* had unfolded. None of the early propagandizing in favour of the 'new economics' appeared in this journal, however. Instead, it was published in 'Conrads Jahrbücher', the *Jahrbücher für Nationalökonomie und Statistik* founded by Hildebrand in 1863 some 14 years before Schmoller's notably *Gründerzeit* journal. Furthermore, the diffusion of Austrian economics began not in the 1870s with the publication of Menger's *Grundsätze,* but later in the 1880s and into the 1890s, through Menger's pupils and not directly via Menger himself. Böhm-Bawerk was an especially assiduous propagandist.[12] He was not alone; in England, for example, James Bonar and William Smart were early adopters of the 'new theory'.[13] By the mid-1890s it would have been impossible to overlook the breaking wave of 'new economics' in a wide range of periodicals.

Contemporary journals also testify to a general upsurge of interest in economics and social reform in the final two decades of the nineteenth century. This coupling was of course one that the German Historical School had made its own since the foundation of the Verein für Socialpolitik in 1872–1873, when Schmoller had argued for a common basis among academics for the reform of social relations, a position from which one might then in turn influence public opinion.[14] It was in part this explicit linkage of social policy to the university, characterized as *Kathedersozialismus,* 'professorial socialism', that gave German economics such a high international profile in the late nineteenth century. This reputation attracted many American students to Germany to complete the doctorates they were unable to undertake in their own universities, which were not on offer in contemporary English universities, while French universities were effectively closed to outsiders. But a displacement occurred: the propagation of economics during the later 1880s and 1890s as an international academic discipline left German economists behind, even though chairs of economics were more firmly anchored in the landscape of the German university than anywhere else.[15] By the early 1900s 'German economics' had lost most of the international authority that it had once enjoyed, and as an academic discipline it was entirely eclipsed by the 1920s.[16] This was a process that began in the 1890s, historical economics polarizing away from the new economics, instead of remaining part of a broad stream.

2. Max Weber's academic career

Max Weber represents precisely this displacement: but rather than cling to 'historical economics' as it marginalized itself, he moved decisively in the opposite direction. As a law student he attended Knies's Heidelberg lectures in 1882 and 1883 (Hennis, 2000a: 128), then in Berlin wrote a dissertation on medieval trading companies and a *Habilitation* on Roman agrarian relations, moving then on this unlikely basis during his period in Freiburg to become by the mid-1890s one of Germany's leading financial economists.[17] His report for the Verein on East Elbian labour relations had been commissioned in 1890; the survey questionnaires were sent out early in 1892, Weber worked on the results through 1892 and they were published at the end of the year, in advance of the (postponed) annual meeting held in March 1893.[18] His public reputation was made by this report, and it formed the basis for his candidacy for the Freiburg chair. Ironically it was subsequently the agrarians who saw to his exclusion in 1897 from the permanent Bundesrat committee on financial affairs on account of what they considered to be his overly close connection to financial interests.[19] All of the foregoing is compatible with historical economics, broadly conceived. But as Weber himself remarked, he heard his first lectures in economics when he delivered them himself as a Professor of Economics.[20] This is certainly no exaggeration if we qualify it as follows: that he heard his first lectures in *modern economics* when he delivered them himself, since what he heard from Knies as a student was broadly representative of the older Classical tradition, as will be shown below. Simply because of his age – barely 30 when appointed to the Freiburg chair – he was capable of moving with the ongoing transition that was occurring in economics at exactly this time. Anyone setting out to teach economics for the first time in 1894 would have at their disposal a range of international journals and new books in the main languages. It was obvious that the discipline was in motion and that for a German-speaker the impulse came from Austria. Furthermore, all that was on offer from the Historical School in the way of economics were indigestible and bulky multipart tomes by the likes of Wagner and Schmoller, which were quite plainly superseded by the latest English, American or even Dutch writing. Why start out teaching with out-of-date textbooks?

This transition is underlined if we consider the course taken by the appointment processes at Freiburg and Heidelberg. The Freiburg vacancy arose from Philippovich's move to Vienna, to the chair of economic policy opposite Menger's chair for economic theory. The Faculty originally proposed two candidates to the Ministry. First place on their list went to Friedrich von Wieser, then teaching in Prague. This might seem to indicate a strong Austrian connection, since Philippovich was going to Vienna and his favoured replacement came from the same direction. Any speculation of this kind is rather undermined when we see that second place on the list was given to Max Sering, an agronomist then teaching at Berlin Agricultural College and whose profile lies entirely outside this Austro-German problematic.[21] In any case, neither of these candidates was available, and so the Faculty had to start again since their list only contained two names. Third place on the new list went to Walther Lotz, then a full professor in Munich. Second went to Carl Fuchs, an extra-ordinary professor at Greifswald.[22] First place was given to Max Weber, who accepted the proposal in July 1893 on condition that no comparable post was offered to him in Berlin, where he lived in his parents' home. Problems then arose because of an intervention by Friedrich Althoff, who reassured the Baden Ministry that it would be a waste of time appointing Weber since he sought only a 'springboard' to greater things; this delayed proceedings and Weber was eventually appointed in April 1894. Althoff's intervention was in fact symptomatic of why Weber wished to move as far as possible from Berlin. It is more than likely that Weber took up the Baden post precisely because it took him away from the capital, not so that he might later return; and he later expressed his profound dislike for the academic politics of Berlin in a series of newspaper articles (Tribe, 1994). Consider in this (geographical) light the chairs that Weber held: Freiburg, Heidelberg, Vienna and Munich.

The subsequent move from Freiburg to Heidelberg was definitely an advancement – the standard nineteenth-century textbook had first been published in the 1820s by the Heidelberg professor, Karl Heinrich Rau, and Knies was his direct successor; Heidelberg and Freiburg were also in the same state of Baden, rendering the move locally sideways, rather than unequivocally upward (to Berlin). By 1896 Knies was 75 and he petitioned the Baden ministry for retirement, at the same time making the unconventional proposal that he be succeeded by Gustav von Schönberg, known principally as the editor of the economics handbook that Weber's *Grundriß der Sozialökonomik* would replace. He supported the suggestion with a claim that he was the only person in his faculty who understood anything about the matter, an argument that was forcefully rejected once the faculty got to hear of it (Hentschel, 1988: 204). They submitted their list in November 1896 after considering the merits of the leading German representatives of 'this most important discipline of modern science'. In first place was Georg Friedrich Knapp (aged 54);

in second Karl Bücher (aged 49); in third Max Weber (aged 32). If it should turn out that the first two turned the appointment down, they added, then the Ministry should offer the better-paid Heidelberg post to Max Weber so that he might be kept in Baden:

> Among the younger teachers of political economy Weber occupies a very special position. [...] If not as a consequence of his youth not yet the equal in inner maturity and clarity of the first two, he nevertheless promises even today to become one of the leading men of his specialism.
>
> (Hentschel, 1988: 205, quoting the Faculty memorandum of 6 November 1896)

Knapp and Bücher did turn the proposal down, and Weber was duly appointed 'Professor of Economics and Finance' in January 1897.

That Weber, whose formal academic qualifications were all in law[23] and who in the early 1890s had certainly contemplated a career in law, could be placed ahead of Fuchs and Lotz on the Freiburg faculty list is related to the fact that economics was in Germany, as everywhere else at the time in Continental Europe, taught only to students of law. A separate qualification in economics was only introduced in 1922/23 (Weber, 1923: 306). In the later nineteenth century, therefore, all German 'economists' had first been students of law, not of economics.[24] As a law student in Heidelberg Weber's own teacher had been Karl Knies. He first attended Knies's lectures on political economy in the summer semester of 1882 and found them boring. By the following semester he acknowledged that Knies on political economy and finance was thorough. By the summer of 1883, having read Adam Smith in the meantime, it all began to make more sense. Knies had devoted a great deal of space to discussion of Smith and the significance of his writings in his *Die politische Oekonomie vom Standpuncte der geschichtlichen Methode*, published 30 years earlier and of course one of the key works of German historical economics (1853). The same year that Knies began to make more sense to Weber a revised edition of this work appeared. Hennis confirms that Weber took detailed notes from this book (Hennis, 2000b: 129, fn. 79) and has linked the materials that Weber found in Knies to the development of his writings right through to *Economy and Society*. Our purpose here is different. We are concerned with the kind of economics to which Weber directed his interest. And we have therefore, in this new edition, a baseline for our understanding of Weber's *own* understanding of the economic sciences of the day, since this was the way he had been introduced to the subject.

3. Knies as a teacher of political economy

Knies's book of 1853 had not been a textbook, or a systematic treatise. One quirk of the book is that the contents page only lists the titles of sections, while the body of the book has no such elementary guide, just numbered sections. The text is organized into three main divisions. The introduction (pp. 1–35) reviews the existing literature of political economy understood as a discourse not only concerning the historical development of economic theory, but also the economic conditions and developments in different nations and periods. The second section (pp. 35–123) emphasizes the historical and ecological context of any given set of economic circumstances. The third and final section (pp. 123–355) opens with a discussion of private property in classical antiquity, then, moves to a discussion of self-interest as the motive of economizing action. In this Knies leans heavily on the work of Smith, placing especial emphasis upon the moral philosophical dimension of his work, locating him with respect to Mandeville and Shaftesbury, Helvetius, Rousseau and Montesquieu. It is this discussion of Smith as a moral philosopher that appears to have caught Buckle's attention and which was elaborated in his *History of Civilization in England* (1861), translated the same year into German and largely responsible in this guise for the development of *Das Adam Smith Problem* (Tribe, 2008).

Knies's text, appearing in the lists of an obscure provincial publisher and rather shoddily set and printed, sold very poorly for many years. When stocks were finally exhausted the publisher suggested a reprint, but instead Knies opted to update the text by cuts and stylistic changes, placing all new material in sections appended to the text of the first edition – *Zusätze* which elaborated or commented upon the existing text. It is this editorial strategy that makes the work so interesting in the present context, for we are able to read out of these additions exactly what Knies himself thought was important or significant in the early 1880s. We can also infer from this text what Knies thought unworthy of mention, so that both the added emphases and the persistent silences of the revised work present us with a record of what he very likely sought to convey to his students, among who was an increasingly receptive Max Weber.

Die politische Oekonomie vom geschichtlichen Standpuncte – the new 1883 edition also bears a revised title, for Knies now has misgivings about 'historical method'[25] – is over 500 pages long, more than half as long again as the original, and the text has been subjected to innumerable detailed changes. It opens on page one with a new addition, stretching to page nine. This is directed to the definition of political economy, and its relationship to other human sciences. 'Politische Oekonomie', he writes, includes all those disciplines referred to in Germany as *Volkswirtschaftslehre, Nationalökonomie, Volkswirtschaftspolitik* and *Finanzwissenschaft*. 'Oekonomie' arises from householding and management (*Haushaltung und Wirtschaftsführung*), but is not a simply technical branch of knowledge:

> It should not be concerned with a mere doctrine of economy (*bloße Wirtschafts-Lehre*), but with 'political' economy.
>
> (1883: 2)

By 'political' he is not making use of the contemporary practise of distinguishing the 'political or statal from the social or the societal':

> Rather should be understood by political economy the sense used previously, as descriptive of the phenomena of social economy, a meaning which could gain wide acceptance; the entire first part of political economy should be solely concerned with the investigation of the economic life of man in society (*das gesellschaftliche Wirtschaftsleben des Menschen*), as manifested in its autonomy from all political influence. It is enough for us here to recognize that the expression 'political economy' also implies 'social economy'.
>
> (1993: 3)

Political economy is part of the science of state and society, and these belong neither to the natural nor the human sciences. The former, argues Knies, study the material observable world, the latter the interior world of human conceptions. By contrast, the proper object of study for the sciences of state and society is instead the actions or labours of men, and the societally and legally ordered life worlds grounded by such actions and labours. Here it is not a question of the inner as contrasted to the external human world; the sciences of state and society are directed to an external world of materially perceptible phenomena distinct to that of the natural sciences and with causal links to the inner life of humans (1883: 6). These are points that Weber would later reprise and upon which his conception of *Verstehen* was constructed.

Despite this addition to the first major section, it is not greatly longer than the original, and this is also true for the second part,

'Volkswirtschaft'. Most of the new additions to the work are to be found in the third section, 'Volkswirtschaftlehre', which now runs from page 157 to page 533. The most significant insertions are towards the end of the book, where Knies updates his account of 'contemporary political economy' from the literature as it stood in 1852. At that time the academic landscape was dominated by one textbook, that of Rau; but by the 1880s this was no longer the case. He noted that political economy had, in the second half of the nineteenth century, undergone a change of direction as significant as that which separated Adam Smith from the work of the 'mercantilists' (1883: 294). Knies did therefore recognize that economic discourse had undergone a profound transformation since the early 1850s. However, he linked this transformation exclusively to the new socialist political economy – Rodbertus, Marx and Lassalle – whose work is associated with conception of labour as the source of all value, hence is continuous with the core principle of classical economics that the 'new economics' abandons.[26] The closing sections of the book then turn to a discussion of historical and comparative method in political economy, with one crucial additional section running from page 590. These pages veer back to points made in the opening sections of the book concerning the proper object of political economy, and the role of ethnographic and statistical work. 'Abstract' political economy, suggests Knies, has no need of such material, for it merely begins from a range of assumptions concerning egoistic action within a given socio-legal order. This method, he writes, was cultivated by the theorists of *laissez-faire*, among whom Ricardo was the most prominent (1883: 497).

Without so much as pausing to start a new paragraph Knies then proceeds directly to an evaluation of Ricardo's account of rent and capital.[27] He allows that a theory of production and distribution can be built upon this, but the difficulty is that any conclusions are logical, not historical, derivatives. He then moves on from his critique of Ricardo to deal with Walras, citing the first (1874) edition of the *Élements*.[28] Walras's approach is presented as merely a further elaboration, this time in mathematical terms, of the same abstract method apparent in Ricardo. The 'applied economics' of Walras is no more than applied mathematics, so far as Knies is concerned. Against this, he asserts that 'politische Oekonomik' deals with the societal formation of prices (*gesellschaftliche Bildung der Preise*); while it might be an interesting exercise to see what would happen to prices should everyone act on the basis of pure self-interest, he states that there is nothing to be learned from such an exercise. Closing this discussion of Walras, he implies that

Walras seeks to construct political economy on the 'natural scientific' basis already rejected in the opening *Zusatz*. With that, he makes some comments on Auguste Walras's work on value and ends the book with a review of recent literature on the older history of political economy.

Nowhere in Knies's book is there a mention, however implicit, of the Viennese school. In 1876 Böhm-Bawerk and von Wieser had attended Knies's lectures and contributed to the seminar,[29] but as Kiichiro Yagi observes in his introduction to a set of Knies's lecture notes from 1886, the conception of market price that he there advances owes nothing to the new theory (Yagi, 2000). Furthermore, the broad similarity of these notes from the period immediately following Weber's attendance at Knies's lectures with another set of notes dating from the summer semester of 1880, two years before Weber's first attendance in the summer semester of 1882, confirms the regular manner in which Knies reproduced the content of his lectures.[30] Knies begins both courses with a systematic overview, starting with the definition of concepts, the relation of the legal order to economics, the divisions of political economy and its literature. In 1880 the textbooks listed are those of Rau, Roscher, Hildebrand, Knies, Schäffle, Lorenz von Stein, Mangoldt and Hermann. In 1886 the list is similar, excluding von Stein and adding Schönberg's *Handbuch der politischen Ökonomie* and Kohn's *Lehrbuch*. The most recent book listed is Bischof's 1876 *Grundzüge eines Systems der Nationalökonomie* (Yagi, 2000: 21). Schäffle was Menger's predecessor in the Vienna chair and Knies adds the comment that his textbook 'is very productive'; while Mangoldt is relegated in this later listing to 'smaller works'. None of the newer work in economics, in German or any other language, is included here.

The lecture notes therefore point in the same direction as the revisions to Knies's textbook. Jevons had famously argued that Ricardo took post-Smithian economics in the wrong direction, building a rigorous theory of production and distribution on a labour theory of value linking the contributions and remunerations of the three classes of labourer, capitalist and landowner (1879: li). The socialist economists named by Knies in his book, especially Marx, shared this fundamental conception. But the new economics was 'new' because it was precisely this which it discarded; not formalism, deductivism nor even inductivism. A focus on 'abstraction' and 'mathematics' appears to have blinded Knies to the manner in which the methodological position that he advanced, placing emphasis upon human action, was entirely compatible with the marginalist position, however 'abstract' or 'concrete-historical' the position one adopted. That he lighted upon Walras as the sole proponent of the new economics, ignoring Menger and Jevons, simply points this out. Walras's formal presentation of the new economics was certainly very different to that of Jevons, and quite at variance with that of Menger, but their underlying conceptions of economic action and structure were very similar.[31]

From this reading of Knies's revisions we can confirm that he was aware that political economy was changing, but that his understanding of how it was changing was faulty. Secondly, he was familiar with the work of Walras, but failed to look beyond the mathematics to the underlying theory of economic action.[32] Thirdly, he made no mention at all of the work of Menger, quite probably because at the time the 'literature of dissemination' had not begun to appear. All of this serves to underline the point that elderly incumbents are unlikely to register change accurately and that academic innovation is the work of the newly appointed.

4. Max Weber as a teacher of political economy

Max Weber began from a different point. As noted above, his initial preparations for his Freiburg lectures on general economic theory were made in the summer of 1894.[33] Economics had moved a long way in the 11 years since Weber had sat in Knies's lectures. His teaching in Heidelberg in the summer semester of 1897 opened with the main course on 'General ("Theoretical") Economics' that he had attended in 1882 when it was called *Nationalökonomie* (*Allgemeine und theoretische Volkswirtschaftslehre*).[34] In the following session he lectured on practical economics and ran a short course on agrarian policy, then for the summer semester of 1898 returned to 'General ("Theoretical") Economics'. In April 1898, the month before his collapse, he prepared and printed a reading guide for the course and a lecture outline for the first section, 'The Conceptual Foundations of Economics'. From these we are able to determine what sort of economics he was interested in.[35]

The reading guide is divided into six 'books' and 20 sections over 23 closely-printed pages.[36] Eliminating the actual references from the guide, we get the following structure:

Introduction: § 1. Tasks and Methods of Theoretical Economics
Book I The Conceptual Foundations of Economics
  § 2. The Economy and its Elementary Phenomena
  § 3. The Economy and its Elementary Phenomena[37]

Book II The Natural Foundations of the Economy
- § 4. The Natural Determinants of the Economy
- § 5. Population
- § 6. The Biological and Anthropological Foundations of Society
- § 7. The Relation of the Economy to other Cultural Phenomena, especially Law and State

Book III The Historical Foundations of Economy
- § 8. The Typical Preliminary Stages of Economy
- § 9. The Economic Development of the Coastal Culture of Antiquity
- § 10. The Agrarian Foundations of the Inland Culture of the Middle Ages
- § 11. Urban Economy and the Origin of Modern Enterprise Forms
- § 12. The Emergence of the Economy (*Volkswirtschaft*)

Book IV The Developmental States of Economic Theory
- § 13. Economic Science up to the Creation of Liberal Economic Theory
- § 14. The Economic Theory of the so-called Classical Economics
- § 15. The Theoretical Bases of Scientific Socialism

Book V Theoretical Analysis of the Modern Exchange Economy
- § 16. Production and its Theoretical Problems
- § 17. Exchange and its Theoretical Problems
- § 18. Distribution and Consumption and its Theoretical Problems
- § 19. The Functions and Developmental Tendencies of the Regulating Principles and Forms of Organization in the Satisfaction of Wants through Trade and Enterprise

Book VI Development and Analysis of Economic and Social Ideals
- § 20. [no title]

Wolfgang Mommsen and other editors of the *Gesamtausgabe* have been rather dismissive of what we can infer from the reading list that went with these headings, suggesting that it involved such a broad swathe of literature that it has to be more a wish-list than any indication of what Weber had read, or even looked at. Even if this view were accepted, it should be noted that the literature cited under these headings amounts to an extraordinarily detailed and precise delineation of 'modern economics' in the mid-1890s, and, as I will show below, 'modern economics' here means 'new economics'. Used as we are to thinking of the 'German Historical School' as an enterprise entirely separate from Austrian or from English political economy, there is a reluctance to recognize that by this time 'national' schools of economics, although still important, were giving way to a more international perspective, a consequence of the rapid and widespread development of university teaching in economics, together with new journals and societies. At this time most leading economists were literate in at least one foreign language, not to mention the Greek and Latin with which they were all familiar. They read each others' work and the journals they edited listed the contents of the leading international periodicals, as noted above. It is not entirely an exaggeration to suggest that economics was more 'international' in this sense a century ago than it is today. And Weber's reading guide entirely reflects this perspective in such detail that we can here only point out some broader conclusions.

While under § 1. Weber lists, with two exceptions, works in the German language, beginning with Roscher's 1843 *Grundriss*, Hildebrand's *Nationalökonomie* (1848) and Knies's *Politische Oekonomie* (both editions), this is because he establishes a 'tradition' of argument that is national, rather than intellectual. Missing from this listing of 'tasks and methods of theoretical economics' is Neville Keynes's *Scope and Method of Political Economy* (1891), a work which lambasted Schmoller as an 'extremist' (Keynes, 1891: 298) and which would therefore have been congenial to Weber. But the principal axis of this section is that of the *Methodenstreit*, presumably a way of easing the way into the rigours of the conceptual foundations that begin with § 2. The ordering is more or less chronological; Cairnes's *Character and Logical Method of Political Economy* (1875) and Cliffe Leslie's *Essays in Moral and Political Philosophy* (1879) are the two exceptions to German-language literature, following on from Knies and preceding Menger's 1883 *Untersuchungen*, which is in turn followed by Schmoller's famous 1883 review of Menger and Dilthey. Cairnes is noteworthy here for his unequivocal rejection of the mathematical method, espoused by 'my friend Professor Jevons' (Cairnes, 1875: vi). Cliffe Leslie sought to promote an understanding of economics as an inductive science; among a wide diversity of topics he argues, contra Buckle, that Adam Smith's work was inductive in spirit (1879: 150). The reference to Schmoller's 1883 essay is in fact sandwiched between Menger's *Untersuchungen* of 1883 and his *Irrtümer* of 1884, followed by Philippovich, Sax and Dietzel, concluding with Schmoller's *Handwörterbuch der Staatswissenschaften* essay on economics and economic method. We might note that so far as the listing of references goes, Weber is quite 'impartial' with respect to the *Methodenstreit*. It is most certainly not the kind of list that a fully-paid up member of the 'German Historical School' would ever have compiled, and of course one that moves considerably beyond Knies's appreciation of German economics in the second half of the nineteenth century.

For the most part the sections of the reading guide order literature under subheadings or with respect to listed points. Book I does not however take this form, being rather an initial list of references combined with the subheadings of § 2 and § 3 that we find in the lecture outline. First, the references:

C. Menger, *Grundsätze der Volkswirtschaftslehre*, Wien 1871.
V. Böhm-Bawerk, 'Grundzüge der Theorie des wirtschaftlichen Güterwerts', *Jahrbücher für Nationalökonomie* N. F. 13 1886.
Pierson, *Leerboek der staatshuishoudkunde*, Haarlem 1884.
M. Block, *Les Progrès de la science économique depuis Adam Smith*,1890
V. Wieser, *Der natürliche Wert*, 1889.
V. Komorzynski, *Der Wert in der isolierten Wirtschaft*.
V. Böhm-Bawerk, *Rechte und Verhältnisse vom Standpunkt der volkswirtschaftlichen Güterlehre*, Innsbruck 1881.
Lexis, Article 'Grenznutzen' im *Handwörterbuch der Staatswissenschaften*, 1 Supplementband.
H. Dietzel, 'Die klassische Werttheorie und die Theorie vom Grenznutzen', *Jahrbücher für Nationalökonomie*, N. F. 20
Dietzel, *Theoretische Sozialökonomik*.
Neumann, *Grundlagen der Volkswirtschaftslehre*, Tübingen 1889.
J. Lehr, *Grundbegriffe und Grundlagen der Volkswirtschaft*, Leipzig 1893.
Auspitz and Lieben, *Untersuchungen über die Lehre vom Preise*, 1889.
Zuckerkandl, *Theorie des Preises mit besonderer Berücksichtigung der geschichtlichen Entwickelung der Lehre*, Leipzig 1889.
Sax, *Die neuesten Fortschritte der national-ökonomischen Theorie*, Leipzig 1889.
Patten, *The Theory of Dynamic Economics*, Philadelphia 1892.
Walras, *Élements d'économie politique pure*, Lausanne 1889.
Gerlach, *Über die Bedingungen wirtschaftlicher Tätigkeit*, 1890.

And from the 'older literature':

Adam Smith, *Untersuchungen über den Nationalreichtum*[38]
Ricardo, *Grundsätze der Volkswirtschaftslehre*
v. Thünen, *Der isolierte Staat*
F. von Hermann, *Staatswissenschaftliche Untersuchungen*
Karl Marx, *Das Kapital*, Bd. 1

Weber therefore understood the 'conceptual development of economics' to be a logical, not a historical matter. And for this he turned almost exclusively to 'Austrian writings'. This was not merely window-dressing, for we have the lecture outline that goes with these writings – we can compare his recommended reading with his lecture notes. Marx here is quite properly assigned to the 'older literature', again diverging from Knies's understanding. It is clear that in the later 1890s Weber directed his students for an understanding of the foundations of contemporary economic theory primarily to Austrian economists. None of these writers sought to moderate the novelty of what they had to say, as did Marshall with respect to classical economics; nor did Weber seek to synthesize their approach with other perspectives in his outline. The Austrians were self-consciously 'modern' and Weber in no respect sought to temper this by drawing parallels with other schools. Even if the lecture course was directed to 'theoretical' economics – Weber making typically free play here with quotation marks to place at a distance a science that on page two of the outline is said to posit an '*unrealistic* man, analogous to an ideal mathematical figure'[39] – Weber shows that he perfectly understands the material he is presenting, even if he does not entirely share its viewpoint.

As we have seen, Knies in the early 1880s understood that contemporary economics was changing quite dramatically, even if his apprehension of exactly how it was changing can be questioned. Veblen also picked up on Marshall's tendency to emphasize continuities with classical economics, describing this new approach as 'neo-classical' to emphasize a continuity, rather than a discontinuity; but then arguing that there was little difference between the Austrians and this 'neo-classical' approach (Veblen, 1900: 261). The Austrian writers never adopted this strategy; theirs was avowedly a new approach, built, as Menger made clear in the opening pages of the *Grundsätze*,[40] upon earlier work, but transforming it. As Sax wrote in the book that Weber cites under § 1:

> Economics finds itself at present in a thoroughgoing process of transformation. The older doctrine, viewed by many to be as incontestable as dogma, is recognized to be in part inadequate, in part untenable. Something new has to be created in its place: a new science, differing from the older sciences in basic perspective, extent, purpose and treatment.
>
> (1884: 1)

Weber's presentation of contemporary theoretical economics in 1898 is entirely in accordance with this sentiment.

Although the sequence in which he orders his presentation might not directly compare with Menger, von Wieser or Sax, it is fairly easy to find matching passages. Summarizing the 'Concept of Economy', Weber writes:

> 'Economy' is the complex of measures brought about by the economizing action of an individual or of a human community.[41]

Compared with Sax:

> Economy is the determination of (technical) action and of the social relationships of men resulting from the endeavour to secure external conditions of existence.[42]

Section 2.3 outlines economic needs as subjectively felt, not objectively given, hence varying from person to person and over time, any one individual having a range of needs felt with varying intensity, degrees of satisfaction of some needs consequently altering the hierarchy of felt need, and also taking into account a discounting of future needs in favour of those in the present. Section 2.4 deals with goods in terms of utilities capable of satisfying these needs, closing with the statement that:

> The standpoint of *man* is decisive. Economics is not a science of nature and its properties, but of man and his needs.[43]

Economic goods are in turn those things which are the objects of economizing activity, divided into consumption and production goods. Having worked through these definition, Weber then turns to 'economic evaluation' (*wirtschaftliche Wertschätzung*) in an isolated economy, the elementary motivations that result in price formation. The assumption is made that in any given time period the supply of non-reproducible consumption goods will be limited, and that an economic subject will first seek to satisfy needs of the greatest urgency first, moving progressively through less urgent needs, equalizing the marginal utilities of the goods employed to satisfy each class of need. For production goods a process of imputation is necessary, Weber noting in passing the erroneousness of the (classical) conception that the value of reproducible goods derives from their costs of production (Book I, § 2.7: 9).

The lecture outline continues relentlessly for 34 dense pages in this vein, through exchange, money, market prices, the regulation of output, supply and demand, enterprise, property and income. Having taken this subjective point of departure, at no point does Weber seek to reintroduce elements of the 'old' theory. The lecture course was never completed, however; in May 1898 he suffered a breakdown and although he taught sporadically over the coming years until his partial recovery by 1903, he never again had the task of presenting the basic principles of economics to students.

5. The genesis of *Wirtschaft und Gesellschaft* Part I

However, this does not mean that he never again found himself in the position of presenting such principles in an orderly manner. Shortly before his death, Weber corrected the proofs to the four chapters of 'Die Wirtschaft und die gesellschaftlichen Ordnungen und Mächte', which finally appeared in 1922 as Part I of *Economy and Society*, the title he gave to section C of Book I of the *Grundriss der Sozialökonomik* that he edited for the publisher Siebeck.[44] At the head of the second chapter, 'Basic Sociological Categories of Economic Action', Weber placed a disclaimer:

> The following is not intended as any kind of 'economic theory', but seeks only to define a few widely-used concepts and determine some very simple sociological relationships within the economy.
>
> (1976: 31)

Here, then, Weber takes up once more the task of expounding the basic principles of economics, while denying that what he is doing is 'economic theory'. So what then, in 1920, did Weber think 'economic theory' was? And if he no longer had the need, or the inclination, to present its principles himself, to whom did he turn for an authoritative exposition? We need look no further than section A Book I, 'Economy and Economic Science'. Published in 1914 as Abteilung I, this was composed of three parts. Karl Bücher briefly outlined stages of economic development; Joseph Schumpeter presented the 'epochs in the history of doctrine and method' that formed the template for his later *History of Economic Analysis*; and Friedrich von Wieser presented his *Theorie der gesellschaftlichen Wirtschaft*. This is what Max Weber thought 'contemporary economic theory' was, even if he no longer practised it; he had especially commissioned von Wieser for this section of the *Grundriss*, and in response Wieser produced what was in many respects the first summary account of 'Austrian economics', a 'modern economic theory that I present', systematically contrasted and compared to classical

English theory, so that the contrast between the new and the classical might be placed in the sharpest contrast.[45]

Weber was rather critical of Wieser's contribution when he finally received it, suggesting that there was a significant weakness when the text made the transition from 'simple' to 'complex' economic relationships, failing to derive the structure of institutions from the social action of individuals (Swedberg, 1998: 160). This latter approach is of course very much the narrative structure of the early chapters of *Economy and Society*, the final form of a project which had altered considerably between 1913 and 1920. In retrospect it does rather seem that Weber sought from Wieser an argument that he alone was in a position to construct, and when he failed to find it in Wieser was prompted to make good the deficiency. This is but one of the issues that will only be made clearer once the editors of the *Gesamtausgabe* have published the papers and correspondence from this period.

Nonetheless, that the account of the 'history and theory' of economics in the *Grundriss* was assigned by Weber to Schumpeter and Wieser respectively is especially significant. The initial schooling that Weber received from Knies made no mention of the work of Menger. That Knies was familiar with Walras is of course something, but as I have shown above, his understanding of Walras's work was flawed in a way that indicates he would not have appreciated the importance of Menger, or of Jevons for that matter. What Weber could have taken from Knies was instead the idea that economic actions were socially constituted – the very conception that he missed in Wieser. In this respect one can indeed trace a line from Knies's conception of 'social economy' to the structure of the *Grundriss der Sozialokonomik*. But any idea that Weber was in the mid-1890s a conventional 'German historical economist' is swept away by close examination of the reading list that he assembled for his main course in theoretical economics, and by an evaluation of the outline of its opening sections that he completed before his breakdown.

A problem that has never been explicitly posed is quite why the first part of *Economy and Society* is structured in the way that it is. It is undisputed that these chapters took shape towards the very end of Weber's life, but argument appears to have exhausted itself debating various explanations of the changing plans for the *Grundriss* and the place that *Wirtschaft und Gesellschaft* occupied within it. What becomes evident, however, in the light of the argument presented above, is that when in the last few months of his life Weber wrote up the second chapter of *Economy and Society*, he recapitulated the concepts and the ordering that we find in his Heidelberg lecture outlines, adumbrating the tenets of the 'modern science' *circa* 1895.

Quite why this happened is suggested by what we know of the genesis of the first chapter. This is a clear revision of his 1913 essay on categories of interpretative sociology. Edith Graber drew attention to the nature of the changes made between 1913 and 1920 in the introduction to her translation (1981: 145–50), remarking that much of the reworking of the treatment of social action occurred in the context of his teaching during the summer of 1918 in Vienna (1981: 147). It is very obvious that the 1913 essay has a discursive, self-clarificatory form, whereas *Wirtschaft und Gesellschaft*, first chapter, is a structured exposition in which definitions are followed by elaborations, and where each definition builds upon the previous one in a logical sequence.[46] Once we grasp this point, then it becomes easier to see that for him to develop the second chapter in the same didactic manner Weber could only have gone back to the last time that he had taught this material – during the summer semester of 1898 at Heidelelberg. Of course, the second chapter also builds upon the concept of social action outlined in the first, but the definition and elaboration of the relevant economic categories resonates with the lectures from the 1890s.[47] When therefore, in his preamble to Chapter 2, Weber disavows any intention of pursuing 'economic theory', what he means is 'economic theory circa 1918' – it is quite plain that he is working with an economic instrumentarium that reflects 'modern economics' circa 1895, that he is conscious of so doing, and that in any case 'economic theory' had already been dealt with in the *Grundriss* by Wieser. What is then added in this chapter is not further elaboration from contemporary economics – to this extent it would be true to say that Weber had 'given up' economics – but the joint threads of rationality and capitalism: how the rationality of modern economic life was a capitalist rationality unique to the Occident; but which had to be constructed *forwards* from basic economic concepts, whose logical construction showed up the institutional conditions for capitalist development and not its evolutionary inevitability. The central sections of Chapter 2 have a direct linkage to Weber's last complete lecture course in WS 1919–1920 – the *Wirtschaftsgeschichte*, whose preliminary conceptual clarifications were so close to the formulations of Chapter 2 WuG that Frank Knight assumed they had been fabricated by Melchior Palyi in his editorial work on the published version.[48] It could be said that in these last writings Weber arrived at a coherent synthesis of the 'modern economics' of the Austrians with the 'historical economics' espoused by the German Historical School, uniting what has, since the *Methodenstreit*, always been considered quite contrasting visions of the future of economics.

Notes

1. Letter cited in Graf (2004: 105).
2. O. Prof. der Nationalökonomie und Finanzwissenschaft, appointed 25 April 1894 – see Biesenbach (1968).
3. He continued as an honorary professor without the right to supervise doctoral candidates or contribute to faculty dialogue (Käsler, 1979: 19).
4. With a course in the summer semester of 1918 entitled 'Wirtschaft und Gesellschaft' ('Positive Kritik der materialistischen Geschichtsauffassung') – Yagi, Ikeda (1988: 104). Ludwig von Mises (at the time Privat-Dozent) was that semester listed for three courses: theory of economic crises, exercises in theoretical economics and Austria's economic policy 1866–1914 (1988: 105).
5. The 'Older School' of German Historical Economics is always associated with Wilhelm Roscher (1817–1894), Bruno Hildebrand (1812–1878) and Carl Knies (1821–1898).
6. Report in *Der Sozialistische Student* Jg. 2 (1898) No. 9, 21 January 1898, p. 139, cited in Mommsen (1993: 45, fn. 171).
7. Underlying the argument of this chapter is the chronology outlined in my essay 'A Lost Connection' (2006a), according to which Classical Economics terminates with the 'Marginal Revolution' in the early 1870s, but is then followed by a period of some decades in which no one approach is hegemonic, but during which period a recognizably 'modern economics' takes shape in Europe and America. The core reasoning during this period I call 'New Economics'. Out of this forms, in the later 1930s, what is today understood as the 'Neoclassical Orthodoxy', fully consolidated in the United States during the 1940s and diffusing across the world in the 1950s and 1960s. 'Neo-classical economics' is hence related to the second half of the twentieth century only. What goes before neo-classicism is a New Economics that has international variants: American, English, Dutch, German, French, Italian, Swedish, Danish. One characteristic of the neo-classical orthodoxy is that it 'supersedes' this sheer variety of New Economics; it quickly became a dogma. Neo-classical economics is therefore treated here as something quite distinct from economics in the aftermath of the 'Marginal Revolution'; as a construct primarily of the mid-twentieth century; and as a template for economic reasoning that always had very great limitations. Importantly, the received doctrines of modern economics provide little insight into economic reasoning in the early twentieth century, which is not to say that a knowledge of economics is irrelevant to its study: quite the contrary.
8. It was stipulated in the terms of sale that the organization of the library as it was at Menger's death be preserved.
9. Böhm-Bawerk argued that such problems could only be adequately dealt with through the combined efforts of practical men, historians and theoreticians (1892a: 6).
10. I have outlined the importance of economic journals in the development of modern economics in Tribe (1992).
11. Schmoller assumed editorial control in 1881.

12. Böhm-Bawerk's first major publication was in 1881; from the later 1880s he published a number of surveys of contemporary theory and expositions of the Austrian approach – see for example (1891a; 1891b; 1892b; 1894b), which is a translation of his 1894a.
13. James Bonar (1888); William Smart (1891a; 1891b; 1892). Significant also is the publication in the very first number of the *Economic Journal* of Friedrich von Wieser's 'The Austrian School and the Theory of Value' (1891).
14. G. Schmoller (2000: 595). Twelve professors and three others had attended a small preparatory meeting in Halle during July 1872; Schmoller described those present as 'a small number of officials, assembly members, professors and journalists' (p. 598) which aptly summarizes the later composition of the *Verein*. There were 159 attendees at the October 1872 meeting, of whom 22 were university professors. The first formal meeting of the *Verein* took place the following year in Eisenach – Lindenlaub (1967: 7).
15. The best account of German Historical Economics in the 1890s is Shiro Takebayashi (2003). Erik Grimmer-Solem (2003) is the most reliable account in English, but is based heavily around the work of Schmoller and ends up sharing Schmoller's prejudices and very real limitations.
16. Although there was an upsurge in the teaching of economics in Germany during the 1920s, the majority of this new generation was diverted overseas by National Socialism – see Harald Hagemann, Claus-Dieter Krohn (1999); and my review essay (2001). There were significant developments in German economics during the 1920s and 1930s, but with one or two major exceptions they came from outside the university system – see J. Adam Tooze (2001).
17. Borchardt (2002); and his stunning *tour d'horizon* of finance in the 1890s in his introduction to Max Weber, *Börsenwesen. Schriften und Reden 1893–1898* (1999).
18. The sequence from appointment to completion of the work is outlined in my essay (1989); see also Martin Riesebrodt's discussion in his introduction to Max Weber, *Die Lage der Landarbeiter im ostelbischen Deutschland* (1984: 22ff.).
19. That is, he argued forcefully that futures trading in grain was an international market and if this was prohibited, as it was in Germany by the new law, then prices would be set in Chicago rather than Berlin. As far as the agrarians were concerned, the fluctuating and falling price of grain was brought about by the machinations of financiers, not of international markets.
20. Borchardt notes that preparation for his Freiburg lecture course on 'General and Theoretical Economics' (four hours a week) was postponed until the summer vacation of 1894, meshing clearly with the chronology of the diffusion of Austrian economics noted above – Borchardt (1999: 102).
21. Biesenbach (1968: 200). See for an example of Sering's writing (1981), which was first published in *Jahrbuch für Gesetzgebung, Verwaltung und Volkswirtschaft* Jg. 23 (1899: 1493–556).
22. Both Lotz and Fuchs were just one year older than Weber, so that none of the candidates on the new list was over 30 at the time it was drawn up.
23. He passed his law exams in 1886, presented his doctoral defence in 1889 on a topic related to Italian commercial partnerships, and published his Habil dissertation on legal aspects of Roman agrarian history in 1891.

24. And the same is true of course for Austro-Hungary, and everywhere else in Continental Europe.
25. K. Knies, *Die politische Oekonomie vom geschichtlichen Standpuncte.*
26. Hence is continuous with the classical theory of value, and does not have any connection with the 'new economics', which is typically the product of university professors, not professional socialists or popular writers on the 'social question'.
27. Well-structured argument is not Knies's forte, one of the reasons that it is so difficult to read his book.
28. Knies (1883: 501ff.). Walras had sent Knies a copy of his book when it was first published – Knies's reply is merely formal without any comment on the substance of the work – letter of Knies to Walras, 22 September 1874, Letter 299 (Jaffé, 1965: 429).
29. Hennings (1997: 10). Böhm-Bawerk's 1876 manuscript has been reprinted in Yagi (1983: 16–35).
30. 'National Oekonomie. Prof. Knies April 1880', Edwin R. A. Seligman Papers Box 86 Notebook IV, Rare Book and Manuscript Library, Butler Library, Columbia University.
31. As Menger himself suggested in a long letter to Walras – Letter from Carl Menger to Walras, February 1884, Letter 602 (Jaffé, 1965: Vol. II: 2–6).
32. And he was unaware of the way that Walras fitted in to the French socialist tradition. Gossen had already demonstrated in the 1850s how the new subjectivist framework was compatible with a kind of free-market communism, and it is important to remember that for Walras 'general equilibrium' was not very general in respect of its extent: land and the railways should for example be excluded from market relations, and be nationalized (see Tribe, 2000).
33. Weber's lectures from Freiburg on *Allgemeine und theoretische Nationalökonomie* were published in May 2009 in MWG III/1, while this essay was in the press. Yet to appear (as of April 2010 announced as "in preparation" on the Mohr website) are his lectures on Finance (MWG III/3) and Money, Banking and Exchanges (MWG III/2). The editors embargo all unpublished papers and letters prior to publication, and require that all editors refuse any discussion of ongoing work on Weber's writings with all interested scholars not part of the editorial group.
34. Weber altered the title and introduced the quotation marks.
35. I have discussed these two outlines in Tribe (2006c: 89–94), directed mainly, however, to establishing what sort of economist Weber was *not*. Here I shift the focus from this negative perspective to the kinds of economics that did interest him and which he sought to promote though his lectures.
36. Exactly how these were to relate to the lecture course is not clear.
37. This is a continuation of § 2, not a misprint, since it occurs in both reading guide and lecture outline.
38. An abbreviation of the title of Stirner's, 1846–1847 translation, not of the edition most recently published, which had the title *Natur und Ursachen des Volkswohlstandes* (1882).
39. Lecture outline of Book I, § 2.2, p. 2. But again, this statement of the abstract nature of the economic agent is not linked to any argument that a more

'realistic' or 'historical' appraisal of this subject should be advanced, and so it should not be read as a criticism of contemporary economic theory.

40. C. Menger (1871) fn. to pp. 2, 5.
41. Lecture outline of Book I, § 2.1, p. 1 – '"Wirtschaft" ist der Complex der Massnahmen, welche durch das Wirtschaften eines Individuums oder einer menschlichen Gemeinschaft veranlasst sind.'
42. Sax (1884: 14): 'Volkswirthschaft ist die aus dem Streben nach Sicherung der äusseren Existenzbedingungen sich ergebende Bestimmung des (technischen) Handelns und der socialen Beziehungen der Menschen.'
43. Lecture outline of Book I, § 2.4, p. 4.
44. Unusually for Weber's writings, these corrected proofs still exist: Wolfgang Mommsen was presented with them in the early 1950s by Else Jaffé-Richthofen, but the first indications of their whereabouts is in a footnote to an essay by Edith Hanke (2006: 32, fn. 19).
45. Friedrich von Wieser (1914: 132). The book takes up pp. 125–444 of the volume.
46. This feature of the text remains hidden from English readers since Talcott Parsons removed the typographical distinction between definition paragraphs and elaborations. See my account of Parsons' translation (2007).
47. And it is only when the Max Weber *Gesamtausgabe* finally published all of these lectures that we will be able to see exactly how this was done.
48. See my discussion of this in the introduction to the translation (2006b: 12).

References

Biesenbach, F. (1968) 'Die Entwicklung der Nationalökonomie an der Universität Freiburg i. Br. 1768–1896', diss. University of Freiburg.

Böhm-Bawerk, E. von (1881) *Rechte und Verhältnisse vom Standpunkte der volkswirthschaftlichen Güterlehre. Kritische Studie*, Innsbruck: Verlag der Wagner'schen Universitäts-Buchhandlung.

Böhm-Bawerk, E. von (1884) *Geschichte und Kritik der Kapitalzins-Theorien*, Innsbruck: Verlag der Wagner'schen Universitäts-Buchhandlung.

Böhm-Bawerk, E. von (1889) *Positive Theorie des Kapitales*, Innsbruck: Verlag der Wagner'schen Universitäts-Buchhandlung.

Böhm-Bawerk, E. von (1891a) 'The Austrian Economists', *Annals of the American Academy of Political and Social Science*, 1(3): 361–84.

Böhm-Bawerk, E. von (1891b) 'Zur neuesten Literatur über den Wert', *Jahrbücher für Nationalökonomie und Statistik*, III. Folge Bd. 1: 875–99.

Böhm-Bawerk, E. von (1892a) 'Unsere Aufgaben', *Zeitschrift für Volkswirtschaft, Socialpolitik und Verwaltung*, 1(1): 1–10.

Böhm-Bawerk, E. von (1892b) 'Wert, Kosten und Grenznutzen', *Jahrbücher für Nationalökonomie und Statistik*, III. Folge Bd. 3: 321–67.

Böhm-Bawerk, E. von (1894a) 'Der letzte Maasstab des Güterwertes', *Zeitschrift für Volkswirtschaft, Socialpolitik und Verwaltung*, 3: 185–230.

Böhm-Bawerk, E. von (1894b) 'The Ultimate Standard of Value', *Annals of the American Academy of Political and Social Science*, 5(1): 149–208.

Bonar, J. (1888) 'The Austrian School and the View of Value', *Quarterly Journal of Economics*, 3(1):1–31.

Borchardt, K. (1999) in Max Weber, *Börsenwesen. Schriften und Reden 1893–1898*, ed. by Knut Borchardt, with Cornelia Meyer-Stoll, MWGA Abt. I, 5(2), Tübingen: J. C. B. Mohr (Paul Siebeck): 1–111.

Borchardt, K. (2002) 'Max Weber's Writings on the Bourse: Puzzling Out a Forgotten Corpus', *Max Weber Studies*, 2(2): 139–62.

Buckle, H. T. (1861) *History of Civilization in England*, Vol. 2, London: Parker, Son, and Bourn.

Cairnes, J. E. (1875) *The Character and Logical Method of Political Economy*, second edition, Macmillan.

Graber, E. (1981) 'Translator's Introduction to Max Weber's Essay on Some Categories of Interpretive Sociology', *Sociological Quarterly*, 22: 145–50.

Graf, F. W. (2004) 'Ernst Troeltsch's Evaluation of Max and Alfred Weber: Introduction and Translation of a Letter by Ernst Troeltsch to Heinrich Dietzel', *Max Weber Studies*, 4(1): 101–8.

Grimmer-Solem, E. (2003) *The Rise of Historical Economics and Social Reform in Germany 1864–1894*, Oxford: Oxford University Press.

Hagemann, H., Krohn, C. D. (eds) (1999) *Biographisches Handbuch der deutschsprachigen wirtschaftswissenschaftlichen Emigration nach 1933*, 2 vols, Munich: K. G. Saur.

Hanke, E. (2006) ' "Max Webers Schreibtisch ist nun mein Altar" Marianne Weber und das geistige Erbe ihres Mannes', in Karl-Ludwig Ay, Knut Borchardt (eds), *Das Faszinozum Max Webers*, Konstanz: UVK.

Hennings, K. H. (1997) *The Austrian Theory of Value and Capital. Studies in the Life and Work of Eugen von Böhm-Bawerk*, Cheltenham: Edward Elgar.

Hennis, W. (2000a) *Max Weber's Central Question*, Newbury: Threshold Press.

Hennis, W. (2000b) *Max Weber's Science of Man*, Newbury: Threshold Press.

Hentschel, V. (1988) 'Die Wirtschaftswissenschaften als akademische Disziplin an der Universität Heidelberg (1822–1924)', in N. Waszek (ed.), *Die Institutionalisierung der Nationalökonomie an deutschen Universitäten*, St. Katharinen: Scripta Mercaturae.

Jaffé, W. (ed.) (1965) *Correspondence of Léon Walras and Related Papers* Vols I & II, Amsterdam: North Holland Publishing Company.

Jevons, W. S. (1879) 'Preface to the Second Edition (1879)', *Theory of Political Economy*, London: Macmillan.

Käsler, D. (1979) *Einführung in das Studium Max Webers*, Munich: C. H. Beck.

Keynes, J. N. (1891) *The Scope and Method of Political Economy*, London: Macmillan.

Knies, K. (1853) *Die politische Oekonomie vom Standpuncte der geschichtlichen Methode*, Braunschweig: C. A. Schwetschke und Sohn.

Knies, K. (1883) *Die politische Oekonomie vom geschichtlichen Standpuncte*, Neue Auflage, Bruanschweig: C. A. Schwetschke und Sohn (M. Bruhn).

Leslie, T. E. C. (1879) *Essays in Political and Moral Philosophy*, Dublin: Hodges, Foster and Figgis.

Lindenlaub, D. (1967) *Richtungskämpfe im Verein für Sozialpolitik, Vierteljahreschrift für Sozial- und Wirtschaftsgeschichte* Beiheft 52/53, Wiesbaden: F. Steiner.

Menger, C. (1871) *Grundsätze der Volkswirthschaftslehre*, Vienna: Wilhelm Braumüller.

Mommsen, W. J. (1993) Introduction to Max Weber, *Landarbeiterfrage, Nationalstaat und Volkswirtschaftspolitik. Schriften und Reden 1892–1899*, MWGA Abt. I, 4(1), Tübingen: J. C. B. Mohr (Paul Siebeck).

Riesebrodt, M. (1984) Introduction to Max Weber, *Die Lage der Landarbeiter im ostelbischen Deutschland*, MWGA Abt. I, 3(1), Tübingen: J. C. B. Mohr (Paul Siebeck).

Sax, E. (1884) *Das Wesen und die Aufgaben der Nationalökonomie. Ein Beitrag zu den Grundproblemen dieser Wissenschaft*, Vienna: Alfred Hölder.

Schmoller, G. (2000) 'Eröffnungsrede auf der Eisenacher Versammlung zur Besprechung der sozialen Frage' [1872], reprinted in J. Burkhardt, B. P.Priddat (eds), *Geschichte der Ökonomie*, Frankfurt: Deutscher Klassiker Verlag.

Sering, M. (1981) 'The Agrarian Question and Socialism', in Athar Hussain, Keith Tribe (eds), *Paths of Development in Capitalist Agriculture*, London: Macmillan: 68–94.

Smart, W. (1891a) *An Introduction to the Theory of Value on the Lines of Menger, Wieser and Böhm-Bawerk*, London: Macmillan.

Smart, W. (1891b) 'The New Theory of Interest', *Economic Journal*, 1(4): 675–87.

Smart, W. (1892) 'The Effects of Consumption of Wealth on Distribution', *Annals of the American Academy of Political and Social Science*, 3(3): 257–92.

Swedberg, R. (1998) *Max Weber and the Idea of Economic Sociology*, Princeton, NJ: Princeton University Press.

Takebayashi, S. (2003) *Die Entstehung der Kapitalismustheorie in der Gründungsphase der deutschen Soziologie. Von der historischen Nationalökonomie zur historischen Soziologie Werner Sombarts und Max Webers*, Berlin: Duncker und Humblot.

Tooze, J. A. (2001) *Statistics and the German State, 1900–1945, The Making of Modern Economic Knowledge*, Cambridge: Cambridge University Press.

Tribe, K. (1989) 'Prussian Agriculture – German Politics: Max Weber 1892–7' in K. Tribe (ed.), *Reading Weber*, London: Routledge: 85–130.

Tribe, K. (1992) 'The Economic Journal and British Economics, 1891–1940', *History of the Human Sciences*, 5(1): 33–58.

Tribe, K. (1994) 'Commerce, Science and the Modern University', in L. Ray (ed.), *Organizing Modernity*, London: Routledge: 141–57.

Tribe, K. (2000) '"The Price is Right": Léon Walras and Economic Justice', *Schweizerische Zeitschrift für Geschichte*, 50(3): 388–402.

Tribe, K. (2001) Review of Hagemann, H., Krohn, C. D. (1999), *Economic Journal*, 111(473): F740–F46.

Tribe, K. (2006a) 'A Lost Connection: Max Weber and the Economic Sciences' in Karl-Ludwig Ay, Knut Borchardt (eds), *Das Faszinosum Max Weber. Die Geschichte seiner Geltung*, Konstanz: UVK Verlagsgesellschaft: 313–29.

Tribe, K. (2006b) 'Max Weber's "Conceptual Preface" to *General Economic History*. Introduction and Translation', *Max Weber Studies*, (1) : 11–38.

Tribe, K. (2006c) *Strategies of Economic Order. German Economic Discourse 1750–1950*, New Edition, Cambridge: Cambridge University Press.

Tribe, K. (2007) 'Talcott Parsons as Translator of Max Weber', *History of European Ideas*, 33: 212–33.

Tribe, K. (2008) '"Das Adam Smith Problem" and the Origins of Modern Smith Scholarship', *History of European Ideas*, 34: 514–25.

Veblen, T. (1900) 'The Preconceptions of Economic Science III', *Quarterly Journal of Economics*, 14(2): 240–269.

Weber, A. (1923) 'Das Diplomexamen für Volkswirte', *Jahrbücher für Nationalökonomie und Statistik*, III. Folge Bd. 65: 289–311.

Weber, M. (1976) *Wirtschaft und Gesellschaft*, 5th edition, Tübingen: J. C. B. Mohr (Paul Siebeck).
Wieser, F. von (1891) 'The Austrian School and the Theory of Value', *Economic Journal*, 1(1): 108–21.
Wieser, F. von (1914) *Theorie der gesellschaftlichen Wirtschaft, Grundriss der Sozialökonomik*, I. Abteilung. Wirtschaft und Wirtschaftswissenschaft, Tübingen: J. C. B. Mohr (Paul Siebeck).
Yagi, K. (1983) *Böhm-Bawerk's First Interest Theory: with C. Menger-Böhm-Bawerk Correspondence 1884–85*, Centre for Historical Social Science Literature, Hitotsubashi University, Tokyo, Study Series No. 3 (March).
Yagi, K. (2000) 'Karl Knies' Heidelberg Lectures on Economics: An Introduction', *Kyoto University Economic Review*, LXIX(1, 2): 1–12.
Yagi, K. and Ikeda, Y. (1988) *Economics Courses at Vienna University 1849–1944*, Faculty of Economics, Kyoto University, February, Vol. 1.

5
The German Historical School, Schumpeter and Ichiro Nakayama: Economic Theory and Economic Sociology

Tamotsu Nishizawa

1. Introduction

Recently the influence of the German Historical School on Alfred Marshall and Joseph Schumpeter has been discussed: both Marshall and Schumpeter were in fact highly influenced by the German Historical School (Hodgson, 2008). In particular, Schmoller's impact on both has been stressed, and Schumpeter's methodological adherence to Schmoller is well known from his 1926 article on Schmoller, *Gustav v. Schmoller und die Probleme von heute*. There have been positive discussions on Marshall and Schumpeter with regard to 'a reasoned history' or 'histoire raisonnee' and on their ideas of economic sociology, further on the legitimate boundaries of economics as a discipline. It has been argued: although both Marshall and Schumpeter admitted the legitimate role of pure economic theory as the economic organon or economic logic, they were not satisfied with it because it was unable to explain the problems of real life, and refused to separate the study of economic factors from that of social, cultural and institutional factors at a more advanced stage of knowledge (Shionoya, 1997, 2001; Nishizawa, 2007; Shionoya and Nishizawa, 2008).

In this chapter I shall focus on mainly Ichiro Nakayama (1898–1980), who studied at Tokyo University of Commerce (now Hitotsubashi University) under Tokuzo Fukuda, then at Bonn University under Joseph Schumpeter, and became a most prominent mathematical and theoretical economist in pre-war Japan by his *Pure Economics* (1933) and *Equilibrium Analysis of the Developing Process* (1939). He was also very deeply involved in the labour problems, industrial relations, in post-war

Japan and wrote many books including *The Economic Sociology of Industrial Relations* (1974).[1] A study in Nakayama might shed fresh light on the relations between economic theory and economic sociology in the German Historical School and Schumpeter.

Nakayama wrote in his autobiography *My Way Economics* (1979) in the year prior to his death:

> Economics, which deals with human being or a study of mankind, seems in necessity to develop into sociology in a broad sense, or humanomics, as we increase our experiences and as we learn as much as from history. It is a good example that Schumpeter's academic system had developed from *Wesen* in 1908 to *Capitalism, Socialism, and Democracy* in 1942, as if a small stream becomes a big river, gathering waters from various sides.
>
> (Nakayama, 1979: 24)

Nakayama's academic studies started from pure economics or mathematical economics and developed into economic sociology; he compared his own academic development to Schumpeter's.

2. Schumpeter on economic history and economic sociology

As Shionoya (1997) put it, in Schumpeter's view, a universal social science is closely connected with a study of history. Schumpeter emphasizes that the subject matter of economics is a unique process in historical time and that the historical materials reflect the development phenomenon and indicate the relationship between economic and non-economic facts, thus suggesting how the disciplines of the social sciences should interact. The recognition of the connection between the unity of social life and historical development was the essence of the German Historical School as he understood it, and constituted his central idea of a universal social science.

Schumpeter thought that economic history, statistics and economic theory made up economic analysis; he added to these three a fourth fundamental field, economic sociology. Of these fundamental fields, 'economic history is by far the most important' for him. He said: if he were told that he could study only one of these but could have his choice, it would be economic history that he should choose. In his view the subject matter of economics was essentially a unique process in historic time, and he stated that most of the fundamental errors currently committed in economic analysis were due to lack of historical experience more often than to any other shortcoming of the economist's equipment. Thus he asserted crucially that

> the historical report cannot be purely economic but must inevitably reflect also 'institutional' facts that are not purely economic: therefore it affords the best method for understanding how economic and non-economic facts are related to one another and how the various social sciences should be related to one another.
>
> (Schumpeter, 1954: 12–13)

Schumpeter added economic sociology to history, statistics and theory: three fundamental fields, while essentially complementing each other, do not do so perfectly. We need economic sociology because 'when we introduce the institution of private property or of free contracting or else a greater or smaller amount of government regulation, we are introducing social facts that are not simply economic history but are a sort of generalized or typified or stylized economic history'. This applies still more to the general forms of human behaviour. We need such an institutional introduction that belongs to sociology rather than to economic history as such. Economic analysis deals with the question of how people behave at any time and what the economic effects they produce by so behaving; economic sociology deals with the question of how they came to behave as they do. If we define human behaviour widely enough so that it includes not only actions, motives and propensities but also the social institutions that are relevant to economic behaviour such as government, property inheritance, contract and so on, that phrase really tells all we need to know (ibid.: 20–21).

Schumpeter appraised Schmoller's research program as the model for economic sociology, and characterized its aims as 'a unified sociology or social science as intellectually ("theoretically") worked up universal history' (*Universalgeschichte*) (Schumpeter, 1926: 382). He defined economic sociology as 'a sort of generalized or typified or stylized economic history' and called it 'reasoned history'. Schumpeter (1926), based upon his methodological evaluation of Schmoller's historico-ethical economics, characterized its approach as an economic sociology that enabled the integration of theory and history (Shionoya, 1997).

The new departure, the distinctive research program and the emergence of a genuine school, Schumpeter said, must be associated with the name of Gustav von Schmoller. The research program of the German Historical School was explicitly formulated by Schmoller as a 'historico-ethical' approach to economics. He always protested against an 'isolating' analysis of economic phenomena and held that 'we lose their essence as soon as we isolate them'. This view was the consequence of his resolve to develop economics through historical monographs. For the materials that such monographs were based on as well as their results were 'refractory to any attempt at isolating – in most cases, in fact, they become meaningless if isolated'. In principle, the Schmollerian economist was 'a historically minded sociologist'. The historico-ethical school associated with Schmoller intended to express 'protest against the wholly imaginary advocacy of the hunt for private profit of which the English "classics" were supposed to have been guilty'. The school professed to study 'all the facets of an economic phenomenon'; hence 'all the facets of economic behaviour and not merely the economic logic of it'; hence 'the whole of human motivations as historically displayed, the specifically economic ones not more than the rest for which the term "ethical" was made to serve, presumably because it seems to stress hyperindividual components' (Schumpeter, 1954: 812).

Marshall also thought of social science as 'the reasoned history of man'. For Marshall, history must be a history of man as the object of philosophy and psychology. In economics we deal with the whole man's nature, though we point out certain special aspects of it. From this it follows that, in so far as we base ourselves upon the history of past times at all, it must be history as a whole.

> We need more than economic history, more than a history of economic institutions and customs, wages and prices, of trade and finance: we want a history of man himself, and economic history as contributing to that.
>
> (Marshall, 1897: 299)

Evaluating Marshall's *Principles*, Schumpeter found out an economic sociology constructed on historical foundations 'behind, beyond, and all around' the core of the analytical apparatus and characterized it as follows:

> His mastery of historical fact and his analytic habit of mind did not dwell in separate compartments but formed so close a union that the live fact intrudes into the theorem and the theorem into purely historical observations.
>
> (Schumpeter, 1951: 94)

In the last two paragraphs of the long essay *Gustav v. Schmoller und die Probleme von heute*, Schumpeter asserts that Schmoller (1900–1904) could write on his book (*Grundriss der allgemeinen Volkswirtschaftslehre*) Marshall's motto '*natura non facit saltum*'. Schumpeter frequently noted the similarity between Schmoller's and Marshall's work. Though Schmoller and Marshall approached different subjects because of their different training and circumstances, they came out of the same world. Marshall and Schmoller eventually wrote the same thing, though their stresses were different. They both overcame the economics of simple postulates and striking results, and showed what the economics of the future would look like. Marshall's *Principles* and Schmoller's *Grundriss* contain in embryo a large majority of what could be done in the present and in the future and what had been done. They continue to be seemingly inexhaustible sources of micro – and macro – social – scientific insights (Schumpeter, 1926: 387–8; Hodgson, 2006: 3).

3. Nakayama and pure economics in Japan

Nakayama was born in 1898 in Mie Prefecture. After attending Kobe Higher Commercial School, he entered the newly opened Tokyo University of Commerce in 1920, which was just promoted from Tokyo Higher Commercial School, located in Hitotsubashi in central Tokyo. There he encountered Fukuda: 'My economics started with teacher Tokuzo Fukuda.' He wrote, 'If I had not attended the lectures of Professor Fukuda at Hitotsubashi, with no mistake, I would not have become an economist' (Nakayama, 1979: 12).[2]

When Nakayama attended Fukuda's lectures, while Fukuda pursued his own welfare economics he also investigated a theoretical and mathematical economics and advised Nakayama to read Cournot, Gossen and Walras; indeed all that Nakayama really read in two years under Fukuda's supervision were the three books, that is, the major works of these three great economists, which were the very classics of mathematical economics. Nakayama published his maiden work, 'On the two tendencies in the mathematical economics and an attempt to synthesize them' (1923), which was probably the first serious article in Japan, insisting the importance of Walras's general equilibrium theory. Fukuda had sought for the core of economics or its theoretical essence; economics as an autonomous science or price theory; therefore Nakayama of his own accord became deeply interested in *Das Wesen und der Hauptinhalt der theoretischen Nationalökonomie* (1908), of which only one copy existed in the university library of Hitotsubashi. Yasuma Takada, another pioneer of equilibrium theory in Japan and a very prominent and prolific writer on economics and sociology, who was then temporarily teaching there, always kept this copy.[3]

Schumpeter had a great impact on Japanese economists. Schumpeter's *Wesen* was translated into Japanese in 1936 by T. Kimura and T. Yasui (the following generation of Nakayama and Takada). Kimura and Yasui were the young scholars at Tokyo Imperial University who attended Schumpeter's lectures in Tokyo in 1931 and the disciples of Eijiro Kawai, who met Schumpeter in December 1924 and arranged his professorship at Tokyo (as successor of Emil Lederer, who taught there for four years) in January 1925. However, Schumpeter soon got an appointment at Bonn, replacing Heinrich Dietzel, and gave up on going to Tokyo. Instead, Alfred Amonn arrived in Tokyo and taught equilibrium theory using Gustav Cassel, whose textbook *Theoretische Sozialökonomie* (1st ed., 1918; English trans., *The Theory of Social Economy*, 1923) was widely read in Japan, as well as in Germany, in the 1920s. Then Schumpeter went to Japan in late January 1931 on the way back from the US, just after the inauguration of the Econometric Society in late December 1930.

Nakayama translated Cournot's *Recherches sur les principes mathématiques de la théorie des richesses* in 1927, then left for Germany, first to Berlin (to study under Bortkiewicz) and then to Bonn to study under Schumpeter. Fukuda had advised his other student Juro Tezuka (who was two years older than Nakayama and taught at Otaru) to work on Gossen and Tezuka published *Studies on Gossen* (of which the substance was an abridged translation of Gossen's *Entwickelung der Gesetze des menschlichen Verkehrs, und der daraus fliessenden Regeln für menschliches Handeln*, 1854) in 1920. Fukuda's student at Keio Gijuku, Shinzo Koizumi (later president there) translated Jevons's *Theory of Political Economy* in 1913. The first full translation of Marshall's *Principles* also appeared in 1926,[4] which was initiated by another disciple of Fukuda, K. Otsuka, who later became a prominent Marxist. Fukuda advised his students to work and transplant the marginal utility theory in Japan in the 1910s and early 1920s, which paved the way to transplant Walras's general equilibrium theory. Yasuma Takada started to lecture at Kyoto Imperial University in 1929 (after a Marxist economist Hajime Kawakami was expelled there) and published *Price Theory* in 1930 as the second volume of *New Lectures on Economics* (in 5 volumes). Miyoji Hayakawa at Hokkaido and Otaru (who studied at Bonn under Dietzel in 1921–1923 and learnt from Schumpeter in Vienna in 1924–1925) published *Introduction to Pure Economic Theory* in 1930. Then Hayakawa, another prominent pioneer of mathematical economics in Japan (and the first Japanese to have a paper accepted by *Econometrica* in 1951), published four other small books on Walras and Pareto by 1932. After coming back from Germany, Nakayama also wrote 'The Method of Mathematical Economics' in 1932, then *Pure Economics* in 1933. Tezuka's translation of Walras's *Élements d'économie politique pure* was also published in 1933, the same year when *Econometrica* and *Review of Economic Studies* started to be issued. The general equilibrium theory had been taking its roots in the Japanese non-Marxian economics academics, who eventually founded the Japanese Economic Association in December 1934 with some 40 people, which celebrated its 75th anniversary in 2009 with some 3400 members. Kei Shibata's *Theoretical Economics* in two volumes appeared in 1935–1936. In the previous ten years mathematical economics had progressed with giant strides in Japan. In this aspect of transplanting the general equilibrium theory, Japan seems to have been well advanced compared even with the Anglophone world, as Yasui later remarked (1979: 79–80).

A 'narrower' definition of economics emerged in the Anglophone world, and it eventually displaced the previous and wider definitions of the subject held by Marshall and the German Historical School (Hodgson, 2008: 94). In Japan also the pure economics and mathematical economics took great strides in the ten years up to 1935 (Tezuka, 1935), but here the Marxian ideas and political economy were very dominant from the late 1920s, particularly in the Imperial Universities such as Tokyo and Kyoto, in contrast with the Universities of Commerce such as Hitotsubashi, where Fukuda and Nakayama worked, as well as Kobe, and Otaru Higher Commercial School.

Nakayama studied under Schumpeter in Bonn during 1927–1929 (though Schumpeter was a visiting professor at Harvard in 1927–1928), then Nakayama met his lifelong friend Seiichi Tohata of Tokyo Imperial University and discussed the essence and *Hauptinhalt* of theoretical economics. Schumpeter (1908) defined the overall subject matter of economics in terms of the formal analysis of exchange relations or catallactics. Nakayama followed in principle Schumpeter's *Wesen* and wrote his 'The Method of Mathematical Economics' and *Pure Economics* in its line. But when Nakayama studied in Bonn, Schumpeter had finished his trilogy works of economic theory and was already lecturing economic sociology, which was to serve as the draft for his later *Capitalism, Socialism and Democracy* (1949). Nakayama found the basis of economics in Schumpeter, who made and introduced the general equilibrium theory of Walras into 'German without mathematics' and parted ways with 'Papa Marx'. Nakayama wrote later that Schumpeter lectured and reviewed a lot on Marx. In fact Schumpeter wrote works such as *The Crisis of the Tax System* (1918), 'The Sociology of Imperialisms' (1918–1919), *Gustav v. Schmoller und die Probleme von heute* (1926), 'The Instability of Capitalism' (1928). Nakayama counted Schumpeter's *Theory of Economic Development* (1912) as his lifelong 'classics'. He translated it with Tohata as early as 1937. They also jointly translated Schumpeter's *History of Economics* in 1950 and *Capitalism, Socialism and Democracy* in 1951–1952.

In so far as economic sociology, institutional economics and evolutionary economics, as distinct from economic statics, take into account non-economic factors along with economic factors, they are all concerned about the interactions between economic changes, on the one hand, and non-economic changes in value, culture and *Zeitgeist*, on the other. For Schumpeter, the analysis of the concurrent evolution of mind and society is the third branch of economics which remains to be explored. The historicity of an economy and social unity in a development process can be addressed only by the apparatus of economic sociology. In his book *Capitalism, Socialism and Democracy*, the major work of economic sociology, he presented the thesis of falling capitalism due to its economic success based on the interaction between the economic and non-economic areas (Schumpeter, 1943).

4. Nakayama, labour problems and economic sociology

In addition to his contributions to pure economics, Nakayama did a great deal for economic and industrial policy making, particularly for industrial peace and stability of labour-management relations in post-war Japan through the economic advisory councils and various intermediate organizations. When Nakayama died in 1980, the then Prime Minister Ohira stated properly his contributions:

> One cannot speak of the recovery and development of our country's post-war economic society without mentioning the Sensei [Professor Nakayama]. Most importantly, during the period when the post-war industrial relations were severely shaken, he expended every effort as chairman of the Central Labour Commission (Chuo Rodo Iinkai). Through the fair and balanced judgment of the Sensei, many major disputes were skilfully brought under control and guided to resolutions [...] In recent times our country's industrial relations have proceeded in a manner more sound than can be seen in any foreign

> country. I believe that this is nothing other than the fruition and realization of the Sensei's long years of guidance in bringing the trust between labour and management together as one.
>
> (Nakayama, 1981: 10–11)

Indeed, no one can discuss Japan's post-war stabilization of industrial relations without noting the Central Labour Commission and the Japan Productivity Centre (Nihon Seisansei Honbu), in particular the latter's Labour-Management Consultation System Committee (Roshi Kyogisei Iinkai). Nakayama served as the chairman of both the Commission and the Committee for many years and played a crucial role in the stabilization of industrial relations and the institutionalization of Japanese management.

Nakayama's deep involvement with labour problems was probably started by Tokuzo Fukuda. Nakayama warmly praised Fukuda's maiden work of pioneering achievement, *Labor Economics* (1899), co-authored with his teacher Lujo Brentano, in his memorial lecture, 'Welfare Economics and Tokuzo Fukuda', delivered on the 100th anniversary of Fukuda's birth. Brentano had researched British labour problems and compared it to the German case. He argued that in order to achieve Britain's level of prosperity and pursue the optimal course of economic development, Germany needed to raise wages, shorten working hours and raise labour productivity. Upon reading this work, Nakayama observed that Japan still faced the problems of one hundred years ago, which were those of whether Japanese economy would surely be able to stand high wages and shortened working hours (Nakayama, 1978: 64–66).

Just as the great economists like Alfred Marshall and A. C. Pigou, Fukuda made actual labour issues the background for his welfare economic studies from the beginning. And, though Fukuda was strongly influenced by Marshall and Pigou's welfare economics, in 'From Price Struggles to Welfare Struggles: Labour Disputes as Welfare Struggles' (1921), he even criticized Marshall and Pigou:

> We conduct research on prices not for its own sake, but in order to know their relationship to economic welfare, so by studying this field we hope to advance research on welfare.
>
> (Fukuda, 1921: 280–81)

Studying prices in market economy was a step towards advancing the studies on welfare, such as human happiness and satisfaction. According to Fukuda, Pigou neglected the issues of whether working hours were judicious and of whether income distribution, and particularly labour's share, was equitable. It was in order to supplement this share that labour disputes or labour movement as welfare struggles occurred. Fukuda believed that labour struggles played the vital role of enabling labour to receive a legitimate share as original income and to ensure proper working hours. This argument appeared in *Labor Economics*, the work which launched Fukuda's welfare economic thinking and social policy making (Nakayama, 1978: 68–72).

Some notes on Nakayama's pre-war activities might be useful here. By the strong recommendation of Fukuda, Nakayama was posted to the Home Office's Social Bureau in 1930, immediately upon his return from studying in Germany. There he developed and conducted surveys on unemployment. Fukuda and a few other people at that time made up the Consultative Council of the Social Bureau and they used it to assist survey research on wages, employment, labour unions and the highly conspicuous unemployment problem. Fukuda had become a counsellor to the Home Office in 1923. He and Hiroshi Ikeda, Toru Nagai and Toyohiko Kagawa, had exerted themselves to produce a proposal for establishing the facilities for labour exchange (the Nationalized Labour Exchange). Fukuda discerned the underlying basis of the unemployment problem and used the Consultative Council to emphasize the need for survey research. The work based on this proposal, from the first draft to the final collection of data, was undertaken by Nakayama at Fukuda's behest. Nakayama believed that the experience he gained in conducting the survey was 'extremely valuable', after until then having 'only meditated at my desk'; it was 'definitely because of it that I [Nakayama] later came to have a multifaceted understanding of surveys and empirical evidence' (Fukuda, 1924: 2; Nakayama, 1972–1973: Vol. 13, ii–iii).

Nakayama's writings in this period indicate the connections between his and Fukuda's thought and that of the German Historical School, as well as an important continuity from Nakayama's pre-war to post-war activities, when he was deeply involved in the labour issues and industrial relations as the second chairman of the Central Labour Commission. After Fukuda's death, Nakayama undertook lectures on economic theory in tandem with Otsuka's Marxist economics. Then Nakayama published *Pure Economics* in 1933. At the same time he wrote many pieces on unemployment and unemployment statistics, and put forth a conception of economic sociology. It was indeed 'Economic Theory and Economic Sociology' which Nakayama wrote in the collected eulogies to Fukuda's death in 1930.

In 'Relations Between Economics and Statistics in the Business Cycle Studies' (*Tokei Jiho*, 1932), Nakayama stated that it was 'the whole of an economic sociology of immense meaning which includes economic theory, and here is nothing other than a very demand for the economics of the present age, that is an age of transition'; and he proposed for 'a program of realistic economics' and argued for 'the creation of universal economic sociology'. The realistic and empirical tendencies in economics were not necessarily those which could be seen first in the current statistical studies, such as those by Wesley Mitchell. They were the essential basis of economics as an empirical science, and 'they were formulated to be a program by the [German] historical school in the history of economics'. It could be easily seen how Mitchell's quantitative economics in the current business cycle studies was similar to Schmoller's economics, and Nakayama referred to Schumpeter's work on *Gustav v. Schmoller und die Probleme von heute* (Nakayama, 1972–1973: Vol. 5, 353–5).

Furthermore, both the German historical school and Mitchell had the very same way of doing things in their aiming for the foundation of economics, which included policies in it, and in their objecting to (or avoiding) the theoretical tendencies of economics in order to attain this aim. In this sense it can be said that the tendencies of modern (current) economics, as shown in the business cycle studies, were a rehabilitation of the economics of the German historical school. The general ground on which the relations between economics and statistics should be discussed had been provided by the German historical school. Many members of the German historical school, such as Wagner, Knapp, Lexis and Conrad, treated a number of problems relating to the relations between economics and statistics, as well as contributing to statistics. Nakayama saw the tendencies of economics shown in the current statistical business cycle studies basically as a re-emergence of the empirical tendencies to a comprehensive economic sociology clearly revealed in the program of the German historical school; and approved the final meaning of statistical method to economics as the indispensable means for the construction of economic sociology.

Nakayama argued about the fundamental problems of how economics as an empirical science would treat and include the problem of judgments and valuations in policy. So far economics seemed to be satisfied with simply expelling the policy problems as normative from scientific economics. However, the empiricism in economics cannot actually come into existence without taking account of policy studies, rather how the policy studies, normative, judgment and valuation problems could be made into academic or scientific problems, should be the final questions of empirical economics (ibid.: 359–60).

He discussed in 'Economic Theory and Economic Sociology' that the relations between economic theory and the given economic conditions were essentially the same as the relations between economic theory and economic sociology. While the autonomy of economic theory was separated from the knowledge concerning the given economic conditions, the main critical tendencies of the current economics were looking towards dissolving this separation. This means that economic theory which came into existence as an autonomous system out of economic sociology in the broad sense was going to take into account once again the relations with economic sociology as its mother's womb. Mitchell's quantitative economics has often been referred to as the most distinct program of this kind of empirical economics, but as Schumpeter acutely pointed out, Schmoller's program representing the economic realism had a lot of similarities to it, that was what Nakayama discussed referring to *Gustav v. Schmoller und die Probleme von heute* (ibid.: Vol. 1, 518–19). Even in the very early days when Nakayama and some Japanese economists were struggling with pure economics, he had economic sociology deeply in his mind.

4.1. Takashima's case for economic sociology

Zenya Takashima (1904–1990), another disciple of Tokuzo Fukuda, learnt a lot from a Marxist Otsuka and, founded a basis of Japan's Adam Smith studies by his *Fundamental Problems of Economic Sociology: Smith and List as Economic Sociologists* (1941), started his studies from Schumpeter. Takashima, who entered Tokyo University of Commerce in 1921, the year after Nakayama, and studied under Fukuda and Otsuka, wrote a graduation thesis called 'The Significance of Economic Statics and Economic Dynamics in the National Political Economy: A Study on Joseph Schumpeter' in 1927. It consists of Chapter 1 'The concept of "natural" and "social" in Wieser', Chapter 2 'Economic statics and economic dynamics in Schumpeter' and Chapter 3 'An attempt to synthesize economic statics and economic dynamics'. Takashima inquired into the relations between pure economics and historical and social matters, and said that for those who would try to synthesize them Schumpeter and Wieser gave some common suggestions of significance. Takashima studied Schumpeter and found the relations between statics and dynamics, pure theory and non-pure theory, the Austrian School (mathematical economics) and the Historical School (social school), and tried to make clear the meaning and limit of pure theory or marginal utility theory (Takashima, 1927).

Under Fukuda's guidance Takashima studied the works of the marginal utility school, the Austrian School, Schumpeter and J. B. Clark. He felt unsatisfied with 'non-social characteristics of those economics', then, at that time, Otsuka came back from studying abroad and insisted on 'socializing the economics' or 'to socialize the theory' and talked of 'social Macht (powers)'. Takashima squeezed out a thesis theme of 'how the marginal utility theory could be socialized' and worked it out methodologically; in a sense Takashima might have tried to integrate catallactics into plutology. Takashima became highly influenced by Otsuka, who was deeply involved in Marxian economics, and Japanese academia was increasingly dominated by Marxism in the 1920s, in particular, the Imperial Universities like Tokyo; where non-Marxian mathematical and theoretical economists such as Yasui and Kimura were very exceptional and isolated. There was a dichotomy between the dominant Marxism and the minority of mathematical general equilibrium theorists.

Takashima investigated methodologically to *aufheben* (sublate) economic statics; criticizing Liefmann's 'circulation theory without value theory', or price theory without value theory based on production process; in a sense Takashima criticized Liefmann's catalactics; Takashima pursued the integration of circulation theory into production theory, he thought that the production process was a primary regulator of circulation process. He thought all the fallacies of the Austrian and mathematical catallactics lied in that they could not understand the real meaning of production process and it was there that social economy as life should start. Takashima studied Edgar Salin and Friedrich List from 'List renaissance' in the 1920s, then found in Werner Sombart a theme to absorb the orthodox school into the Historical School. Takashima worked over and shaped his ideas of economic sociology from re-examining the Historical School. He said that once Menger had criticized Schmoller, now Schmoller criticized Menger. Now that mathematical and theoretical economics came to a deadlock, so people could reconsider the meaning of the Historical School in historical perspective (see Nishizawa, 2000).

5. Epilogue

Later in the post-war period, Nakayama started his activities with deep involvement in the issues of labour-management relations through the

Central Labour Commission. While working for Hitotsubashi as professor (up to 1961) and president (1949–1955), he was closely involved in industrial relations and industrial disputes from the stormy post-war times through the age of stability, making contributions to stabilizing labour-management relations, and in so doing promoting industrial development in general. It is stated:

> [Nakayama,] over a period of fifteen years following the war, [at the Central Labour Commission], provided a leadership unsurpassed in the area of labour-management relations for our country, and was the man who produced an epoch in industrial relations.
>
> (Central Labour Commission, 1981: 5)

After resigning from the Central Labour Commission, he was named president of the Japan Labour Association (now the Japan Institute of Labour).

In addition to the Central Labour Commission, Nakayama served on the Central Wages Council, preparing a proposal that became the basis for establishing the minimum wages law. He was also named as vice-chairman of the Japan Productivity Centre when it was founded in 1955. In this capacity he co-headed the first productivity mission to the US in the same year. In 1957 he was appointed as chairman of its Standing Committee for Labour-Management Consultation System, a position in which he served until his death. Beginning in the autumn of 1957 Nakayama wrote a series of articles 'Industrial Relations Henceforward' for *Asahi Newspaper* and in 1958 he published *New Managers, New Workers* (1958a) and *The Labour-Management Consultation System* (1958b). In this and other ways he greatly contributed to the propagation and diffusion of the labour-management joint consultancy system.

Further, in the 1 January 1959 edition of *Yomiuri Newspaper*, he published his well-known article 'A Proposal for Wages Doubling: It's not a Dream if Production Increases'. Nakayama says:

> When thinking about the future of Japan's economy, in abstract form the most comprehensive phrase is welfare state. [...] But how can we move toward the ideal of the welfare state just when we are poor? When facing this problem, in concrete form, I want to boldly advocate wages doubling.
>
> (Nakayama, 1972–1973: Vol. 16, 32–34)

Just two months after Nakayama's article, the future Prime Minister Ikeda's article appeared in the *Nihon Keizai Shinbun* (9 March 1959): 'A Proposal for Doubling my Salary'. It is said that Nakayama's article was the intellectual basis of Prime Minister Ikeda's national income doubling policy (see Nishizawa, 2002).

Through his practical career Nakayama wrote numerous further works on industrial relations and human relations such as *Japan's Industrialization and Labour-Management Relations* (1959), and *The Economic Sociology of Labour-Management Relations* (1974). Thus his pure economics evolved to become 'a social and human science in a broad sense' or economic sociology, or even economic sociology in practice, as he stated in his autobiography, *My Way Economics*.

For Nakayama the problem of industrial relations was his life-long subject; he often speaks of it as human relations, he might have thought of the ideas of Marshall on economic, social and human progress and Fukuda's ideas on labour issues, welfare and 'democratic control of industry'. Marshall had warned that the sectional selfishness of the unions or the employers would be the 'Achilles' heel' of Britain's industries, that the labour market would be the 'Achilles' heel' of the efficiently working (functional) market system. Nakayama might have followed this message.

As a reviewer remarked (Nakayama, 1981: 37), for Nakayama the making and establishment of Japan's industrial relations was his mission as an economist, and the quest for their normal position was a quest for a general equilibrium model in the real world which would make it possible for the efficiency and distribution (equity) to coexist. Japan's industrial relations were the canvas on which he should draw a picture, or they were the place to practice his economic theory, or the place to apply his theory in the real world, which generated his economic sociology in practice. Nakayama did not write a systematic work on economic sociology like Schumpeter's *Capitalism, Socialism and Democracy*. Rather the whole of his numerous works on industrial relations brought forth by his activities as a man of practice seems to have composed his economic sociology in practice.

Notes

1. Nakayama's writings referred in this chapter are in Japanese, unless otherwise indicated.
2. For Tokuzo Fukuda, see Nishizawa (2010).
3. Takada had written a paper 'Leon Walras and the Lausanne School' early in 1912 (*Journal of National Political Economy [Kokuminkeizai Zasshi]*, Vol. 13,

Nos. 5–6), which was actually a translation of 'Leon Walras und die hedonistisch-mathematische Schule von Lausanne' (*Archiv für Sozialwissenschaft und Sozialpolitik*, 1911).

4. The first translation of Marshall's *Principles* by Otsuka was published in 1919 without Book V, which was the very core of the pure economics. Fukuda's *Lectures on Economics* (1909), which was based on Marshall's *Principles*, was also only on Book I to Book IV. These seem to reflect the state of economics in Japan at those days, when the Japanese Society of Social Policy was the major society for economists. Economics was not yet pure economics, it was largely rather related to the given social conditions, or to the social and political elements.

References

Brentano, L. and Fukuda, T. (1899) *Labor Economics* [*Rodo Keizairon*], Tokyo: Dobunkan.

Central Labour Commission (ed.) (1981) *Professor Nakayama Ichiro and the Labour Commission* [*Nakayama Ichiro Sensei to Rodo Iinkai*], Tokyo: Chuo Rodoiinkai.

Fukuda, T. (1921) 'From Price Struggles to Welfare Struggles: Especially Labor Struggles as Welfare Struggles' ['Kakaku toso yori kosei toso e'], in T. Fukuda (ed.), *Collected Works on Economics [Keizaigaku zenshu]* Tokyo: Dobunkan, Vol. 5.

Fukuda, T. (1924) *Principles and Recovering Economies and Some Problems* [*Fukko keizai no genri oyobi jakkan mondai*], Tokyo: Dobunkan.

Hodgson, G. (2006) 'Schmoller's Impact on the Anglophone Literature in Economics', *Schmollers Jahrbuch*, 126(2): 163–76.

Hodgson, G. (2008) 'Marshall, Schumpeter and the Shifting Boundaries of Economics and Sociology', in Y. Shionoya and T. Nishizawa (eds) (2008): 93–115.

Marshall, A. (1897) 'The Old Generation of Economists and the New', in A. C. Pigou (1925) (ed.), *Memorials of Alfred Marshall*, London: Macmillan.

Nakayama, I. (1932) 'Relations Between Economics and Statistics for Business Cycle Studies' ['Keiki kenkyu ni okeru keizaigaku to tokeigaku to no kosho'], in Nakayama (1972–1973), Vol. 5.

Nakayama, I. (1933) 'Economic Theory and Economic Sociology' ['Keizai riron to keizai shakaigaku'], in Nakayama (1972–1973), Vol. 1.

Nakayama, I. (1958a) *New Managers, New Workers* [*Atarashii keieisha, Atarashii rodosha*], 2nd edition 1963, Tokyo: Nihon Rodo Kyokai.

Nakayama, I. (1958b) *The Labor-Management Consultation System* [*Roshi kyogisei*], Tokyo: Nihon Seisansei Honbu.

Nakayama, I. (1959) 'A Proposal for Wages Doubling: It's not a Dream if Production Increases' ['Chingin nibai wo teisho'], in Nakayama (1972–1973), Vol. 16.

Nakayama, I. (1972–1973) *Collected Works of Ichiro Nakayama* [*Nakayama Ichiro zenshu*], 18+1 Vols, Tokyo: Kodansha.

Nakayama, I. (1974) *The Economic Sociology of Industrial Relations* [*Roshi kankei no keizai shakaigaku*], Tokyo: Nihon Rodo Kyokai.

Nakayama, I. (1978) 'Welfare Economics and Fukuda Tokuzo' ['Kosei keizaigaku to Fukuda Tokuzo'], in T. Minoguchi and T. Hayasaka (eds), *Modern Economics and Japan* [*Kindai keizaigaku to Nihon*], Tokyo: Nihon Keizai Shinbunsha.

Nakayama, I. (1979) *My Way Economics* [*Waga michi keizaigaku*], Tokyo: Kodansha.

Nakayama, I. (1981) *A Straight Way for Eighty Years: Collected Essays in the Memory of Professor Nakayama Ichiro* [*Ichiro hachijunen: Nakayama Ichiro Sensei Tuiso Kinen Bunshu*], privately published.

Nishizawa, T. (2000) 'Takashima Zenya: A Quest for Economic Sociology' ['Takashima Zenya: Keizaishakaigaku no tankyu'], in M. Watanabe (ed.), *Takashima Zenya: His Academic World* [*Takashima Zenya: Sono gakumontekisekai*], Tokyo: Kobushi-shobo.

Nishizawa, T. (2002) 'Ichiro Nakayama and the Stabilization of Industrial Relations in Postwar Japan', *Hitotsubashi Journal of Economics*, 43(1): 1–18.

Nishizawa, T. (2007) *Economic Thought of Alfred Marshall and the Historical School* [*Marshall to Rekishigakuha no Keizaishiso*], Tokyo: Iwanamishoten.

Nishizawa, T. (2010) 'The Ethico-Historical Approach Abroad: The Case of Fukuda', in R. Backhouse and T. Nishizawa (eds), *No Wealth but Life. Welfare Economics and the Welfare State in Britain,1880–1945*. Cambridge and New York: Cambridge University Press.

Schmoller, G. (1900–1904) *Grundriss der Allgemeinen Volkswirtschaftslehre*, Munich and Leipzig: Duncker & Humblot, Vol. I, 1900, Vol. II, 1904.

Schumpeter, J. (1918) *Die Krise des Steuerstaats*. Graz and Leipzig: Leuschner & Lubensky; reprinted in J. Schumpeter, *Aufsätze zur Soziologie*, edited by E. Schneider and A. Spiethoff, Tübingen: J. C. B. Mohr.

Schumpeter, J. (1918–1919) 'Zur Soziologie der Imperialismen', *Archiv für Sozialwissenschaft und Sozialpolitik*, 46; reprinted in J. Schumpeter, *Aufsätze zur Soziologie*, edited by E. Schneider and A. Spiethoff, Tübingen: J. C. B. Mohr.

Schumpeter, J. (1926) 'Gustav v. Schmoller und die Probleme von heute', *Schmollers Jahrbuch*, 50, reprinted in J. Schumpeter, *Dogmenhistorische und biographische Aufsätze*, 1954, Tübingen: J.C.B. Mohr.

Schumpeter, J. (1928) 'The Instability of Capitalism', *Economic Journal*, 38(151).

Schumpeter, J. (1943) *Capitalism, Socialism and Democracy*, London: George Allen & Unwin.

Schumpeter, J. (1951) *Ten Great Economists from Marx to Keynes*, London: Allen & Unwin.

Schumpeter, J. (1954) *History of Economic Analysis*, New York: Oxford University Press.

Shionoya, Y. (1997) *Schumpeter and the Idea of Social Science: A Metatheoretical Study*, Cambridge: Cambridge University Press.

Shionoya, Y. (ed.) (2001) *The German Historical School. The Historical and Ethical Approach to Economics*, London: Routledge.

Shionoya, Y. and Nishizawa, T. (eds) (2008) *Marshall and Schumpeter on Evolution. Economic Sociology of Capitalist Development*, Cheltenham and Northampton: Edward Elgar.

Takashima, Z. (1927) 'The Significance of Economic Statics and Economic Dynamics in the National Political Economy: A Study on Joseph Schumpeter' ['Keizai-seigaku to Keizai-dougaku no Kokuminkeizaigakuteki-igi: Joseph Schumpeter no Ichikenkyu'], in *Collected Works of Zenya Takashima* [*Takashima Zenya Chosakushu*], Tokyo: Kobushi-shobo, 1998, Vol. I.

Tezuka, J. (1935) 'Mathematical Economics in Japan in the Last Ten Years' ['Suginishi saikin no junen-ni okeru konokuni no surikeizaigaku'], *Shogaku Tokyu* (Otaru Higher Commercial School), 10: 61–100.

Yaui, T. (1979) *Economics and Its Surroundings* [*Keizaigaku to sono shuhen*], Tokyo: Bokutakusha.

Part III

Some Methodological Problems

6
Friedrich von Wieser on Institutions and Social Economics

Richard Arena

1. Introduction

In a former essay dedicated to a part of Wieser's contribution to economics and economic sociology (Arena, 2003), we noted that, within the triumvirate of the founders of the Austrian School, Friedrich von Wieser is certainly not the one who is the most esteemed by modern historians of economic thought. On the one hand, he is frequently considered as a mere and faithful follower of Carl Menger; and his theoretical originality is supposed to be much weaker than that of Böhm-Bawerk. On the other hand, his observations on human races and his inclination in favour of authoritarian political regimes did not contribute to making him very likeable. These circumstances led certainly to an undervaluation of his economic works. Wieser's economic theory, however, offers a very interesting mixture of economic analysis and economic sociology and its insights strongly contributed to the development of the intellectual achievements of the second generation of the Austrian School (see Streissler, 1986: 85, 91–3, 1988: 195). Moreover, if a part of Wieser's work contributed to the formation of what was later called the 'Marginal Revolution' (see for instance Wieser, 1889/1893), another part certainly participated in the process of transition which favoured the emergence of an original Austrian approach. In this contribution we would like to focus mainly on this second part of Wieser's social and economic theory, also because it is too often ignored.

2. Wieser's general perspective

Der natürliche Wert (*Natural Value*) and the *Theorie der gesellschaftlichen Wirtschaft* (*Social Economics*), which are certainly the most famous of

Friedrich von Wieser's works, seem to contain two different fundamental analytical messages.

In the first book (Wieser, 1889/1893), individuals are supposed to live in a 'communist state'. They have analogous natural endowments and abilities, as well as identical consumer preferences and the same marginal utility of income. Individuals are characterized as utility maximizers but, although they do not really differ from their Walrasian cousins, Wieser's 'natural state' is, however, clearly distinct from Walras's pure exchange economy. Exchange, as well as money, is actually absent and a central authority directs national economic activity and, especially, the distribution of wealth among agents. Natural value is determined by marginal utility and is not disturbed by 'human imperfection', 'error, fraude, force, chance', 'order of society', 'private property' or distributional factors (Wieser, 1893: 61–2). Moreover, individual agents do not belong to social classes, they are not constrained by institutions and they cannot exert (or suffer) power effects on (or from) other individuals. In other words, *Der natürliche Wert* offers a theory of 'this most unnatural of all imaginable states of nature, i.e., with perfect competition and equal incomes for all' (Streissler, 1986: 88–9). To put it in another way, in spite of the differences between his approach and the Walraso-paretian approaches, in *Natural Value*, Wieser seems to accept the idea that the explanation of the working of the economic system first requires the construction of a basic model which offers a simplified broad view of the main analytical components of the real world, namely, a theory of income distribution based on imputation and on marginal utilities and productivities. The common point with Walras and Pareto is that this basic model is a *real* and *natural* economy from which money is entirely excluded. Therefore, *Natural Value* seems to belong to the tradition of economics which began with Adam Smith and corresponds to the Keynesian definition of a 'real exchange economy': according to this tradition, money does not matter and the foundations of economic analysis are purely real.

By contrast, the second book (Wieser, 1914/1927) first describes a 'simple economy' which resembles but is not completely analogous to a 'natural state'. In Volume I of *Social Economics* (called 'the theory of the simple economy'), for instance, individuals are again supposed to express identical preferences and incomes. Therefore, according to Wieser, they can easily be replaced by a single economizing individual who, however, cannot be assimilated to a Robinson Crusoe. 'Millions of persons' are replaced by a 'masses unit', which presents holistic features (Wieser, 1927: 9). As Wieser wrote,

> In the theory of the simple economy we shall examine only the effects of economic purposes on economic processes. We shall not consider the conditions that accompany the formation of the socio-economic powers except to remark the condition of fatigue that attends the expenditure of personal energy.
>
> The simple economy [...] is the economy of a single subject. Here one does not find the contrasts that are manifest in the social formation of forces. But we do not have in mind the scant economy of an isolated householder. Rather we envisage an economy that has the breadth of a national economy with all its wealth, technical knowledge and problems of economic calculus. But this broad economy is guided by a simple mind.
>
> (Ibid.: 19)

Quite logically, exchange and money are still absent in those 'simple economies'. However, there is another more radical difference between 'natural states' and 'simple economies'. In *Social Economics*, the theory of a 'simple economy' is not a subject for studies *per se* but only a logical step in the construction of a 'social economy'. To put it differently, 'simple economies' refer to what Wieser calls 'the most abstract isolating and idealizing assumptions' (ibid.: 6). Therefore, they are only introduced to define, by contrast, 'social economies' which appear to correspond to a 'decreasing abstraction to conditions of reality' (ibid.: 9). Now, contrarily to 'natural states', in social economies individuals cease to have analogous natural abilities and identical endowments. They belong to social classes, are constrained by institutions and especially by money and credit, and can exert (or suffer) power effects on (or from) other individuals. Therefore, individual decisions now also depend on social inequalities and constraints. They contribute, however, to institutional changes, even if it is in an unintended way and if these changes affect, in turn, subsequent economic behaviours. Thus, in *Social Economics*, a simple economy no longer plays the role of a real exchange economy as it is defined by Keynes and as it was the case for natural states. It is only a preliminary and pedagogical step towards monetary economies which constitute the very topic of economic analysis: in *Social Economics*, Wieser is certainly more Wicksellian than Walrasian.

This apparent divergence between the messages of Wieser's two main books is the result of the evolution of his own thought. It has, however, the merit of showing, that Wieser's final conception consisted in taking institutions and money seriously into account and giving up the idea that the model of a 'real economy' was able to capture the main features of the economic system. If our interpretation is right, Wieser's theories of money and institutions thus appear to be crucial. Indeed, few historians of economic thought paid attention to them and this is certainly a pity. Before entering into more detail, it is necessary to raise the issue of Wieser's view of the connection between individuals and society.

3. Wieser on individualism

Wieser's position on methodological individualism is carefully described in the following passage of *Social Economics*:

> What valid substitute may we offer for the individualistic theory of society? In its naïve formulation it has became inadequate. But one cannot get away from its fundamental concept, that the individual is the subject of social intercourse. The individuals who comprise the society are the sole possessors of all consciousness and of all will. The 'organic' explanation, which seeks to make society as such, without reference to individuals, the subject of social activity, has patently proved a failure. One must hold himself aloof from the excesses of the individualistic exposition, but the explanation must still run in terms of the individual. It is in the individual that one must look for those tendencies that make the social structure that dove-tail (if we may use that expression) in such a manner as to give the firm cohesion of social unity and at the same time provide the foundation for the erection of social power.
>
> (Ibid.: 154)

It is clear that Wieser expresses strong doubts on what he calls 'naïve' individualism. Classical economists were not in fact 'naïve' individualists but, in a way, they opened a road in this direction. Of course, they did not explain *all* economic phenomena by *mere* individual behaviours and found them on a *limitless* self-interest. Wieser noticed that

> when they dealt with freedom of action, they conceived of personal egoism as controlled by law and modality. Moreover, they clearly recognized that certain dangers inhered in personal egoism and that certain precautions must be taken against them.
>
> (Ibid.: 153)

But Wieser considered that classical economists only took into account a part of the individual determinants of economic behaviours, namely the 'forces of freedom' ('*Freiheitsmächte*').[1] They ignored the 'forces of compulsion' related to the existence of power in economics and this omission led them to cope with individuals as if they were perfectly autonomous, free and equal. Wieser interprets this view of individuals as a logical prerequisite for the construction of a theory of pure exchange based on individual equality and price equivalence, which he attributes to the classical approach. He disagreed, however, with such a theory.

On the one hand, he denied that exchange relations were independent from the existence of what he called 'social power':

> As in all other activity, so in the negotiation of economic contracts, the average man is governed by the social power of the associative principle. In his individual dealings he uses the type of contract that has been generally developed. As a rule he adds nothing more to this form than a specification of the particular persons and values involved [...]. If one looks more closely, one finds that as a rule even in the selection of persons and the specification of consideration he is governed by class and social powers; and his legal freedom of contract as a matter of fact shrinks into an extremely limited freedom of choice. If one points to private contract as the unifying medium of the national economy, and if one seeks to faithfully reproduce actual conditions, one must add that the private contracts are themselves governed by class and social powers.
>
> (Ibid.: 162)

On the other hand, Wieser considered that individuals were generally unequal and that 'compulsion' reduced their degree of freedom and autonomy. This is why he attributed to classical economists the 'error' of having given 'too much room for the play of personal freedom' (ibid.: 53). A different conception of individuals and individualism had therefore to be introduced and to consider both types of social forces which we already mentioned: natural controls [forces of freedom] and compulsion. Forces of freedom correspond to self-will and self-interest. It is only when individual motives strictly coincide with pure 'forces of freedom' that we can consider agents as Classical economists looked at them. Therefore, freedom does not consist in total lack of control. It rather consists in a relation of the individual to society. Compulsion, on the other hand, is recognized as a restriction on the individual life.

It takes various forms from 'the armed force which has subdued the vanquished to the will of the victor' to the more subtle but ordinary notion of social influence.

Such a distinction between 'natural controls' and 'compulsion' deserves some comments. It is first clear that Wieser does not see those two concepts as the poles of a strict opposition:

> Between the natural controls and compulsion – between the latter and domination – there are imperceptible gradations, extraordinarily difficult to distinguish, whether subjectively by those who are controlled or objectively by those who observe from without. There may be cases where a power is still regarded by its victim as a natural control, although it already operates by compulsion, in that it restricts the development of its life.
>
> (Ibid.: 155)

This embeddedness of free choice within a compulsory system does not forbid, however, the distinction between both types of forces. In other words, even if it is not always easy to make this distinction *in practice*, there is no doubt that it *must* be done *analytically*.

This is why Wieser did not deny that individuals were searching for their self-interest, in *Natural Value* as well as in the *Theory of the Simple Economy* (Book I of *Social Economics*). However, in the context of social economies, Wieser's conception of individualism allows him to define a conception of the individual which differs from the one that he attributes to the Classical approach. Wieser's individual is no longer an atom; he is now a social individual:

> In his economic conduct also the individual is determined by social forces. Law and morals, of which the classicists made mention, are not the only forces. A man is also influenced in all those relations where law and morals leave him free. He is a creature of his period and his environment – of his nation, his class and his profession [...].
>
> Also the impulses to activity are not purely personal. For the average man they are entirely dependent upon the practice of his time and environment for their direction and their strength.
>
> (Ibid.: 159)

It is therefore necessary to take into account the national differences which are essentially related to the diversity of cultures; the 'horizontal division of economic society' (that is, the distinction between producers belonging to different activities, namely 'professions', to use Wieser's own words) (ibid.: 158) as well as the 'vertical' one (that is, the distinction between 'classes' or leaders and masses) (ibid.). National, vertical and horizontal stratifications form what Wieser calls the 'social order' (ibid.: 161).

4. Wieser on power and institutions

Social economies do not only include social stratifications but also social power related to the forces of 'compulsion'. Wieser quoted Spinoza to define power 'as command over the human mind' (1926: 3), social power meaning 'command over the minds of the members of society' (ibid.). In *Das Gesetz der Macht*, he referred to two types of social power. 'External power' is the power that some persons or some groups exert on people with the help of 'external' means such as 'numerical superiority, arms or wealth' (ibid.: 2). 'Internal power is viewed as impersonal and anonymous' (ibid.: 3). It corresponds to ideas, feelings or beliefs 'to which one ascribes power' (ibid.: 3). The processes which permit internal power to exert its influence are various.

The first of them is *mimetism*. On the one hand, economic agents belonging to a specific nation, class or profession try to behave according to the average behaviour they attribute to the stratification to which they belong. Now, this average behaviour may be often analogous to the pursuit of self-interest:

> The goals of the economy are derived from the needs; its powers come from the impulses and will. Therefore, the direction and standard of economic endeavour cannot be determined entirely personally. The injection to achieve the highest utility with the lower cost is interpreted by everyone in the light of his social environment. The spirit of his times led him. For the mass of average men the economic principle that they follow is simply to 'be as economical as your associates': i.e., fulfil the law of lowest costs and highest utility as far as is customary in the circle to which you belong and in which you would maintain yourself [...].
>
> Economic leaders raise themselves above the mass of their associates but they themselves cannot get away entirely from the social concept of the economic principle.
>
> (Wieser, 1927: 160)

As Samuels pointed out, Wieser's concept of 'success' plays a crucial role in the choice of mimetic behaviours. Success is not defined in an abstract way as the achievement of the fittest economic state. It can be actual or perceived. Success

> constitutes the mechanism, as it were, of historical selection. The course of history is marked by a path of success *vis-à-vis* other paths which might have been. Success in this context signifies survival. [...] Success, in Wieser's analysis, has no independent positive or normative, ex ante, test. It is circumstantial, episodic, and without external or internal value basis independent of the fact of survival. It is the sequence of successes, however, which mark the course of history.
>
> (Samuels, 1983: XXXI)

Even if Hayek's positive feedback of mimetic attitudes differs from Wieser's success, there is, however, something common in both concepts: agents imitate their neighbours *ex ante* and the revision of their beliefs depends on the issue generated by the social interaction of the innovative and the mimetic attitudes. Wieser's view of this interaction is clearly non-deterministic: in accordance with the Austrian tradition, economic states appear to be the unintended consequences of decentralized voluntary actions.

On the other hand, economic agents are very sensitive to the social image they create among the economic community. From this angle, individual behaviours *cannot be* defined independently of each other since the definition of any of them depends theoretically on the definition of all of them. This is the reason why individual behaviours are also necessarily social. Without mentioning them, Wieser actually revives Smith (and his concept of 'self-love') and Say (and his concept of 'vanité'):

> [The] Ego [of the socially educated individual] is not satisfied unless it finds itself in all important respects at one with society. If one is truly socially educated, his Ego departs from him and finds its end in society; it ceases to be purely personal and becomes social egoism; it wishes to conform in all respects to law and custom and in general to the social forces of the economy; it demands only so much for itself as social precept indicates that it may and should demand. This statement holds true not only of those cases in which a man clearly feels himself bound to social conscience but also where he believes himself

> to be entirely independent. In most matters, a man accepts the social code of the industrial or social group of which he is a member; it is only in certain major relationships, that are uniform for the whole of society, that a universally accepted rule obtains. By reason of the social egoism a man is ready to fit into a social order which includes both submission and domination. The feeling of fellowship makes easier the submission of the masses to the historically maintained power or domination of a class of leader – one submits more readily when others are seen also to submit. In a class of servitors, content with its lot, there arises a class-spirit which regards submission as a point of honor and creates the good will of the faithful servant.
>
> (1927: 161)

This quotation also shows the importance of 'historical education' in Wieser (see again Samuels, 1983: XXII): education contributes to the creation of the social interactions which support social internal power.

This conception of economic individuals obviously differs from the atomistic vision of the first generation of the marginalists. This is the reason why Wieser criticized them as he criticized the Classical School, although he made a systematic use of marginal tools. Wieser's critique does not provide, however, a support of methodological holism. As we have stressed, considering Wieser's individualism, there is no superhuman will, mind or subject in his contributions:

> One must firmly emphasize that the habitat of the mind is in the individuals and remains there even in conjunction with all collective relationships. In truth there is no popular mind and no popular will.
>
> (Wieser, 1926: 56)

This means that, like most of the Austrian economists (see Arena and Festré, 2002), Wieser did not accept the assumption of collective beliefs as such, namely of beliefs which might be generated by social groups. According to Wieser, social beliefs (as distinct from collective ones) are only generated by individuals and could therefore be defined as shared individual beliefs (1927: 4). These beliefs are often the results of the influence of internal power. They reflect the variety of individual agents. Therefore, they exclude the assumption of 'a single mind', leaving it for the context of simple economies (ibid.: 19). Often too, social beliefs are the beliefs of the 'powerful persons' (ibid.: XVII), especially when these persons are able to convince ordinary agents that their own interests coincide with the interests of the former.

We mentioned earlier Wieser's quotations using the concepts of 'leaders and masses'. It is now time to define these concepts since they play a fundamental role within Wieser's conception of social power. 'Leaders' and 'masses' emerge within 'social economies' since 'simple economies' only relate equal individuals. From this viewpoint, the distinction is not provisional or casual. It presupposes a national community in which agents are fundamentally unequal (ibid.: 157).

'Social economies' are more complex than 'simple ones' since, within them, 'individual units meet from all directions' and 'clash with great forces' (ibid.: 153). This complexity, according to Wieser, implies a necessity of coordination which is solved by social power. Thanks to it,

> the individual search of whom independently follows his own law, are held to a common purpose and enabled to work to a single end.
>
> (Ibid.: 152)

Wieser indeed considers that 'masses' are unable to generate a spontaneous coordination and, therefore, they have to be directed and controlled by 'leaders':

> Even in those cases of social intercourse where a legal right of self-determination is preserved to the individual and in which leadership plays no part, leadership and the accompanying power of leadership do develop. Even in their personal affairs, the mass of individuals are too weak to rely upon themselves alone. [...] Everything that man has accomplished whether in spiritual or physical evolution, has been attained only through social relations, in that the best leadership has furnished the example, the advice and the knowledge; and that others were induced to follow them because of the success which these leaders have attained.
>
> (Ibid.: 156)

This very general definition implies various types of social leadership (Ibid.: 38). According to Wieser's conception of the social economy, leaders are autonomous and their energy permits them to behave according to their individual aims. However, masses are not passive. They may accept or reject what leaders decided and their decisions and reactions are essential. If masses agree with the actions and innovations of the leaders, they are led to copy them. Therefore,

> [t]hrough the initiative of leaders and through initiative acceptance by the masses, society develops certain institutions serving the common needs so well as to seem like the creation of an organized social will. Money, markets, division of labour, the social economy itself are such creation.
>
> (Mitchell, 1927: 104)

Wieser introduces two different behaviours. One is *innovative*: it corresponds to leaders decisions. The other one is *imitative*: it refers to the attitude of masses. This distinction is obviously close to the one pointed out by Schumpeter in the first German edition of his *Theory of Economic Development*, when he contrasted what he called 'energetic' and 'hedonistic' economic behaviours. The mechanisms of innovation in the subsequent editions of the book are also an echo of this opposition, since new products of new techniques are introduced and diffused within the economy through a combination of innovative and initiative behavioural patterns. These observations are not really surprising since we know how much Wieser influenced Schumpeter's ideas (Kauder, 1957: 422; Streissler, 1986: 92).

The intervention of masses cannot be interpreted, however, as a pure act of recognition of the social utility of leaders' decisions. It generally transforms an individual invention into a real social device. Therefore, masses tend to create a final rule 'far beyond [leaders'] expectations' (Wieser, 1927:165). This is the meaning Wieser attributes to Menger's idea according to which economic institutions are the 'unintended social results of individual teleological tendencies' (ibid.).

Two cases may be faced according to the interests privileged by leaders. Wieser indeed observes that

> powerful persons are merely in a position, in building up the economic organization, to carry through their personal interests rather than the general interest. Thus they are able, at those points which they regard as critical, to replace the social mind by their own. By these means the social consciousness is falsified and made to appear contradictory.
>
> (Ibid.: XVII)

In this case, Wieser observes that the intervention of the State (XVII) or of the masses is necessary. If this intervention does not occur and if, on the contrary, masses approve their actual leaders some general interest is therefore defended by the latter. Social classes, for instance, derive from a systematic and permanent leadership. They are acceptable if they do not 'lead to the oppression of the masses' (ibid.: 157).

5. From simple to social economies

Among the institutions which are associated with social economies and contribute to reducing the relative weight of the 'forces of freedom', *money* plays a special role since it contributes to changing the nature of social interaction among individual agents:

> The enormous advantage offered by money in the community of exchange is explained solely from the fact that it dissolves the entire turnover into links of such individual transactions of one exchanging couple each. The effect of it is that men, in their acquisitions, are never tied down to the one contracting party with whom they have just dealt. They altogether turn to any other man who may have the stock required.
>
> (Ibid.: 169)

But money is not present in all economies. We already noted that its emergence is related to the process of transition from simple to social economies described in Volume II of *Social Economics* ('The Theory of the Social Economy'). Noticeable for us, exchange *and* money finally appear in this volume:

> The second section, the theory of exchange, presupposes a social economy, unhampered by interferences on the part of the state. The theory of the simple economy having shown in what manner a single subject manages and calculates his economic affairs, we now show the numerous juridical subjects, who meet in the course of exchange, as they seek their economic advantage, determine prices and thus erect the structure of a social economy.
>
> (Ibid.: 10)

Wieser assigned to social as well as to simple economies the same fundamental objective, which is strictly analogous to the one that the Classical School defined for the first time in the history of economic thought. This objective is economic self-reproduction and it reflects what Wieser calls 'the law of the unity of the economy' (ibid.: 68). In compliance with the classical tradition, simple and social economies must ensure, with or without any exchange process, that a net product is created:

> An economy aspiring to enduring service must distinguish between gross-yields and net-yields. It must lay aside: sufficient reserves to entirely renew its capital, treating only the residue as net-yield [...]. Net-yield may be defined as the residue left after deducting reversal-costs from the gross-yield.
>
> (Ibid.: 131)

This stress on self-reproduction is increased by the transition process from simple to social economies and explains the first 'typical' feature which permits distinction between both types of economy. Streissler indeed emphasized the importance given by Wieser to production within social economies:

> It is also correct that [Wieser] also had a strong inclination for the production side of the economic process. And that made him the only truly neo-classical author in the first two generations of the Austrian School and together with Fritz Machlup one of only two neo-classical authors in the school altogether. He thereby also provided a link with Anglo-American economic thought, particularly with Alfred Marshall, with whom he had the strongest affinity and who also appreciated him most. His strong 'neo-classical' bent of thought (in the narrower sense) can best be seen in the disposition of his material in *The Theory of Social Economics*. It reflects John Stuart Mill's *Principles*: the analysis of the factors of production is placed nearly at the beginning; distribution, on the other hand, is treated, as in Mill, much later, in the case of Wieser nearly at the end. The classical vein runs very strong in Wieser: in his habilitation thesis he gives Ricardo, Marx, Engels, Jevons and Menger as his authorities; and in the textbook of his maturity Ricardo out-distances Menger in text references by 25 to 18 and Marx is the author most frequently quoted in footnotes, four times among only twelve footnotes in all.
>
> (1986: 96)

More precisely, Wieser dedicates an entire paragraph of his *Social Economics* (Book I, § 10) to what he calls the 'unity of the economy'. Among the three determinants of this unity – money, market, production – the first two only unify the economy 'externally' (ibid.: 49) but the fundamental 'internal' link which allows one to define the economy 'as a whole' is production:

> However, despite its extreme differentiation and manifold contrasts, the economic process of today is actually a whole. It is not a unit in the truer sense of the term; and yet it functions with an all-embracing homogeneity which may be idealized and represented as unity. This condition is founded in production. All productive stems are related to one another.
>
> (Wieser, 1927: 50)

More fundamentally, production is, in turn, based on the existence of a process of division of labour which exhibits two dimensions. The first, horizontal, was already emphasized by the Classical School, according to Smithian lines. The second one, vertical, refers to the division of social classes. Wieser considers its importance is not inferior to the one related to horizontal division of labour (ibid.: 310). Now, money did not generate division of labour but is only its 'concomitant' (ibid.: 170). This is probably the reason why it only unifies the economy 'externally'.

The existence of a vertical division of labour provides one of the main foundations of what Wieser calls *social stratification*, namely the second typical feature of social economics. As we already noticed, stratification implies both the division *between* and the division *within* social classes. These divisions exert various and substantial effects on the economic activity. They do not only concern production but also exchange. For instance, in a social economy, prices are also stratified, reflecting the evolution of the different types of goods in relation with the social groups which consume them. Thus, the existence of three classes implies that the group of 'mass-commodities' has to be evaluated by the marginal utility of the poor: the set of 'intermediate goods', by the preferences of the middle classes and the group of 'luxury goods', by the valuations of rich people (ibid.: 157–8). Social stratification also appears through the social role played by entrepreneurs:

> The legally independent acquisite enterprises are instruments of a great social productive and acquisitive process following a division of labour.
>
> (Ibid.: 151)

This process allows entrepreneurs to act frequently as 'leaders', not only because 'commodities, as things, are controlled by the owners' (ibid.: 42) but also because

> the institution of enterprise is the organ of the modern economic stratification [. . .]. In its simple forms, it invests the entrepreneur merely with personal superiority; later, when large enterprises develop, it gives him a degree of power that finally swells to capitalist supremacy [. . .]
>
> He is not merely the legal head; he is also at all times the economic leader. His legal power of disposition reaches its full significance in securing him complete freedom of economic management. His economic leadership commences with the establishment of the enterprise; he supplies not only the necessary capital but originates the idea, elaborates and puts into operation the plan, and engages collaborators.
>
> (Ibid.: 324)

Firms are not the only institutions in social economies. We have already noticed how they were generated by the interaction between leaders and masses. We have also to recall that this interaction is only understandable in a permanent process. Leaders create social devices which correspond to their needs and aims. Masses imitate leaders and, therefore, transform those devices into social rules or institutions. These institutional patterns then become constraints for further individual behaviour. The aggregate results of the various agent decisions change, in turn, and contribute to institutional change and so on. This approach, therefore, introduces a process of institutional change able to imply feedback effects on the economic sphere. This kind of process occurs in historical time and, therefore, it has to be considered step by step. From this standpoint, institutional impulses

> are entirely dependent [for the average man] upon the practice of his time and environment for their direction and their strength.
>
> (Ibid.: 159)

The emergence of new leaders can, however, change institutions, if they are allowed by masses.

One of the main institutions of a social economy is *market* or, to be more precise, *markets*, since Wieser refers to 'institutions of exchange' (ibid.: 150). Wieser's view of exchange substantially differs from that of Walras. Indeed, Wieser does not consider that the scheme of pure bilateral exchange offers a kind of universal foundation for any economic system. Quite the contrary, he stresses that the mutual wills of individual economic agents do not provide the only determinant factors of exchange:

> The exchange contract [...], although it is made as a rule only between two parties, has manifested itself the coordinating instrument that binds the individual economies into the rational economy [...] our main task is to describe the institutions of exchange and erection of the national economic body that is brought about by these.
>
> (Ibid.: 150)

In this context,

> the market is a social institution, where the freedom of exchange operates as a freedom of choice.
>
> (Ibid.: 172)

The existence of markets is implied by the coexistence of private property and (both horizontal and vertical) division of labour. Production is indeed implemented by 'legally independent' individual 'producers', helped by 'workers' (ibid.: 150). Now,

> in a fully developed money economy, in which individual self-sufficiency disappears, all households must finally turn to the market for a satisfaction of their needs.
>
> (Ibid.: 150)

In other terms, *markets are fundamentally monetary*. They form what Wieser called 'the great circulation of the national economy' (ibid.: 151).

On one hand, households demand consumption goods to firms and they are then 'faced with the necessity of securing a monetary income' (ibid.: 150). This income is a money wage paid by producers. Money holding is, therefore, a prerequisite of demand for wage-earners. They are submitted to a kind of Clowerian liquidity constraint. They cannot buy goods directly through barter with their labour.

On the other hand, for firms, money holding is a prerequisite of production. Firms must hold the amount of money due to wage-earners and, therefore, they also demand liquid resources. Contrary to a simple economy, they are now structurally parted from households.

Again, Wieser's conception of market is entirely different from Walras's one. While Walras starts from a basic scheme of market economy based on barter between two commodities and then generalizes it progressively to general pure exchange, production, capitalization and, in the end, money and credit, Wieser considers that there is no market without money. To use Hicks's modern words, his theory of markets is a monetary theory of markets, since, for Wieser, markets are logically inconceivable if money as an institution is not presupposed. But Walras's and Wieser's conceptions of market do not only differ according to the part they attribute to money within the exchange process. Walras stresses the universal character of pure exchange economies as a general logical device on which it is necessary to build the whole edifice of general economic equilibrium. On the contrary, Wieser does not emphasize the homogeneity of concrete markets but their heterogeneity. This attitude is not surprising. Wieser first considers markets as an institution:

> The market is a social institution, where the freedom of exchange operates as a freedom of choice.
>
> (Ibid.: 172)

Considering markets as an institution, Wieser notices that it is necessary to distinguish various 'institutions of exchange' and he dedicates the whole Part II of Book II of his *Social Economics* to their study.

Markets must therefore be distinguished according to their specific institutional set-up or, to use Wieser's (but also Marshall's) own words, to their proper 'organizations of markets'. Market organization is indeed central in Wieser's approach, as it was in Menger's. The formation of prices does not follow the same rules, according to the fact that the market is organized or 'disorganized' (ibid.: 195).

Markets might be characterized, however, by a common feature but also by their diversity.

The common feature of markets is the predominant part played by producers and supply within the working of exchanges. On one hand, the freedom of exchange is indeed counterbalanced, at least partially, by the forces of compulsion. Wieser observes that, often, in the process of exchange, agents do not have their 'full economic strength' (ibid.: 168) and therefore, as in the contracts of 'labour' or 'usurious loan', an asymmetry exists among the parties. Producers may, therefore, profit from compulsion and they are also able to impose their 'supply prices' (ibid.: 175) as a prerequisite imposed by producers to consumers (ibid.: 175).

Markets, however, are not identical. They are all different:

> Theoretically, we have to distinguish in the universal economic market as many varieties of partial markets as there are varieties of market-indices.
>
> (ibid.: 175)

This stress on the diversity of markets was not introduced by Wieser, but by Menger, within the Austrian tradition (Arena, 1999).

As we pointed out earlier, it first refers to what Wieser calls 'the stratification of prices' (Wieser, 1927: 186). In other words, markets are not all accessible by any type of agents. Thus, the quantities of 'mass-commodities' brought to markets depend on the volume of consumption needs of all social strata which are expected to consume these goods. Therefore, in mass-commodities markets, prices are determined by the poorest agents and only by their marginal utilities. On the contrary for luxury goods markets, 'prices are offered according to a standard induced by the purchasers' ability of members of the higher and highest income-strata who are bent on excluding the competition of all other rivals' (ibid.: 187). Finally in intermediate goods markets, prices are determined according to the purchasing power of the middle classes. Therefore, markets are *socially stratified* according to the diversity of consumer purchasing powers.

Markets are also differentiated according to their organization. Here the Mengerian influence is direct. Several causes might be related to the: degree of speculation (ibid.: 173), type of competition (ibid.: 173–4), distance to the final consumer (ibid.: 176), mechanisms of bids (ibid.: 174–6) or quality of organization (ibid.: 195). These causes permit one to distinguish a set of main markets. The labour market is the first described by Wieser, who notices that 'labour is not a product' (ibid.: 176). Market products are differentiated according to their modes of exchange: natural barter (ibid.: 174) or monetary exchange (ibid.: 175). Money markets include the loan and the stock markets; they do not allow product exchanges; they permit to satisfy investment needs (ibid.: 176). Finally, the price variations on the 'market of agricultural or urban real estate' often follow the price variations of the money market (ibid.: 176).

Last, but not least, then comes *money* as a distinct feature of social economics. If we combine it with production, we obtain the two most distinctive typical features of a modern economy. That is why we may credit Wieser, without any hesitation, with having built a theory of monetary production economies within the Austrian tradition. It is now time to focus on money as such.

6. Wieser on money and credit

As already stressed, Wieser clearly considers money as one of the founding institutions of social economy:

> For complicated social institutions the historical explanation requires further refinement. We shall show this by the classic illustration of money, whose unknown origin has provoked almost as much interest among men as the origin of the state or of speech. But we must also show that the more subtle explanation at which one finally arrives, necessarily involves a reduction of individualistic stress.
>
> The long series of writers who sought to explain money as an individualistic institution ends with Menger's penetrating investigation. He uses the phenomenon of money as a paradigm by which he assumes to show that all social institutions of the economy are nothing more than 'unintended social results of individual-teleological factors'. (Untersuchungen, Menger 1883: 171–87)
>
> (Wieser, 1927: 163)

The reference to Menger is obviously essential. For our purpose, it is not however necessary to remind ourselves here of Menger's conception at length. We shall confine ourselves to two substantial quotations taken respectively from Menger's *Principles of Economics* and *Problems of Economics and Sociology*:

> Money is not the product of an agreement on the part of economizing men nor the product of legislative acts. No one invented it. As economizing individuals in social situations became increasingly aware of their economic interest, they everywhere attained the simple knowledge that surrendering less saleable commodities for others of greater saleability brings them substantially closer to the attainment of their specific economic purposes. Thus, with the progressive development of social economy, money came to exist in numerous

> centres of civilization independently. But precisely because money is a natural product of human economy, the specific forms in which it has appeared were everywhere and at all times the result of specific and changing economic situations. Among the same people at different times, and among different people at the same time, different goods have attained the special position in trade described above.
>
> (Menger, 1871: 262–3)

> It is clear [...] that the origin of money can truly be brought to our full understanding only by our learning to understand the *social* institution discussed here as the unintended result, as the unplanned outcome of specifically *individual* efforts of members of a society.
>
> (Menger, 1883: 155)

These two quotations provide a significant outlook on Menger's theory of money. Wieser accepted it only partially. He indeed considered that money is something more than this 'intended result' (ibid.: 165). To put it briefly, for Wieser, Menger's story is substantially correct if we interpret 'individual efforts' as the efforts of the 'leaders'. In other words, Wieser implanted his theory of the interaction between leaders and masses within Menger's approach. According to him, within the market process, the members of the society who were in charge of the organization of exchanges very quickly realized the importance of the drawbacks implied by a barter economy. These drawbacks, which are familiar to economists, convinced 'leaders' to introduce a simpler system which would have avoided the necessity of multiplying indirect and costly exchanges. Through a process of learning, little by little, they created several means of substitution according to their historical and cultural environment. Therefore, those leaders who only had in mind their own interests, indeed contributed to create a true unintended new monetary system. But, in Wieser's conception, these means only formed a system when masses approved them by imitating leaders, in other words, when everyone, in the least exchange processes, used the means introduced by the main participants to the market.

> The function of the masses consists in the case of money as in all other social activity in that their imitation establishes the universal practice which gives to a rule its binding force and social power.
>
> (1927: 104)

Money is therefore an institution which is not understandable only by means of an individualistic approach. Wieser, however, did not only pay attention to the problem of the origin of money. He also faced the main questions of monetary theory. We shall not consider here those related to the value of money. Wieser's only innovation is related to the link he sets up between the value and the utility of money, in contradiction with the usual original quantity theory of money. We shall not consider either the problem of a monetary system based on a metallic commodity. We shall rather stress the different forms of money distinguished by Wieser which correspond, in modern terms, to the various types of liquid assets. The first one is 'money-capital'. Money-capital

> includes not only cash reserves but also those much large sums which are held in other liquid form, especially those already invested at interest during the process of accumulation, provided that they may be cashed or transferred on short notice.
>
> (Ibid.: 293)

Therefore, it is easy to understand why 'the formation of money-capital is accomplished by saving or by laying aside money' (ibid.: 300). 'Money-capital' indeed corresponds to 'saving deposits' in Keynes's *Treatise* (Keynes, 1930), namely, to firms' monetary saving. Money-capital has to be distinguished from loan-capital:

> All capital lent, that is not money-capital is loan capital, from short-term business credits to long-term or perpetual mortgage loans and annuities which are usually spoken of as capital investments.
>
> (Ibid.: 294)

Loan capital corresponds to the bank or money deposits firms obtain by the means of short-term or long-term credit. It is therefore analogous to Keynes's 'finance' and 'business deposits'. 'Entrepreneur's capital' is, then, the sum of 'liquid cash items which are to cover payments of wages and other current operating expenses, that part outstanding as loan capital and also the remainder which has been transformed into natural capital and further the enterprise as such' (ibid.: 294). 'It means the entire capital which has been invested and is actively used in the enterprise' (ibid.). It corresponds to the classical volume of 'advances'.

Finally, 'the ready money of the household' 'is to be used directly to cover domestic needs' (ibid.: 293). It therefore corresponds to income deposits in Keynes's *Treatise*. When consumers form saving deposits, the usual language avoids to call them money-capital but land or housing acquisitions by households have to be included within national saving (ibid.: 295, 300).

What is striking here is obviously the analogy between Wieser's and Keynes's classifications. It reveals a connection related to the will of describing the same reality which is a monetary production economy. This parallel goes on with the introduction of credit:

> The establishment of the credit system did not introduce a fundamentally new set of conditions; it is not even desirable to speak of a special credit economy. What men refer to as the credit economy is merely an extension of the money economy; it might be called the credit-and-money economy.
>
> (Ibid.: 261)

A 'credit-and-money economy' is therefore nothing other than the modern form of an exchange economy. In other words, credit and money institutions correspond to the contemporary stage of the process of emergence of money market economies:

> the development is within the money economy; credit transactions are an institution of exchange.
>
> (Ibid.: 238)

The introduction of credit within money market economies facilitates the activities of production and this is the reason why 'leaders' created it and 'masses' accepted it. It strongly increases the performances of the economy:

> By means of loans and credits in their various forms individuals other than those owning property are given control of the property. In particular the group of entrepreneurs is renewed. By means of payment by credit the form of money is expanded; developing natural values offer a commercial security and themselves furnish the means of payment which facilitate their sale. Thus the avenues of production are enlarged. These are great results but they rest on a monetary economy within which they function.
>
> (Ibid.: 261)

Credit, therefore, appears to be both the modern form of exchange and facilitator of production. However, these two roles are not so distinct;

they merge into the assertion that, in a credit-and-money economy, credit supplies entrepreneurs with the liquidity they need to organize production. Anticipating Keynes's finance motive, Wieser shows that bank money or credit provides the very condition of production within a money market economy. In this prospect, Wieser indeed remarks that, thanks to credit, the entrepreneur (and not the capitalist!)

> is enabled for the entire period to continue an economic process which, in the absence of the loan, he could not have begun or continued.
>
> (Ibid.: 240)

Credit takes a variety of forms in real life. We shall not enter, however, here into the description of the different concrete types of credit by Wieser since it only presents a historical interest. We shall rather consider the economic principles according to which the credit system is organized.

The foundation of this organization is Fullarton's principle, which assumes the strict necessity of the periodical reflux of credit creation:

> Notes which are paid out in discounting loans are subject to a law which has been called after its discoverer, 'Fullarton's law'. When the credit granted by the bank expires the bank either receives its note or, if repayment is made in cash, an amount of cash which covers the note remaining in circulation. The notes which the bank issues in discounting commercial paper are no longer lived than the draft of acceptance itself. [...] They come into existence when the draft is discounted; they die when the draft is honoured.
>
> (Ibid.: 245)

In compliance with the Banking School approach, the adoption of Fullarton's principle obviously implies a distinction between credit defined as a temporary means of payment and money defined as a definitive one. Wieser states:

> Finally commercial paper is a means of only provisional payment. Notes [of the Central Bank – R.A.] are a means of final and conclusive payment just as is money.
>
> (Ibid.: 245–6)

It is then natural that Wieser conceives bank money supply as endogenous:

> The amount of the unsecured balances, to the extent of which money does double work, fluctuates as elastically with the monetary requirements of trade as does the amount of unsecured notes. In periods with large financial requirements, the bank will increase its loans. As the requirements drop off, there takes place a return flow of bank funds which is quite analogous to that described by the law of the return of bank notes.
>
> (Ibid.: 248–9)

Within the theoretical framework that we have just described, the fulfilment of Fullarton's principle and the respect of the rule of endogeneity of bank money imply a strict equality between the money values of supply and demand. This equality ensures, in its turn, that the values which finally prevail on the market, as well as in the production sphere, are *natural*:

> It is his personal loss, when one of the contracting parties errs and surrenders a greater value in the one form than he receives in the other. The equation of values in the total, however, is not affected by this error, for what he overpaid becomes the gain of the other party to the contract.
>
> (Ibid.: 256)

7. Money and circulations

As one of the economists at the beginning of the twentieth century interested in the field of monetary theory, Wieser describes the national economy as a 'community of payment'. This community, which derives from the existence of money and credit, involves two different types of circulation.

The first circulation might be called the income circulation. It is described by Wieser as 'the exchange of natural values for money' (ibid.: 250). It is the circulation which, according to the prevailing form of the division of labour, allows households and firms to buy the different consumers and capital goods with the incomes they earned in the process of production and exchange. Wieser describes this circulation as a means for society to attribute social utility to produced goods. There is certainly here a possible parallel with Marx. Marx characterized exchange as the process of transformation of concrete labours into parts of the social abstract labour. Therefore, exchange was a means of confirming the social utility of goods which were produced earlier in a purely private sphere. Now, Wieser writes:

> In disposing of his products for money, the producer effects a transition from the narrow field of his particular process – a limitation imposed by the division of labour – to the entire wealth of values in the market. He surrenders the natural form of a specially conditioned product for which the market possesses only a limited capacity of acceptance. In return he receives money, the general medium of exchange, which enjoys a mass-habit of acceptance and by which he is left to a greater or less degree master of the market. He may now come forward in the market with his demand. It is this shift from a restricted to a general command of the market that is significant in the concept of payment. In this sense payment is a monetary performance in exchange.
>
> (Ibid.: 251)

Through exchange, 'natural values' are therefore becoming 'social values', as 'concrete labour' used to become 'abstract labour' in Marx. Therefore, the income circulation is not only the means to ensure the renewal of production in a social economy involving private property and division of labour. It is also a social set-up which permits society to include (or exclude) private productions within (or from) the set of the national product.

Wieser also admits the existence of a second type of circulation. He indeed uses the word 'original' to specify the natural income. But this original income does not sum up the whole economic activity. Besides 'price payments' which characterize the circulation of income, Wieser also defines 'payments by assignment', 'which are made under any title outside the market of natural values' (ibid.: 253). These payments are rather heterogeneous. They refer to transactions related to changes of ownership, as it is the case when a financial asset (a share or a bond) is transferred to another agent. Payments to banks or to creditors are also included in 'payments by assignment' because

> the party paying as the assignor [...] surrenders a certain general market control, considered as money, to an assignee.
>
> (Ibid.: 253)

This category also entails gifts or tax payments. The incomes to which these 'payments by assignment' give birth form what Wieser calls the 'derived income'. Within the sphere of the derived income a specific mention must be made of the capital market (ibid.: 303). This market is subdivided into the 'money' and the 'investment markets' (ibid.).

The money market is the liquidity market. It allows banks and firms to meet and determine the conditions of short-term production credits. It provides the means which permit market economies to organize their credit system.

The investment market ensures the funding of investment by saving. Capital-Goods and unsold commodities are assumed to form a part of firms' saving, while sold commodities appear as monetary balances within firm endowments (ibid.: 295–6). The investment market involves the market of stocks and bonds, on the one hand, and the real estate market, on the other hand. This view of 'investment market' may present some resemblances with Keynes's 'financial circulation', but they are only superficial: no real Keynesian speculative motive is assumed to exist in Wieser's theory.[2]

The money and investment markets 'are mutually connected' (ibid.: 304). Therefore, one could expect the emergence of a single long-run rate of interest, as the result of 'equalizing movements' (ibid.: 304). But, in practice, this is not the case:

> Even with complete security on the loans, the interests of the different groups composing the supply and the demand are too diverse as regards the period of the loan and a number of other conditions for a central market to form in which the law of the unity of price might prevail.
>
> (Ibid.: 304)

The rate of interest on the money market is 'more mobile' than the 'steadier' interest rate on the investment market (ibid.: 304).

8. Concluding remarks: Wieser's influence and legacy

Very often, in some ill-informed papers or books, Wieser's legacy is limited to his contribution to the elaboration of the concept of marginal utility or to his introduction of the notion of opportunity cost in economic theory. Wieser is therefore presented as a minor founding father of the Marginal School. Our contribution, however, stresses many other contributions to the advancement of economic analysis which must not be forgotten and which paved the way to the transition from Menger's work to modern Austrian theories. To conclude, let us just mention two of them.

Wieser pointed out how economics and economic sociology could be combined to allow a better understanding of the emergence of rules and institutions. Wieser did not introduce the idea that social and economic institutions are the result of unintended consequences of human voluntary action. He found it in Menger's theory. Yet, he developed it, introducing the role of masses, namely of ordinary agents (by contrast with leaders) which Menger had neglected, and showed how they could prevent leaders' innovations in some given circumstances. Moreover, he stressed that if institutions were created and developed by human actions, they could also exert some feedback effects constraining individual choices later on. Undoubtedly, Hayek, Mises and Schumpeter shared these views. Hayek was strongly influenced by Wieser and explicitly recognized this influence (1994: 57). He expressed it through the role he gave to imitation and creation in his analysis of the 'market process discovery' as well as in his theory of the emergence of social rules. Mises never studied under Wieser, though it is likely that after 1903, when Wieser succeeded Menger at the University of Vienna, he was probably one of his academic examiners. It is clear that Mises's views on spontaneous market order were developed in relation with Wieser's theory of the emergence of institutions. Concerning Schumpeter's real indebtedness to Wieser, it is true that Wieser's *Social Economics* was first published in 1914, that is, three years after the first German edition of Schumpeter's *Theory of Economic Development*. However, as we already noted, Wieser strongly influenced Schumpeter. Schumpeter accepted Wieser's 'principle of continuity' (Schumpeter, 1934: 9) when he welcomed the fact that in the circular flow framework, economic systems together are made up of habits, routines and long experience. It was Wieser, Schumpeter argued, who first realized the full importance of habitual and traditional behaviour in economic life. In the field of economic development, he seemed to develop his theory of endogenous economic change *against* the background of the 'principle of continuity' (ibid.: 5–6). However, in Wieser's view, strict reliance on habits and tradition does not pre-empt the possibility of change because of the role of leaders who are the cousins of Schumpeterian entrepreneurs. Finally Wieser's and Schumpeter's economic sociologies share a family likeness.

Wieser also contributed to the emphasis on the original nature of monetary economies. He stressed the role of credit and banks, as Wicksell before him, and shared this emphasis with Mises, Schumpeter and Hayek. In a neo-Wicksellian perspective, he showed that money was not mainly a specific commodity devoted to being more and more utilized as an exchange medium. In accordance with Carl Menger's theory, money was an institution, among others, which permitted the transition from simple to social economies. Money had allowed both the creation of credit and of finance. Now, credit and finance played in their turn the role of supporting entrepreneurship. On these different issues, Wieser's approach foreshadows modern Austrian monetary theory and shares the mistrust Hayek and Schumpeter developed regarding the quantity theory of money. What is more surprising is the analytical proximity between Wieser's monetary theory and later Keynes's views on monetary economies. However, is not this proximity further evidence of Wieser's analytical depth?

Notes

1. A. Ford Hinnichs's English translation (Wieser, 1927) used the word 'natural controls' (see Translator's note 1, in Wieser, 1927: 154). We prefer the literal translation accepted by Mitchell (1917: 104).
2. Wieser describes speculation but does not see the importance of its financial dimension (1927: 363–7).

References

Arena, R. (1999) 'Austrians and Marshallians on Markets: Historical Origins and Compatible Views', in S. Dow and P. Earl (eds), *Economic Organization and Economic Knowledge: Essays in Honour of Brian J. Loasby*, Cheltenham: Edward Elgar, Vol. I.

Arena, R. (2003) 'Economic Agents and Social Beliefs in the Austrian Tradition: the Case of Friedrich von Wieser', *Rivista Internazionale di Scienze Economiche e Commerciali*, 50(3): 291–309.

Arena, R. and Festre, A. (2002) 'Connaissance et croyances en économie: l'exemple de la tradition autrichienne', *Revue d'Economie Politique*, 5: 635–57.

Hayek, F. A. (1994) *Hayek on Hayek*, edited by S. Kresge and L. Wenar, Chicago: The University of Chicago Press.

Kauder, E. (1957) 'Intellectual and Political Roots of the Older Austrian School', *Zeitschrift für Nationalökonomie*, 17(4): 411–25.

Keynes, J. M. (1930) *A Treatise on Money – The Pure Theory of Money*, Vol. V *Collected Writings of John Maynard Keynes*, London: MacMillan, Cambridge University Press, 1971.

Menger, C. [1871] (1950) *Grundsätze der Volkswirtschaftslehre*[*Principles of Economics*], Glencoe: The Free Press.

Menger, C. [1883] (1963) *Untersuchungen über die Methode der Sozialwissenschaften und der Politischen Oekonomie insbesondere* [*Problems of Economics and Sociology*], Urbana: University of Illinois Press.

Mitchell, W. C. (1927) *Foreword* to F. von Wieser (1927).
Samuels, W. (1983) *Introduction* to F. von Wieser (1926); XIII–XXXVII.
Schumpeter, J. A. [1911] (1934) *The Theory of Economic Development,* Harvard Economic Studies Series, Cambridge: Harvard University Press.
Streissler, E. (1986) 'Arma Virumque Cano: Friedrich von Wieser, the Bard as Economist', in N. Leser (ed.), *Die Wiener Schule der Nationalökonomie,* Vienna: Hermann Böhlau.
Streissler, E. (1988) 'The Intellectual and Political Impact of the Austrian School of Economics', *History of European Ideas,* 9(2): 191–204.
Wieser, F. von (1889/1893), *Der Natürliche Werth,* Vienna: Hölder; English translation as *Natural Value,* London 1893: Macmillan, reprinted, New York 1956: Kelley & Millmann.
Wieser, F. von (1926) *Das Gesetz der Macht,* Vienna: Springer, English translation as *The Law of Power,* Bureau of Business Research, University of Nebraska-Lincoln, 1983.
Wieser, F. von (1914) *Theorie der gesellschaftlichen Wirtschaft,* Tübingen: Mohr Siebeck, 2nd ed. 1923; English translation as *Social Economics,* New York 1927: Adelphi Company, reprinted by Augustus M. Kelley Publishers in 1967.

7
From Menger to Polanyi: The Institutional Way

Michele Cangiani

1. Introduction

The crisis of the institutions of liberal capitalism dates back to the last decades of the nineteenth century. Economics was thenceforth forced to radically reconsider its achievements and even its basic presuppositions, to the extent that they were linked to a free-market and perfect-competition model.

Two alternative ways were opened to economists. The first was to carry on the institutional approach, in order to explain the economic process from an 'evolutionary' perspective, in the sense Thorstein Veblen indicates. It is indispensable not only to analyse the economy as an institutional reality, but also 'to think constructively about economic institutions', as, for instance, Wesley Mitchell (1924: 21) maintains after the turning point of the First World War. However, a second way out of the crisis of economics prevailed. It consisted in making theory more abstract and formal, and thereby independent from institutional transformations. No matter if, as a consequence, its history became 'a tale of evasions of reality' (Balogh, 1982: 32).

Karl Polanyi contributed to a revival of the debate during and after the Second World War, though with no chance of overthrowing the hegemony of the mainstream neo-classical tendency. One of the issues he raised in this connection was that the novelty of the revised version of Carl Menger's *Grundsätze der Volkswirtschaftslehre* (1923), in comparison with the original 1871 version, had been underrated; and that this had happened because Menger's tentative opening to some aspects of the institutional paradigm could not but be ignored by the prevailing opposite tendency.

The present inquiry, starting from Polanyi's remarks, intends to investigate some results of Menger's revision of his 1871 book, on the basis of Polanyi's suggestions (Section 3). A synthetic analysis of Polanyi's method accounts for his interest in Menger's work (Section 2). The problem of situating Menger's revision within the history of economics is summarily considered in Section 4. Section 5 deals with the concepts of *value* and *scarcity*, on the basis of the arguments expounded in the preceding sections.

2. Polanyi's institutional approach

The 1957 publication of *Trade and Market in the Early Empires* – a collection of essays inspired by Polanyi's research and teaching at Columbia University – set off a wide debate, at first between 'substantivist' and 'formalist' economic anthropologists. The issue was the method of comparative analysis of economic systems. Anthropologists and historians nowadays still consider that book a seminal work.

Polanyi's interest in ancient and primitive societies, however, was stimulated by his concern for the nature and transformations of the market society; a critical analysis of this society is both the motive and the objective of his comparative approach. Further, this approach also supports his critique of economics; while market society is defined as a specific and contingent organization, the 'habits of thought' (to use Thorstein Veblen's phrase) on which it is grounded are revealed as the actual source of the false generalizations of economics.

The anthropological point of view Polanyi adopts does not simply mean that he makes use of anthropological research in order to prove his theses or to highlight particular problems. His approach is first and foremost anthropological, in the sense that it is holistic and at the same time historical. He considers each society, starting with market-capitalist society, as a historically specific whole, and the economy as a process which is specifically instituted within each social system. Thus, to study the economy means, according to Polanyi, to raise the problem of its social organization: the problem of 'the place of the economy' within any given social system.

Two interrelated questions emerge at this point: that of the object and method of economic theory and its relation to other social sciences, and that of a general definition of the economy.

The problem of 'the theoretical handling of early economies that possess no market systems' (Polanyi, 1971: 16) immediately causes Polanyi to question the very concept of 'economy'. This is precisely what he does at the beginning of his essay 'The Economy as Instituted Process', included in the above-mentioned book (Polanyi (ed.) 2001), where 'formal' and 'substantive' definitions are contrasted. In a revised version of a 1953 paper, Polanyi refers the formal meaning 'to a definite situation of choice, namely, that between the different uses of means induced by an insufficiency of means' (Polanyi, 1968: 216). There is here a reference to Lionel Robbins's definition, according to which the subject-matter of economics is 'human behaviour', and more precisely the 'form of choice' it assumes, when 'scarce means which have alternative uses' are to be employed for given ends (Robbins, 1962: 14–16). In opposition to that formal definition, according to Polanyi,

> [...] the substantive meaning of economic derives from man's dependence for his living upon nature and his fellows. It refers to the interchange with his natural and social environment, in so far as this results in supplying him with the means of material want satisfaction.
>
> (Polanyi (ed.) 1957: 243)

As Rhoda Halperin observes, 'the concept of the substantive economy has two analytically separable but empirically related components: one is ecological and technological, while the other is institutional' (Halperin, 1984: 253). The distinction between the two components becomes more precise in Polanyi's later writings. 'The substantive economy', we read in the posthumous volume edited by H. W. Pearson (Polanyi, 1977: 31), 'must be understood as being constituted on two levels: one is the interaction between man and his surroundings; the other is the institutionalization of that process'. And more concisely, in an article written in the years 1958–1960: 'The economy as a sub-system in society may be defined as a process of continuous material supply channelled through definite institutions' (Polanyi, 1971: 19).

To distinguish the institutional aspect of economic activities is Marx's purpose too. Thus he comes to a definition where the same 'two related components' as in Polanyi's definition can be found:

> Every production is an appropriation of natural resources [*der Natur*] by the individual within and through a given social organization [*Gesellschaftsform*].
>
> (Marx, 1974: 9)

Marx's concept of *Form* (structure, organization) initiated an innovative institutional tendency in the social sciences. Its meaning is the opposite of that of Robbins's economic (or rather, as he calls it, 'economizing') 'form' of behaviour. This latter form typically rids economics of the problem of social, historical and institutional arrangements of the economy, by establishing an immediate connection between the general characteristic of the economy – the use of resources to meet human needs – and 'economizing' individual activity. Robbins repeatedly refers in his *Essay* to the 'Crusoe Economy', to that 'isolated man' who 'has to choose', 'has to economize' (Robbins, 1962: 10ff., and *passim*). Obviously Robinson Crusoe did have to do so. But is it possible to deduce a general definition of the economy and the economic attitudes from the behaviour of an 'isolated man'? Marx calls this kind of reasoning a *Robinsonade*. His point is that the image of the isolated man is typical of the modern epoch; it corresponds to the fact – the 'historical result', as he says – that social subjects have become *individuals*. This is possible on the basis of a market society where in fact economic subjects (both entrepreneurs and workers) act as individuals. Robinson – Marx observes – brought his market culture, his society, with him to the island. The market system, despite the illusionary independence of individuals and the fetishist character of commodities and their value, is, like any other social system, a way of *socially* organizing the economy – though its typically economic, indeed *economizing* form makes it difficult to perceive its social, institutional nature. This conclusion is the starting point of Marx's 'critique of political economy': economists are interested only in relative values of commodities; they do not consider the specific form of economic organization, the system of social relations which explains the very existence, the historical occurrence of prices, of markets and of the economizing behaviour.

Polanyi similarly maintains that economists try to understand the working of the 'market-organized livelihood', but not this kind of organization as such; as a consequence, undue generalizations are advanced. His criticism of the 'formal' conception of the economy can be summarized thus. Firstly, the logic of rational choice connecting means to ends applies to any aspect of human activity, and is therefore inadequate to define the economic activity in its specificity. Secondly, economic activity does not necessarily imply choice (see, for example, Max Weber's concept of 'traditional' behaviour) and economic choice does not always imply scarcity. When the economy is organized through the *institutions of market and capitalism* choice and scarcity become instead essential features of the economic system.

'Conventional wisdom', Polanyi observes, has adopted 'the axiom of gainfulness as a universal principle of human behavior', as well as 'the ambiguous terms of supply and demand', with 'commercial trade and commercial money as logical corollaries' and 'utilitarian psychology' as a background (Polanyi, 1971: 17). Modern man has 'absolutized the motive of economic gain in practice'; this is why 'he loses the capacity of mentally relativizing it again' (Polanyi, 1977: XLVI).

The same 'habits of thought' permeate both daily life and economic science. The generalization of such categories as 'rational choice' and 'scarcity' is revealed as fallacious, to the extent that it discards their historical, institutional peculiarity. Polanyi (ibid.: 6) calls 'the economistic fallacy' the logical error of 'equating the human economy in general with its market form'. We could say that the general concept, the concept of the set of all economic systems, is entangled in the concept of an element of the set, the market system. Moreover, Polanyi's analysis of the 'market system' as an 'economically' instituted economy, and of the 'market society' as a society where the economic system becomes differentiated, autonomous and dominant, enables him to explain the real basis, the very origin of the 'economistic fallacy'.

If in all societies, however primitive, there is an economy, and if the market-related, utilitarian and, as Polanyi says, 'catallactic' concept of economy cannot be generalized, we need another concept, a truly general one: the 'substantive' concept. This is the crucial problem Polanyi raises. In dealing with it, he interprets Menger's decades-long and never completed revision of the first edition of his *Grundsätze* as an attempt in this direction. Polanyi's acknowledgement of Menger's achievement in the posthumous edition of 1923 is rather isolated; yet, the way it indicates is in my opinion worth following.

3. Menger's attempt to define the 'two meanings of "economic"'

Polanyi acknowledges the importance of Menger as a founder of neoclassical economics. According to him, Menger's premise that the 'appropriate concern' of economics is 'the allocation of insufficient means to provide for man's livelihood' constitutes an early statement 'of the postulate of scarcity, or maximization', 'of the logic of rational action'. Furthermore, Polanyi continues, it was with his 'brilliant and formidable achievements in price theory' that Menger revealed 'the new "economizing" or formal meaning of economic' (Polanyi, 1971: 17–18). There seems to be full agreement on this point. For instance, Menger's *Grundsätze* – first edition – is the first among the cited sources in a footnote added by Robbins to the famous statement of his definition of economics (Robbins, 1962: 16).

However, Polanyi observes, in the second edition Menger distinguishes two 'basic directions' of the economy, as if he desired 'to limit the strict application of his *Principles* to the modern exchange economy (*Verkehrswirtschaft*)'. One direction is 'the economizing direction stemming from the insufficiency of means, while the other is the "techno-economic" [...] deriving from the requirements of production *regardless of the sufficiency or insufficiency of the means*' (Polanyi, 1971: 18).

In the latter direction, as distinct from the former, Polanyi finds an element of that substantive meaning of 'economic', which is inherent in the institutional approach and which is required if market and pre-industrial non-market economies are to be compared. While market economies, according to Polanyi, are 'readily identifiable by the dominance over the whole of a network, a self-regulating system of price-making markets' which constitutes 'a widely integrative exchange pattern unique to our times', non-market economies are organized by a great variety of socio-cultural institutions that can be referred to 'two basic patterns: reciprocity and redistribution, or a combination of the two' (ibid.: 19). These patterns (or 'forms of integration') allow us to understand how the 'stability and unity' of the economic process are established, how this process is 'integrated' (that is, organized). The 'economic process' can thus be 'conceived as a locational or appropriational movement of things while the institutional integument consists of "persons in situation" causing the movements to happen' (ibid.: 20).

For Menger, too, the economy consists of goods that are moving as well as of persons who set them in motion. Persons find themselves in given situations, and the next step is – or should be – to recognize the cultural-institutional aspect of those situations. Polanyi is aware that it is true that economics is basically the theory of 'the system of prices and the system of markets', but he maintains that Menger tried to go beyond these boundaries, 'to find an even more general theory', in order to 'make a place for history, anthropology, and sociology'; this is why in the 1923 edition 'he stated that there are two meanings of "economic"' (ibid.: 21). In other words, according to Polanyi, the fundamental purpose of the revision and expansion of the *Grundsätze* would have been to provide a 'substantive' definition of the economy, one that could be truly general, and not an undue generalization of the characteristics of the market system.

Apart from the additions Polanyi stresses, the first four chapters of the 1923 edition of Menger's *Grundsätze* seem as a whole to deal with a general theory of the economy, with the economy in general, with everything that can be said in general about human wants and the endeavour to meet them with disposable resources. In the fifth chapter (on the theory of value) some concepts specifically concerning the market society are also introduced. In the following chapters these two levels of analysis appear more and more interwoven. In fact, Menger's attempt to distinguish 'between the economy as the sphere of man's livelihood, and the different forms of integration through which the economy as a unit was institutionalized' (Polanyi, 1971: 22) is scarcely discernable beyond the first four chapters, where changes and additions are by far more important.

In Section 3 of Chapter 4, which is completely new in the 1923 edition, Menger actually identifies 'two directions' or elementary tendencies of the economy: the 'economizing' tendency in a condition of scarcity, and the 'techno-economic' tendency in the absence of scarcity. The latter, too, according to Menger, consists in employing information necessary for organizing the use of resources and satisfying human needs.

But immediately following this Menger adds that, in reality, the economy will never be able to supply all the goods needed for full satisfaction, even in the absence of inequality among members of society and of inefficiency in the use of resources. Therefore, if we consider society as a whole – any society – the problem is *in general* that of *maximizing* the quantity and quality of disposable goods. In spite of the theoretical distinction between the economizing and the techno-economic tendencies, scarcity as a universal trait of the economic activity seems to return through the back door. It can be absent, Menger admits, in case of overabundant availability of natural resources or if working does not constitute a sacrifice: but these appear as enclaves in the economic system, or as exceptions proving the rule of scarcity.

In fact, it is difficult to find in Menger's distinction all the meanings Polanyi attributes to it, if we restrict our survey to Section 3 of Chapter 4, where that distinction is traced. Polanyi's, as it were, wishful interpretation alludes to his own conception of the economy and the comparative analysis of economic systems, notions that imply a deeper acknowledgement of the specificity of the market-capitalist society. While Menger's distinction is analytical, within a general economic theory, Polanyi's distinction is grounded on empirical knowledge of societies different from ours. Beyond the anthropological research he cites, that of Malinowski for example, we could refer to more recent archaeologists and anthropologists who have been inspired by Polanyi, such as Marshall Sahlins, who describes the 'original affluent societies' (Sahlins, 1972). These are primitive societies where there is evidence neither of scarcity nor of an economizing attitude, in the sense they have in the market society.

Nevertheless, a more comprehensive study of the 1923 edition of Menger's book, particularly of what is new in the first four chapters, enables us to discover passages that give some support to Polanyi's interpretation.

In Chapter 2 on the 'general theory of goods' Menger says that utility, as the quality that transforms things into goods, is not an objective quality of things themselves, but depends on the relationship of things to human beings (Menger, 1923: 10). We also encounter a distinction between free workers, within a contractual relationship, and slaves or servants in the Middle Ages; the latter, Menger observes, can be regarded as goods possessed by other people (Menger, 1923: 11, note*). Could these be considered as premises in the direction Polanyi alludes to, that of the 'distinctive determination' of modes of production?

More interesting in this sense is Chapter 3 on 'the measure of needs and goods'. In order to clarify this point, two interrelated aspects should be considered.

The first is that here, as well as in the first two chapters, Menger's analysis remains at an extremely high level of abstraction, a level at which it is possible to speak about the economy without considering any specific social organization. At this level the theory of value is necessarily *subjective*: value depending on how needs and disposable resources are known and evaluated. Polanyi appreciates the general significance of the subjective theory of value, and in particular Menger's idea that value 'is not an attribute of the item but of the person and of the social relationship' (Polanyi, 1971: 21). He adopts this concept of value precisely because it fits any social organization. For instance, in a socialist society too, he argues in the 1920s, the value of goods would depend on individual and social evaluations concerning the utility of goods and painfulness of work (see, for example, Polanyi, 1922). This general concept of value applies to pre-modern economies as well as to the utopia of a self-regulating market and to an economy more or less organized in the (more or less democratic) political sphere. The question shifts, then, from the general concept to the *social forms*, constituting the core issue of social *and economic* theory. And if this is the problem to be solved, clinging to the general subjective concept is not sufficient. We will see to what extent Menger himself is aware of that.

Thus we are led to the second aspect of the importance of Chapter 3. In Section 5, Menger briefly considers *given institutional conditions*, and precisely the 'present-day social situation', in relation to the general concept of 'social wants', understood as 'the sum total of goods that are necessary for the quantitative and qualitative full satisfaction of the individual and social needs of all members of a given society' (Menger, 1923: 48). In 'a true social economy', he writes, 'that is in an economy whose purpose would be the highest welfare (the fullest satisfaction of needs) of all the members of society [...] political authorities should be strongly concerned in taking into account social wants' (ibid.: 49). Polanyi considered this problem as that of the *Übersicht* (oversight, implying the *Durchsichtigkeit,* that is transparency, a clear and shared vision of individual needs and the conditions of production) in his political reflections during the inter-war period. The solution he was looking for was not a centralized administration, but a political organization that would allow conscious individual choices and democratic social choices. A difficult problem indeed: and an even more difficult solution. However, according not only to Polanyi, but also to Menger, the very possibility of confronting the task of achieving 'the highest welfare for all members of society' is compromised in the current social relations, '*unter unseren heutigen sozialen Verhältnissen*', as Menger says.

> In presently existing society, whose economy is based on exchange, and particularly among people belonging to the business milieu, social needs are not understood as the real wants of the members of society. [...] In our social organization, the object of the zealous concern of the business world is not the *real* needs of the population, but only those endowed by the *capacity and will to pay*. In the present study, in which I consider the fundamental principles of human economy in general, and not those of a given form of it, I could not overlook social wants [*Volksbedarf*] in the true sense of the word, for they are so much more essential for a deeper understanding of economic problems, and obviously also for the solution of them regarding our current economic organization.
>
> (Ibid.: 49–50)[1]

An immediate and pertinent reference for this issue is Friedrich Wieser's 'natural value' (*Der natürliche Wert*, 1889). Wieser considers Menger's 1871 *Grundsätze,* and more precisely his theory of price, as a starting point. The inquiries of the two authors seem thereafter to follow parallel paths. I would like to mention here just a few relevant points.

Wieser tries to explain value 'absolutely and by itself' (Wieser, 1956: 53, note 1); to the extent that goods are useful but 'not free', they have value in any society. However, they would be exchanged at their 'natural value' only in a situation where 'the social relation between amount of goods and utility' would not be biased by social organization or individual irrationality: that is, in 'a completely organic and most highly rational community', in a 'communist state' (ibid.: 60–1). In this ideal situation the 'subjective value' would be perfectly known by individuals, and would coincide with 'objective value', that is, with price. In 'the present order of society', Wieser observes, prices are systematically distorted: demand is biased by differences in purchasing power and the correlative 'valuation of money' of the buyer; this is why the value in exchange – which constitutes the market value, the 'objective value' – does not generally correspond to the value in its proper, subjective concept, which depends on utility. A distorted demand structure involves a distortion in the supply side of the economy and vice versa: the way in which supply is organized conditions its reaction to demand, and demand itself. This is due, as Wieser says, to 'the economic order, under which society exists'; the private entrepreneur, in particular, 'is not concerned to provide the greatest utility for society generally; his aim is rather to obtain the highest value for himself – which is at the same time his highest utility' (ibid.: 55).

The awareness that both Menger and Wieser have of the deviation of real prices from ideal, 'natural' values inevitably results in raising the issue of the specific social organization of the economy, of its being socially instituted. But let us move on to Chapter 4 of Menger's *Grundsätze*, and more precisely to Section 1 ('On the nature of the economy'), which is new in the 1923 edition. There we find further evidence of substantive and institutional aspects, or at least potentialities, in Menger's thought. Any institutional economist would agree with the definition he gives here of economic activity as an 'organizing activity', and with the reference he makes to natural, social and legal conditions of choice, and not reductively to the scarcity-plus-economizing condition affecting individual behaviour.

According to Menger, the economy is to be considered from two points of view. From the *subjective* one it is the activity of organizing the use of goods, of disposing of them with the purpose of satisfying our wants. From the *objective* point of view it is 'the whole of the goods and work (his own and other people's) that a person or a group of persons do or expect to dispose of, depending on natural or legal conditions' (Menger, 1923: 60). There is 'an indissoluble bond' between those two aspects. Menger maintains that they are both essential, in the sense that neither of them, taken alone, constitutes the economy. On the one hand, he emphasizes the novelty of the neo-classical approach: the economy as related to subjective utility, as the activity of choosing and organizing. In fact, in the subsequent development of economics the objective aspect, which depends on natural and social conditions, will be increasingly neglected, even up to its being excluded from the scope of economics, by Robbins for instance.

On the other hand, though Menger's theory has actually been one of the roots of the neo-classical-formalist tendency, it did not fail to consider 'the economy in the objective sense'. And it is typical of the institutional tendency to take into consideration the objective conditions which constitute the presupposition of individual choices: actually available resources and knowledge, and the institutional process on which that availability depends. According to the institutional approach, this concern for objectively existing resources and institutions is complementary to the 'substantive' statement – made by Menger not only in the following lines (of Chapter 4, Section 1) but throughout his book – that the goal of the economy is 'the covering of needs', the production of consumer or 'first-order' goods. This is the ground on which, according to Menger, value is – or should be – based, also of capital goods.

It is worth noting that the way is thus open to a crucial substantive question, which can be raised on the basis of the premise that the economic process is always socially organized, that it is objectively instituted: how efficiently does a given institutional arrangement provide for social wants, in given natural and technical conditions? To what extent, how and why do subjective and objective values diverge? Marginalist and formalist developments of economics tend to avoid this question. Veblen's early and radical criticism of the neo-classical paradigm should be recalled in this regard: if 'serviceability' (of goods, for 'society at large') is 'construed in terms of marginal utility or some related conceptions, [...] the outcome is a tautology' (Veblen, 1901: 309).

Menger's ability to distinguish between subjective choices and the natural and social conditions in which they are made allows us to credit him with a measure of institutional sensitivity. Not only the institutional constraints of choice, but even the very possibility of choosing are *objective* issues to be raised. In given social conditions, for instance, labour is an object of economic activity rather than its subject, to the extent that working does not require choices. Slaves did not perform an economic activity, Menger observes; and modern wage workers act economically when they sell their work-force on the labour market, but not at all when they are working (Menger, 1923: 62). What is appreciable here is Menger's ability to identify that specific social situation in which, as Polanyi says, labour becomes a 'fictitious commodity' and, as Marx says, 'the worker is there for the production process, and not the production process for the worker' (Marx, 1979: 514). Menger's acknowledgement of the social reality of labour as a commodity sets him in opposition to those neo-classical developments in economics that have continued to consider labour merely in relation to the problem of its cost as a factor of production – corresponding to its marginal contribution, and so on.

4. Two opposed tendencies of economics

Polanyi considers it revealing that the original 1871 version was chosen for both the reprint with Friedrich Hayek's Introduction in 1933 and the first translation into English in 1950 with Frank H. Knight's Introduction. The ideological bias of those choices is confirmed by the fact that, as Polanyi observes, the German term *wirtschaftend*, which means 'exercising an economic activity', was translated as *economizing*. In the 1923 edition of the *Grundsätze*, however, the term *sparend* is introduced to indicate the economizing activity in conditions of scarcity, as distinguished from economic activity in general (Polanyi, 1977: 19–20).

The First edition was in fact the only one Menger completed, but this was probably not the only reason for its being chosen. Another and more important reason derives from the nature of the problems economists are usually interested in. Thus, for example, Knut Wicksell's brilliant review of 1924 (Wicksell, 1958) considers as unimportant the innovations of the second edition. This follows from the idea that Menger's main achievement is to settle the question of 'the correct concept of value and the relation between utility and value', thus allowing a better understanding of 'the phenomena of exchange and pricing', of 'the measure of value'. In conclusion, according to Wicksell 'what is fundamental and really original in the book [...] is to be found in the short chapters on value and exchange' (Wicksell, 1958: 197, 198 and 203). These are Chapters 3 and 4 in the first edition; they become Chapters 5 and 6 in the second edition, *without any conceptually important change*.

Friedrich Hayek in his turn emphasizes Menger's ability to extend the analysis of utility-based value of goods 'from the case of given quantities of consumers' goods to the general case of all goods, including the factors of production'. With his consideration of consumer-behaviour and producer-behaviour, the structures of the means-ends relationship and 'the logic of choice or economic calculus', Hayek continues, Menger laid the foundations of 'modern micro-economic price theory' (1973: 7). The revolution in the theory of value, in the direction of a true 'economic analysis', is considered the principal merit of Menger also by Joseph Schumpeter, who does not miss the opportunity to recall the principle that the specifically 'economic' characteristic of economics is the issue of price formation (Schumpeter, 1951).

Different cultural and political suggestions were also traceable, however, in the epoch in which Menger revised his work. Max Weber's *Wirtschaft und Gesellschaft* was published, also posthumously, one year before the second edition of Menger's work. Weber's monumental work is typically a complex organization of concepts at different levels of abstraction, where the issue is raised of the distinctive features of 'modern capitalism', to be determined within more general definitions and concepts, and in comparison with pre-modern societies (see Weber, 1968). Such themes were as common in that period as they are neglected in ours; in this sense, the work in progress of both Menger and Weber is meaningful. And it is obvious to refer also to a variety of socialist and institutional economists, or to such anthropologists as Marcel Mauss and Bronislaw Malinowski who in the first two decades of the twentieth century were still seriously challenging the kind of economic science which was to prevail.

Moreover, mention should be made in this connection of the loss of theoretical complexity and institutional sensibility that characterizes twentieth-century developments in neo-classical economics, and of the Austrian School in particular, compared with its original achievements. Adolf Löwe observes – in his 1935 book of collected lectures given at the London School of Economics, which represents the opposite of Robbins's point of view – that from the end of the nineteenth century on,

> the economists tried to eject just those substantial elements of their doctrines that before had linked economic research with political science, law, psychology and history – striving after 'pure economics' as an independent body of exact knowledge.
>
> (Löwe, 1935: 26)

Basically, according to Löwe, economics had to get rid of the general concept of the economy as a socially instituted and historically specific system. As a consequence, it becomes impossible both to explain the dynamics of the capitalist economic system, and to question its efficiency from the point of view of its relationships with its social, human and natural environment. As to this last point, we may add to what has been said in the preceding section that the issue both Menger and Wieser raise, by distinguishing between 'natural value' and 'objective' exchange value, is taken up and further developed throughout the history of institutional economic thought: from Veblen's distinction between 'vendibility' and 'serviceability' (Veblen, 1901: 309) to K. W. Kapp's theory of 'social costs' (1963) and François Perroux's concept of '*coûts de l'homme*' (Perroux, 1964).

A radical critique of the market efficiency and the 'fundamental limits' of capitalist and market rationality can also be found in Weber. The presence of this kind of issue in Menger's revised work corresponds in fact to a widespread exigency in the epoch of the crisis of liberal capitalism. Also the Polanyian 'substantive' conception of the economy, with its institutional implications, is rooted in that political and intellectual situation.

On the basis of Menger's and Wieser's work, and in particular of their acknowledgement of the existence of different social-economic orders, a dynamic analysis of the economic process was still conceivable. As Löwe points out, however, the dominant tendency was to concentrate on the formal 'maximum-minimum calculation' (1935: 45), concerning *data* which are always given and never a problem, as if they were always external, and never a result of the (specific social organization of the) economic process itself.

Menger's and Wieser's theories, although lacking a full 'institutional' capacity to analyse the basic laws and dynamics of the market-capitalist society, nonetheless show – at the origin of the Austrian School – appreciation of a range of problems that was later to be reduced by the prevailing Austrian, and in general neo-classical, tendency. Any theory raising the question of the 'efficiency' of the price system 'in the general business economy' (Wieser, 1956: 55) risks, in fact, being unsuited to the support of 'the present order of society'.

5. Two meanings of *value* and *scarcity*

Polanyi's theory, and in particular his remarks on Menger, imply the need to retain – together with the subjective concept of value, at the analytical level of the economic activity in general – the objective concept of value, which concerns the social conditions of that activity. Thus the market and capitalist system can be analysed as a specific way of socially integrating individual labour and realizing the general, substantive economic function of meeting human wants. Besides, this is the starting point for the '"distinctive determination" of modes of production' Polanyi was seeking in Menger.

Like value, scarcity also has two meanings, at two levels of abstraction, corresponding to the two meanings of value. This can be the way out of Menger's difficulty in establishing his distinction between the two concepts of economy. The first meaning of scarcity concerns in general the human Paradise-Lost condition: the general necessity of organizing the livelihood of man, and the dependence of the individual 'upon nature and his fellows' for the satisfaction of his wants. The concept of scarcity, at this level, corresponds to the general, substantive concept of the economy, the concept of the set of all possible historical forms of economic activity.

The second meaning of scarcity belongs rather to a specific element of the set, to the market-capitalist form of the economy, whose fundamental features are connoted by the 'objective' concept of value. In that situation, money, either as capital or as wages, becomes in general the means and universal medium – scarce by definition, and requiring choice between different uses. The expansion of the market provides the opportunity for rational choice. On the one hand, in the 'market situation', individuals can no longer unconditionally rely on their community for their needs, which, moreover, cease to be predetermined by traditional culture; on the other hand, it becomes not only lawful but institutionally possible to employ money in order to get more money and, in particular, to produce value by means of the commodity 'work-force'.

As a consequence of this social mutation, scarcity becomes systematic and *systemic*; it acquires a specific institutional meaning, in addition to the general, substantive one. This specific meaning is inherent in the economic organization itself, in the historically specific way of employing resources and meeting needs. Everybody must *economize*; furthermore, as profit is, in Polanyi's words, 'the organizing force in society', economizing is carried out for its own sake. Thus, scarcity appears as a presupposition of economic behaviour because it is a consequence of the social form of that behaviour, of the way it is objectively institutionalized.

Note

1. This as well as any other quotation from the 1923 *Grundsätze* is translated into English by the author of this chapter.

References

Balogh, T. (1982) *The Irrelevance of Conventional Economics*, New York: Liveright.

Halperin, R. H. (1984) 'Polanyi, Marx, and the Institutional Paradigm in Economic Anthropology', in B. L. Isaac (ed.), *Research in Economic Anthropology. A Research Annual 6*, Greenwich, Conn. & London: JAI Press.

Hayek, F. A. (1973) 'The Place of Menger's *Grundsätze* in the History of Economic Thought', in J. R. Hicks and W. Weber (eds), *Carl Menger and the Austrian School of Economics*, Oxford: Clarendon Press.

Kapp, K. W. (1963) *The Social Costs of Business Enterprise*, Bombay: Asia Publishing House.

Löwe, A. (1935) *Economics and Sociology*, London: George Allen & Unwin.

Marx, K. (1974) *Grundrisse der Kritik der politischen Ökonomie*, Berlin: Dietz.

Marx, K. (1979) *Das Kapital*, I. K. Marx, F. Engels, Institut für Marxismus-Leninismus (ed.), Berlin, Dietz, Vol. 23.

Menger, C. (1923) *Grundsätze der Volkswirtschaftslehre*, edited by K. Menger, Vienna & Leipzig: Hölder-Pichler-Tempsky & G. Freytag.

Mitchell, W. C. (1924) 'The Prospects of Economics', in R. G. Tugwell (ed.), *The Trend of Economics*, New York: Alfred Knopf.

Perroux, F. (1964) *L'économie du XXème siècle*, Paris: PUF; first edition, 1961.

Polanyi, K. (1957) *Trade and Market in the Early Empires. Economies in History and Theory*, edited with C. M. Arensberg and H. W. Pearson, Glencoe, Ill.: The Free Press.

Polanyi, K. (1922) 'Sozialistische Rechnungslegung', *Archiv für Sozialwissenschaft und Sozialpolitik*, 49(2): 377–420.

Polanyi, K. (1968) 'Anthropology and Economic Theory', in M. H. Fried (ed.), *Readings in Anthropology* (New York: Crowell).

Polanyi, K. (1971) 'Carl Menger's Two Meanings of "Economic"', in G. Dalton (ed.), *Studies in Economic Anthropology*, American Anthropological Association, 16–24.

Polanyi, K. (1977) *The Livelihood of Man*, edited by H. W. Pearson, New York: Academic Press.

Polanyi, K. (2001) *The Great Transformation*, Boston: Beacon Press.

Robbins, L. (1962) *An Essay on the Nature & Significance of Economic Science*, London: Macmillan, and New York: St. Martin's Press (first edition, 1932; second edition, revised and extended, 1935).

Sahlins, M. (1972) *Stone Age Economics*, Chicago: Aldine-Atherton.

Schumpeter, J. A. (1951) *Ten Great Economists from Marx to Keynes*, New York: Oxford University Press.

Veblen, T. (1901) 'Industrial and Pecuniary Employments', in *The Place of Science in Modern Civilisation*, New York: Russell & Russell, 1961; originally in *Publications of the American Economic Association*, Series 3, Vol. II).

Weber, M. (1968) *Economy and Society*, edited by G. Roth and C. Wittich, 3 volumes, New York: Bedminster Press (*Wirtschaft und Gesellschaft*, 1922).

Wicksell, K. [1924] (1958) 'The New Edition of Menger's *Grundsätze*', in E. Lindahl (ed.), *Selected Papers on Economic Theory*, Cambridge, MA: Harvard University Press.

Wieser, F. von (1956) *Natural Value*, New York: Kelley & Millman (*Der natürliche Wert*, 1889).

8

A Note on Menger's Problem Situation and Non-essentialist Approach to Economics

Karl Milford

1. Basic principles of Menger's economic theory

Philosophical interpretations of Menger's approach to economics can be divided into two groups: one considering his approach from a more 'technical' point of view; and one considering possible philosophical influences on his position. Authors belonging to the first group consider questions such as whether Menger regards inductivist or deductivist techniques as primarily appropriate for economics (Schmoller, 1883; Keynes, 1891; Kerschagl, 1925). Authors belonging to the second group try to establish the influence of specific philosophical theories upon Menger's economic theories and methodological positions. They suggest that Menger's economic theories and methodological positions reflect influences of the philosophy of Kant (Dobretsberger, 1949) or opine that they reflect principles of rationalism and intellectualism, such as represented by the philosophy of Wolf (Boos, 1986). But the most prominent group among those interpretations asserts that Menger defends an Aristotelian essentialist position. It also seems that this interpretation has become a kind of standard interpretation of his economic, philosophical and epistemological positions (Kauder, 1958, 1962; Hutchison, 1973; Alter, 1990; Smith, 1990; Campagnolo, 2008).

However, an internal critique of 'technical' and 'philosophical' interpretations, based on an internal reconstruction of Menger's main works, shows that both kinds meet serious difficulties (Milford, 1989, 1990). Especially the standard interpretation of Menger defending an Aristotelian essentialist position is most counterintuitive if one regards the open problems of economic theory as well as the epistemological and methodological problems Menger wants to solve, his problem situation, and the philosophies of history of German idealism and German historism.

In his *Grundsätze* Menger (1871, 1981) explicitly writes that the prime problem he intends to solve is to develop a unified price theory,

> [...] a price theory based upon reality and placing all phenomena (including interest, wages, ground rent, etc.) together under one unified principle.
>
> (Ibid.: 49)

His solution to that problem consists of two components: a theory of subjective evaluations (subjective value theory) and the position of methodological individualism. These two components, however, are in conflict with any essentialist approach to economics.

2. Essentialist and non-essentialist explanations of goods

According to the Aristotelian version of essentialism, essences reside within objects, are real and, like seeds, contain some potential characteristics that are observable in concrete historical situations (Popper, 1966: chapter 11). Due to their being observable in concrete situations essences can be uncovered by different methods, for instance by intuition or by observing the historical development of objects or other entities such as institutions. An essentialist theory of goods asserts a special characteristic or essence inherent in a physical object which through that essence transforms that physical object into a good thereby demarcating it from physical objects which are not goods. For instance, labour theories explain that physical objects are goods only if they are labour products, labour being the essence that transforms physical objects into goods. That labour is the essence of goods is in fact observable in concrete situations of exchange, because the observable and unique price at which goods exchange indicates that individuals in fact exchange equivalents, that is, equal quantities of labour. In contrast, Menger bases his price theory on a theory of subjectivist evaluations which explains the evaluating behaviour of humans. According to that theory goods are not physical objects characterized by special properties, essences or characteristics inherent in them, but by the result of evaluating judgments of humans in different circumstances or social situations. Its aim is to establish 'laws' that describe the evaluating behaviour of individuals under different conditions and specify the conditions under which individuals evaluate physical objects (human actions) as goods (services). In contrast to an essentialist theory a nominalist theory is not trying to uncover essences, special properties or constitutive characteristics inherent in physical objects transforming them into goods, but one that establishes laws and conditions of human behaviour such that in certain conditions or in certain social situations individuals evaluate physical objects as goods and under different conditions or in different social situations not. Menger emphasizes that

> [...] economic theory is concerned [...] with the *conditions* under which men engage in provident activity directed to the satisfaction of their needs. [and that it investigates] [...] under what conditions a thing [...] is a *good*, whether and under what conditions it possesses *value* and how large the *measure* of this value is [...] [and] whether and under what conditions an *economic exchange* of goods will take place between two economizing individuals, and the limits within which a price can be established if an exchange does occur [...] [and on that basis] [...] the phenomena of economic life, like those of nature, are ordered strictly in accordance with definite laws.
>
> (Menger, 1981: 48)

But Menger not only describes a nominalist approach to economic theory in general. In the course of developing his price theory he explicitly and frequently rejects special essentialist theories referring to special problems. For instance; after having stated the conditions under which individuals evaluate physical objects as goods he explicitly rejects any essentialist notion of the 'good' saying

> From this it is evident that [the] goods character is nothing inherent in goods and not a property of goods, but merely a relationship between certain things and men, the things obviously ceasing to be goods with the disappearance of this relationship.
>
> (Menger, 1981: 52)

In other passages, not referring to the explanation of goods in general, but to more special problems such as the distinction between economic and non-economic goods or the differences between theories of objectivist and subjectivist evaluations, Menger also rejects any essentialist approach. With respect to the distinction between economic and non-economic goods he argues that an essentialist approach can not establish that distinction because this distinction can only be established on the basis of the idea of scarcity. However, Menger points out that the idea of scarcity itself depends on the individualist and subjectivist evaluations of humans with respect to goods and wants and maintains that

> [...] it is also evident that the economic or non- economic character of goods is nothing inherent in them, and that therefore every good, without regard to its internal properties or its external attributes, attains economic character when it enters into the quantative relationship explained above, and looses it when this relationship is reversed.
>
> (Ibid.: 101)

Likewise he rejects any essentialist notion of goods in his discussion of value theory. He writes

> Value is nothing inherent in goods, no property of them, nor an independent thing existing by itself. It is judgment economizing men make about the importance of the goods at their disposal for the maintenance of their lives and well-being. Hence value does not exist outside the consciousness of men. It is, therefore, also quite erroneous to call a good that has value to economizing individuals a 'value' as of independent real things, and to objectify value in this way. For entities that exist objectively are always only particular things, and their value is something fundamentally different from the things themselves; it is a judgment made by individuals [...] Objectification of the value of goods, which is entirely *subjective* in nature, has nevertheless contributed very greatly to confusion about the basic principles of our science.
>
> (Ibid.: 121)

These are just two examples among others which show Menger's non – or even anti-essentialist approach to economics. Other examples are his criticism of the classical explanations of exchange and of classical price theory as well as his explanation of their seeming plausibility. And then there is of course his price theory itself and its construction which rigidly adheres to the principles of a theory of subjective evaluations and to those of the methodological position of methodological individualism.

3. Essentialist and non-essentialist explanations in the social sciences

In contrast to the theory of subjective evaluations which is an empirical theory explaining the evaluative behaviour of individuals, methodological individualism is a methodological position defining the structure of a satisfactory explanation in the theoretical social sciences. It is not an empirical theory asserting something about the world, but a methodological position asserting something about science, that is, about the structure of satisfactory theoretical explanations. According to this position, social facts, processes or institutions have to be explained as the unintended result of the interplay of intended individual actions. In order to be regarded as satisfactory, explanations in the theoretical social sciences have to be structural explanations, which explain markets, prices, money or other institutions by referring to the preferences and evaluations of individuals.

Like the empirical theory of subjective evaluations, the methodological position of methodological individualism conflicts with an essentialist approach to economics. Methodological essentialism objects to methodological individualism in that its rigorous application necessarily triggers an infinite regress of explanations. It is argued that individuals always act within a given social and cultural framework and that any individualist explanation of that framework again presupposes some socio-cultural framework. This, however, conflicts with the nineteenth-century essentialist ideal that in order to be accepted as genuine scientific explanations, explanations must be ultimate explanations, explanations that are absolutely certain and verified (Popper, 1962: chapter 3). From such considerations it is concluded that the kind of explanation of the social and cultural framework in which individuals act must be non-individualistic and that in order to explain the origin and development of that framework an essentialist approach is needed. In order to provide such explanations some representatives of historism, like for instance Ranke, and of German idealism like Hegel reanimate Aristotelian essentialist ideas and regard concrete social and cultural institutions as emanations of real but hidden essences residing in those institutions. Since concrete social and cultural institutions emanate from some kind of essence, for instance from the '*Volksgeist*' of a people, essences become observable and can be uncovered by studying their historical development. Social and cultural institutions are regarded as holistic entities and although they are perceived as unintended human products which grow and develop 'organically' they nevertheless cannot be explained as the unintended result of the interplay of individual human intentions but are governed by their own specific regularities and laws (Popper, 1966: chapter 11).

Note, however, that only methodological individualism contrasts an essentialist methodological approach to economics; psychological individualistic positions are not sufficient to contrast essentialist methodological positions. As Menger shows, psychological individualism may even be regarded as an outcome of essentialist explanations of goods. Although quite different with respect to their epistemological status the methodological position of methodological individualism and the empirical theory of subjective evaluations seem to require each other. If the position of methodological individualism is not combined with a theory of subjective evaluations it remains quite blind since then social processes, facts or institutions cannot be explained as human but unintended products by way of the interplay of individual intentions. However, if the theory of subjective evaluations is not combined with the position of methodological individualism it becomes quite empty: the theory of subjective evaluations then is a psychological theory only, explaining social facts, processes and institutions not as unintended but as intended products referring to psychological motivations explaining the agreement upon which they are based. As Menger shows in his discussion of the so-called 'pragmatic' explanations the coherence of social facts and social institutions can then only be explained on psychological grounds, for instance by introducing a psychological hypothesis referring to human motives (motif causality) or in general to the (psychological) nature of humans (Menger, 1883, 1985: book III). On that basis social institutions can only be explained as the intended results of intended human behaviour, or as results of human agreement and design. Accordingly this view rejects the notion of an autonomous theoretical social science and regards it as a sub-discipline of psychology.

4. Problem situations

The history of science or of any scientific discipline is a history of problem situations, of problems and their solutions which frequently trigger new problems and new solutions which in turn change problem situations. The description of a problem situation consists of several different elements. These elements are the problems an author wants to solve as well as the formulation of that problem; the prevailing formulations of that problem by other authors, the different solutions of that problem suggested by different authors and the different research questions or research traditions triggering different solutions of that problem. In addition a kind of 'rationality principle' is required in order to make the problem situation 'work', that is, in order to explain the proposal of a particular problem solution suggested by some author on the basis of that problem situation. This rationality principle asserts that an author aims at solving a certain problem or wants to improve already existing solutions to a problem. This of course requires the development and application of certain quality standards in order to appraise the quality of a particular suggested solution in comparison to other solutions.

Note that such an internal description of a problem situation is completely devoid of psychological, sociological, political or other 'external', that is, non-scientific factors. Whether an author suffered from an inferiority complex which he wanted to compensate by extraordinary scientific efforts, or whether he was motivated by other psychological motives in order to develop a solution for an open problem is entirely irrelevant with respect to quality of that solution, that is, whether it is better than the prevailing ones or whether that solution is in fact a solution of that problem at all. In addition internal descriptions of problem situations clarify the role and the importance of forerunners as well as of influences in the development of science. In accounts of scientific development forerunners are frequently mentioned in order to show that a particular author was not as ingenious as it is generally assumed and that other authors developed ideas along lines similar to those of that author. In addition the study of influences is also regarded as important because authors do not develop their ideas in a scientific and social void.

Both views are triggered by the insight that scientific development is a social process and the result of human interaction and discussion. Accordingly it is thought that psychological, sociological, political or economic factors, so called 'external' explanations, provide better insights into the development of science than internal investigations. However, it is rather difficult to establish psychological-intellectual influences of different authors upon each other. Hypotheses about influences are always highly speculative because they assume psychological reactions of authors to intellectual stimuli, which hardly can be tested, if they can be tested at all. Referring to the books an author has read cannot establish any influence in a certain direction, simply because an author might not have grasped what he has read and may have found the solution of the problem he wants to solve precisely for that reason.

However, the importance of forerunners or the importance of influences on an author can be established if it can be shown that certain problems and their formulations as well as their suggested solutions are part of the problem situation of that author. It may of course happen that an internal analysis providing an internal 'rational' reconstruction of a problem situation yields 'irrational' results. For instance when in contrast to what would have been a certain 'rational' solution of a problem in a given problem situation an author chooses a solution of perhaps lower quality; one, which is rather unexpected in relation to what would have been a rational outcome in that problem situation. Such cases may at first be explained on an internal basis as well, for instance by referring to certain research traditions or to autonomous developments of a discipline. Particular solutions of problems may trigger new problems which require new solutions and stimulate new questions of research thereby triggering new research traditions which substitute old ones. Yet internal descriptions and explanations of problem situations may not always be successful and one may have to turn to external, that is, non-scientific elements such as psychological, economic, political or ideological factors in order to attain plausible explanations. However, internal investigations of problem situations regard problem situations as the unintended outcome of scientific developments and discussions. Accordingly they reject psychological or other external explanations of scientific development because such explanations explain principally too much. In contrast to internal explanations they suggest that problem situations can be determined and are the intended results of, for instance, intended political decisions. But even intentions to create specific problem situations trigger unforeseen consequences and feedbacks which can only be explained by internal investigations. Accordingly internal explanations regard external explanations as fruitful supplements in the rather unlikely case that internal explanations prove to be unsuccessful.

5. Menger's problem situation

Both, the theory of subjectivist evaluation and the position of methodological individualism conflict an essentialist approach to economics. But it is precisely this non-essentialist combination of an empirical theory explaining the intentions of humans on a subjectivist basis and a methodological individualistic position upon which Menger bases his nominalist and non-essentialist economic theory. His non-essentialist approach to economics is therefore strongly reflected by his problem situation and by the critique of the positions he rejects. In both of his major works (Menger, 1871, 1883) he tries to show that the reasons for

Smith's as well as for the German Historical School authors' unsuccessful attempts to develop a successful unified price theory lie in their basically essentialist approach to economics and that progress of economics is much hampered unless that approach is given up.

Roughly Menger's problem situation can be described by four different elements, each consisting of a combination of an empirical theory and a methodological position. The empirical theories are theories explaining the evaluative behaviour of individuals, that is, the theory of subjective evaluations and the theory of objective evaluations respectively. Whereas the theory of subjective evaluations explains that individuals evaluate situations, physical objects and human actions as goods and services according to their subjective and individual preferences, the theory of objective evaluations claims that individuals evaluate physical objects as goods only if they have certain objective properties which can be measured according to some objective standards. According to that theory individuals do not regard physical objects as goods unless they have these inherent properties, characteristics or essences. The two methodological positions are the positions of methodological individualism and methodological (inductivist) essentialism or collectivism. Methodological individualism requires that social institutions, facts and processes are explained as the unintended outcome of the interplay of individual intended actions; and methodological (inductivist) essentialism or collectivism asserts that there exists at least one social institution, fact or process which for principal reasons cannot be explained according to the principles of methodological individualism.

It is interesting to note that the four possible combinations of these two empirical and methodological positions have been represented by different authors in the history of economic ideas. The non-essentialist combination of a methodological position of methodological individualism and an empirical theory of subjective evaluations is represented by Menger and before Menger, by G. Hufeland (1807). The combination of an essentialist theory of objective evaluations and an, in its intentions, individualistic methodological position is represented by A. Smith. Marx may be regarded as a representative of the third possible essentialist combination, that is, of methodological inductivist essentialism and an essentialist theory of objective evaluations. The fourth combination, constituted by the theory of subjective evaluations and methodological inductivist essentialism is represented by different authors of the German Historical School of economics, such as Roscher (1838, 1842), Hildebrand (1848), Knies (1853) and Schmoller (1900–1904).

Graphically Menger's problem situation may be described as follows

Table 8.1 Menger's Problem Situation

		Theories of evaluating behaviour	
		subjective	objective
Methodological positions	individualism	Hufeland 1807 Menger 1871	A. Smith 1776
	inductivist essentialism	German historical school Roscher 1842	K. Marx 1867

Menger's solution of a unified price theory is based upon the combination of a theory of subjective evaluations and the methodological position of methodological individualism. According to him this combination is decisive for finding a satisfactory solution for the problems of finding an acceptable explanation of exchange and of finding a unified price theory. In his view many attempts to solve those problems failed, simply because their authors did not base their attempts on that combination. In the course of developing his own solution Menger especially criticizes Smith's combination and the combination represented by the authors of the German Historical School, especially by Roscher. He provides no explicit criticism of the fourth combination, that is, the combination of a theory of objective evaluations and the methodological position of methodological inductivist essentialism, presumably because he regarded that combination as completely refuted by his arguments against the positions of Smith and of Roscher.

According to Menger, Smith, by developing a theory of objective evaluations, defends an essentialist theory of goods and an individualistic methodological position, which, however, cannot meet the requirements of methodological individualism. In his view Smith's essentialist theory of goods as well as his individualistic position have to be rejected. The former because it cannot explain the evaluative behaviour of individuals and therefore provides an unsatisfactory theory of goods only; the latter because it is a psychological individualistic position which is capable of explaining social facts such as social institutions on the basis of psychological investigations but not as unintended outcome of the interplay of individual intended actions. With respect to the authors of the German Historical School of economics, Menger observes that their price theories although fruitful because based on a theory of subjective evaluations, nevertheless cannot provide a satisfactory unified price theory. In his view they are reservational price theories only, describing the factors determining reservational demand and supply prices but unable to explain how individuals evaluate concrete quantities of concrete goods and how prices emerge as the unintended outcome of the interplay of demand and supply on a market. That the German authors were unable to develop these fruitful beginnings into one successful price theory is, according to Menger, the result of their peculiar methodological position, that is, methodological inductivist essentialism.

Against the position of Smith, Menger directs one empirical and two methodological arguments. According to him Smith and other representatives of a theory of objective evaluations cannot explain exchange. He explains that according to Smith individuals exchange equivalents when exchanging goods. And he observes that in Smith's view individuals exchange equivalents because they are labour products and evaluate them according to the labour quantities measured in time needed to produce them. However, Menger emphasizes that this explanation of exchange is empirically false because it cannot explain observations such as the termination of exchange processes as well as their irreversibility. If individuals were to exchange equivalents, so Menger, exchange cannot be explained by referring to the different individuals' evaluations of goods. Exchange of equivalents therefore has to be explained on a different basis and according to Menger Smith provides that basis by introducing a psychological hypothesis about the nature of man, that is, a special psychological inclination of humans to truck and barter. This, however, means that the process of exchange itself provides pleasure, since it satisfies a human need, that is, to truck and barter. To this hypothesis, however, Menger objects that it has no explanatory power with respect to the explanation of exchange. He emphasizes that

> [if] trading were a pleasure itself [and] hence an end in itself [...] there would be no reason [...] why [men] should not trade back and forth an unlimited number of times.
>
> (Menger, 1981: 177)

According to Menger the reason for this unsuccessful attempt to explain exchange lies in the essentialist character of any theory of objective evaluations. In order to show this he tries to explain the causes that may have led to the development of a theory of objective evaluations and to the idea that individuals exchange equivalents. He suggests that the idea that individuals exchange equivalents may have been triggered by the observation that goods exchange at one observable price and that consequently economists sought to uncover of what it is that makes goods equivalents. Observable prices may have been regarded as observable manifestations of an essence that makes goods equivalents, an essence which lies within the physical objects that transforms them into goods; and some authors, according to Menger, regarded this essence to be labour. In his view physical objects were regarded as values or goods because it was thought that they have that objective inherent property, characteristic or essence of being a labour product, which as such can be objectively measured. Menger writes

> But since prices are the only phenomena of that process that are directly perceptible, since their magnitudes can be measured exactly, and since daily living brings them unceasingly before our eyes, it was easy to commit the error of regarding the magnitude of price as the essential feature of an exchange, and as result of this mistake, to commit the further error of regarding quantities of goods in an exchange process as equivalents.
>
> (Ibid.: 192)

And he proceeds, explaining that

> [t]he result was incalculable damage to our science since writers in the field of price theory lost themselves in attempts to solve the problem of discovering the causes of an alleged *equality* between two quantities of goods. Some found the cause in equal quantities of labor expended on the goods. Others found it in equal costs of production. And a dispute even arose as to whether the goods are given for each other because they are equivalents, or whether they are equivalents because they are exchanged. But such an equality of the values of two quantities of goods (an equality in the objective sense) nowhere has any real existence.
>
> (Ibid.: 192)

However, in a footnote to this passage (Menger, 1981: 305, appendix F) Menger not only emphasizes that already Aristotle committed that error, that is, regarding goods in an exchange process as equivalents. He also points out that such an essentialist approach of explaining goods has rather serious and disastrous consequences for the progress of economics because it implies unfruitful research questions and triggers a barren research tradition leading to obsolete and false research results. According to him an essentialist approach of explaining goods which attempts to uncover some essence or inherent property of physical things transforming them into goods necessarily leads to research questions regarding the origin of physical objects and not to research questions regarding the evaluative behaviour of individuals under different conditions. In his view an essentialist approach substitutes the basic research question of any theoretical social science, that is, that of explaining the evaluative behaviour of individuals for research questions regarding the origin of physical objects the answer to which, however, is rather irrelevant for the theoretical social sciences. He points out that

> In general, no one in practical life asks for the history of the origin of a good in estimating its value, but considers solely the services that the good will render him and which he would have to forgo if he did not have it at his command. [...] Comparison of the value of a good with the value of the means of production employed in its production, an act of *past* human activity, was appropriate or economic. But the quantities of goods employed in the production of a good have neither a necessary not a directly determining influence on its value.
>
> (Ibid.: 146, 147)

An essentialist approach to economics attempting to uncover the essence or characteristic inherent property of physical objects transforming them into goods, for instance by studying their historical development, necessarily leads to questions regarding the origin of that historical process and therefore to questions regarding the origin of physical objects and not to questions regarding the evaluative behaviour of individuals and thus of goods. But according to Menger the task of economics is to study the evaluative behaviour of individuals because only human judgments or evaluations transform already existing physical objects into goods. According to Menger

> Value is nothing inherent in goods, no property of them, nor an independent thing existing by itself. It is a judgment economizing men make about the importance of the goods at their disposal for the maintenance of their lives and well-being. Hence value does not exist outside the consciousness of men. It is therefore, also quite

> erroneous to call a good that has value to economizing individuals a 'value' or for economists to speak of 'values' as of independent real things, and to objectify value in this way. For the entities that exist objectively are always only particular things, and their value is something fundamentally different from the things themselves; it is a judgment made by [...] individuals [...] Objectification of the value of goods, which is entirely subjective in nature, has nevertheless contributed very greatly to confusion about the basic principles of our science.
>
> (Ibid.: 121)

Menger's critique of Smith's and other authors' combination of an essentialist theory of objective evaluations and an intended individualistic methodological position shows that essentialist explanations of exchange are empirically false, falsified by experience and lead to unwanted methodological consequences in the form of uninteresting and unwanted research questions delaying the progress of economics. But it also shows that any explanation of exchange or relative prices on an essentialist basis, that is, on the basis of a theory of objective evaluations necessarily requires the introduction of a psychological hypothesis about the psychological nature of humans. Menger points out that if it is explained that individuals exchange equivalents, exchange cannot be explained at all, unless such a psychological hypothesis is introduced. However, according to Menger, this means that in order to explain social institutions investigations with respect to the psychological motivations of individuals have to be carried out and that social institutions have to be explained as agreements settled by humans, that is, as intended results of intended human actions. Explanations such as these Menger calls 'pragmatic' explanations (1985: book III), and he emphasizes that if social institutions are explained in the 'pragmatic modus' as the intended result of an agreement among humans, social science can only explain the motives and aims of individuals which resulted in that agreement. Menger emphasizes, however, that psychological individualistic explanations of social institutions violate the task of any genuine theoretical social science which is to explain social institutions according to the principles of methodological individualism, that is, as the unintended results of the interplay of intended actions. By introducing an additional psychological hypothesis about the nature of humans, Smith not only introduces additional and redundant psychological assumptions, but rejects also the idea of a genuine theoretical social science, though perhaps unintentionally. Menger writes:

> In this one-sidedly pragmatic view of the nature of social institutions, the sphere of ideas of A. Smith and his closest followers comes into contact with that of the French writers of the French Age of Enlightenment in general and of the French physiocrats in particular. Adam Smith, also, and his school predominantly strive for the *pragmatic* understanding of economy, even where such understanding is not adequate for the objective state of affairs. The result is that the broad realm of unintentionally created social structures remains closed to their theoretical comprehension.
>
> (Menger, 1985: 172)

The second major element in Menger's problem situation consists of positions which may be described as a combination of a theory of subjectivist evaluations and the methodological position of methodological inductivist essentialism or methodological collectivism. In his critique of that combination, he, quite similar to his critique of the combination represented by Smith, tries to show that it is also the result of an essentialist approach to economics. He directs his criticism mainly against versions given to it by the authors of the so called German Historical School of economics and in particular by Roscher whose works are considered to have constituted that school. However, unlike his criticism of the objective theory of value, which he considers to be an outcome of essentialist ideas, Menger regards the first component of the combination of a theory of subjective evaluations and the position of methodological inductivist essentialism as uncommonly inspiring and emphasizes its extraordinary fruitfulness (Menger, 1981: 49). However, he also points out that the prevailing explanations of the evaluative behaviour of humans, as well as the explanations of goods and of relative prices on the basis of that theory are quite unsuccessful. According to Menger they remain so called reservational price theories enumerating the factors determining the reservational supply and demand prices. But these theories, so Menger claims, are incapable of explaining exchange and relative prices because they lack explanations regarding the individuals' evaluative behaviour of concrete quantities of goods in order to satisfy concrete needs.[1]

Menger is of course aware that the attempt to base the explanation of prices upon theories of subjective evaluations has a long tradition in German economics. His criticism of the prevailing but unsuccessful attempts by German authors to establish a satisfactory price theory therefore tries to explain that rather unexpected failure. However, according to him this failure results from the peculiar methodological positions the German authors defend, especially that of methodological inductivist essentialism, developed by Roscher. In other words, Menger regards the failure of the German authors' explanation of prices as an indirect outcome of an essentialist approach to economics.

A problem still regarded as unresolved among many German economists was the question of explaining the coherence of social institutions on an individualistic basis and on the basis of a theory of subjective evaluations. It was thought that an individualistic explanation of social institutions, like for instance markets, on the basis of individuals trying to achieve their subjective aims in the possibly best manner can only explain antagonistic tendencies in society, not however the coherence of social groups or institutions. In order to solve that problem some German economists introduced special psychological hypotheses, not unlike Smith, about the psychological nature of humans. Roscher (1886: 22), for instance, claims a special '*Gemeinsinn*' which checks the egoistic actions of individuals and which explains why social institutions or even society is not drifting apart although it is inhabited by egoistic individuals.[2] A second argument, already mentioned previously in Section 3, was that self interested individuals always act within a given social and cultural framework which has to be explained by a non-individualistic, that is, a collectivist or 'organic' approach.[3]

Menger's criticism of the first argument is quite similar to his criticism of Smith's attempt to explain exchange by way of introducing a special psychological hypothesis about humans. If psychological hypotheses are required only 'pragmatic' explanations are possible. Menger's criticism of the second argument, however, is twofold because he discusses especially Roscher's version of the argument that the origin and development of the social framework within which individuals act has to be uncovered by historical research.

In order to develop a non-individualistic approach with respect to the explanation of the social and cultural framework, Roscher draws upon philosophical and epistemological ideas developed by authors defending historism, especially by Ranke. Ranke, like Hegel and other representatives of German idealism and historism reanimated some Aristotelian essentialist ideas in his philosophy of history (Iggers, 1997: 86). According to Ranke social and cultural institutions are concrete emanations of the essence of a people or a nation. Not unlike Aristotle's essentialist philosophy, he explains that the essence of a thing resides within that thing, is real and contains some potential characteristics which come to existence in concrete historical situations. Thus the essence of a thing becomes at least partly observable and by studying its historical development may finally be described by some historical law. Accordingly true scientific knowledge of a people, a nation or of social institutions or of economic systems can be obtained by describing a nation's, or people's, or social institution's historical development by some kind of historical law.

The doctrine that essences unfold in change and can be observed by studying the historical development of its emanations is only one among others following from Aristotle's essentialism (Popper, 1966: chapter 11). It provides the possibility of combining empirical research and of obtaining genuine scientific knowledge about a changing observable universe, that is, knowledge which according to nineteenth-century standards is proven true and absolutely certain. Roscher defends such a doctrine in order to solve the problem of explaining the origin and development of the social framework in which individuals act on a non-individualistic basis. Like many other nineteenth-century authors he regards the method of induction to be the method for acquiring empirical knowledge and explains that the empirical basis of the theoretical social sciences is the history of mankind. According to him the task of the theoretical social sciences is to uncover laws of historical development describing the social and cultural framework in which individuals act according to their subjective evaluations. The methodological position of methodological inductivist essentialism and the empirical theory of subjective evaluations are seemingly quite compatible (Milford, 1995).

Although Roscher draws on essentialist Aristotelian ideas in the form Ranke has given to them, he nevertheless is much more interested in its empirical and inductivist transformation.[4] Roscher (1838, 1842) tries to carry out this transformation by developing a philosophy of history and a philosophy of the social sciences explaining the role of history as an empirical basis for the social sciences. His philosophy is inductivist and although it describes content-enlarging and truth-preserving inferences, that is, logical relations between statements, it is formulated in 'naturalistic' or sociological terms. He describes the activities of historians collecting historical data and facts establishing the empirical basis of the social sciences from which historical and social laws are inferred by inductive inferences. However, Roscher also emphasizes, like Ranke, that although science is capable of establishing social and historical laws of development it cannot explain them. For in his view the attempt of explaining natural and social laws governing the world means attempting to uncover God's design which is blasphemous since humans are not divine.

Like with 'pragmatic' explanations, Menger's criticism of the argument that social and cultural frameworks cannot be explained on an individualistic basis refers to the principal methodological requirements of methodological individualism. According to him social and cultural institutions cannot be regarded as holistic and organic entities, for if they are only vacuous explanations of their origins and developments are possible (Menger, 1985: book III). Menger points out that without providing structural explanations of such entities on the basis of methodological individualism such explanations simply amount to saying that social and cultural institutions have originally and organically developed. Menger emphasizes that

> [T]his theory [...] indeed avoids the error of those who reduce all institutions to acts of positive common will. Still, it obviously offers us no solution of the problem discussed here, but evades it. The origin of a phenomenon is by no means explained by the assertion that it *was present from the very beginning* or that it *developed originally*.
>
> (Ibid.: 149)

Holistic entities such as nations or a national economy or money do not exist, are pure fictions, and establishing seeming laws between such fictions will not add to social science knowledge. Menger also draws upon the epistemological and methodological similarities of the positions of Smith and the authors of the German Historical School with respect to the explanation of social institutions. Both are drawn into 'pragmatic' explanations as a result of their essentialist positions. Smith, perhaps unintentionally, because he bases his explanation of exchange on an essentialist theory of goods; and the authors of the German Historical School because they regard the introduction of essentialist and inductivist methods to be most fruitful for the progress of social science (ibid.: 196).

Due to Roscher's inductivist position Menger not only discusses the essentialist nature of that position but its inductivism as well. Although Menger, like Roscher shares the prevailing nineteenth-century idea that the method of induction characterizes empirical science, he nevertheless opposes Roscher's idea that history constitutes the empirical basis of the theoretical social sciences. Menger argues that the German

Historical School's essentialist conceptions of social science explanations is flawed and discusses the different structures of theoretical and historical explanations. He points out that in contrast to genuine historical explanations, theoretical explanations are interested in finding some strictly universal statement or law from which the singular statement describing the observation or process one wants to explain can be logically deduced. Historical explanations, however, are not interested in finding new laws but apply social or economic laws in order to provide an explanation of a singular historical fact (ibid.: 44–5). Menger emphasizes that this conception of a satisfactory historical explanation strongly contrasts with the 'pseudo-historical orientations of theoretical research' (ibid.: 102) of the German Historical School, that is, its 'national and historical conception of theoretical science' (ibid.: 24) and its 'historical-philosophical and statistical-theoretical orientation of research' (ibid.: 25).

Menger, however, not only points out that the essentialist and inductivist approach of the German Historical School is pseudo-historical. He also emphasizes that it has to be rejected on logical grounds. In his analysis of the positions of the authors of the German Historical School he shows that they infer at least three different methodological principles from the argument that individuals act within a given socio-cultural framework. First, if the socio-cultural framework develops in the course of history and if individuals act within that framework individual actions can only be explained by referring to the values and standards of a particular, historically given framework. Accordingly the aim of social science to establish a universal valid theory explaining individual behaviour has to be rejected because it cannot be attained for principal reasons. Secondly, if social regularities can be found in a developing historical process at all, their validity is confined to special historical periods only. Accordingly, genuine, that is, strictly universal, laws must be laws of historical development determining that historical process; theoretical social science is the theory of history whose task it is to establish laws of historical development. Thirdly, an absolute certain emprico-historical basis from which social regularities are inferred by content-enlarging and truth-preserving inductive inferences, requires that abstract concepts have to be avoided; the formation of abstract concepts by generalization from given facts endangers the truthfulness of the empirico-historical basis and that of the regularities and theories derived from that basis; accordingly the social sciences ought to avoid the formation of universals.

With respect to the last principle Menger shows that it is logically false, since even singular observational statements necessarily include universals, that is, 'exact types' (Menger, 1985: 56–7). However, with respect to the problem of establishing social laws that are strictly universal and empirical Menger shows that so called 'exact laws' can only be established on the basis of an induction principle, 'a rule of research' and that the naïve inductivist position of Roscher also has to be rejected on logical grounds (Menger, 1985: 57, 60; Milford, 1990, 1995).

6. Some concluding remarks

That Menger defends an Aristotelian essentialist position is simply a myth. He defends a position which consists of a theory of subjectivist evaluations and the methodological position of methodological individualism which are both non-essentialist. In both of his works he aims at showing that precisely this combination conflicts with essentialist positions, whether they are empirical theories or methodological positions. His price theory is nominalist and empirical as well as inductivist. He justifies social and economic laws by referring to experience and observation as many passages in his work (1981) show. For instance his formulation of the idea of 'marginal utility' is negative and based on a loss principle because one may observe that individuals abstain from satisfying a concrete need if the available stock of a good is decreased by one concrete quantitative unit. Yet it is hardly possible to observe the additional utility an individual receives by consuming an additional quantitative unit of ice cream. Similarly his formulation of the so-called equimarginal principle is justified by observation and not derived from an optimizing calculation under linear constraints as in modern theory. His theoretical considerations even lack the explicit formulation of a budget constraint. That he discusses induction and tries to solve the problem of induction is due to Roscher's formulation of the position of methodological essentialist inductivism. And in his considerations with respect to the 'organic understanding of social phenomena' he also tries to show the non-essentialist character of methodological individualism.

However, the myth that Menger defends an Aristotelian essentialist position has to be rejected not only on grounds referring to his economic theory and methodological analysis. It also has to be rejected on grounds regarding the general history of ideas. German idealism and German historism reanimated Aristotelian essentialist ideas in order to solve methodological problems of historical and social science explanations and there cannot be much doubt on the basis of Menger's writings that he opposed their ideas. It is indeed true that Menger frequently uses the term '*das Wesen*'. But it is quite impossible to infer any philosophical theory defended by Menger from the frequency of his using this term. In German language the term '*das Wesen*' frequently only refers to the definition formula (*definiens*) of a definition and thus is completely neutral. But whether the term to be defined (*definiendum*) simply is a nominalist summary of the content described by the definition formula or whether it is claimed that the definition formula provides genuine knowledge of essences of the *definiendum* cannot be decided without a philosophical theory. Yet it is hard to find an Aristotelian essentialist philosophy in Menger's works.

Notes

1. Cf. Menger (1981: 292, appendix C). In this passage Menger critically discusses alternative theories of subjective evaluations and explains their failure.
2. The argument is false because it confounds methodological individualism and the theory of subjective evaluations.
3. This approach is also called 'ethical' approach, not because its representatives evaluate economic and social situations from a present day ethical point of view, but because individuals act within a historically given socio-cultural framework of historically given norms and traditions which influence their actions.
4. For a detailed analysis of that transformation, cf. for instance Weber (1975) and Milford (1995). Also cf. Menger's (1985) analysis in the fourth book of his where he discusses the principles of Roscher's position. Due to Roscher's emphasis on history as the empirical basis of the theoretical social sciences, Menger, emphasizes that Roscher's claim that his position transfers the essentialist ideas of Savigny and of W.v. Humboldt into economics is rather unwarranted.

References

Alter, M. (1990) *Carl Menger and the Origins of Economics*, San Francisco and Oxford: Westview Press.

Boos, M. (1986) *Die Wissenschaftstheorie Carl Mengers*, Wien: Böhlaus Nachf.

Caldwell, B. J. (ed.) (1990) *Carl Menger and His Legacy in Economics*, Durham, N.C.: Duke University Press.

Campagnolo, G. (ed.) (2008) *Carl Menger, Discussed on the Basis of New Findings*, Frankfurt am Main: Peter Lang.

Dobretsberger, J. (1949) 'Zur Methodenlehre C. Mengers und der österreichischen Schule', in *Neue Beiträge zur Wirtschaftstheorie. Festschrift anläßlich des 70. Geburtstages von H. Mayer*, Wien.

Hildebrand, B. (1848) *Die Nationalökonomie der Gegenwart und Zukunft*, Frankfurt am Main.

Hufeland, G. (1807) *Neue Grundlegung der Staatswirthschaftskunst*, Gießen and Wetzlar: Tasche und Müller.
Hutchison, T. (1973) 'Some Themes from Investigations into Method', in J. R. Hicks and W. Weber (eds), *Carl Menger and the Austrian School of Economics*, Oxford: Oxford University Press.
Iggers, G. (1997) *Deutsche Geschichtswissenschaft*, Vienna: Böhlau.
Kauder, E. (1958) 'Intellectual and Political Roots of the Older Austrian School', *Zeitschrift für Nationalökonomie*, 17(4): 411–25.
Kauder, E. (1962) 'Aus Mengers nachgelassenen Papieren', *Weltwirtschaftliches Archiv*, 89(1): 1–28.
Kerschagl, R. (1925) *Einführung in die Methodenlehre der Nationalökonomie*, Vienna: Hölder-Pichler-Tempsky.
Keynes, J. N. (1891) *The Scope and Method of Political Economy*, New York: A. M. Kelley, reprint 1955.
Knies, K. (1853) *Die Politische Ökonomie vom Standpunkt der geschichtlichen Methode*, Braunschweig: Schwetschke.
Menger, C. (1871) *Grundsätze der Volkswirthschaftslehre*, Vienna: Wilhelm Braumüller.
Menger, C. (1883) *Untersuchungen über die Methode der Socialwissenschaften und der Politischen Ökonomie insbesondere*, Leipzig: Duncker & Humblot.
Menger, C. (1981) *Principles of Economics*, New York: New York University Press.
Menger, C. (1985) *Investigations into the Method of the Social Sciences with Special Reference to Economics*, New York: New York University Press.
Milford, K. (1989) *Zu den Lösungsversuchen des Induktionsproblems und des Abgrenzungsproblems bei Carl Menger*, Österreichische Akademie der Wissenschaften, Veröffentlichungen der Kommission für Sozial- und Wirtschaftswissenschaften, Bd 27, Verlag der Österreichischen Akademie der Wissenschaften, Wien.
Milford, K. (1990) 'Menger's methodology', in Caldwell (ed.) (1990).
Milford, K. (1995) 'Roscher's Epistemological and Methodological Position: Its Importance for the Methodenstreit', *Journal of Economic Studies*, 22(3/4/5): 26–52.
Popper, K. R. (1962) *Conjectures and Refutations*, London: Routledge & Kegan Paul.
Popper, K. R. (1966) *The Open Society and its Enemies*, London: Routledge & Kegan Paul.
Roscher, W. (1838) *De historicae doctrinae apud Sophistas majores vestigiis*, Göttingen: Vandenhoeck und Ruprecht.
Roscher, W. (1842) *Leben, Werk und Zeitalter des Thukydides*, Göttingen: Vandenhoeck und Ruprecht.
Roscher, W. (1886) *Grundlagen der Nationalökonomie*, Stuttgart: Cotta.
Schmoller, G. (1883) 'Zur Methodologie der Staats- und Sozialwissenschaften', *Jahrbuch für Gesetzgebung, Verwaltung und Volkswirthschaft*, 7: 975–94.
Schmoller, G. (1900–1904) *Grundriss der Allgemeinen Volkswirtschaftslehre*, Vol. I 1900, Vol. II 1904, Munich and Leipzig: Duncker & Humblot.
Smith, B. (1990) 'Aristotle, Menger, Mises: An Essay in the Metaphysics of Economics', in Caldwell (ed.) (1990).
Weber, M. [1903] (1975) *Roscher and Knies: The Logical Problems of Historical Economics*, London: Collier Macmillan.

Part IV

Dissemination of the Austrian School of Economics

9
The Austrian School in the Interwar Period

Harald Hagemann

1. Emigration of the Austrian economists

The dismissal of academics from German universities under the Restoration of Civil Service Act from 7 April 1933, which enabled the Nazis to fire scientists because of racial and/or political reasons, and the expulsion of academics from Germany, and after the 'Anschluss' in March 1938 also from Austria, interrupted or destroyed promising developments in economics as well as in physics and other fields. This caused a negative turning-point for the long-term development of sciences at German-speaking universities. German and Austrian economics fell behind internationally and had to undergo a laborious catching-up process after 1945 without being able to fully compensate the loss of qualified personnel in the following decades. In contrast, the economists who had been driven out of Germany and Austria not only enriched the development of their specialized areas in their host countries, but also made decisive contributions to the international standard of research. This holds in particular for the United States, which was the direct or indirect destination for some two-thirds of German-speaking émigré economists, and which also became the new home for 'Austrian economics'.

The relative importance of Austrian economics within the German language area and the enormous loss due to the political development in the interwar period can also be seen by taking a look at the quantitative figures (see Hagemann and Krohn, 1999). Out of 253 dismissed economists, 221 emigrated. Of those 32 scholars who stayed one half was killed in the Holocaust, concentration camps or Gestapo prison, for example, Carl Grünberg and Rudolf Hilferding. Of the émigré economists, 51 had achieved their doctorate at an Austrian university.

With the exception of one scholar who received a doctorate from the University of Innsbruck, all the others did their PhD at the University of Vienna, 13 before and 37 after 1918. This shows that the University of Vienna had almost monopolized academic education in Austria, a situation substantially different from the situation in Germany.

However, Hitler's occupation of Austria in March 1938 did not cause dramatic changes in the development of economics insofar as it was institutionalized at Vienna University, where economics in the interwar period was still taught at the law faculty, which even in the years of the Republic was not inclined to offer greater career prospects to Jews, social democrats, liberals or other 'suspicious' persons. A good indicator of the limited career opportunities for qualified young economists is the new appointments to the three chairs in economics which all became vacant in the period between 1919 and 1926. These include the chairs formerly held by Eugen von Böhm-Bawerk, Friedrich von Wieser (who had succeeded Menger in 1903 and retired in 1922),[1] and the socialist Carl Grünberg (1861–1940) who had received a new chair of economic history through the strong support of Böhm-Bawerk and Wieser in 1912. The two outstanding candidates Joseph A. Schumpeter and Ludwig von Mises, who both had the right age for being appointed and were already well known internationally since their pre-war publications such as *The Theory of Money and Credit* and respectively *The Theory of Economic Development*, were systematically overlooked. Instead the three chairs were given to Othmar Spann, a reactionary and anti-semitic supporter of the corporatist state who strongly opposed the methodological individualism of the Austrian School and favoured a holistic intuitive universalism instead, Hans Mayer and Count Ferdinand Degenfeld-Schonburg, who is hardly remembered today.[2] Of these three professors only Mayer, Wieser's handpicked successor, stayed within the Austrian tradition of methodological individualism. However, his contributions on value, price and utility theory and the imputation problem did not make a lasting impact. The appointments of these professors, none of whom is remembered today for having made important contributions to economics, sent clear signals to the most outstanding representatives of a new young generation of economists with a keen interest in modern theoretical analysis to look elsewhere for professorships.

Following Hayek who in 1923/1924 had spent 14 months at Columbia University (listening to John Bates Clark and Wesley Mitchell) and had studied the Federal Reserve System, most of the outstanding young economists, such as Gottfried Haberler, Oskar Morgenstern, Fritz Machlup or Gerhard Tintner, took a two-year-fellowship from the Rockefeller Foundation to study at leading American universities. There they established intensive international contacts which were very helpful for their later academic careers. When the Nazis occupied Austria in March 1938 many of them had already left the country years before. Schumpeter who had become professor in Bonn in 1925 moved from there to Harvard in 1932. In 1934 Mises had become professor of international economics at the Institut Universitaire des Hautes Etudes Internationales in Geneva. In summer 1940 he took an adventurous flight from Switzerland via France, Spain and Portugal to the USA, where he settled at New York University founding an American Austrian School of Economics, with Israel Kirzner and Murray Rothbard as his main students.[3] Hayek moved to the London School of Economics in 1931 where his *Prices and Production* lectures qualified him for the Tooke Professorship. Haberler worked for the League of Nations in Geneva, surveying the modern literature on business-cycle theory in his famous *Prosperity and Depression* (1937). In 1936 he immigrated to the USA where he became full professor and a colleague of Schumpeter at Harvard University. Machlup and Tintner were among the younger economists who were appointed professors at the State University of New York at Buffalo in 1935 and Iowa State University at Ames in 1937, respectively.

With the deep economic depression, the menace of Nazi rule across the border in neighbouring Germany, and the authoritarian regime in Austria which consolidated in the civil war situation of February 1934, many economists had already left when the *Anschluss* happened in 1938. This had the greatest negative impact at the Austrian Institute for Research on Business Cycles in Vienna. At the initiative of Mises it had been founded in 1927 with Hayek becoming the first director who, after his move to the L.S.E., was succeeded by Morgenstern from 1931–1938. Shortly after the Anschluss the Vienna Institute lost its independence and became a branch office – specializing in South-Eastern Europe – of the German Institute for Business-Cycle Research, which was headed by Wagemann in Berlin. The Vienna Institute now suffered severe losses. Besides its director Morgenstern, who accepted the offer from the Institute for Advance Study in Princeton, we find such outstanding scholars as Alexander Gerschenkron (1904–1978) and Abraham Wald (1902–1950) among the Institute's researchers who immigrated to the USA in the same year. The younger Josef Steindl (1912–1993) got a position at Balliol College in Oxford with the support of Hayek and Haberler. Among the young students who emigrated immediately after the Anschluss there are such later excellent economists as Bert(hold) Frank Hoselitz (1913–1995), Kurt W. Rothschild (*1914) and Paul Streeten

(*1917). Most of the remaining members of the Mises circle or of Hayek's friends emigrated from Austria in 1938. The long list includes Martha Stephanie Browne (Braun) (1898–1990), Ilse (Schüller-)Mintz (1904–1978) and Joseph Herbert Furth (Fürth) (1899–1995).

1938 also implied the end of the Vienna-based *Zeitschrift für Nationalökonomie* as a leading international journal. With Morgenstern as the managing editor since 1930 (until 1934 with his friend Paul Rosenstein-Rodan), it had become the most important scholarly journal in economics in the German-language area in the 1930s.[4] The journal published important contributions to business-cycle theory, capital theory, general equilibrium theory and

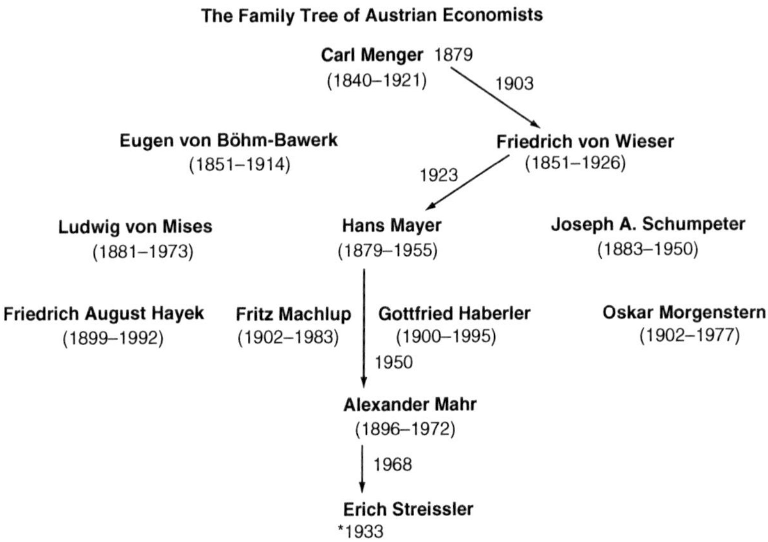

the role of time in economics. The long list of outstanding international economists among the contributors includes Aftalion, Fanno, Frisch, Knight, Lange, Marget, Myrdal, Ohlin, Tinbergen, Zeuthen and many others. A particularly interesting case is Hicks's article (1933) 'Gleichgewicht und Konjunktur' in which the author, who was a young lecturer at the L.S.E. when Hayek arrived in 1931, grappled with the latter's *Prices and Production* and Hayek's concept of inter-temporal equilibrium. Against the background of modern equilibrium theories of the business cycle inspired by Lucas, it wasn't until 1980 that Hicks's article was retranslated into English and published in an American journal. No

German-language journal in economics after the Second World War ever became as important as the *Zeitschrift für Nationalökonomie* had been in the 1930s.

2. Some important contributions of Austrian economics in the interwar period

2.1. Monetary theory

Since Menger's article 'On the Origin of Money' (Menger 1892) and his contribution on 'Money' to the *Handwörterbuch der Staatswissenschaften* monetary theory had been a major subject of Austrian economics.[5] Ludwig von Mises's *Theory of Money and Credit* may be regarded as a typical outcome of the ideas of the Austrian School. Major sources of inspiration were

- Böhm-Bawerk's conception of the production sphere of the economy as a sequence of stages of production in which original inputs are transformed into a single output of consumable commodities, and where capital goods only appear as intermediate products or 'working capital';
- Wicksell's path-breaking distinction between the natural and the money rate of interest charged by the banks; and
- a view of the operation of banking which was strongly shaped by the insights of Lord Overstone and other members of the British Currency School into the circulation of (even convertible) bank-notes and credit.

Against the background of the hyperinflationary processes in Austria and Germany after the end of the First World War Mises made important revisions in the second edition of the book published in 1924. Whereas in 1912 Mises still had stressed that the primary impulse for a boom does not proceed from excessive credit creation, and located only one of several possible causes for economic fluctuations in the credit sector (see ibid.: 434), he now identified banks as the main culprits responsible for an excessive credit creation by artificially lowering the rate of interest on loans below the natural rate, thereby inducing a period of unsustainable expansion. The inevitable consequence of such a credit-induced boom is a bust. It is a central element of Mises's, and later Hayek's, monetary theory of business cycles that the banking system grants a volume of credit which transcends the level of voluntary savings in the economy, thereby causing a misallocation of resources. The boom thus contains the seeds of its later correction.

Mises's argument that excessive credit by the banking sector is the decisive cause of cyclical fluctuations is most clearly stated in his *Monetary Stabilization and Cyclical Policy* (1928). The natural rate of interest is that rate which tends towards equilibrium on the market or, what Mises later preferred to call 'the final state of rest'. Any prosperity brought about by the availability of easy credit according to Mises could be logically proved to be an illusory one. The 'mania for lower interest rates' generates a monetary policy which, sooner or later, must necessarily always lead to crisis and depression. Thus the banks, by reducing the money below the natural rate of interest, generate the problem of crisis which inevitably will break out in the moment when the banks stop undercutting the natural rate and change their conduct in discontinuing the issuing of more fiduciary media. This will lead to the liquidation of businesses and enterprises which were misguided by the artificial stimulus of the boom period. Mises saw a remedy against the mania for lower interest rates and excesses of credit creation in the free banking alternative. There bankers would recognize soon that it is in their own interest to restrain the issue of fiduciary media. While not entirely eliminating economic fluctuations, economic crises would be much reduced. Mises (1928) thus became an early advocate of free banking as the alternative to a centralized monopolistic banking system, which some years later became the subject of investigation in the doctoral dissertation of Vera Smith (1936) written under the supervision of Hayek at the LSE.

The main reason that Hayek received the Bank of Sweden Prize in Economic Sciences in Memory of Alfred Nobel in 1974 was his pioneering work in the theory of money and economic fluctuations – besides the penetrating analysis of the interdependence of economic, social and institutional phenomena. Hayek shared the Nobel Prize with Gunnar Myrdal who had published the German version of his path-breaking analysis *Monetary Equilibrium* in the volume *Beiträge zur Geldtheorie* (1933) edited by Hayek.

2.2. Business-cycle theory

Some of the most outstanding contributions to business-cycle theory in the interwar period were written by Austrian economists. Haberler's *Prosperity and Depression* has already been mentioned. In 1926 Schumpeter had published the second revised edition of his opus magnum *The Theory of Economic Development* in which innovations, entrepreneurs and credit constitute the three decisive elements. All three main ideas existed already in the German and Austrian literature, but Schumpeter combined the three themes in an innovative way and gave a novel twist to these arguments. In Schumpeter's view not only the final chapter but in fact any single page of his *Theory of Economic Development* deals with the business-cycle problem, and analyzing business cycles 'means neither more nor less than analyzing the economic process of the capitalist era' (Schumpeter, 1939: V). Schumpeter contributed a series of articles to leading international journals in the interwar period and marked the end of an era with the publication of his monumental study *Business Cycles* (ibid.).

However, the trademark for an *Austrian* business-cycle theory was set by Hayek, in particular his Vienna habilitation thesis *Monetary Theory and the Trade Cycle* and the subsequent *Prices and Production*. In his business-cycle theory Hayek combined five key elements already existing in an innovative way:

(1) Böhm-Bawerk's theory of capital with its emphasis on the time structure of the production process.
(2) Wicksell's theory of the cumulative process where price changes are caused by the discrepancy between the market rate and the natural (equilibrium) rate of interest.
(3) Mises's theory of money and credit in which banks artificially lowering the money (market) rate of interest are responsible for overinvestment and a misallocation of resources which necessarily has to be corrected.
(4) Cantillon effects of changes in the money supply on the price structure and hence on the structure of production (non-neutrality of money).
(5) 'Ricardo' effects of a shortage of consumption goods on the production of investment goods (disproportionality).

It is important to notice that *Monetary Theory and the Trade Cycle* was published in German as early as 1929, two years before the *Prices and Production* lectures were given at the London School of Economics. The historical order matters for two reasons. First, there were important differences in the theoretical traditions in Britain and in the German language area at the time. Whereas Hayek in his German writings was fighting to establish that changes in money and credit were attached importance in the context of business-cycle theory, in his English lectures and publications he was distancing himself from monetary explanations of cyclical fluctuations which only emphasized changes in the *absolute* level of prices instead of changes in the structure of production that arise as a consequence of a distortion in the structure of *relative* prices due to excessive credit creation, that is, because the price system communicates false information about consumer preferences and resource availability. Second, with regard to the role of technical progress, we find a significant change in Hayek's writings over time. In *Monetary Theory and the Trade Cycle*, Hayek supported Wicksell's argument that monetary expansion is frequently induced by changes in the 'capital rate', that is, from improvements in profit expectations. Hayek (1933: 191–2) mentioned that technical progress was a major factor behind such changes. Thus he recognized the importance of technical progress as part of the impulses and implicitly also of the propagation mechanism for cyclical fluctuations. In later writings he paid little attention, if any, to technical progress. Apparently he did not want to modify his insistence on the inevitability of crisis and the return to the original equilibrium position. However, reducing the Ricardo effect to a choice of technique problem required a switch in the assumptions about the cause of monetary expansion, from technological change to an autonomous lowering of interest rates. Thus Hayek refers to Mises's villains in the piece: the banks which arbitrarily lower the money rate of interest. However, although his business-cycle theory is a monetary overinvestment theory, the distinctive line of Hayek's argument can be characterized as a combination of the Cantillon effect of monetary expansion on the price structure and the Ricardo effect of a shortage of consumption goods on the production of investment goods which also serves the function of restoring equilibrium.[6]

In contrast to his two compatriots Hayek and Mises, who were adherents of the orthodox doctrine that only voluntary savings can create sustainable capital and held the view that the granting of a credit volume by the banking system which transcends the amount of voluntary savings inevitably leads to a crisis in which the reallocation of resources to excessively roundabout methods of production during the credit-induced boom is corrected, in Schumpeter's view the creation of money and credit is an essential condition for the financing of innovational activities and thus development in competitive capitalism. Schumpeter made it very clear that for him the spending of credit for innovative investments is decisive, not for increased consumption. The quality of new purchasing power generated by a credit volume exceeding the amount of money saved in the economy is, however, supported and limited not by *existing* goods but by *future* goods.[7] Since Schumpeter also emphasized that the role of the credit system is not a very active but a rather passive one, because it adapts itself to the changing demands coming from entrepreneurs, he may be regarded as a 'horizontalist'.

2.3. The socialist economic calculation debate

A key topic of Austrian economists in the interwar period was the question of how socialist planners might grapple with the allocative problems of a complex society. The question had already been discussed by several economists at the turn of the century, and Barone (1908) had made an important contribution in which – by avoiding all mention of utility and the concept of indifference curves – he had established the formal equivalence of the basic economic concepts between a socialist society and a capitalist society with private property and perfect competition. It was Ludwig von Mises (1920) who in a famous paper developed the thesis that economic calculation in a socialist commonwealth is impossible because there is no price formation on free markets, and therewith launched the socialist calculation debate in the German-language area in the 1920s, which found its sequel in Britain in the 1930s when Hayek became involved in a controversial debate with Lange, Lerner and Dickinson. The intensity of the controversial debates can only be explained against the historical background of the dominance of planning elements in the war economies, the bolshevist revolution in Russia in 1917, and the foundation of socialization committees in Austria and Germany at the end of the war. Besides Joseph Schumpeter and Emil Lederer, the Austromarxists Otto Bauer, Rudolf Hilferding and Otto Neurath had been prominent fellow students of Mises in Böhm-Bawerk's seminar at the University of Vienna in 1905. Lederer became scientific director of the Austrian Socialization commission which was chaired by Otto Bauer and, together with Hilferding, also a member of the German Socialization Commission where they were joined by Schumpeter for the short period from January to March 1919 when the latter had to resign due to his appointment as Austrian minister of finance.

As Streissler (1994) has emphasized, with Mises's contributions the socialization debate shifted from restrictions to questions of the incentive compatibility to the human reason side of socialism, culminating in Hayek's writings on information and knowledge.[8] However, it should be pointed out, that Mises only fully developed his essential argument that the economy is in a process of permanent change and that therefore the data necessary for efficient planning are not available, in the second

1932 edition of his book on socialism (*Gemeinwirtschaft* 1922), in which he sharpened his thesis not least because of the critique which had been raised against his views by Jacob Marschak, Karl Polányi and others. All the more so this holds for Hayek's important writings since 1935 in which he developed the argument on the dispersion of knowledge and the problem of decision making with uncertainty and incomplete information (see Hayek, 1935, 1937, 1940, 1945).

2.4. Capital theory/the role of time in economics

According to Machlup (1982) the essential components of Austrian economics consist of

(1) methodological individualism
(2) methodological subjectivism
(3) tastes and preferences
(4) the concept of opportunity costs
(5) marginalism
(6) time structure of production.[9]

The last element is particularly relevant for questions of capital theory, which in its Austrian form, first discussed by Menger, had been mainly shaped by Böhm-Bawerk. The Austrian theory of capital and Böhm-Bawerk's concept of the average period of production played a significant role in the famous 'triangle chapter' of Hayek's *Prices and Production*. However, the 1930s were characterized by a capital controversy which was as fierce as the later Cambridge-Cambridge controversy in the 1960s. A key axis of the capital debate in the 1930s was the Hayek-Knight controversy (Cohen, 2003). It was Oskar Morgenstern in particular who gave contributions on capital theory and the role of time in economics, to which his friend Paul Rosenstein-Rodan[10] (1930) had already made an important contribution in the very first issue, prominent space in the *Zeitschrift für Nationalökonomie*. Morgenstern himself also published an important paper in which he contributed to the critique of the average period of production (Morgenstern, 1935a), a concept which Hayek finally gave up in his *Pure Theory of Capital* (1941), a project into which Hayek had embarked in 1934 to defend the core of Austrian capital theory against Knight and other critics. His adoption of the notion of a multidimensional heterogeneous capital structure left the readers puzzled over the remains of an Austrian theory of capital.

2.5. The theory of international trade

Haberler's work in international economics in the interwar period has been often and rightly celebrated for brilliant theoretical innovations.[11] Undoubtedly, his most important theoretical contribution was the reformulation of Ricardo's theory of comparative costs in his article 'The Theory of Comparative Costs and its Use in the Defence of Free Trade' (Haberler, 1930), in which he introduced the 'production substitution curve', today's production-possibility frontier or transformation curve, allowing for several factors of production. Haberler's contribution revolutionized the theory of international trade and paved the way for the subsequent work of Ohlin, Samuelson and others. In his later textbook *The Theory of International Trade* (1933) Haberler made full use of his new concepts and, moreover, integrated real and monetary aspects of international economics, also employing supply and demand functions in the analysis of currency markets. He also integrated international aspects into his theory of economic fluctuations. In this respect the chapter on the international aspects of business cycles in *Prosperity and Depression* has to be regarded as a highly innovative contribution. Haberler's discussion of how the degree of capital mobility and the exchange rate system influence the international transmission of business cycles is particularly noteworthy.

2.6. Game theory

Another challenging new area was game theory, for which the basis was shaped by the joint work of Oskar Morgenstern and John von Neumann culminating in their *Theory of Games and Economic Behavior* (1944). The roots of game theory can be traced back to Morgenstern's Vienna habilitation thesis on economic forecasting (Morgenstern, 1928), which had been written while Morgenstern was a Rockefeller Foundation Fellow in the USA 1926–1927, and to his 1935 article on 'Perfect Foresight and Economic Equilibrium'. In these writings Morgenstern emphasized the incompatibility of perfect foresight and economic equilibrium. Morgenstern had early on recognized that in the great majority of human actions the decision maker faces one or more other decision makers who can either cooperate with him, compete with him or confront him. In contrast to 'dead variables', which do not reflect the actions by other individuals, the 'live variables' do, so that the decision maker is not in full control of all the factors that affect the outcome. Morgenstern (1928, 1935b) discussed already the famous Sherlock Holmes-Moriarty case of interacting decision makers which can be considered the first example of a two-person zero-sum game with no saddle point in pure strategies, and which has proved seminal for later analyses of optimal decision making.

Morgenstern had been an early activist in the 'Vienna Circle', a group of outstanding intellectuals led by the philosopher Moritz Schlick. There he developed a close friendship with the mathematician Karl Menger and the logician Kurt Gödel. He also gave a job to the mathematician Abraham Wald at the Business Cycle Institute. Morgenstern became aware that the problems raised by him in the analysis of interacting decision makers resembled those treated by John von Neumann in the latter's 'Theory of Games of Strategy' (1928). The Budapest-born mathematician von Neumann had studied in Berlin, Göttingen (with Hilbert) and Zurich (with Weyl and Polya) since 1921, had become Privatdozent in Berlin in 1927 from where he went to Hamburg in 1929 and permanently moved to Princeton (where he had been active since he first was invited in 1930) only after the Nazis' rise to power. Although von Neumann and Morgenstern had developed a mutual interest in their works, and the former presented a paper on the general economic equilibrium of an expanding economy in the mathematical colloquium of Karl Menger at the University of Vienna in 1936 (when Morgenstern could not be present), the long sought-after cooperation between the two could only occur in an intensive form at the Institute for Advanced Study in Princeton in the years 1939–1943.[12]

2.7. General equilibrium theory

The most important works by Austrian scholars for the long-term development of economics were Morgenstern and von Neumann's laying the foundations of game theory and several important contributions presented in the Mathematical Colloquium of Karl Menger (1902–1985) in Vienna in the 1930s. It was the Hungarian-born banker Karl Schlesinger, who committed suicide on the day of the Anschluss 13 March 1938, who gave a seminar 'On the Production Equations of Economic Value Theory' in March 1934, in which he discussed the question of a general, positive and unique solution of a general equilibrium system. He stimulated his friend Abraham Wald to give the first consistent proof for the existence of a general equilibrium for a stationary economy a year later. It was then John von Neumann who in 1936 in Menger's Vienna Colloquium expanded the proof for the general case of a growing economy.[13] Von Neumann's paper (1937/45), which laid the foundations for multisectoral linear models, however, had been conceptualized already in 1932 in Princeton and cannot be placed into the Walrasian tradition.

Considering most Austrian economists' neglect of and often hostility towards mathematical methods, it is not without a certain irony that the two areas of game theory and general equilibrium theory are highly mathematical and that Carl Menger's son Karl played a major role in the latter field.

3. Conclusion

Austrian economics in the interwar period was certainly wrestling with capital and time, equilibrium and business cycles as well as the possibilities and limitations of economic socialism. The preceding short survey of important contributions of Austrian economics in the interwar period has shown that Boehm (1992: 1) was right in his assessment that 'interwar Austrian economic thought is a venture of many dimensions that does not easily lend itself to a reduction to some invariable standard. The label "Austrian economics" is merely a shorthand expression for what is, in fact, an ill-defined body of ideas with many facets'. Boehm also pointed out 'that in the 1930s Austrian economics [...] suffered from a series of blows it proved rather difficult to recover from [...], notably in the Hayek–Sraffa exchange, the capital controversies, and the debates with the Keynesians' (ibid.: 3), an assessment which is heavily strengthened by Mark Blaug in his commentary.

Whereas judgments on the socialist economic calculation debate may differ between the majority of modern economists and many contemporary economists in the 1920s and 1930s, Haberler's work on international trade theory, Morgenstern's contribution to game theory and the contributions to modern general equilibrium theory presented in Karl Menger's *Mathematisches Kolloquium* certainly had a major impact on the long-term development of economics. However, for the greatest part they lie outside the scope of the research programme of contemporary Austrian economics in North America.

Notes

1. For a sequence of the 'Menger chair', which until recently was held by Erich Streissler, see the family tree of Austrian economists. The chair had been newly founded in 1763 when Joseph von Sonnenfels was appointed professor of police and cameralistic sciences. Menger received this chair in political economy in 1879.
2. See Craver (1986) and Milford and Rosner (1997) on the appointment policy and for an assessment of the contributions by Degenfeld-Schonburg, Mayer and Spann.

3. See the three-volume collection edited by Stephen Littlechild (1990) for a good overview on the contributions by a new generation of modern 'Austrians' coming out of this school, who reject much of mainstream economics including general equilibrium theory, mathematical economics and econometrics.
4. For greater details see Hagemann (1991).
5. For a modern assessment of Menger's contribution on money in the history of economic thought see Streissler (2002).
6. For a detailed analysis of the Cantillon and Ricardo effects in Hayek's business-cycle theory see Hagemann and Trautwein (1998).
7. See Schumpeter (1926: 165).
8. On Hayek see also Caldwell (2004).
9. From the perspective of late twentieth-century Austrian economics Kirzner (1994, I: XIX) criticizes Machlup for the absence of emphasis on markets and competition as *processes* of learning and discovering in an environment of Knightian uncertainty.
10. Rosenstein-Rodan (1902–1985), who later in Britain in the early 1940s became one of the founders of Development Economics, in 1927 had already written a brilliant article on 'Marginal Utility' which surveyed the key arguments pro and con.
11. See, for example, Baldwin (1982) and Samuelson (1996).
12. For a detailed analysis of the cooperation between Morgenstern and von Neumann see Morgenstern's own reflections (1976) and Leonard (1995).
13. For a full documentation and modern assessment of the influence on economic theory of Karl Menger's 'Mathematisches Kolloquium', held at the university of Vienna from 1928 to 1936, see K. Menger (1998).

References

Baldwin, R. E. (1982) 'Gottfried Haberler's Contributions to International Trade Theory and Policy', *Quarterly Journal of Economics*, 97(1): 141–59.

Barone, E. (1908) 'Il Ministro della Produzione nello Stato Collettivista', *Giornale degli Economisti*; English translation as 'The Ministry of Production in the Collectivist State', in Hayek (ed.) (1935).

Blaug, M. (1992) Commentary to Boehm (1992).

Boehm, S. (1992) 'Austrian Economics Between the Wars: Some Historiographical Problems', in B. J. Caldwell and S. Boehm (eds), *Austrian Economics: Tensions and New Directions*, Dordrecht and Norwell, MA: Kluwer, Academic Publishers.

Caldwell, B. (2004) *Hayek's Challenge: An Intellectual Biography of F.A. Hayek*, Chicago & London: The University of Chicago Press.

Cohen, A. J. (2003) 'The Hayek/Knight Capital Controversy: The Irrelevance of Roundaboutness, or Purging Processes in Time?', *History of Political Economy*, 35(3): 469–90.

Craver, E. (1986) 'The Emigration of the Austrian Economists', *History of Political Economy*, 18(1): 1–32.

Haberler, G. (1930) 'Die Theorie der komparativen Kosten und ihre Auswertung für die Begründung des Freihandels', *Weltwirtschaftliches Archiv*, 32(2): 349–70; English translation as 'The Theory of Comparative Costs and its Use in the

Defense of Free Trade', in A. Y. C. Koo (ed.), *Selected Essays of Gottfried Haberler*, Cambridge, MA: MIT Press, 1985.

Haberler, G. (1933) *Der internationale Handel*, Berlin: Julius Springer; revised English translation as *The Theory of International Trade with its Applications to Commercial Policy*, London: William Hodge & Co, 1936.

Haberler, G. (1937) *Prosperity and Depression*, Geneva: League of Nations.

Hagemann, H. (1991) 'Learned Journals and the Professionalization of Economics: The German Language Area', *Economic Notes*, 20(1): 33–57.

Hagemann, H. and Krohn, C. D. (eds) (1999) *Biographisches Handbuch der deutschsprachigen wirtschaftswissenschaftlichen Emigration nach 1933*, 2 vols, Munich: K. G. Saur.

Hagemann, H. and Trautwein, H. M. (1998) 'Cantillon and Ricardo Effects: Hayek's Contributions to Business Cycle Theory', *The European Journal of the History of Economic Thought*, 5(2): 292–316.

Hayek, F. A. (1929) *Geldtheorie und Konjunkturtheorie*, Vienna: Hölder-Pichler-Tempski; English translation as *Monetary Theory and the Trade Cycle*, London: J. Cape, 1933.

Hayek, F. A. (1931) *Prices and Production*, 2nd edition, 1935, London: Routledge & Kegan Paul.

Hayek, F. A. (ed.) (1933) *Beiträge zur Geldtheorie*, Vienna: Springer.

Hayek, F. A. (ed.) (1935) *Collectivist Economic Planning: Critical Studies on the Possibilities of Socialism*, London: Routledge.

Hayek, F. A. (1937) 'Economics and Knowledge', *Economica*, N.S. 4(1): 33–54.

Hayek, F. A. (1940) 'Socialist Calculation: The Competitive Solution', *Economica*, 7(26): 125–49.

Hayek, F. A. (1941) *The Pure Theory of Capital*, London: Routledge & Kegan Paul.

Hayek, F. A. (1945) 'The Use of Knowledge in Society', *American Economic Review*, 35(4): 519–30.

Hicks, J. (1933) 'Gleichgewicht und Konjunktur', *Zeitschrift für Nationalökonomie*, 4(4): 441–55; English translation 'Equilibrium and the Trade Cycle', *Economic Inquiry*, 18(4), 1980: 523–34.

Kirzner, I. M. (ed.) (1994), *Classics in Austrian Economics: A Sampling in the History of a Tradition*, 3 vols, London: Pickering & Chatto.

Leonard, R. J. (1995) 'From Parlor Games to Social Science: von Neumann, Morgenstern, and the Creation of Game Theory, 1928–1944', *Journal of Economic Literature*, 33(2): 730–61.

Littlechild, S. (ed.) (1990) *Austrian Economics*, Schools of Thought in Economics X, 3 vols, Aldershot: Edward Elgar.

Machlup, F. (1982), 'Austrian Economics', in D. Greenwald (ed.), *Encyclopedia of Economics*, New York: McGraw-Hill.

Menger, C. (1892) 'On the Origin of Money', *Economic Journal*, 2(June): 239–55.

Menger, K. (1998) *Ergebnisse eines Mathematischen Kolloquiums*, edited by E. Dierker and K. Sigmund, with a Foreword by G. Debreu and an Afterword by F. Alt, Vienna and New York: Springer.

Milford, K. and Rosner, P. (1997) 'Die Abkoppelung der Ökonomie an der Universität Wien nach 1920', in H. Hagemann (ed.), *Zur deutschsprachigen wirtschaftswissenschaftlichen Emigration nach 1933*, Marburg: Metropolis: 479–502.

Mises, L. von (1912) *Theorie des Geldes und der Umlaufsmittel*, Munich and Leipzig: Duncker & Humblot; 2nd edition 1924; English translation as *The Theory of Money and Credit*, London: Jonathan Cape, 1934.

Mises, L. von (1920) 'Die Wirtschaftsrechnung im sozialistischen Gemeinwesen', *Archiv für Sozialwissenschaft und Sozialpolitik*, 47(1): 86–121; English translation as 'Economic calculation in the socialist commonwealth', in Hayek (ed.) (1935).

Mises, L. von (1922) *Die Gemeinwirtschaft. Untersuchungen über den Sozialismus*, 2nd edition, 1932, Jena: Gustav Fischer; English translation as *Socialism: An Economic and Sociological Analysis*, London: Jonathan Cape, 1936.

Mises, L. von (1928) *Geldwertstabilisierung und Konjunkturpolitik*, Jena: Gustav Fischer; English translation as 'Monetary Stabilization and Cyclical Policy', in P. L. Greaves (ed.), *Mises on the Manipulation of Money and Credit*, Dobbs Ferry, NY: Free Market Books, 1978: 57–107.

Morgenstern, O. (1928) *Wirtschaftsprognose. Eine Untersuchung ihrer Voraussetzungen und Möglichkeiten*, Vienna: Julius Springer.

Morgenstern, O. (1935a) 'Zur Theorie der Produktionsperiode', *Zeitschrift für Nationalökonomie*, 6(2): 196–208.

Morgenstern, O. (1935b) 'Vollkommene Voraussicht und wirtschaftliches Gleichgewicht', *Zeitschrift für Nationalökonomie*, 6(3): 337–57; English translation as 'Perfect Foresight and Economic Equilibrium' in A. Schotter (ed.), *Selected Economic Writings of Oskar Morgenstern*, New York: NYU Press, 1976: 169–83.

Morgenstern, O. (1976) 'The Collaboration of Oskar Morgenstern and John von Neumann on the Theory of Games', *Journal of Economic Literature*, 14(3): 805–16.

Neumann, J. von (1928) 'Zur Theorie der Gesellschaftsspiele', *Mathematische Annalen*, 100: 295–320; English translation as 'On the Theory of Games of Strategy', in A. W. Tucker and R. D. Luce (eds), *Contributions to the Theory of Games. Vol. 4*, Princeton: Princeton University Press, 1959: 13–42.

Neumann, J. von (1936) 'Über ein ökonomisches Gleichungssystem und eine Verallgemeinerung des Brouwerschen Fixpunktsatzes', in K. Menger (1998), 8: 73–83; English translation as 'A Model of General Economic Equilibrium', *Review of Economic Studies*, 13(1), 1945: 1–9.

Neumann, J. von and Morgenstern, O. (1944) *Theory of Games and Economic Behavior*, Princeton: Princeton University Press.

Rosenstein-Rodan, P. N. (1927) 'Grenznutzen', in *Handwörterbuch der Staatswissenschaften* IV, Jena: 1190–223; English translation as 'Marginal Utility', *International Economic Papers*, 10(1), 1960: 71–106.

Rosenstein-Rodan, P. N. (1930) 'Das Zeitmoment in der mathematischen Theorie des wirtschaftlichen Gleichgewichts', *Zeitschrift für Nationalökonomie*, 1(1): 129–42; English translation as 'The Role of Time in Economic Theory', *Economica*, N.S. 1(1): 77–97.

Samuelson, P. A. (1996) 'Gottfried Haberler (1900–1995)', *The Economic Journal*, 106(439): 1679–87.

Schumpeter, J. A. (1911) *Theorie der wirtschaftlichen Entwicklung*, Munich and Leipzig: Duncker & Humblot; 2nd edition, 1926; English translation as *The Theory of Economic Development*, Cambridge, MA: Harvard University Press, 1934.

Schumpeter, J. A. (1939) *Business Cycles. A Theoretical, Historical and Statistical Analsyis of the Capitalist Process*, 2 vols, New York: McGraw-Hill.
Smith, V. C. (1936) *The Rationale of Central Banking and the Free Banking Alternative*, reprinted with a Preface by L. B. Yeager, Indianapolis: Liberty Fund, 1990.
Streissler, E. W. (1994) 'Hayek on Information and Socialism', in M. Colonna, H. Hagemann and O. F. Hamouda (eds), *Capitalism, Socialism and Knowledge: The Economics of F.A. Hayek. Vol. II*, Aldershot: Edward Elgar: 47–75.
Streissler, E.W. (2002) 'Carl Menger's Article "Money" in the History of Economic Thought', in M. Latzer and S. W. Schmitz (eds), *Carl Menger and the Evolution of Payment Systems: From Barter to Electronic Money,* Cheltenham: Edward Elgar.

10
Ludwig von Mises's Business Cycle Theory: Static Tools for Dynamic Analysis

Arash Molavi Vasséi

> In the thirty-one years which have passed since the first edition of my *Theory of Money and Credit* was published no tenable argument has been raised against the validity of what is commonly called the 'Austrian' theory of the credit cycle.
>
> – Mises, 1943: 251

1. Introduction

This article discusses Ludwig von Mises's attempt to frame his business cycle analysis by an essentially stationary apparatus. It pays special attention to his choice to take sides with Frank Fetter ([1902] 1997) and his theory of interest and highlights some unpleasant consequences for his study of monetary dynamics. The article provides a simple model to depict and clarify Mises's major shortcomings in real analysis. It is shown that in *Human Action*, his magnum opus first published in 1949, Mises has fallen far behind the frontiers of economic analysis, including major contributions of economists within or close to the Austrian tradition, like F.A. Hayek and Knut Wicksell.

Of course, problems associated with the immense task of integrating money into real accumulation processes are numerous. Neither Mises's contemporaries, nor modern economists, have found satisfactory solutions. The particular significance of Mises's idiosyncratic framework is due to the fact that his major prediction – any money-induced traverse necessarily reverses – ultimately depends on his barren analytical device. This prediction proves little robust in the light of even small variations of the underlying framework.

Section 2 introduces the problem, starting with Böhm-Bawerk's initial exposition of the theory of interest. Section 3 provides a simple model of Mises's peculiar outline. Section 4 analyses the traverse as a genuine disequilibrium phenomena and the role of forced saving therein. Section 5 discusses Mises's business cycle theory. Section 6 concludes.

2. The problem

Mises's difficulty with economic dynamics roots deep, going way back to Böhm-Bawerk's original exposition of his theory of interest. There, Böhm-Bawerk poses the question of why there is interest at all, of why capital earns an 'excess value' arising from 'the fact that the sum of the products created with its help is regularly of greater value than the sum of the costs of the goods expended in the course of production' ([1889] 1959: 6). If, in equilibrium, the services of labour and land are paid according to their marginal product, and if capital has no productive power of its own (ibid.: 80), the cost of producing or purchasing capital goods eats up the entire revenue generated by their use. In long-run competitive equilibrium, the value of total product should be accordingly exhausted by outlays to the original factors. Mises retains this perspective ([1949] 1998: 490): the marginal value productivity of capital is introduced as a riddle.

Obviously, this formulation of the interest problem leads attention to stationary states. What Böhm-Bawerk attempts to answer are the questions of why interest is not annihilated by the accumulation of capital, why the marginal utilities of present and future consumption are not thereby equalized, and thus, why the return on capital is positive even after the stock of capital has reached its long-run equilibrium level.

To answer the enigma of interest, Böhm-Bawerk introduces three causes for positive interest. The first cause is the 'difference between the relation of supply and demand as it exists at one point in time and that relation as it exists at another point in time' (Böhm-Bawerk, [1889] 1959: 265–6). Thus, interest is due to relative physical scarcities. Relatively abundant future goods suffer a discount, or relatively scarce present goods earn a premium. As Fisher ([1907] 1997) points out, only Böhm-Bawerk's second reason – the 'fact' that 'we systematically undervalue our future wants and also the means which serve to satisfy them' ([1889] 1959: 268) – is able to account for a positive rate of return on capital in stationarity, putting a break upon the accumulation process before capital's value product, the third cause, vanishes. Böhm-Bawerk believes that the first two causes 'work cumulatively', independent of the third (ibid.: 283–4). Also for Mises, determination and causation are analytically separate concepts.

After a first but unsuccessful attempt in 1927, Hayek attacks the Böhm-Bawerkian formulation of intertemporal choice in 'Utility Theory and Interest', published in 1936. Hayek attributes the 'confusion' characterizing the subsequent controversies about the proper relationship between Böhm-Bawerk's three ingredients, especially the relation between subjective and objective data, to the original formulation of the problem. The 'pseudo-problem' of a positive net return on capital in equilibrium, so Hayek, roots in the improper conceptualization of intertemporal choice. He criticizes the Böhm-Bawerkian framework for treating the utility function as primitive by resorting to the comparison of absolute marginal utilities (Hayek, 1936: 48). Marginal utilities are not simultaneously determined by subjective and objective data, including, besides preferences, the state of technology and the levels and structure of endowment (ibid.: 44–5).

Also in Mises's outline, marginal utilities are purely intrinsic phenomena disentangled from objective data. They are introduced independent of relative physical scarcities and are as such given data to the economic system. Indeed, even though Mises categorizes action as a choice among alternative means to a variety of ends, scarcity is introduced as an absolute. It is because any quantity of a given good 'can only produce a limited effect, some things are considered scarce and treated as means' (Mises, [1949] 1998: 120). Mises's ordinal measure of this 'limited effect', his utility function, is negative. He refers to 'felt uneasiness', which is to be minimized.

> Utility means in this context simply this: causal relevance for the removal of felt uneasiness.
>
> (Ibid.: 120)

The term 'causal' is meant to exclude simultaneous determination. Marginal utilities are disproportionally attached to 'the various portions of a supply of homogenous means (diminishing marginal utility). *Each portion is valued separately*' (ibid.: italics mine). Small quantities of any given stock satisfy the most important pleasures or reduce the most unbearable pain. High quantities can additionally satisfy less urgent ends or reduce more tolerable disutility.

This, of course, affects the conceptualization of general equilibrium. Prices coordinate the excess demand relations of consumers. In an exchange economy, each consumer's excess demand relation is directly derived from the primitive utility function. Single prices are thus independent of each other, and relative prices therefore also primitive. The only mechanism needed is the law of one price. Thus, market process theory is treated as a substitute for general equilibrium analysis. This is also true for Mises's treatment of intertemporal preferences. Indeed, it is exactly here where we find the very hawkish prediction of his business cycle theory: time preference as a primitive, directly determining optimal intertemporal allocation independent of any other economic data, is responsible for his overemphasis on consumer sovereignty and mean-reversion.

Hayek's critique highlights the consequences of such utility analysis for Böhm-Bawerk's theory of intertemporal choice, especially given the choice to assume total consumption over time to be homogenous. Thus, according to the underlying utility framework, intertemporal exchange is reduced to analysis of the law of one price. At zero rate of time preference, general equilibrium is restored on a single market for a given total quantity of homogenous supply. Because physically identical commodities at different dates are treated as perfect substitutes, the equilibrium condition is fulfilled at equal *absolute* marginal utilities of present and future consumption for each date, indicating stationary equilibrium consumption at constant prices (Hayek, 1936: 44–8).

Mises theory of interest attempts to provide reason for the fact that the law of one price fails to establish a single price and resumes to Böhm-Bawerk's second cause. The relative intertemporal price, the rate of interest, is directly imposed by the rate of time preference, the exogenous subjective rate of discount on future consumption. The 'originary' rate of interest is thus a pure value phenomenon, independent of the level and growth rate of consumption, identical with the prevailing rate of time preference. Objective data is unable to alter intertemporal equilibrium allocation. Whatever the supply of total consumption, and whatever its initial distribution in time, the long-run equilibrium allocation is unidirectionally determined by an unexplained rate of time preference.

In stationarity, Böhm-Bawerk's first cause of interest is absent. Right because its sign is contingent on the data of the system, Mises dismisses the rate of time preference due to changing future consumption (1940: 442–4). Instead the second source, the systematic undervaluation of future consumption, is introduced as a categorical aspect of human action so that 'the very act of gratifying a desire implies the gratification at the present instant is preferred to that at a later instant' (Mises, [1949] 1998: 481). Thus, Mises superimposes the intertemporal preference relation. In fact, however, the dominant role of a positive rate of time preference is an embarrassment to Mises's analysis (Hayek, [1927] 1984: 55). In marginalist analysis it is illegitimate to presume that agents categorically discount future consumption at a constant rate whatever other primitives are, as it is illegitimate to assume ad hoc that agents always prefer apples to bananas, independent of other data. As Hayek points out:

> The fact is that the assumption of identical utility curves at all successive moments states not merely the general postulate that the choice between present and future will be made in the *same* way at different moments, but implies beyond that that the choice will be made in a *particular* way. [...] It is impossible to decide on a priori grounds what the actual attitude of the person in any given position will be.
>
> (1936: 48, 51; his italics)

Ironically, Hayek's decisive innovation of dated commodities ([1928] 1984: 73) – brought to general attention by John Hicks's *Value and Capital* (1939) and by now standard in Arrow-Debreu-type analysis – is inspired by Mises's treatment of physically identical commodities at different locations as heterogeneous (Mises, [1934] 1980), which also became part of Gerard Debreu's *Theory of Value* (1959).

Growth is thus abandoned from equilibrium theory and analysed within an essentially timeless framework. Here, intertemporal allocation is discussed for a non-dated vertical two-sector model, the investment good sector representing the future. Net saving and net investment are a disequilibrium phenomena guided by pure profits (and losses). Accordingly, Mises introduces the 'evenly rotating economy' (ERE), the infinite perpetuation of a timeless economy under certainty, in which 'today does not differ from yesterday and tomorrow will not differ from today' (Mises, [1949] 1998: 248, Cowen and Fink, 1985). Given stationarity, the systematic rate of discount of future consumption and a given initial level of subsistence fund control the gross ERE-levels of saving and investment. The subsistence fund determines the feasible set of techniques, together forming a long-run aggregate production function pointing to different feasible ERE's (if the subsistence fund is empty, nature provides the feasible set). The net rate of time preference determines the choice between feasible techniques and thus determines the golden long-run consumption level of the economy. Net saving and net investment can then be derived ex-post by subtracting the ERE-level from the initial level of subsistence (Mises, [1949] 1998: 487).

Mises's theory rests on a set of identities. He thus chooses a framework that allows for no more than to compare different stationary equilibria, one for each arbitrarily chosen rate of time preference. Original factors, with the usual emphasis on common labour, are called 'future goods', earning their marginal product defined in terms of present consumption. Mises is explicit: capital earns has no value productivity in ERE. The value productivity of capital has fallen victim to the law of one price.

> [...] it becomes evident that it is absurd to speak of a 'rate of profit' or a 'normal rate of profit' or an 'average rate of profit'. Profit is not related to or dependent on the amount of capital employed by the entrepreneur. Capital does not 'beget' profit. Profit and loss are entirely determined by the success and failure of the entrepreneur to adjust production to the demand of the consumers. There is nothing 'normal' in profits and there can never be an 'equilibrium' with regard to them.
>
> (Ibid.: 295)

Thus, in ERE, all net income is then computed to the non-produced factors. However, since consumption goods are part of the Austrian capital stock (free capital), the income appropriated by original factors first remains in the hand of capitalists. Very close to classical theory, ownership relations are indeed decisive in Mises's theory of distribution.

Interest is indeed introduced as a tax on non-ownership: net income to capital is viewed as a *transfer payment* that non-owners pay to owners of capital (including the total stock of consumption goods) for the *maintenance* of the given level of total net consumption (gross profits are distributed by investors). Since maintenance means 'food and shelter' for original factors during the average period of production, owners with positive time preference are categorically biased to consume the real savings necessary to sustain the even provision of services over time. Indeed, the entire initial subsistence fund is in danger. At zero interest, yet positive time preference, capitalists eat up the maintenance fund, each time consumption goods mature until the entire fund has successively depleted. To induce them not to do so, non-owners earn discounted wages at a rate given by the rate of time preference. At zero time preference, all gross income is distributed for free (ibid.: 481). Given the initial subsistence fund, capitalists' unidirectionally regulate the level of ERE, the bliss level of consumption. In fact, the ERE is a golden-rule economy – at least golden for those with non-productive ownership. All this turns out to be significant for Mises's business cycle theory.

3. The model

Mises takes the size of the subsistence fund, the supply of original factors (here just labour), technological knowledge and the utility function as given. As noted above, Mises's utility function does not monotonically transform some underlying preference preordering, but measures utility directly. Primitives are themselves hierarchical, the utility function dominating all equilibrium outcomes. Utility (U) – the negative of 'felt uneasiness' – is monotone in total consumption (C). The rate of net time preference (ρ) is defined for stationary consumption only, that is, it is a *net* rate of time preference (Böhm-Bawerk second cause). In terms of the Fisher Diagram, by means of which Hayek formulates his critique, the indifference surface is only defined for the bisecting line. Thus, Hayek rightly criticizes the absence of a theory of rational intertemporal choice in the Böhm-Bawerkian framework (1936: 44–5). Measuring the proportional increase in the 'disutility' of waiting for a given level of consumption, the utility function is linear and the net rate of time preference its gradient (Figure 10.1).

The choice dimension, however, is '*more* but later' and thus has a quantity dimension. Unlike in Fisherian theory, however, the future cannot be broken up into sub-periods, allowing for multi-period choices and the consideration of the time shape of income. Compounding is

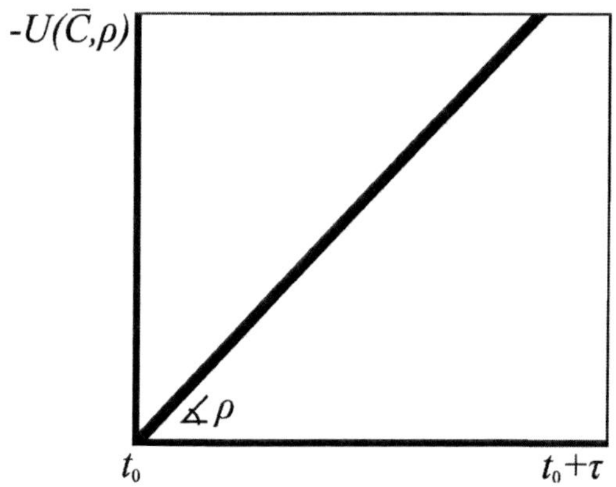

Figure 10.1 Time Preference

dispelled. The future is collapsed into single point in time, being 'later' only in respect to the average period of production (τ), a technological variable. Mises's equilibrium outline sheds no light on the processes during the waiting period. The concavity of Mises's utility function has thus nothing to do with the modern, that is, Fisherian concept. Modern intertemporal utility functions are concave due to the convexity imposed on the preference preordering. Concavity indicates the increasing rate of gross time preference or marginal rate of intertemporal substitution, measuring – in addition to the net rate of time preference – the degree of resistance against postponements, depending on the level and growth rate of consumption (Böhm-Bawerk's first cause of interest as embodied with the second in the Keynes-Ramsey rule).

Mises, in contrast, introduces concavity indirectly, not as a characteristic of intertemporal choice. Indeed, by introducing disutility as an absolute cost, the utility function can only be linear. It is rather the decreasing physical productivity of waiting, a technological parameter, which diminishes the marginal utility of income at higher consumption levels (Figure 10.2): costs increase proportionally with waiting time, but higher levels of consumption come only by more than proportional increases in the average period of production. The subsistence fund, the embodiment of aggregate waiting-capacity, becomes the limiting factor that causes increasing real costs to the lengthening of the average period of production. The choice of the optimal period of production is directly controlled by the utility function for a given subsistence fund,

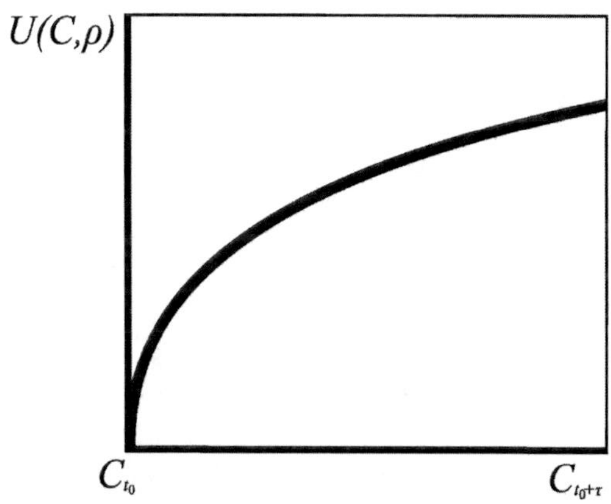

Figure 10.2 Utility Function

inherited from the immediate past. For each level of initial subsistence ($\overline{W}_{t_0}$), Mises defines a utility function ([1949] 1998: 480–99):

$$U: C_{\text{Bliss}} = U(\overline{W}_{t_0}, \rho), \quad 0 < \rho < 1$$

$$C_{\text{Bliss}} = U(\overline{W}_{t_0}, \rho), \quad \frac{dC_{\text{Bliss}}}{d\rho} < 0, \quad \frac{d^2 C_{\text{Bliss}}}{d^2 \rho} > 0,$$

$$\lim_{\rho \to 0} U = -\infty; \quad \lim_{\rho \to \infty} U = 0.$$

Adopting Böhm-Bawerk's aggregate production function, Mises maps the cost-minimizing combination of a non-produced or original factor (labour) and an initial subsistence fund – measured by the average period of production (τ) – to efficient or long-run net output (C):

$$C = f(\tau), \quad \frac{dC}{d\tau} > 0; \quad \frac{d^2 C}{d\tau^2} < 0.$$

The introduction of capital as a subsistence fund is attempted to homogenize and then to aggregate capital as stored-up waiting-capacity (Mises, [1934] 1980: 399, [1949] 1998: 483–4). Measuring aggregate capital as an average period of production, however, reduces the time dimension to a scalar in an essentially timeless framework. To substitute some average waiting time for the volume or value of capital and then to treat it *pari passu* with labour does not turn static analysis dynamic.

The underlying production processes are of a flow input – point output type. Capital goods are goods-in-process, transformed to a lower level intermediary of 'lower' order over time. In stationarity, all stages have to be regarded as being fully vertically integrated production process. Thus, given the perishable nature of capital (working capital), original factors like common labour and 'virgin soil' (Wicksell, [1934] 1977: 145) can appropriate total consumption in the ERE (Bliss, 1975: 173). Mises reacts by rejecting the value productivity of capital ([1949] 1998: 490). He thereby illegitimately generalizes his restrictive model.

A priori, the services and marginal products of the original factors are evenly distributed over time. Single processes are thus linear. Investors (firms) distribute gross profits to control by ownership. The feasible production set for the economy contains blueprints with divergent investment periods. Longer processes require more previously accumulated waiting-time to feed and shelter labour. In comparison, shorter and more productive processes and longer and less productive processes pose no economic problem. The former are always superior; the latter always inferior. The decision problem arises with more productive but longer processes. At margin of choice, we find the longest period of production still feasible given the subsistence fund. As indicated above, varying levels of subsistence fund then derive the production function with diminishing returns. The case of shorter but less productive process is blinded out, since it is related to the saving process and to the speed of transition (Hayek, 1936, [1941] 2007). Long-run or net productivity of labour, and thus the wage rate (w), is a positive function of the average period of production. The sheer number of investment opportunities guarantee continuity.

What makes Mises's model idiosyncratic is the source of interest. Here, he follows Frank Fetter ([1902] 1977) and adopts a 'Pure Time Preference Theory of Interest' (Kirzner). It is based on two-stage reasoning. First, as shown, all net income is assumed to be appropriated by original factors. Then, in a second step, Mises discusses the distribution of this total among owners of capital and original factors. Consumption is distributed between the owners of the means of subsistence (C_P) and non-owners (the wage bill: C_W), who, however, supply a fixed quantity of original factors ($\bar{L}$). Even though Mises computes total consumption to original factors, the saving decision is by the capitalist. Indeed, the capitalist still seems to own the consumption goods in the ERE, to have the privilege to control something that is not his or hers. This obscurity results from the treatment of consumption goods as advances to labour, so as to maintain the chosen bliss level of consumption constant (Wicksell's 'free capital'). Working well within the classical outline, the concept of advanced capital in conjunction with Mises's rejection of positive value productivity of capital is the root cause of Mises's idiosyncratic theory. On the one hand, competition between capitalists is assumed to exhaust net profits, while on the other, it is the capitalist who decides what fraction of total consumption to consume (C_P). The remaining wage bill (C_W) is his or her gross saving (S_g):

$$Y_n \equiv C \equiv C_P + C_W \equiv C_P + S_g$$

The identity is entirely controlled by the owning classes. It is their time preference that is expressed by the fraction of total consumption advanced (Mises, [1949] 1998: 488):

$$\rho = \frac{C_P}{C} = \frac{C - S_g}{C} = 1 - s_g.$$

Accordingly, Mises's reformulation of his apparatus in *Human Action* introduces interest as a tax on non-ownership – a transfer payment – a fact unrecognized by modern Austrian scholars, probably due to Mises's diffused exposition.

Note that with the rate of time preference, the optimality criterion directly enters the equation that determines the actual level of ERE-consumption. The 'originary rate of interest' (r) is introduced as both, a warranted rate and an actual rate. Thus, an identity bridges the gap between preferences and outcomes:

$$r \equiv \rho$$

$$r = \frac{p_{t_0} - p_{t_0+\tau}}{p_{t_0+\tau}} = \frac{p_{t_0}}{p_{t_0+\tau}} - 1 = 1 - s_g.$$

Relative intertemporal prices do not figure as Hayekian knowledge-surrogates, signalling a simultaneous balance between preferences, technology and endowments. Given the supply of labour, the wage rate is just a residual:

$$C \equiv rC + wL$$

$$w \equiv (1 - r)\frac{C}{L} = (1 - r)c$$

$$w = w(r), \quad \frac{dw}{dr} < 0.$$

A change in the rate of net time preference is associated with net saving and treated as a disequilibrium phenomenon outside the reach of disequilibrium analysis (see below).

$$S_g = S_g(\rho), \quad \frac{dS_g}{d\rho} = \frac{S_n}{d\rho} < 0.$$

Mises assumes Say's identity:

$$S_g \equiv I_g; \; S_n \equiv I_n.$$

Investors are passive. The rate of originary interest suffices to determine their choice of technique:

$$\tau = \tau(r), \quad \frac{d\tau}{dr} < 0.$$

Indeed, impressed by all these ex post identities, Mises himself formulates the 'close of his system':

> Originary interest is not a price determined on the market by the interplay of the demand for and the supply of capital or capital goods. Its height does not depend on the extent of this demand and supply. It is rather the rate of originary interest that determines both the demand for and the supply of capital or capital goods.
>
> [...] People do not save and accumulate capital because there is interest. Interest is neither the impetus to saving nor the reward or the compensation granted for abstaining from immediate compensation. It is the ratio in the mutual valuation of present goods as against future goods.
>
> ([1949] 1998: 523–4)

The equilibrium-condition asks for the equality between the actual and the bliss levels of consumption. This is trivial: since economic behaviour is introduced by a set of identities and since each of these identities contains originary interest or time preference as the dominating primitive, ERE exists per definition at all rates of time preference, given the initial stock of subsistence. Q.E.D.

Because of Say's Identity, the choice of technique and actual consumption is determined by the subjective premium on present consumption, the single subjective data that alone provides the optimality condition:

$$C = C(r), \quad \frac{dC}{dr} < 0$$

$$C_{\text{Bliss}} = U(\rho), \quad \frac{dC_{\text{Bliss}}}{d\rho} < 0.$$

Since $\rho \equiv r$,

$$C_{\text{Bliss}} \equiv C.$$

Within the boundaries imposed by time preference, all ERE are by definition utility maximizing. Q.E.D. Ex post identities are turned into ex ante identities. Can anyone imagine a more barren and unpromising starting point for business cycle analysis?

4. The traverse

As shown above, Mises is well aware of the stationary nature of his real analysis. He, however, believes that equilibrium analysis can do no more than this.

> It is [...] preposterous to maintain that the construction of the evenly rotating economy does not elucidate conditions within a changing universe and to require the economists to substitute the study of 'dynamics' for their alleged exclusive occupation with 'statics'. The so-called static method is precisely the proper mental tool for the examination of change.
>
> ([1949] 1998: 248)

Not only business cycle theory, he insists, but any analysis of economic change must be embedded into the framework provided by his 'evenly rotating economy'. Net saving becomes a source of pure profits, per definition unexpected, due to exogenous increase in the average rate of time preference. Mises defines 'net profit' (P_n) as the excess of aggregate pure profits (P) over aggregate losses (L), being positive only if net savings are positive, indicating a change in the rate of time preference ([1949] 1998: 292–3).

$$P_n \equiv P - L \equiv \frac{dS_g}{d\rho} \equiv \frac{I_n}{dr} \equiv \frac{S_n}{dr}$$

All uncertainty usually associated with windfalls, is relegated to the composition of consumption. The level of net profits is always and by necessity equal to the rate of change in the rate of originary interest. Over time, Mises is confident, factors combined in new processes can appropriate more and more of their contribution to long-run equilibrium, until stationarity is finally reached and net saving and thus net profit again disappear. The economy is stable:

> What happens in the short-run is precisely the first stages of the chain of successive transformations which tend to bring about the long-run effects. The long-run effect is in our case the disappearance of entrepreneurial profits and losses. The short-run effects are the preliminary stages of this process of elimination which finally, if not interrupted by a further change in data, would result in the emergence of the evenly rotating economy.
>
> (Mises, [1949] 1998: 294)

Mises, very much in contrast to his Austrian companion Hayek, fails to realize the advantages of general equilibrium theory as a conceptualization of an interdependent, simultaneously determined global system. Also changes in economic data have to be grasped by such interdependence. The decision space is complete only if all primitives do equally matter in determining general equilibrium solutions. A choice-theoretic intertemporal framework is at best incomplete, if it cannot display rational answers to the optimal time shape of income.

Not a 'rational theory of saving', as developed by Wicksell ([1928] 1997) and Hayek (1936) – but the law of supply and demand regulates Mises's traverse from one stationary state to another. Excess demands and price adjustments, of course, do not fit the use of ex ante identities. Mises escapes into monetary analysis and introduces the capital market. Money is a veil, yet weakening the link between time preference and the rest of his system in the case of changes in (circulating) money. But also in the absence of additions to money, net saving becomes an excess supply of capital. Net savings drive down the market rate of interest, so that the market price reflects the underlying primitive during the traverse. The dominant capitalists thereby feed the money-price system with their preferences, signalling a change in the optimal technique.

A lower rate of interest induces an excess demand for labour in higher stages of production, the competition between entrepreneurs driving up the net income of higher-order labour. The excess demand for labour in roundabout process is matched by an excess supply of labour in stages of lower order. Reallocation is driven by the law of one price on the labour market. The rising profit of using labour in lower stages of production reduces the supply of consumption and interrupts processes with below average period of production. More and more labour moves upwards in the vertical chain of production, each time leaving interrupted processes that otherwise would have matured, yet at different points in time depending on their respective maturities. The decrease in the production of consumption goods is initiated by a decrease in the capitalists consumption, the tax on wages falling with the rate of time preference, allowing labour to consume at the initial level over the longer period of production. The price level remains constant until the new processes ripen and total consumption is distributed to the original factors by a falling price level (minus the lower fraction consumed by the capitalist).

The investor's only job is to transform capital and to control the composition or structure of capital, not to control the growth of capital. They are entrepreneurs only with regard to the cost-minimizing combination of heterogeneous inputs, while savers determine the period of production (Mises, [1949] 1998: 555). They rely on the interest rate to reflect such local information. Savers, in turn, lack any detailed technological knowledge related to their choice of technique and therefore depend on the investors' entrepreneurial abilities.

When coming to money's non-neutrality, Mises subscribes to the classical version of forced saving, which emphasizes the impact of disproportional additions to the supply of money on the social rate of net time preference by initiating a redistribution of wealth and income among households with different saving propensities, that is, by Cantillon-effects[1] (Mises, [1934] 1980: 386, [1949] 1998: 545–7), with saving and investment however being always equal. This concept of forced saving must be distinguished from its post-classical version, especially prominent during the interwar period and employed by Hayek ([1931] 1935). This later version of forced saving rests on the existence of macroeconomic disequilibria, of excess aggregate expenditures, and which Keynes accordingly calls 'investment over saving' ([1931] 1978; see also Hayek, 1932: 133). Here, Say's Law is an equilibrium condition.

Very much like the British monetary analysis he admires, Mises's credit market simply allows investing in other people's productive opportunities ([1949] 1998: 543–4).

Mises asserts to be empirically evident what his business cycle theory attempts to prove analytically, namely, 'that "forced savings" [in his sense] can reduce the "natural rate of interest" only fractionally, as compared with the reduction in the "money rate of interest" which produces the "forced savings"' ([1928] 2006: 112) Thus, Mises derives the business cycle from a spread between the money rate of interest and a new, lower equilibrium level of the originary rate, 'indirectly' reduced by a money-induced redistribution of wealth and income. Mises's measure of macroeconomic disequilibria is not a spread between the money rate of interest and the marginal productivity of capital, but the spread between the net rate of time preference and the market rate of interest. If the money rate of interest is lowered below the reduced social rate of time preference, capital gains turn positive and investors aim at income above the warranted level. This gap between the money and the new rate of time preference induces what Mises names the 'direct effect' of credit expansion, which 'at first exerts a stronger influence than the displacement of the social distribution which occurs as a consequence of it' ([1934] 1980: 391).

5. The business cycle theory

The 'Austrian' tradition in business cycle theory begins with Ludwig Mises's *Theorie des Geldes und der Umlaufsmittel* in 1912. It arises from his attempt to integrate British monetary theory into Carl Menger's marginal utility analysis. Always threatened to sink into oblivion, yet unfading, the Austrian Business Cycle Theory originates as an isolated chapter (chapter 19 of the English edition; [1934] 1980). It is a corollary of Mises's more comprehensive endeavour to overcome the classical dichotomy. In the first edition of *Theorie des Geldes*, yet only here, Mises is explicit: 'A theory of business cycles is not the purpose of this study' (1912: 433).

Mises introduces his business cycle theory as a refinement and extension of classical monetary orthodoxy. He adores the Currency School, especially David Ricardo and Samuel J. Loyd (Lord Overstone since 1850) for their analyses of monetary cycles. Triggered by the creation of inconvertible banknotes and checked by the specie-flow mechanism, the classical business cycle allegorizes money's short-run non-neutrality. Correcting for what he considers to be the gravest analytical error of the Currency School – the exclusion of deposits from effective money supply (Mises, 1912: ix) – Mises envisions a world beyond the gold standard, where commercial and central banks can freely manipulate the money supply, unconstrained by the costs of obtaining gold. What mechanism, if any, imposes a check on monetary expansion in a closed or global economy, in the absence of international choice and the threat of external drain? What constrains the creation of credit in excess of savings in Wicksell's Pure Credit Economy? Here, internal drains are excluded by definition and no rise in absolute prices and credit demand provides the incentive to increase interest rates (Mises, [1934] 1980: 394). The supply of finance is perfectly elastic, 'the credit-issuing banks are able to extend their issues indefinitely' (ibid.: 396). Aggregate expenditure increases in excess of real output, reflecting the excess supply of credit, and deteriorates money's purchasing power.

It is only in *Theorie des Geldes* where Mises makes extensive use of Wicksell's relation between the money and the natural rate of interest.[2] Wicksell states three conditions for macroeconomic equilibrium (neutrality): first, the equality between the loan rate of interest and the equilibrium rate on capital, second, the equality between saving and investment, and third, the stability of the price level (Myrdal, 1933: 387; Wicksell, [1935] 1978: 193, 207). Either of the first two conditions suggests a constant level of aggregate expenditures. Obviously, for all three conditions to prevail simultaneously, the economy must be stationary. Otherwise, Wicksell's first two conditions do not coincide with the third (see Davidson, 1906; Hayek, [1929] 1933, [1931] 1935; J. Koopmans, 1933).

In contrast to Wicksell, however, Mises declines the study of price-level dynamics and applies Wicksell's interest rates gap to analyse the impact of money-induced income effects on relative prices. Insofar, Mises focuses on the impact of money and credit expansion on intertemporal coordination. Given stationary intertemporal preferences, money-induced excess demand for consumption goods will sooner or later reverse and annihilate the accumulative impact of any prior excess in investment spending. This hawkish prediction of Mises's business cycle theory is placed on new ground in *Human Action*: mean-reversion becomes the outcome of the dominance Mises attributes to ownership relations. If capitalists do not save voluntarily, that is, do not advance consumption to labour so as to keep wages constant over a longer period of production and instead consume, whereas investors choose longer investment periods due to the false price of intertemporal exchange, the subsistence fund depletes before the new processes can mature. Even if total demand remains constant, somehow unaffected by increases in nominal spending, the excess demands for consumption goods turn positive, driving down the price of future goods (that is, labour) in terms of present consumption. This implies a rise in the market rate of interest to the level predetermined by the rate of time preference. The traverse reverses to the initial level of consumption. To assert that additions to money and nominal demand can permanently increase output above its long-run equilibrium value – so the essence of Mises's cycle theory – is to assume that the increase can be maintained against public will and resistance.

Thus, supply-driven credit expansion only temporarily disconnects the money rate of interest from the rate of time preference and imposes a signal-extracting problem. Mises's investors blindly follow the ups and downs of the loan rate, systematically fooled by the banking system that, in turn, is driven by a wrong mercantilist worldview, reinforced by the fact that the general public persistently tends to fall victim to inflationist ideologies. Even in the first German edition of *Theorie des Geldes*, where Mises still allows for credit demand to exert some influence on the supply of credit, it is only by the entrepreneurs' 'call for cheap money' to circumvent the limitation imposed by thrift and their pressure on political processes that banks create excess credit.

What Mises has in mind is the pressure exerted by the sovereign and rent-seekers on the banking system to overcome established 'routines' and 'conservatism', which is the pressure *to move first* (1912: 435). Mises claims that 'according to the Circulation Credit Theory [his label for the business cycle theory], it is clear that the direct stimulus which provokes the fluctuations is to be sought in the conduct of the banks' ([1928] 2006: 120). Accordingly, the regularity of cycle is due to ideological ups and down, to the struggle of ideas and to 'the mania for lower interest' (ibid.: 121; Mises, [1949] 1998: 569) as substitutes for the waves of optimism and panic of older analysis that Mises condemns as unscientific. The only way out comes by a general understanding of Mises's business cycle theory ([1928] 2006: 123–4).

Further, it is unclear how malinvestments due to forced saving can possibly occur. As Hicks points out against Hayek's early version of business cycle theory, all dynamic analysis is built on time-lags, on frictions in market adjustments (1967: 207–8). Mises refers to the money-induced distributional effects, which allow those who receive the money first to have a temporary gain at the cost of those who receive money later. All prices, including wages, are perfectly flexible. Yet, if prices are flexible, and if all new processes begin with the employment of original factors alone, consumption demand increases in proportion to their higher nominal incomes. Investment spending initiating new processes is not associated with the purchase of capital, but with outlays to labour and land, to wages (and rents). Given the strict verticality of Mises's production processes, any excess supply on the money market is immediately reflected by an excess demand on the labour market and, according to the prevailing rate of time preference, by an inflationary excess demand for consumption goods. Thus, overinvestment – in nominal terms – implies nominal wage hikes. In this light, Mises's business cycle theory depends on a price-lag, on nominal wages increasing while the prices of final outputs remain temporarily constant (the boom). Otherwise, forced saving could not drive the economy away from its trend path. But this cannot be. If, at full-employment, the circulating supply of money increases, flexible wages and prices increase together.

Mises himself is explicit that there is no time-lag between the increase of capital goods prices and the increase of consumers' goods prices. 'With the rise in wage rates the prices of consumers' goods rise too' ([1949] 1998: 550). It is indeed this initial rise of consumption-goods prices that accounts for the boom.

> The general upswing in prices spreads optimism. If only the prices of producers' goods had risen and those of consumers' goods had not been affected, the entrepreneurs would have become embarrassed. They would have had doubts concerning the soundness of their plans, as the rise in costs of production would have upset their calculations. But they are reassured by the fact that the demand for

> consumers' goods is intensified and makes it possible to expand sales in spite of rising prices.
>
> (Ibid.: 550–1; see also 554)

> At any rate, the *immediate* consequence of credit expansion is a rise in consumption on the part of those wage earners whose wages have risen on account of the intensified demand for labor by the expanding entrepreneurs.
>
> (ibid.: 553; italics mine)

Mises's claim that a more than proportional increase in the supply of money can prolong the boom is again inconsistent with his use of original factors of production ([1949] 1998: 552). Even if money grows at an accelerating rate, the increase in nominal incomes increases in proportion to the excess funds at any point in time. From the onset, consumers are equipped with additional purchasing power to defend their chosen consumption level.

Wicksell did not apply his apparatus for price-level dynamics to the analysis of business cycles. He is well aware of the fact that increases in nominal wages reduce profit, if prices remain constant, that is, if aggregate demand is fixed. In such a case, investors switch technique, favouring more capitalistic processes. As soon as the level of expenditures shifts, and this is the starting point of Mises's business cycle theory, the economy faces real-wage rigidities. As he points out in his critical review of *Theorie des Geldes* (Wicksell, 1914: 147–8), and what is equally true for all of Mises's later formulations of business cycle theory, it remains to be proven that excess credit and the loan rate below its neutral rate induce a switch in technique towards longer processes. In this case, there is nothing left of Mises's business cycle theory.

6. Concluding remarks

A most astonishing fact about Mises is that the solution to the proper relationship between the three causes of interest is right in front of him, elaborated by the most prominent of his contemporaries. For instance, the excellent general equilibrium theorist Fisher stresses the simultaneous determination of interest, treating intertemporal preference and investment opportunities pari passu as primitives ([1907] 1997, [1930] 1997). Others are even close to or within the Austrian tradition like

Wicksell and Hayek. In *Zur Zinstheorie – Böhm-Bawerk's dritter Grund*, written in 1926 and published *post mortem* in 1928, Wicksell refers to Böhm-Bawerk's 'cardinal error'. He correctly says that during the accumulation process all three causes of interest collaborate. Very early, Wicksell insists on a 'rational theory of saving' (Wicksell, [1893] 1954). Indeed, as Boianovsky (1998: 145) points out, 'in his suggested rule for the determination of saving Wicksell all but wrote Ramsey's equation.' Wicksell, like Ramsey, assumes that until stationary conditions prevail, it is the marginal productivity of capital that determines the rate of interest. Net time preference, important to determine bliss, does not bear the burden of adjustment. Over time, the return on new capital approaches the exogenous rate of net time preference until the two rates become equal and Böhm-Bawerk's first cause evaporates (Wicksell, [1934] 1977: 209).

Most importantly, Ramsey's bliss is not the starting point of analysis, but becomes the long-term goal of optimizing individuals who do not only care about the size of equilibrium income, but also about its time shape during the transition process. As Ramsey (1928: 548) points out, 'the most remarkable feature of the [his] rule is that it is altogether independent of the production function [...], except in so far as this determines bliss, the maximum rate of utility obtainable.' The dynamics of capital formation become separated from the aggregate production function which determines the long-run equilibrium level of income, given the rate of net time preference.

Mises, however, treats all attempts to improve on the underlying equilibrium framework by reaching beyond the classical long-run concept as a waste of time. It is of course true that optimal growth theory and Ramsey's prominence are post Second World War phenomena. However, Mises read extensively and surely knew the works of Wicksell, Fisher and Hayek. And yet, in subtlety and analytical depth, *Human Action* falls short of Wicksell's *Lectures* ([1914] 1934), Fisher's *Theory of Interest* (1930) and Hayek's introduction of intertemporal general equilibrium analysis in 1928 and his detailed exposition in *The Pure Theory of Capital* ([1941] 2007). Hicks's *Value and Capital* (1939), published ten years before *Human Action* and partly motivated by Hayek, is neither mentioned, nor has it left any discernible impression on Mises's general outline. In siding with Frank Fetter once and continuing to do so ever after, Mises persistently declines all major contributions to our present understanding of economic growth since Böhm-Bawerk. In fact, Mises's apparatus falls behind.

Acknowledgement

I thank Harald Hagemann, Hansjörg Klausinger, Peter Spahn and Hans-Michael Trautwein for their valuable suggestions. The usual disclaimer applies.

Notes

1. For a more detailed account of Cantillon-effects as a building block in ABCT see Hagemann and Trautwein (1998).
2. Wicksell, however, carefully avoids applying his apparatus to the analysis of business cycles (Boianovsky, 1995; Laidler, 1991).

References

Bliss, C. (1975) *Capital Theory and the Distribution of Income*, Amsterdam: North Holland.

Boianovsky, M. (1995) 'Wicksell's Business Cycle', *The European Journal of the History of Economic Thought*, 2(2): 375–411.

Boianovsky, M. (1998) 'Wicksell, Ramsey and the Theory of Interest', *The European Journal of the History of Economic Thought*, 5(1): 140–68.

Böhm-Bawerk, E. (1889/1959) *Capital and Interest*, South Holland: Libertarian Press, Vol. 2.

Cowen, T. and Fink, R. (1985) 'Inconsistent Equilibrium Constructs: The Evenly Rotating Economy of Mises and Rothbard', *American Economic Review*, 75(4): 866–9.

Davidson, D. (1906) 'Nagot om begreppet "penningens varde"', *Ekonomisk Tidskrift*, 8: 460–8.

Fetter, F. (1902/1977) 'Review of Böhm-Bawerk's Positive Theorie des Kapitals', in M. Rothbard (ed.), *Capital, Interest, and Rent – Essays in the Theory of Distribution*, Kansas City: Sheed Andrews and McMeel, 1977.

Fisher, I. (1907/1997) 'The Rate of Interest', in W. Barber (ed.), *The Works of Irving Fisher*, Vol. 3, London: Pickering & Chatto.

Fisher, I. (1930) 'The Theory of Interest', in W. Barber (ed.), *The Works of Irving Fisher*, Vol. 9, London: Pickering & Chatto, 1997.

Hagemann, H. and Trautwein, H.–M. (1998) 'Cantillon and Ricardo Effects: Hayek's Contributions to Business Cycle Theory', *The European Journal for the History of Economic Thought*, 5(2): 292–316.

Hayek, F. A. (1928) 'Das intertemporale Gleichgewichtssystem der Preise und die Bewegungen des Geldwertes', Weltwirtschaftliches Archiv, July, 33–79.

Hayek, F. A. (1929/1933) *Monetary Theory and the Trade Cycle*, New York: Sentry Press.

Hayek, F. A. (1931/1935) *Prices and Production*, 2nd edition, London: Routledge and Kegan Paul.

Hayek, F. A. (1932) 'A Note on the Development of the Doctrine of Forced Saving', *The Quarterly Journal of Economics*, 47(1): 123–33.

Hayek, F. A. (1936) 'Utility Analysis and Interest', *The Economic Journal*, 46(181): 44–60.
Hayek, F. A. (1941) *The Pure Theory of Capital*, Chicago: Chicago University Press, 2007.
Hicks, J. (1939/1965) *Value and Capital*, Oxford: Oxford University Press.
Hicks, J. (1967) 'The Hayek Story', in J. Hicks (ed.), *Critical Essays in Monetary Theory*, Oxford: Clarendon Press, 203–15.
Keynes, J. M. (1931/1978) 'A Treatise on Money, Vol. 1', in D. Moggridge (ed.), *The Collected Writings of J. M. Keynes*, Vol. 8, Cambridge: Cambridge University Press.
Koopmans, J. (1933) 'Zum Problem des "Neutralen" Geldes', in F. A. Hayek (ed.), *Beiträge zur Geldtheorie*, Vienna: Springer.
Laidler, D. (1991) *The Golden Age of the Quantity Theory*, Princeton: Princeton University Press.
Mises, L. von (1912/1924) *Theorie des Geldes und der Umlaufsmittel*, 1st edition, Munich: Duncker & Humblot, 2nd edition, Berlin: Duncker & Humblot.
Mises, L. von (1928) 'Monetary Stabilization and Cyclical Policy', in P. L. Greaves Jr. (ed.), *The Causes of the Economic Crisis – and other essays before and after the Great Depression*, Auburn: Ludwig von Mises Institute, 2006.
Mises, L. von (1934/1980) *The Theory of Money and Credit*, Indianapolis: Liberty Fund.
Mises, L. von (1940) *Nationalökonomie*, Geneva: Editions Union.
Mises, L. von (1943) ' "Elastic expectations" and the Austrian Theory of the Trade Cycle', *Economica*, New Series, 10(39): 251–2.
Mises, L. von (1949/1998) *Human Action: A Treatise in Economics*, Scholar's edition, Auburn: Ludwig von Mises Institute.
Myrdal, G. (1933) 'Der Gleichgewichtsbegriff als Instrument der geldtheoretischen Analyse', in F. A. Hayek (ed.), *Beiträge zur Geldtheorie*, Vienna: Springer.
Ramsey, F. (1928) 'A Mathematical Theory of Saving', *Economic Journal*, 38(152): 543–59.
Wicksell, K. (1893/1954) *Value, Capital, and Rent*, London: Allen & Unwin.
Wicksell, K. (1914) 'Review of L.v. Mises: Theorie des Geldes und der Umlaufsmittel', *Zeitschrift für Volkswirtschaft, Sozialpoltitik und Verwaltung*, 23: 144–9.
Wicksell, K. (1928/1997), 'On the Theory of Interest – Böhm-Bawerk's "Third Ground" ', in B. Sandelin (ed.), *Knut Wicksell – Selected Essays in Economics*, London: Routledge.
Wicksell, K. (1934/1977) *Lectures on Political Economy – General Theory*, Vol. 1, New York: Kelley.
Wicksell, K. (1935/1978) *Lectures on Political Economy – Money*, Vol. 2, New York: Kelley.

11
Hayek on Practical Business Cycle Research: A Note

Hansjoerg Klausinger

1. Introduction

On 11 December 1926, Friedrich August Hayek wrote to Oskar Morgenstern, then at Harvard on a Rockefeller Research grant:

> You will wonder that it is just Professor Mises and me, having always been rather sceptical of such research methods based on statistical inquiries, who are responsible for creating this thing.[1]

The 'thing' to which Hayek referred was the *Österreichisches Institut für Konjunkturforschung* (Austrian Institute for Business Cycle Research), of which Hayek would soon become the first director, and as it turned out Morgenstern in due time his successor. Moreover, the scruples Hayek expressed were rather typical for both their approaches towards business cycle research. Indeed, for Hayek his position as director of the Institute was just to be a transition phase before his outright venture into business cycle theory earning him in the 1930s a professorship at the much renowned London School of Economics and for a short time the reputation of one of the most prominent among contemporary economists. Yet in this note we concentrate on Hayek's directorship at the Institute and on the tension that developed from the methodological position he embraced and his venture into the practice of business cycle research.

2. The Austrian Institute for Business Cycle Research

In 1923/1924 Hayek had spent 15 months in the United States, and during this time had become acquainted with the empirical approach towards economic research as propagated by Wesley Mitchell and the

National Bureau of Economic Research. Although Hayek was rather sceptical towards its fruitfulness as a contribution to economic *theory*, he had acquired a working knowledge of the new statistical techniques used in the analysis of time series. Thus back in Vienna when he jointly with Mises, in the latter's capacity as the Secretary of the Vienna Chamber of Commerce, advanced the idea of founding an institute for economic research,[2] he felt most qualified to do this job.[3] Eventually, after Mises had succeeded in securing the necessary funds from the relevant economic 'corporations', the Institute was founded in 1926 and started its work with Hayek as the first director in January 1927. In June 1927 after a few months of preparatory work the first of its Monthly Bulletins (*Monatsberichte*) was published, with for some time Hayek being the sole author.[4]

The Institute had been established after some discussion neither as a government agency nor as part of the Chamber of Commerce, but for the sake of its independence as a private society. In order to demonstrate that the Institute should not be dominated by any political party or special interest its board included members from a broad spectrum of Austria's political landscape. For example, the Executive Board (*Ausschuss*) consisted of the President of the Chamber of Commerce (as President of the board), the President of the Chamber of Labour (as its Vice-President) and a representative of the scientific community, Richard Reisch, then President of the Austrian National Bank. Besides that, there existed a Board of Trustees (*Kuratorium*) of no less than 51 members, somewhat in contrast to the staff of the Institute's scientific office of just two, Hayek and a secretary. At the end of 1928 Morgenstern became the second member of the scientific office (and deputy director of the Institute), and when in 1931 Hayek left the Institute for the London School of Economics, Morgenstern succeeded him as director. The main sources of finance came from the Chambers of Commerce, of Labour and of Agriculture, the Austrian National Bank, various industry and banking groups, and the Federal Railroads. Anyway, the close relation not only between Hayek and Mises, but also the Institute and the Chamber of Commerce, became evident from the fact that the Vienna Chamber provided, free of charge, the rooms for the Institute in its building. Finally, in a happy turn of events and due to the initiative of Mises, from 1931 onwards a substantial Rockefeller Foundation grant supplemented the funds available for the Institute.[5]

Although the place where the Institute's work was done bore the name of a 'scientific office', its task was defined not primarily as scientific, but more prosaically as providing information and decision support to the public, in particular serving business and policymakers. In its emphasis on practical business cycle research the Austrian Institute followed the precedence set by similar institutes for economic research, the founding of which blossomed in the 1920s. The most important of these were of course the Harvard Economic Service, and in Germany the recently founded institute in Berlin and the new department for research on business cycles at the Kiel Institute of World Economics.[6] In view of the decidedly empirical (or 'practical') nature of the research pursued in these institutes and in Vienna, too, our focus will be on the tensions thereby created for Hayek's interpretation of his own work. Or put differently, how he managed to reconcile the tasks of the Institute with his opinion in matters of methodology and his work on business cycle theory, to which he soon was to make a major contribution.

3. Theory and practice of business cycle research

The odd position of adherents to the Austrian School of Economics founding an Institute mainly dedicated to doing practical business cycle research comes to the fore when comparing the official pronouncements with the reservations expressed in private correspondence. In particular, with regard to Hayek we have, on the one hand, his statements on the role and the tasks of the Institute as published in economic weeklies and later on in the *Monatsberichte*.[7] On the other hand, the views expressed in his correspondence with Morgenstern certainly came closer to his true feelings.[8] For example, Hayek confessed: 'Least of all am I pleased [...] that it [the funding of the Institute] was only possible by this kind of adaptation to a fashion of thought so that the funds cannot be spent as I would do it if they were provided without any restriction of its intended use.'[9] Moreover, the methodology espoused in his habilitation thesis (Hayek, 1929, translated 1933) also squared awkwardly with the agenda of the Institute.

What, then, were the tasks assigned to the Institute and how should these be accomplished? According to its bylaws the aim of the Institute was prescribed as 'advancing and disseminating knowledge about the conditions and tendencies of the Austrian economy'.[10] A prospectus on the tasks and organization of the Institute (Anon., 1927)[11] made clear that the Institute's role was seen in improving the information and thus supporting the decisions of business and, to a lesser degree, of policymakers. The need for such information being provided by the Institute was justified in the following, quite remarkable, way: The success of firms depends on industry- or firm-specific as well as on economy-wide factors. One of these economy-wide factors is the endogenous movement of the business cycle. Yet, entrepreneurs are much better equipped to deal with the processing of specific information than with that on the cycle, so that 'almost always business has been caught unprepared by the alteration of good and bad trade' (ibid.: 1). Thus information on the state of the economy should be provided, objectively and regularly, by an organization like the Institute, and by doing so it would indeed make possible a 'more rational management of firms' (ibid.) and thus contribute to a more stable course of the economy; and similarly so for the decisions of policy-making bodies.

Indeed, this concurred with a wide-spread view among contemporary economists on the improvement of information as a proper means for combating industrial fluctuations. Hayek (1926: 48) in his 'propaganda piece' argued that a correct identification of the prevailing phase of the cycle might prevent firms from excessive investments in the boom period exacerbating cyclical fluctuations. In Hayek (1933: 192) he confirmed that the 'knowledge of the actual phase' is an important condition for the mitigation of the cycle, although now he put the emphasis not on the results from business cycle research, but on increased publicity requirements for firms, in particular banks.[12] To cite but another example, Joseph Schumpeter was rather outspoken in declaring that 'the most important remedy á la longue [...] is the improvement of business cycle prognosis' (1926: 367, as translated 1934: 253), adding, not quite prophetically: 'The ever-increasing familiarity of businessmen with the cycle is [...] the chief reason why the real crisis phenomena [...] are becoming weaker' (ibid.).

The means and methods to be developed by the Institute derived from the tasks specified above. These were, in ascending order of ambition, the collection of quantitative information and its statistical processing (for example, adjusting for the seasonal or trend components in time series), the detecting of regularities in the movements of the economic variables throughout the cycle, this in turn should make possible both the diagnosis of the present phase of the business cycle and eventually the prediction of its future course. Postponing for the moment the discussion of the possibility of forecasting, we see that Hayek did not – at least in his official pronouncements – challenge the adequacy of the other less ambitious tasks. Besides the technical aspect of information gathering he described the practical task of business cycle research as bringing about an 'amplification, with the aid of special statistical devices, of our knowledge of the course of particular phases of trade fluctuations' (Hayek, 1933: 27), and furthermore, as ascertaining 'the point in this wave-like motion [of the business cycle] where the economy is actually located' (Hayek, 1927a: 5). It should be noted that in this regard the 'practical' tasks and the scientific tasks overlapped but were not wholly congruent. In particular, with regard to the scientific foundation for the Institute's practical work Hayek insisted – in accordance with the Austrian view in general – on the primacy of theory.

The primacy of theory had been, of course, a well known theme of Austrian economics in its controversy with the German Historical School.[13] Mises emphasized its particular relevance to business cycle research by pointing out that: 'Nowhere else is it clearer that there can be no understanding of the facts without theory' (1928: 39, as translated 1978: 112). Hayek (1933: 38) followed suit: 'The oft-repeated assertion that statistical examination of the Trade Cycle should be undertaken without any theoretical prejudice is therefore always based on self-deception.'[14] Thus, starting from the selection of the variables to be observed, and the time series data to be collected, a theoretical preconception is needed for deciding which information might be relevant for the (practical) purpose in mind, and of course the same is true for being able to distinguish between seasonal, cyclical and trend movements. Similarly, for diagnosis and prognosis a theory establishing a link between variables as cause and effect is indispensable.[15] Furthermore, as regards their potential contribution to scientific knowledge: 'Empirical studies [...] can, at best, afford merely a verification of existing theories; they cannot, in themselves, provide new insight into the causes or the necessity of the Trade Cycle' (Hayek, 1933: 27).[16]

The issue where the conflict between the scientific and practical aspect of business cycle research, and thus Hayek's personal opinion and the Institute's official task, became most visible was the question of economic prediction. As long as Hayek approached the problem of prediction in its most general terms there is no indication that he considered economic prediction impossible for reasons of principle. He started his argument with pointing out that a proper prediction must rest on a well-elaborated theory of the business cycle. Yet, even then such a prediction could only single out the endogenous tendencies immanent in the cycle (cf. Hayek, 1927b: 5). Moreover, he continued, presently there is no such theory available, and even if it were, it would not be of much use for predicting the evolution of the cycle due to changes in economic data exogenous to the theory used (cf. Hayek, 1927a: 11–12). So he arrived at the modest suggestion that the Institute should 'without formulating its own judgment of the prospects of the economy [...] just arrange in a suitable form the evidence on which such a judgment must be based and point out the most important tendencies discernable from it' (Hayek, 1927b: 5). Note that in this statement we not only find modesty for what could be expected from the Institute's predictions, but also eclecticism with regard to the theory on which such predictions should be based.[17] Even in his 1929 book, which devoted a whole chapter to methodological discussion, Hayek did not exclude the logical possibility of predicting the business cycle but rested his scepticism again on the fact that presently 'such forecasts are attempted in too unconditional a form, and on an inadmissibly over-simplified basis' – yet he stated quite apodicticly 'that statistical research in this field is meaningless except in so far as it leads to a forecast, however much that forecast may have to be hedged about with qualifications' (Hayek, 1933: 36n.). In thus upholding the goal of economic prediction Hayek's position was in contrast to Morgenstern. In his *Wirtschaftsprognose* Morgenstern (1928a) had argued that apart from other difficulties predictions will as a rule turn out as self-destroying because of the interdependence between (publicly available) predictions and the anticipations of economic actors, thus demonstrating their logical impossibility.[18] In this regard, the crucial role of the Holmes-Moriarty paradox for Morgenstern's reasoning is well known.[19] In any case, Hayek did not share this belief in the logical impossibility of economic predictions and consequently criticized Morgenstern on that account.[20]

Yet, as the Austrian Institute had been modelled on its American and German predecessors, such modest ambitions as Hayek had formulated would not have fulfilled what the public did expect the Institute to deliver. The prospectus formulated very clearly as one of the aims of the work of the Institute 'to provide, similarly to the American "economic barometers", a direct *basis for predictions*' (Anon., 1927: 5; emphasis in the original). Hayek had already complained that 'for the time being these people [who are providing funds] only appreciate the work on an Austrian business barometer', and it was just 'these business barometers which are somewhat dubious and burden my conscience as a theorist'.[21] However, as the bare existence of the Institute was linked to it Hayek as its director could not escape from elaborating and publishing such an economic barometer.

The most famous of these barometers was that published by the Harvard Economic Service. This so-called Harvard barometer consisted of three types of indicators, leading, current and lagging, displayed graphically as A-, B- and C-curves. These curves in turn represented indices of the stock market, the commodity market (called the Index of General

Business Conditions) and the money market, respectively. Observing the relative positions of these curves was meant to give a clue on the phase of the cycle which the economy was presently in and consequently on its course in the future. Within only a short time after its foundation the Austrian Institute began to apply all of these instruments to the Austrian economy: In July 1928 it started to calculate an Index of General Business Conditions (*Index des allgemeinen Geschäftsganges*) (Hayek, 1928b), and in December for the first time published all three curves for the Austrian economy (Hayek, 1928c). Yet, Hayek never stopped stressing the particular circumstances that made the construction of a Harvard-like barometer for the Austrian economy especially difficult, mainly due to the still considerable interdependence among the economies of Central Europe.[22] Finally, from February 1929 onwards the Institute also regularly reported, and commented upon, the short-term forecasts of the Harvard Economic Service with regard to the American economy.

Not surprisingly, Hayek's attempt at a methodological justification for the use of these barometers was not very convincing. His main thrust of argument was that as long as a fully developed theory of the business cycle was lacking in its stead one must take refuge to 'rules of thumb' like those provided by the barometers in question. Although methodologically of a lesser rank than a full-blown theory, such a 'simple interpretative rule' might serve as 'a useful guide' if it is recommended by its reasonable success in the past (cf. Hayek, 1927a: 12). Therefore, these barometers seemingly covered a kind of middle ground between high-brow deductive (equilibrium) theory and purely inductive research that merely consisted in data-gathering. And indeed, some justification for the use of the Harvard barometer for diagnosis and prediction was drawn from the fact that the Austrian economists apparently considered the Harvard barometer not only as based on some theory, but specifically on the broad outlines of their own monetary theory of the cycle. For example, Mises despite all his reservations against the idea in general flatly stated: 'The Harvard barometer does provide the statistical verification of the circulation credit theory' (1978: 152 [cf. 1928: 69], my emendation of the translation).[23] Thus interpreted, a defence, if possibly just a superficial one, had been found to accommodate business cycle research as practiced at the Institute with the Austrian emphasis of the primacy of theory and of the deductive method. However, this interpretation was in contradiction to how the Harvard barometer had been conceived by its inventors, who prided themselves for not having thereby presupposed any specific theory.

Yet, a still greater contrast (than with regard to Harvard) existed between the Austrian approach and the type of business cycle research advocated by the Berlin Institute under the directorship of Ernst Wagemann. When Mises (1978: 112 [cf. 1928: 39]) spoke of 'modern students of cyclical movements [who] are contemptuous of theory – not only of this or that theory but of *all* theories – and [who] profess to let the facts speak for themselves', it appears that in all probability not Harvard (or Mitchell) but Wagemann was the real target of this attack.[24] For the distinguishing characteristic of the Berlin Institute was to collect as many data as possible and when forming its predictions to decide from case to case which weight to attach to the specific items. In comparison, the merit of the barometer approach lay in its rigidity in specifying in advance, and that is in accordance with some prior 'theory', the rules of how to derive predictions from the variables observed. This was so for the Harvard barometer,[25] and also for a rival German project, the so-called Spiethoff barometer.[26] The latter had been introduced in 1928 jointly by Arthur Spiethoff and the economic weekly *Wirtschaftsdienst*, based on Spiethoff's theory of the cycle, which considered the relation between the production of raw iron and the volume of capital formation an indicator of prime importance. The Spiethoff project is noteworthy not so much for itself – it soon had to be abandoned for lack of success – but for the controversy to which it gave rise between Spiethoff and Wagemann (or more precisely their associates, Kurt Singer and Adolf Löwe). In substance this controversy centred on the necessity for such empirical work to be based on theoretical foundations. Whereas the Spiethoff barometer was modelled on its patron's theory, and thus could have been seen as an attempt at verification (of which it failed), the approach of the Berlin Institute came close to a mere collection of data from which the respective prediction was derived more or less by discretion. Thus, going back to Hayek's methodological point of view, it was Wagemann (more so than the various barometers) who indeed challenged the Austrian position by the pursuit of a programme that strongly resembled that of the German Historical School.[27] As the enmity between Spiethoff and Wagemann persisted, Wagemann, consequently, conceived the Spiethoff *Festschrift* of 1933 (Clausing, 1933) – with significant contributions by Mises and Hayek – being less 'Pro-Spiethoff' than 'Anti-Wagemann' (see Kulla, 1996: 132).

4. The Institute and the prediction of the American crisis of 1929

Keeping in mind the veritable extent of self-denial that was demanded of Hayek and his Austrian credentials to preside over an Institute that saw its ultimate goal in predicting the course of the business cycle, it seems curious that present-day fame of the same Institute appears to be based to some extent on the alleged success of a concrete prediction. For in his Foreword to *Prices and Production* Lionel Robbins singled out Austrian business cycle theory, and in particular Hayek, for having been able – contrary to the contemporary mainstream of economic thought – to correctly predict the American crisis of 1929 (as the onset of what came to be known as the Great Depression). Robbins claimed 'that the Austrian *Institut für Konjunkturforschung*, of which Dr. Hayek is director, was one of the very few bodies of its kind which, in the spring of 1929, predicted a setback in America with injurious repercussions on European conditions' (Robbins, 1931: xi–xii). Indeed, contemporaries considered (and some present-day historians of thought still do so) this prediction as evidence of the soundness of the Austrian approach and as one of the sources of its success in the early 1930s.[28]

The phenomenon that had puzzled economists during the long American boom of the 1920s was that it had not as usual been accompanied by a rising but instead by a more or less stable price level. From this, adherents to the monetary approach of the business cycle, that is at least those who equated stabilization of the price level with that of the cycle itself, had drawn comfort that a crisis could not be imminent. Conversely, their opponents questioned the validity of the monetary explanation as it appeared to have been disproved by a lack of association of the boom with rising prices. Doubting the monetary nature of the cycle, these latter economists as a rule were also not so sanguine with regard to the danger of a crisis because a breakdown could well ensue from non-monetary causes alone. In comparison, the position of Hayek was insofar unique as he shared the belief in the monetary origin of the cycle, but discarded the norm of a stable price level. Instead monetary neutrality and thus the absence of business cycles required that in case of technical progress and growth of output the price level ought to fall. Thus, even stable prices as they had characterized the American economy during the 1920s might be interpreted as signalling an unsustainable boom, which must end in a crisis. This was the view Hayek put forward in his habilitation thesis and already earlier in a report to the Zurich meeting of the *Verein für Sozialpolitik* (cf. Hayek, 1928a, 1929).[29]

In the above sense, Hayek – and also some other authors – might be credited with having 'predicted' the American crisis. In retrospect, Hayek's success in this regard appears aptly to conform to the notion of a 'pattern prediction', which he developed later in his career (cf. Hayek, 1967) in contrast to the notion of the concrete forecast of an event in time and place. Yet, Robbins's claim appears to have been just that, maintaining that Hayek's Institute had accurately predicted the breakdown of the American boom, not as a pattern but as a concrete event. Now such a feat should somewhere have left its traces. However, browsing through the monthly bulletins of the Institute, it is difficult to discover anything that comes close to corroborating Robbins's statement. In fact, from February 1929 onwards the reports in the bulletin had made extensive use of the predictions of the Harvard Economic Service as well as of the Harvard barometer, and rarely went beyond an eclectic interpretation of these. However, as the Harvard barometer has ever since become infamous as one of the most egregious failures of economic research in *not* predicting the crisis of 1929,[30] the Institute's persistent use of it is difficult to reconcile with Robbins's claim for just such a prediction. The most dramatic warning to be found in the *Monatsberichte* dated from April 1929 when, noticing an inflationary movement in the United States, the author cautioned of the 'unpleasant consequences' to be expected (Anon. [possibly Hayek], 1929a: 69). And in August 1929 addressing the prospect of an American recession the report conceded that 'as has been repeatedly been pointed out' such a backlash 'would facilitate the situation of the European economy' (Anon. [possibly Hayek], 1929b: 142) – in contradiction of the predicted 'injurious repercussions on European conditions', to which Robbins would refer later on.

Thus, convincing evidence of a prediction that conformed to what Robbins suggested in his foreword, is still lacking.[31] Yet, this accords well with the sceptical view towards the feasibility of prediction, which to some extent can be ascribed to Hayek even before he left the Institute.

5. Conclusion and outlook: from Hayek to Morgenstern

This note on Hayek and business cycle research has highlighted the tension that arose between the tasks officially assigned to the Institute and the methodological and theoretical views of Hayek, its founding director. On the one hand, practical business cycle research aimed at the diagnosis and prognosis of cyclical movements, on the other hand, the primacy of theory, as advocated by the Austrian economists in general, limited the role allowed for economic prediction, in particular as derived from statistical investigations. In principle, these conflicting views could not be resolved, but only camouflaged. In any case, after his rather short spell as director of the Institute, Hayek turned to pure theory and nevermore actively participated in the type of business cycle research practised at the Austrian Institute.

Under the directorship of Morgenstern, who succeeded Hayek, the activities of the Institute and its staff greatly expanded, thanks to the extension of the Rockefeller grant and to Morgenstern's venture into the business of policy advice.[32] He also broadened the fields of inquiry of the Institute well beyond that of the business cycle. Methodologically, loosening his ties to the Austrian school, on the one hand, Morgenstern advocated an axiomatic foundation for economic theory, formulated mathematically as fit for an 'exact science'. On the other hand, he also emphasized the necessity of enlarging the empirical base and in fact he appreciated his experiences in policy advice for inspiring his theoretical thought. Yet, for the practice of business cycle research as presented in the *Monatsberichte* this methodological reorientation had not much of an effect. Morgenstern retained his negative view on the possibility of economic prediction, reinforced by a further inquiry into the incompatibility of perfect foresight and equilibrium (Morgenstern, 1935). As his scepticism towards the Austrian approach to the business cycle increased, yet without developing a specific theory of his own, the reports in the *Monatsberichte* became ever more eclectic. With regard to the statistics reported, they visibly gained in volume, if not necessarily in depth, and occasionally also included some curiosities, for example, using the sales figures of the Vienna coffeehouses as an indicator for the curtailing of private consumption (see Anon., 1932).

In sum, though superficially the activities of the Austrian Institute resembled to a large extent those of other similar institutes elsewhere, it stood out from the beginning for addressing the relationship (and, behind the scenes, the tension) between statistical research and economic theory. In particular for Hayek – the main object of this note – there existed a real conflict between the tasks of the Institute and his (and his mentor Mises's) methodological position. This conflict remained virtually unsolved despite the occasionally used argumentative twist of claiming an intermediary position, between full-blown theories and atheoretical data-gathering, for the economic barometers used cautiously for diagnosis and prediction. This innate tension reflected the awkward fact that both the directors of the Austrian Institute entertained severe doubts on the feasibility of the very task the Institute was designed to fulfil, that is, predicting the business cycle. This came out nicely in Frank Knight's observation:

> I remember being struck by the incongruity of the author of Morgenstern's *Wirtschaftsprognose* being engaged in prognosis [...][33]

Yet, in any case, this incongruity had been no less significant for Hayek than for Morgenstern.

Acknowledgement

I am grateful to Bruce Caldwell, the general editor of the *Collected Works of F. A. Hayek*, for permission to quote from the correspondence of Friedrich August Hayek and for his comments on a preliminary version. Moreover I am indebted to the staff of the Special Collections Library at Duke University and of the Hoover Institution Archives at Stanford University for assistance in locating the requested material. If not indicated otherwise, all translations from German-language sources are my own.

Notes

1. Hayek to Morgenstern, 11 December 1926, Oskar Morgenstern Papers [= OMP], box 2; this passage has already been quoted in Rellstab (1992: 128).
2. Cf. the *Denkschrift* by Mises and Hayek (1926). In the following I draw in this section also on Craver (1986), Fleck (2000), Leonard (2002), Leube (1999), Nemschak (1967), Reichmann (2007), Schmidt (1931) and Schweiger (2006).
3. So we are told by Hayek (1983: 143, 1984: 69).
4. In the early period the authorship of all articles in the *Monatsberichte* can be safely attributed to Hayek, who then was the only member of the Institute's scientific office. Yet since the end of 1928, when Morgenstern had entered the office, anonymous articles henceforth originated either from Hayek or Morgenstern.
5. See Craver (1986) and Leonard (2002: 9–13).
6. On the Harvard Economic Service cf. Bullock and Crum (1932) and Mason (1982: 414–18), and on the beginnings of business cycle research in Germany cf. Kulla (1996).
7. Cf. Hayek (1926, 1927a, 1927b, 1928d). Hayek himself admitted that his 1926 article was a piece of 'propaganda for the sake of founding the Institute' and that it did 'in no way contain all aspects of my own scientific position' (Hayek to Morgenstern, 11 December 1926, OMP, box 2); cf. also the critique by Morgenstern (1927).
8. Cf. in addition Hayek to Morgenstern, 25 March and 13 October 1927, OMP, box 2. However, as one purpose of these letters was to persuade Morgenstern to join the work at the Institute, they may also not be entirely free from second thoughts.
9. Hayek to Morgenstern, 11 December 1926, OMP, box 2.
10. Cf. Schweiger (2006: 33).
11. Hayek attached the prospectus to his letter to Morgenstern of 25 March 1927 (in OMP, box 2).
12. Cf. also Hayek (1933: 238–9 and 1931a: 109) and already earlier Morgenstern (1928a: 123–4).

13. For a broader perspective on Hayek's work in this regard cf. Caldwell (2004: ch. 3).
14. In the accompanying footnote Hayek referred as an example to the adverse opinion of Charles Bullock, the founder of the Harvard Economic Service. Significantly, in an otherwise friendly report on the Austrian Institute Bullock was later on to comment that: 'The German [*sic*] writers on the business cycle seem to be nuts on the matter of equipping themselves with a lot of theories about the subject before they go to work to study the facts ...' (Letter to Edmund E. Day, 22 May 1930, as quoted in Craver, 1986: 212–3).
15. Although, later on, Hayek would not have upheld his view (as in Hayek, 1933: 28–9) that the theory in question must be an 'equilibrium theory'. Cf. also Caldwell (2004, 159).
16. Hayek (1933: 32–3) identified as the criteria for the validity of a theory its logical consistency and its corroboration with the facts as established by statistics.
17. Indeed in its *Monatsberichte* the Institute did not advance a specifically 'Austrian' position; cf. on this Rosner (1999).
18. Cf. also Morgenstern (1928a: 121–4, 1928b: 344–5) for the consequences on the tasks assigned to institutes for business cycle research, which was in short: 'They shall give up predictions' (1928a: 121).
19. Cf. Morgenstern (1928a: 98; cf. also 1976: 173–4 [1935: 343–4]). It should be noted that in this example Morgenstern rested his conclusion on a special case, where perfect foresight and equilibrium are indeed incompatible, yet which is not generically true.
20. Cf. Hayek (1933: 36n.). In his later writings Hayek would stress another, more fundamental reason for the unpredictability of concrete events (as compared to patterns), namely the complexity of the phenomena to be explained by economic theory. Therefore, on the one hand, the economist never will have the knowledge of all the individual data that would be needed as initial conditions jointly with a covering law for an exact prediction. On the other hand, the problem cannot be solved by recourse to statistical methods as the relations between individual elements with different attributes cannot be reduced to averages. Cf. on this Hayek (1967).
21. Hayek to Morgenstern, 11 December 1926, OMP, box 2.
22. This had already been emphasized in Anon. (1927: 5); ideally, a close cooperation among the business cycle research institutes of all the countries of this region would have been required.
23. However, he was anxious to add that neither did modern empirical research accomplish anything that was principally novel nor did it make the task of banking policy essentially easier (see Mises, 1978 [1928]: 164–5). For the more explicit criticism in his later writings cf. for example, Mises (1949: 868).
24. Mises continued: 'The delusion that theory must be distilled from the results of an impartial investigation of facts is more popular in business cycle theory than in any other field of economics' (ibid., my emendation of the translation).
25. Nevertheless the predictions of the Harvard Service contained an element of discretion as they left room for expert judgment to supplement the tendencies as derived from the barometer statistics. Allegedly (cf. Bullock and Crum,

1932: 137), it was this element of discretion that more than the barometer itself contributed to the failure to predict the crash of 1929.

26. The following is based on Kulla (1996: 111–35); cf. also Janssen (1998: 312–21).
27. Remarkably, Kulla (1996: 51) reports of a plan, never realized, that the Berlin Institute be sponsored by a society named the 'Gustav Schmoller Society'.
28. When in 1974 the Nobel Prize was awarded to Hayek, the press release referred to Hayek's prediction of the 1929 crisis (Royal Swedish Academy of Sciences 1974: 470); for similar recent statements see, for example, Laidler (1999: 44) and Horwitz (2001: 102).
29. For a more extensive review of this debate on the possibility of an everlasting boom see Klausinger (2007: sec. 3.5).
30. On the failure of the Harvard Barometer cf. Bullock and Crum (1932) and Dominguez, Fair and Shapiro (1988).
31. Hayek's own claim in this regard had been much more modest when he referred to passages in his 1925 article (Hayek, 1925: 260, 271 and 275–6 [1999: 105, 114 and 118]) for having already pointed out 'the immense possibilities of credit expansion created by the Federal Reserve System and the dangers of a policy directed towards the stabilization of the price level' (Hayek, 1931b: x–xin.).
32. On Morgenstern as a policy adviser cf. Klausinger (2008).
33. Frank Knight to Morgenstern, 19 December 1932, OMP, box 6 (quoted in Rellstab, 1992: 123).

References

Anonymous (1927) 'Aufgaben und Organisation des Institutes', mimeo. in OMP, box 2.

Anonymous [Hayek, F. A.?] (1929a) 'Vereinigte Staaten', *Monatsberichte des Österreichischen Instituts für Konjunkturforschung*, 3(4): 65–71.

Anonymous [Hayek, F. A.?] (1929b) 'Österreich', *Monatsberichte des Österreichischen Instituts für Konjunkturforschung*, 3(8): 133–42.

Anonymous (1932) 'Rückblick auf das Jahr 1931', *Monatsberichte des Österreichischen Instituts für Konjunkturforschung*, 6(2): 17–27.

Bullock, C. J. and Crum, W. I. (1932) 'The Harvard Index of Economic Conditions: Interpretation and Performance, 1919–31', *Review of Economic Statistics*, 14(3): 132–48.

Caldwell, B. (2004) *Hayek's Challenge: An Intellectual Biography of F. A. Hayek*, Chicago and London: University of Chicago Press.

Clausing, G. (ed.) (1933) *Der Stand und die nächste Zukunft der Konjunkturforschung. Festschrift für Arthur Spiethoff*, Munich: Duncker & Humblot.

Craver, E. (1986) 'Patronage and the Directions of Research in Economics: The Rockefeller Foundation in Europe, 1924–1938', *Minerva*, 24(2–3): 205–22.

Dominguez, K. M., Fair, R. C. and Shapiro, M. D. (1988) 'Forecasting the Depression: Harvard Versus Yale', *American Economic Review*, 78(4): 595–612.

Fleck, C. (2000) 'Die gescheiterte Gründung eines Zentrums für sozialwissenschaftliche Forschung in den 30er-Jahren in Wien', *AGSÖ Newsletter*, 20: 15–29.

Hayek, F. A. (n.d.) Papers. Hoover Institution Archives. Stanford University.
Hayek, F. A. (1925) 'Die Währungspolitik der Vereinigten Staaten seit der Überwindung der Krise von 1920', *Zeitschrift für Volkswirtschaft und Sozialpolitik*, 5(1): 25–63, (2) 254–317; English translation as 'Monetary Policy in the United States after the Recovery from the Crisis of 1920' in Hayek (1999: 71–152).
Hayek, F. A. (1926) 'Die Bedeutung der Konjunkturforschung für das Wirtschaftsleben', *Der Österreichische Volkswirt*, 19(1): 46–9.
Hayek, F. A. [Anon.] (1927a) 'Die Methoden der Konjunkturforschung und ihre Anwendung in Österreich', *Monatsberichte des Österreichischen Instituts für Konjunkturforschung*, 1(1–6): 2–20.
Hayek, F. A. (1927b) 'Konjunkturforschung in Österreich', *Die Industrie*, 32, 30 (22 July): 3–5.
Hayek, F. A. (1928a) 'Einige Bemerkungen über das Verhältnis der Geldtheorie zur Konjunkturtheorie', in *Verein für Sozialpolitik*, 1928: 247–94; English translation as 'Some Remarks on the Relation of Monetary Theory to Business Cycle Theory', in H. Hagemann (ed.) (2002), *Business Cycle Theory. Selected Texts 1860–1939*, Vol. III: Monetary Theories of the Business Cycle, London: Pickering & Chatto, 163–97.
Hayek, F. A. [Anon.] (1928b) 'Österreich', *Monatsberichte des Österreichischen Instituts für Konjunkturforschung*, 2(7): 101–9.
Hayek, F. A. [Anon.] (1928c) 'Österreich' *Monatsberichte des Österreichischen Instituts für Konjunkturforschung*, 2(12): 179–89.
Hayek, F. A. (1928d) 'Die Aufgaben der wissenschaftlichen Konjunkturforschung' Incomplete typescript of a radio lecture (dated 5 October 1928) in Friedrich August Hayek Papers, box 104, folder 32.
Hayek, F. A. (1929) *Geldtheorie und Konjunkturtheorie*, Vienna: Hölder-Pichler-Tempsky; reprinted Salzburg: Neugebauer, 1976. English translation as Hayek, 1933.
Hayek, F. A. (1931a) *Prices and* Production, 2nd edition, London: Routledge, 1935.
Hayek, F. A. (1931b) *Preise und Produktion*, Vienna: Springer; reprinted 1976.
Hayek, F. A. (1933) *Monetary Theory and the Trade Cycle*, London: Jonathan Cape.
Hayek, F. A. (1967) 'The Theory of Complex Phenomena', in F. A. Hayek (ed.), *Studies in Philosophy, Politics, and Economics*, Chicago: University of Chicago Press: 22–42.
Hayek, F. A. (1983) *Nobel Prize-Winning Economist. Friedrich A. Hayek*. Oral History Program, University of California, Los Angeles, mimeo.
Hayek, F. A. (1984) *Hayek on Hayek: An Autobiographical Dialogue*, S. Kresge and L. Wenar (eds), Chicago: University of Chicago Press, London: Routledge.
Hayek, F. A. (1999) *Good Money. Part I: The New World* (*The Collected Works of F. A. Hayek*, vol. 5), S. Kresge (ed.), Chicago: University of Chicago Press, London: Routledge.
Horwitz, S. (2001) 'Review Essay – Hayek: Good Money', *Journal of the History of Economic Thought*, 23(1): 99–104.
Janssen, H. (1998) *Nationalökonomie und Nationalsozialismus. Die deutsche Volkswirtschaftslehre in den dreißiger Jahren*, Marburg: Metropolis.
Klausinger, H. (2007) 'The Making of F. A. Hayek's *Monetary Theory and the Trade Cycle*', Paper presented at the 11th ESHET Conference in Strasbourg (July 2007), mimeo.

Klausinger, H. (2008) 'Policy Advice by Austrian Economists: The Case of Austria in the 1930s', *Advances in Austrian Economics*, 11: 25–53.

Kulla, B. (1996) *Die Anfänge der empirischen Konjunkturforschung in Deutschland 1925–1933*, Berlin: Duncker & Humblot.

Laidler, D. (1999) *Fabricating the Keynesian Revolution. Studies in the Inter-War Literature on Money, the Cycle, and Unemployment*, Cambridge: Cambridge University Press.

Leonard, R. (2002) 'Risk, Foresight – Flight. Morgenstern's Vienna in the 1930s', Working Paper, University of Quebec at Montréal.

Leube, K. R. (1999) 'On the Foundation of the Austrian Institute for Business Cycle Research and the Methodological Problems of Economic Forecasting', *Journal des Economistes et des Etudes Humaines*, 9(2–3): 321–40.

Mason, E. S. (1982) 'The Harvard Department of Economics from the Beginning to World War II', *Quarterly Journal of Economics*, 97(3): 383–433.

Mises, L. von (1928) *Geldwertstabilisierung und Konjunkturpolitik*, Jena: Gustav Fischer. English translation in Mises, 1978, 57–171.

Mises, L. von (1949) *Human Action: A Treatise on Economics*, 1st edition, New Haven: Yale University Press; 3rd revised edition, Chicago: Regnery 1966.

Mises, L. von (1978) *On the Manipulation of Money and Credit*, P. L. Greaves (ed.), New York: Free Market Books.

Mises, L. von (2003) *Der unbekannte Mises. Reden und Aufsätze zur österreichischen Wirtschaftspolitik der Zwischenkriegszeit*, Kurt R. Leube (ed.), Frankfurt am Main: Frankfurter Allgemeine Buch.

Mises, L. von and Hayek, F. A. (1926). 'Denkschrift betreffend der Einrichtung eines österreichischen Konjunkturbeobachtungsdienstes', Report at the Meeting of the Chamber of Commerce (November); reprinted in Mises 2003: 109–17.

Morgenstern, O. (1927) 'Die andere Seite der Konjunkturforschung', *Der Österreichische Volkswirt*, 19(1): 393–5.

Morgenstern, O. (1928a) *Wirtschaftsprognose. Eine Untersuchung ihrer Voraussetzungen und Möglichkeiten*, Vienna: Springer.

Morgenstern, O. (1928b) 'Aufgaben und Grenzen der Institute für Konjunkturforschung', *Verein für Sozialpolitik*, 1928, 337–53.

Morgenstern, O. (1935) 'Vollkommene Voraussicht und wirtschaftliches Gleichgewicht' *Zeitschrift für Nationalökonomie*, 6(3): 337–57. English translation as 'Perfect Foresight and Economic Equilibrium', in Morgenstern, 1976, 169–83.

Morgenstern, O. (1976) *Selected Economic Writings of Oskar Morgenstern*, A. Schotter (ed.), New York: New York University Press.

Morgenstern, O. Papers [= OMP]. Special Collections Library. Duke University.

Nemschak, F. (1967) (Untitled contribution), in *40 Jahre Österreichisches Institut für Wirtschaftsforschung*, Manfred Mautner Markhof and Franz Nemschak et al. (eds), Vienna: Überreuter.

Reichmann, W. (2007) ' "Die Gezeiten der Wirtschaft". Institutionalisierung und Methoden der Beobachtung wirtschaftlicher Zyklen in Österreich bis 1945', *Österreichische Zeitschrift für Geschichtswissenschaften*, 18(4): 39–58.

Rellstab, U. (1992) *Ökonomie und Spiele. Die Entstehungsgeschichte der Spieltheorie aus dem Blickwinkel des Ökonomen Oskar Morgenstern*, Chur: Ruegger.

Robbins, L. (1931) 'Foreword' to Hayek (1931a), vii–xii.

Rosner, P. (1999) 'The Austrian Research on Business Cycles', *History of Economic Ideas*, 7(1–2): 195–226.

Royal Swedish Academy of Sciences (1974) 'The Nobel Memorial Prize in Economics 1974', *Swedish Journal of Economics*, 76(4): 469–71.

Schmidt, C. T. (1931) 'The Austrian Institute for Business Cycle Research', *Journal of Political Economy*, 39(1): 101–3.

Schumpeter, J. A. (1926) *Theorie der wirtschaftlichen Entwicklung*, 2nd edition, Munich and Leipzig: Duncker & Humblot.

Schumpeter, J. A. (1934) *The Theory of Economic Development*, Cambridge, MA: Harvard University Press.

Schweiger, M. (2006) *Wirtschaftsforschung in Österreich: Zwischen Liberalismus und Sozialpartnerschaft*, unpublished Doctoral Disseration, University of Graz.

Verein für Sozialpolitik (1928) *Beiträge zur Wirtschaftstheorie*, Karl Diehl (ed.), Zweiter Teil: *Konjunkturforschung und Konjunkturtheorie*, Schriften des Vereins für Socialpolitik, 173/2, Munich and Leipzig: Duncker & Humblot.

12

Involvement of an Austrian Émigré Economist in America

Chikako Nakayama

In the interwar period, the Austrian School of economics neither did nor could stay in Austria; hence, most of its members emigrated, mainly to the United States. A precursory work on this emigration points out the economic and political reasons.

> (In the circle of Hayek and Fürth) the topic of emigration often came up during the fortnightly meetings. [...] the difficulties faced in finding permanent employment must have been one of the primary reasons why this was so. But there was obviously concern with the deteriorating political situation as well.
>
> (Craver, 1986a: 16–17)

And this author further cites the statement made by Engel-Jánosi, one of their contemporaries, that the decision was necessary for three men, namely, Hayek, Morgenstern, and Machlup. Here we investigate the case of Oskar Morgenstern for the following reason. On the one hand, he has made major collaborative contributions to economic theory after he immigrated to the United States, the first being the collaboration with John von Neumann on the theory of games,[1] and the second being that with C. W. T. Granger on the random-walk hypothesis for stock exchange markets (cf. Morgenstern and Granger, 1970).[2] Judging from these outcomes, his emigration to and new acquaintances with people in the new continent have certainly been significant for Morgenstern. However, on the other hand, it is also known that Morgenstern was not as motivated to emigrate from his Vienna as the others: he had a respectable job as the Director of the Institute for Business Cycle Research as Hayek's successor and also had his habilitation at the University of Vienna. Further, he was not a Jew and was rather reluctant, according to a reply in a later interview, to break away from his cosmopolitan life in Vienna (Craver, 1986a: 22). He was largely successful in his profession in Vienna and was obtaining greater responsibility as the central figure of the Austrian School, utilizing his international intellectual network in the academic world of economics, until the late thirties. Symbolically, this is most evident in his role as the managing editor of the journal *Zeitschrift für Nationalökonomie*.[3] However, perhaps because of this apparently contradictory situation, it is all the more interesting to closely scrutinize his intellectual activity in Vienna to find the conjunctive phases, that he was gradually involved in the United States and emigrated in the end. So we are going to investigate this, especially focusing on Morgenstern's thoughts in the first half of the thirties.

1. The international-oriented attitude of the Austrian School

Since our theme of emigration of the Austrian School can be included in the research interest of the internationalization and dissemination of economics, it might be worth understanding the general circumstances of this school in the international context. As Hayek points out, the methodological debate in the nineteenth century between the founder of the School, C. Menger, and the leader of the German Historical School, G. Schmoller, had a considerable influence on the situations of the disciples.

> Schmoller went so far as to declare publicly that members of the 'abstract' school were unfit to fill a teaching position in a German university, and his influence was quite sufficient to make this equivalent to a complete exclusion of all adherents to Menger's doctrines from academic positions in Germany.
>
> (Hayek, 1934/1992: 81)

From this episode we can imagine that the members of the Austrian School did not have any of hope of securing a position in Germany; instead, they endeavoured to catch up with the 'international' tendency outside German-speaking academia. Hayek recounts that 'we in Vienna of any note were busy very early with merely absorbing the flood of new ideas which were coming in from elsewhere, mainly from England, but increasingly also from the United States' (1963/1992: 38).

An example of their orientation is seen in the first volume of the four-volume series *The Economic Theory of Today* (*Die Wirtschaftstheorie der Gegenwart*), edited by Hans Mayer and published between 1927 and 1932. This series explores the state and trend of economics in several countries including Germany and other European countries, the United States, Russia and India. It is remarkable that Schumpeter (1910), who wrote the section on Germany, had already written an article describing the economic situation in the United States in Schmoller's journal, where he mainly discusses pure theoretical issues, referring to Clark, Fetter, Fisher, F. W. Taussig, R. T. Ely and A. W. Flux. He characterizes the German Historical School as the precursor of American Institutionalism (Schumpeter, 1927: 4–5; and more explicitly, Schumpeter, 1926/1954: 164–5). This interpretation of German economics with the auxiliary perspective of American and international situation might intend to mitigate emotional antipathy among the Austrians. Moreover, Schumpeter also contributed to building personal bridges between the Austrians and Americans. He is believed to have made considerable efforts to introduce young and relatively unknown Austrian researchers to famous American economists (Hayek, 1963/1992: 34–5).

Interestingly, the above mentioned volume edited by Mayer shows that the Austrian school has gradually earned international reputation. It was Fetter who provided an introduction to the situation in America in this volume. He was born in rural Indiana and studied at Cornell. Thereafter, he went to Germany and received his doctorate from the University of Halle, and then worked as professor at Cornell University from 1910 to 1911 and at Princeton University from 1911 to 1931. As is shown by an anthology of his articles and as Rothbard also explains in the introduction, in his early days, Fetter's major research focused on capital, rent and interest or on the roundabout process in the interest theory, analyzing Böhm-Bawerk's works (Fetter, 1977).[4] In this sense, Fetter can be regarded as the leader of the early Austrian Economics in the United States[5] (Rothbard, 1977: 1). Fetter describes the situation after the 1890s when the economic thoughts of the Austrian School were brought into America via Böhm-Bawerk's model, though there were also counterarguments by the supporters of Ricardo's or Clark's theories (Fetter, 1927: 37). Hence, the relation between the Austrian School and economic theories in the United States was also bilateral. In order to more precisely describe and analyze this bilateral relation, we are going to focus on one pivotal figure in relation to Morgenstern in the following sections.

2. Research interests of Morgenstern in the early 1930s

First we have to ascertain that Morgenstern showed a talent for making international connections from an early stage of his professional career.[6] As has sometimes been pointed out, his first research interest was the role of the time element in economic theories (Leonard, 1995; Rellstab, 1992; Nakayama, 1997), in which he intended to combine the business cycle theory and the concept of general equilibrium. There can certainly be an institutional explanation, in view of Morgenstern's work and directorship of the Institute for Business Cycle Research,[7] but his sincere interest in dynamic problems cannot be explained only by this factor. He seems to have acquired this idea much earlier as a combinatory outcome of the investigation of Böhm-Bawerk's works on the one hand and his visits to foreign countries on the other, especially to the United States, in 1925 with the financial support of the Rockefeller Foundation.[8]

In the United States, Morgenstern became acquainted with well-known economists such as Mitchell, Burns, Bullock and Fetter.[9] In particular, he participated in Mitchell's seminar and absorbed ideas and became involved in discussions (Leonard, 2004: 292–3). One outcome of this, for example, is his paper on Mitchell and Pigou, which appeared later in 1928 and which shows his serious interest in dynamic problems.[10] Moreover, it also shows his interest in the problem of adopting either the quantitative or qualitative method, which he later reconsiders.[11] Anyway, after having published his first book on economic forecasting *Wirtschaftsprognose* in 1928 (1928a), which endowed him with the habilitation at the University of Vienna, he intended to write another book that was to have the title *Time and Economic Equilibrium*. However, this project was never completed.

It is known that members of the Austrian School in the 1920s and 1930s were generally engaged in the problem of imputation, borrowing from the contributions of Böhm-Bawerk and Wieser, and Morgenstern was no exception. Further, the research interest aroused by the experience in the United States was also shared by some members of the School, such as Hayek and Haberler.[12] However, the exploration gave Morgenstern the incentive to develop his ideas further, which, in the end, brought him far away from the tradition of the School. By the beginning of 1935, he had become so strongly aware of this fact as to write in some personal letter:

> For the moment I work on a book about 'time and economic equilibrium' and will have to deal with the period of production and all of these kinds of things in detail in it [...]. I myself am very critical of the orthodox opinion of Viennese School [...].
>
> (Morgenstern to Knight, 4 January 1935, Morgenstern Papers, Box 6)

The important point is that, owing to his interest in the time element, since the publication of the first book in 1928, Morgenstern started paying attention to a particular kind of subjectiveness which means that individuals' decisions are mutually influenced and not independently taken. In his view, this is crucial for analyzing dynamic processes.

The idea of subjectiveness was originally inspired by his contemporary discussions, since it was definitely one of the traditional concepts of the School, and Vienna seems to have also provided a stimulating interdisciplinary atmosphere. For instance, Morgenstern refers to Weber's sociological concept of *Verstehen* (understanding) and emphasizes the idea of rationality and the mutual dependence of individuals' decisions. Further, he was also largely influenced by theories of mathematics and logics during that period, through his contact with the members of the so-called Vienna Circle, who were discussing ideas, methods of logical positivism and rationality. Morgenstern gave a talk in one of their meetings in the late 1920s.[13] In this connection, his contact with Karl Menger was especially important. Menger was a member of the Vienna Circle for a while but then separated from it and independently organized other interdisciplinary 'mathematical' colloquia.[14] Menger remembers that it was Morgenstern who, upon listening to Menger's talk at some meeting and, in complete contrast to other members of the Austrian School, immediately understood its importance and encouraged him to write an article. This was realized in 1934 and they kept good contact from then onwards.[15] It would not be unreasonable to assume that Morgenstern's development of the idea was, at least partly, influenced by Menger.

However, what mostly differentiates Morgenstern from the Viennese tradition was an American collaborator, Frank H. Knight: He played an important role in inducing Morgenstern to develop his own view of subjectiveness, to examine the theoretical tradition of the Austrian School in detail, and to separate him gradually from this school in the 1930s.[16] In fact, the letter quoted above was sent to Knight by Morgenstern.

At first glance, their contact seems to have been that between an editor and an author. The name and theory of Frank Knight should have already been known among Austrian economists in general, since his name was on the list of authors for one of the volumes edited by Mayer mentioned above (Knight, 1932a), but when it had not yet been published, before 1932, it was Morgenstern who, as the editor, took initiative and contacted Knight.[17] Besides this, three articles by Knight were published in the journal *Zeitschrift für Nationalökonomie*. We have evidence that at least two, namely, 'Statik und Dynamik. Zur Frage der mechanischen Analogie in den Wirtschaftswissenschaften' in Volume 2 in 1931, 'Bemerkungen über Nutzen und

Kosten' in Volume 6 in 1935, which was split into two parts: 'Teil I: Kritisches und Dogmengeschichtliches', and 'Teil II: Versuch einer Neugestaltung der Kostentheorie', were published with the strong support of Morgenstern.[18] Nonetheless, the correspondence between them shows that their intellectual contact was not exhausted by this kind of relationship.

From the early 1930s, Morgenstern and Knight continued to discuss problems that were of fundamental interest to both of them. These primarily concern the problems of time and equilibrium in economic theory, the satisfactory structure of dynamic theories and economic forecasts. It seems that, due to their correspondence, Morgenstern's ideas were influenced by Knight's ideas on risk, profit, interest and uncertainty. However, this influence was not one-directional: Knight seems to have been introduced into the theoretical problems of business cycle theory since 1932, probably after reading articles by the Austrians, although he found their results unsatisfactory.[19] Further, this interchange of ideas might be more meaningful than personal ones since this was the interchange of ideas between two major schools of liberalism in the 1930s, the Vienna and Chicago Schools.[20] However, we restrain ourselves from broadening our examination too much and rather focus on Morgenstern here.

The fact is also evident that Morgenstern placed considerable confidence in Knight since he had asked Knight in the early 1930s whether it would be possible for him to get a position at a university in the United States. This might seem contradictory to Morgenstern's later observation, mentioned in the first section of this paper, that the prospect of immigration to America was not very attractive to him. However, the correspondences with Knight show us that there was at least one opportunity in 1932 when Knight introduced him to a position for an economic theorist at the University of California at Berkeley, where Knight's brother worked as professor, and that Morgenstern, after showing keen interest in it, had to decline this offer, owing to the conditions of employment.[21] We could imagine that Morgenstern might have taken this offer had the conditions been better. Further, it is clear that the contact with Knight for Morgenstern was already symbolic of the academic life in the United States.[22]

3. Starting point for Morgenstern: consideration of production

The decisive issue was the judgment on the concept of the period of production proposed by Böhm-Bawerk, with regard to the concept of capital and interest, as is mentioned in Morgenstern's letter declaring his conscious separation from the Austrian School. However, before this very concept became the main focus, the theories of cost and production that used the idea of marginal productivity, widely discussed at that time, motivated Morgenstern to investigate them, which led him to examine the rule of thumb for production, the law of rate of returns. This arouses the necessity to fundamentally re-examine the meaning of 'production'. Morgenstern writes a survey article about these theories of cost and production in 1931, expressing his thanks to Haberler and Hayek for having held a common seminar at the University of Vienna on this topic during the winter semester in 1929/1930 (Morgenstern, 1931: 481), which indicates that it was a shared interest among them. Although Morgenstern told Knight that this was just a survey article, neither new nor interesting (a letter from Morgenstern to Knight on the 24th of January in 1931), he himself seems to have derived much insight from this investigation, especially on the period of production and on production in general.

In this article, Morgenstern inspects ideas and theories of marginal productivity, referring not only to the writings of Wieser, Mayer and other Austrians, but also to international literature by Anglo-Saxons, Italians and others, such as Marshall, Pigou, Edgeworth, Clark, Barone, Pareto, Sraffa, including Knight. This was partly aimed at criticizing the domestic situation in Germany (Morgenstern, 1931: 482), which provoked a counter-argument from the German side (Liefmann, 1932), but Morgenstern's major intention seemingly was to compare the theory of the Austrian School with those of others and to place the Austrians in the international context. He finds it disappointing that Böhm-Bawerk's 'famous' model of greater productivity in roundabout production has not been very influential in England and the United States (Morgenstern, 1931: 505). From this passage, we cannot infer that he was critical of Böhm-Bawerk's theory at this time. What he only emphasizes is that it should be distinguished whether the lower increase in the rate of return is caused by the longer roundabout production process or by the greater number of units of factors of production, which needs more investigation. This is a distinction that later, after Morgenstern further examines Böhm-Bawerk's theory and becomes rather critical of it, separates the concept of overinvestment from that of overproduction.

Besides, even though Morgenstern had then shifted his attention to exploring the concept of the period of production, the general rule or the law of the rate of returns continued to attract research interest. In 1936, Karl Menger wrote an article in *Zeitschrift für Nationalökonomie*

(Menger, 1936/1979), on which Schlesinger (1936) wrote a commentary. Both give exact mathematical formulations and Menger directly shows a possible model by refining Böhm-Bawerk's description, which is different from the descriptive style of the original.

4. Critics of the theory of period of production: the decisive issue for the separation

Around 1932, the contact with Knight began to have a strong influence on Morgenstern's attitude toward the Austrian School. It mainly began with a question and an advice from Knight to Morgenstern in a letter, in which the former asked the latter not to give too much consideration to the Austrian tradition and to hold on to his own belief in the impossibility of forecasting. Knight writes:

> I often think of your situation there and wonder how you feel about it since Hayek is gone. I remember being struck by the incongruity of the author of Morgenstern's *Wirtschaftsprognose* being engaged in prognosis; you produced the 'alibi' that you were only doing the statistical work and that Hayek was the 'prognoser'!
>
> (A letter from Knight to Morgenstern dated 19 December 1932)

Thereafter, Knight presents his criticism of the Austrian School, referring to Morgenstern's own work and stance:

> One conviction I do have [...] is that any theory of cycles or any other phase of economic life based on Böhm-Bawerk's theory of capital is necessarily and egregiously wrong. [...] there is no such thing as a time length of the production process, still less any possibility of defining capital in such terms. [...] I was a little disappointed with your article in 'Probleme der Wertlehre'. It seems to me more of an apologetic for the Austrians and their position than a critically balanced survey. I wondered how much you were influenced by personal loyalty to Mayer [...].
>
> (Ibid.)[23]

We know that in these passages, not only Böhm-Bawerk but also Hayek is implicitly the opponent. Hayek integrated Böhm-Bawerk theory of capital into his own business cycle theory (Cohen, 2003: 470 also points this out) and vigorously committed himself to the similar research field as Morgenstern. In fact, Hayek criticizes Morgenstern's 'denial' of forecasting,[24] although he uses, at the same time, Morgenstern's idea presented in the article on business cycle theory in 1928b, for critically investigating Pigou's trade cycle theory of errors of forecast or the psychological theory (Hayek, 1933: 83). Knight would later oppose Hayek's concept of capital, which would be publicly stated in a series of articles on the so-called capital controversy since then (Knight mentions this in a letter to Morgenstern dated 26 July 1934. cf. also, Boettke, P. and Vaughn, K., 2002.). However, around 1932, the criticism was rather directed at Böhm-Bawerk's concepts of capital and interest and of the idea of 'roundaboutness', which Knight later refers to as 'Böhm-Bawerkism' (this is a term used by Knight in one of his letters to Morgenstern dated 31 January 1937). Knight tells Morgenstern that he has made his own elaboration explicit in the article entitled 'Interest', in the *Encyclopedia of the Social Sciences* (Knight 1932b. Then he further investigates this theme in other articles: Knight, 1933, 1934 and so on).

This article comprises the following three parts: (1) the history of doctrine, (2) general theory and (3) historical, dynamic and sociological aspects, the themes of which imply his criticism that 'there is no reason to believe in the reality of "impatience" or of preference of present to future as a general principle of conduct' (ibid.: 137). Knight tries to prove this from the perspective of the history of economics as well as from the sociological and cultural viewpoints. The criticism of Böhm-Bawerk's theory, following Jevons's theory, is mainly discussed in the second part of the article, but even in the first part, it is referred to as being at the centre of the interest theories preceding the First World War. What also attracts our attention is that Knight explains Böhm-Bawerk's great influence, especially in the United States, and mentions Fetter and Fisher as its supporters there. Knight stated that Böhm-Bawerk's view might be appropriate for theoretical analysis, but it is 'fatally handicapped by the lack of a general and accurate conception of the length of the production process' (ibid.: 135). The point of issue is the difference of their recognitions of the time dimension.

What Knight finds crucial and what may also have had much influence on Morgenstern is the existence of uncertainty in the production process. Knight emphasizes that there is no working distinction between capital and other factors if there were no element of uncertainty. However, in reality, there are unpredicted changes that determine what capital goods are, so that 'in the production of any capital goods the use of pre-existing capital goods is always involved' and thus, neither the starting point nor the ending point of the production process can be precisely defined (ibid.: 136). The unpredicted changes include technological, sociological and cultural ones. It is hence of no use to think that the production process has a computable time length or, what is still less true, an average length. Moreover, in his explanation of savings and accumulation, which supposedly influences the interest rate, Knight finds it more realistic to consider social factors such as living standards, forms of social emulation, the general movement of taste, or social changes like the increase in population, development of natural resources and invention of new technical processes. And this idea explains the presence of the third part of Knight's article, 'historical, dynamic and sociological aspects', where he more directly discusses uncertainty or the changes and divergence of various interest rates.

> Uncertainty affects more or less every loan or investment, depending especially how far into the future the commitment looks... the subjective and individual element of uncertainty is not susceptible to standardization; it is a matter of how much confidence one feels in his opinions about the future course of events and of how much courage he has in acting upon his convictions.
>
> (Ibid.: 141)

For Knight, the subjectiveness or the limited extension of time in foreseeing the future includes people's anticipation of unpredicted changes. It is natural that this argument is followed by the discussion of 'imperfect foresight', which determines foreknowledge of conditions during the period of the loan, with regard to the general price level. Knight argues that people do not have the necessary foreknowledge but rather tend to consider the value of money to be absolute, even when confronted with actual changes. This reminds us of a very similar investigation of imperfect foresight by Morgenstern around the same period. Their mutual stimuli and motivation seems to have been high.

Morgenstern also tried to show his agreement with Knight in his elaboration of the time element in 1934a[25] and directly expressed his opposition to the concept of the production period in two articles published in 1935.[26] One of these was explicitly so entitled (Morgenstern, 1935b) and the other one investigated the relation between perfect foresight and the concept of equilibrium (Morgenstern, 1935a/1976). Morgenstern received much reputation for this second article,[27] where his criticism of timeless equilibrium was considerably sharpened and directed toward Hayek who abstracted the element of time and removed foresight from the theory of equilibrium.[28] Morgenstern asked Knight for comments on this article (a letter from Morgenstern to Knight dated November 18, 1935) and received a favourable one; Knight commented that with this article Morgenstern has 'done a major piece of work' (a letter from Knight to Morgenstern dated 23 December 1936). As is well-known, Knight translated this article into English, which seems to confirm his positive evaluation. However, upon checking the correspondence between Knight and Morgenstern, we find that there is one reservation, in that Morgenstern wanted to write an article in English related to the topic of perfect foresight and attempted to have this article translated and published in the *Journal of Political Economy*.[29] Knight seems to have helped him much.[30]

In the first article on the subject of production period, Morgenstern's investigation of the production period and of the roundabout production in connection to the intensity of capital and to the fluctuations of the business cycles, with explicit reference to Böhm-Bawerk, corresponds to Knight's criticism. He endorses Knight's reasoning of uncertainty, claiming that there are no clearly determined points of starting and ending for production. Further, he criticizes the idea that a longer roundabout production has an increasing rate of return, citing the differences between usual observations of nature and those of the modern large industry with production goods. This distinction aims at criticizing Böhm-Bawerk's idea of 'original factors of production' (A letter from Knight to Morgenstern dated 1 May 1936: 199) and refers to Knight's discussion of pre-existing capital goods. In the latter half of the article, Morgenstern emphasizes the distinction between the intensity of capital or the degree of capitalization, which relates to the rate of interest on the one hand and the intensity of production or business itself on the other. In the case of affluence, these two conditions, respectively, possibly lead to 'overinvestment' and 'overproduction', the discussion of which is presented in connection with the theory of business cycles or, more exactly, with the theory of crisis.

In connection with this theory of crisis, the passage attracts our attention where Morgenstern explicitly refers to Ellis (1935) as well as Knight (a letter from Knight to Morgenstern dated 1 May 1936: 202). Ellis is the author of an article 'The meaning of the period of production for the theory of crisis' published in the same volume of *Zeitschrift für Nationalökonomie*.[31] This article complements the rather modest and short one by Morgenstern, giving special consideration to economic crisis in the business cycle. Ellis classifies eight kinds of concepts of production period including those proposed by Böhm-Bawerk, the Vienna School of monetary theory and Knight,[32] discussing the characters of each theory and judging which ones are important and useful for dynamic analysis. He pays special attention to Böhm-Bawerk's theory and explains the distinction of increase of capital or of production, as is the claim of Morgenstern. From the correspondence, we know that it was Knight who first introduced Ellis to Morgenstern in 1933, calling Ellis as 'the bearer' and appreciated as 'one of my first students in economics and has been my favorite of all of them ever since.'[33] In 1935, Knight expresses his gratitude to Morgenstern, seemingly replying to Morgenstern's positive judgment of Ellis's contribution, where Knight takes 'a certain "paternal" interest and pride' (a letter from Knight to Morgenstern dated 15 August 1935). As a result, volume six of *Zeitschrift für Nationalökonomie* in 1935, in which Knight also contributed two articles, shows Morgenstern's remarkable aptitude for editorship. Their articles correspond with each other in that they show a tendency toward a theory that is considerably different from that of the Austrian School. Still in Vienna, Morgenstern refers to his separation from the Austrian School or a kind of 'inner' emigration, mostly in the direction of the United States, where Knight and Ellis hailed from. In fact, this talent and contribution of Morgenstern seems to have appealed to Knight so much that the latter enquired about Morgenstern's intention to immigrate to the United States again. In a letter in 1936, Knight told Morgenstern:

> Another thing that I have been wanting to take up with you is the fact that the market for high grade economists in this country seems to be quite 'bullish' at the moment. Are you interested? I wish you would write me frankly about your state of mind on the subject.... Ellis and I rather agreed that you probably wouldn't and shouldn't care to move unless you got a pretty good position....
>
> (A letter from Knight to Morgenstern dated 12 March 1936)

Unfortunately several letters sent after this one, which are important for determining the decisive moment of Morgenstern's immigration, seem to be missing. However, we know that, after a while, Morgenstern did move to the United States as a guest professor and, by chance or by intention, he did not or could not go back to Austria in 1938.[34] Based on the entire available correspondence, it is certain at least that Knight had long been aware of Morgenstern's inner desire to move out of Austria, especially after the political situation became uncomfortable around 1934. Even though they did not come much closer after Morgenstern's arrival in the United States, contrary to our expectation from their friendship until then, it is still not an exaggeration to state that Knight was a very important figure in Morgenstern's separation from Austria and the Austrian School and his involvement in the United States.

Notes

1. My claim is that this holds true even though the division of labour could have been unbalanced and von Neumann might have worked almost independently. The wide knowledge and sincere interest in the new ideas of Morgenstern surely attracted and stimulated von Neumann.
2. Malkiel (1973/2003: 32–3) points out that 'Oskar Morgenstern was a leading champion. The views he expressed in *Theory of Games and Economic Behavior*, of which he was co-author, have had a significant impact not only in economic theory but also on national security decisions and strategic corporate planning. In 1970 he co-authored another book, *Predictability of Stock Market Prices*, in which he and his colleague, Clive Granger, argued that the search for intrinsic value in stocks is a search for the will-o-the-wisp. In an exchange economy the value of any asset depends on an actual or prospective transaction. Morgenstern believed that every investor should post the following Latin maxim above his desk: Res tantum valet quantum vendi potest (A thing is worth only what someone else will pay for it)'.
3. Morgenstern was the managing editor (*Schriftleiter*) of *Zeitschrift für Nationalökonomie* from 1930 to 1938. In the first volume, he was named after Rosenstein-Rodan, while he occupied the first position from the second volume onwards. As to the international network, we have explored his relation with Italian economists, especially with L. Einaudi (Pavanelli, Nakayama, 2008).
4. This is a collection of articles written between 1897 and 1937.
5. In fact, even in the abovementioned article written by Schumpeter in 1910, Fetter is mentioned many times in relation to the theory of capital and interest.
6. We see some of these outcomes in the volume of collected works of Morgenstern, such as an article on Edgeworth and another on Young (Morgenstern, Schotter and Nadiri, 1976: 477–80, 487–8, respectively). We can find more evidence in the Morgenstern Papers; For example, in Boxes 2 and 3, we can find several letters of correspondence with economic theorists and editors of journals in English-speaking countries, such as Bowley, Mitchell, Young and Taussig.
7. We use the term 'business cycle research' rather than 'trade cycle research' as the equivalent of the German term *Konjunkturforschung*. In fact the engagement in this institute itself reflects Morgenstern's interest in measuring international economic phenomena.
8. Based on Morgenstern's reading of Böhm-Bawerk in his earlier days, cf. Morgenstern, 1976: 805. He received the scholarship between 1925 and 1928, travelling to the United States, England, France and Italy (Rockefeller Foundation, 1933: 76–7, Craver 1986b).
9. According to the reconstructive essay by Leonard, Morgenstern saw Fetter frequently (Leonard, 2004: 301).

10. Morgenstern wrote this article as part of his investigations on the problems of time and equilibrium in economics. Further, he criticized Mitchell for not having integrated cyclical movements into a framework of general equilibrium: '*Er* (Mitchell) *sagt ausdrücklich,* "It is no part of my task to determine how the fact of cyclical oscillations [...] can be reconciled with the general theory of equilibrium" ' (Morgenstern, 1928b: 67). Referring to Pigou's position, he maintains that Pigou's emphasis on the role of psychological factors as well as on the 'expectations of profit from industrial spending among business men' (Pigou, 1927: 35), constitutes major elements in satisfactory explanations of business cycles and economic fluctuations. However, he objects to a certain vagueness of that analysis. According to him, this imprecision is due to the 'Marshall Tradition' (Morgenstern, 1928b: 71–2), which constitutes the framework of Pigou's reasoning, and to which Morgenstern objects. According to him, this Marshall tradition is a type of compromise between common sense and statistics and lacks scientific precision.
11. Morgenstern begins to adapt himself to the quantitative direction of research (1943), which reminds us of his earlier contribution of 1927. However, in the 1920s, he was generally against the quantitative or empirical method. Rellstab (1992, Ch. 3) deals with this issue. Leonard (2004: 292) points out that it was Mises who introduced the idea to Morgenstern that Mitchell's institutionalism was 'an American reincarnation of the German historical method.'
12. Hayek himself remembers his interest in the business cycle theory in the similar reasoning and mentions Haberler as the representative author on the theme (Hayek, 1963/1992: 34–8). Hayek went to the United States in the early 1920s with recommendation letters by Schumpeter. Haberler got the scholarship from the Rockefeller Foundation between 1927 and 1929 (Rockefeller Foundation, 1933: 46–7).
13. Morgenstern (1976: 806) recalls that he was invited by the representative, Moritz Schlick, to give a talk on the theme of his 1928 book.
14. In the 1930s several economists also took part in these colloquia, including Morgenstern.
15. Menger (1934/1979: 259), Leonard (1995) and Nakayama (1997) point this out. The presentation has become Menger's article in 1934 and their contact continued even after both of them immigrated into the United States.
16. The material is found in Box 3 (correspondence of Morgenstern 1930–1932), Box 6 (correspondence 1928–1939, the parts of Knight), Box 13 (Diaries 21 January 1928–3 August 1944) and Box 47 (subject; Knight) of the Oskar Morgenstern Papers.
17. In the letter dated 2 January 1931, Knight asked Morgenstern how his article for the volume was progressing, and Morgenstern replied in the letter dated the 24th of the month, with the reserve that he was not responsible for this publication, although the volume had almost been completed. Morgenstern seems to have taken the effort to ask the publisher or the editor for the state of publication.
18. In a letter to Knight dated 12 September 1934, Morgenstern thanks Knight for the 'wonderful' article, although the American was half-sceptical of publication of these articles. (The scepticism is shown in a letter from Knight to Morgenstern dated 26 July 1934.)

19. 'I have been dipping into this business cycle literature and find the result depressing. It reflects very able work, but I cannot see that any of them are giving us [...] conclusive answers to vital problems [...]' (a letter from Knight to Morgenstern dated 8 January 1932). In an earlier letter, he expressed his desire to discuss with these people' (a letter from Knight to Morgenstern dated 10 November 1931).
20. There are not many researches on this topic, and some of them, Skousen (2005) for example, do not look into Morgenstern very much.
21. Letters from Knight to Morgenstern dated 8 January and 23 May 1932, and Morgenstern's replies dated 27 January and 14 July, respectively, show the process of discussion on this matter.
22. Later in 1937, when Morgenstern was about to move to the USA, Knight wrote – in a hand-written sentence after the entirely type-written text of the letter – 'I will entirely be glad to welcome you to the USA' (a letter from Knight to Morgenstern dated 31 July 1937).
23. However, the influence of Mayer on Morgenstern could have been not only a personal one but also a theoretical one, which is different from Knight's ironical suggestion. Leonard (2004) suggests this influence, pointing out Mayer's emphasis on the time element in his seminar (Leonard, 2004: 291–5).
24. 'Dr. O. Morgenstern's recent categorical denial (*Wirtschaftsprognose* [...] 1928) of the possibility of forecasting seems to be due only to the fact that he demands more from forecasting than is justifiable. Even the ability to forecast a hailstorm would not be useless...' (Hayek, 1933: 36).
25. In a letter, Morgenstern told Knight that he would see Morgenstern's scepticism of the so-called production period in his article on time element in 1934 (a letter from Morgenstern to Knight dated 12 September 1934) and asked for comments (a letter from Morgenstern to Knight dated 4 January 1935). Unfortunately, Knight did not appreciate this article very much.
26. Besides, he repeated this criticism in another article in 1936 (Morgenstern, 1936/1976: 402).
27. For example, Hutchison (1938) paid attention to Morgenstern's work in his book. Morgenstern also paid attention to Hutchison, which is seen, for example, in a letter to Knight dated 24 September 1939.
28. 'Hayek thinks that the equilibrium theory has been erected by abstracting the element of time and hence without inclusion of an element of foresight' (Morgenstern, 1935/1976: 170–1). Here Morgenstern also criticized Hicks, but made some reservation, pointing out that Hicks was aware of the possibility that 'monetary theory lied outside equilibrium theory because the use of money existed only in close association with imperfect foresight' (ibid.).
29. 'I am now thinking of adding a series of observations on risk and of somewhat changing the exposition of the whole and offering you the article in English for publication in the J. P. E. Will you please let me know soon, whether you are interested to have this article (app. 28 printed pages) or not and if you would publish it very soon. I have a certain interest to have this article appear in English because Mr. Keynes is preparing a book on the theory of money largely based on the element of expectation and anticipation'

(a letter from Morgenstern to Knight dated 12 March 1936). By the way, this quotation is interesting also because it shows Morgenstern's consciousness of Keynes's contribution to the theory of expectation and, in relation to it, forecasting.

30. 'Viner (who was one of the editors) says: "I see no reason why we shouldn't invite Morgenstern to submit the article to us, provided it is not too obviously a translation of the original article [...]" I should personally be most happy to see it published in the Journal' (a letter from Knight to Morgenstern dated 1 May 1936).
31. From the footnote of the article, we see that Ellis presented a paper at the Society of Economics in Vienna (*Nationalökonomische Gesellschaft*) on 1 February 1935.
32. When he mentions the Vienna School of monetary theory, Ellis refers to Mises and Hayek (Ellis, 1935: 154). He deploys some criticism of Knight's idea that it allows no room for 'period' at all (ibid.: 158–9).
33. This was a letter requesting Morgenstern to take care of Ellis who was going to visit Vienna with his family (A letter from Knight to Morgenstern dated 12 September 1933).
34. 'In January 1938, I left for the United States, invited by the Carnegie endowment for International Peace as a Visiting Professor at four American universities. [...] The Nazis took over in Vienna in March 1938. I was dismissed as "politically unbearable" from the University as well as from my Institute [...]' (Morgenstern, 1976: 807).

References

Boettke, P. and Vaughn, K (2002) 'Knight and the Austrians on Capital, and the Problem of Socialism', *History of Political Economy,* 34(1): 156–76.

Cohen, A. J. (2003) 'Hayek/Knight Capital Controversy: The Irrelevance of Roundaboutness, or Purging Processes in Time?', *History of Political Economy,* 35(3): 469–90.

Craver, E. (1986a) 'The emigration of Austrian economists', *History of Political Economics,*18(1): 1–32.

Craver, E. (1986b) 'Patronage and the directions of research in economics, the Rockefeller Foundation in Europe, 1924–1938', *Minerva,* 24(2–3): 205–22.

Ellis, H. S. (1935) 'Die Bedeutung der Produktionsperiode für die Krisentheorie', *Zeitschrift für Nationalökonomie,* 6(2): 145–69.

Fetter, F. A. (1927) 'Amerika', in H. Mayer (ed.), *Gesamtbild der Forschung in den einzelnen Ländern, Die Wirtschaftstheorie der Gegenwart,* 1: 31–60.

Fetter, F. A. (1977) *Capital, Interest, and Rent: Essays in the Theory of Distribution,* Kansas City: Sheed Andrews and McMeel, Inc.

Genechten, R. van (1931) 'Über das Verhältnis zwischen der Produktivität des Kapitals, den Löhnen und Zinsen,' *Zeitschrift für Nationalökonomie,* 2(2): 200–20.

Hagemann, H. (ed.) (1997) *Zur deutschsprachigen wirtschaftswissenschaftlichen Emigration nach 1933,* Marburg: Metropolis.

Hagemann, H (1999) 'Oskar Morgenstern', in H. Hagemann and C. D. Krohn (eds), *Biographisches Handbuch der deutschsprachigen wirtschaftswissenschaftlichen Emigration nach 1933*, Munich: K. G. Saur.
Hayek, F. A. (1933) *Monetary Theory and the Trade Cycle*, translated by N. Kaldor and H. M. Croome, London/Toronto: Jonathan Cape.
Hayek, F. A. (1934/1992), 'Carl Menger (1840–1921)', in Klein (ed.) (1992).
Hayek, F. A. (1963/1992) 'The Economics of the 1920s as Seen from Vienna', in Klein (ed.) (1992).
Hutchison, T. W. (1938) *The Significance and Basic Postulates of Economic Theory*, London: Macmillan.
Klausinger, H. (2006) '"In the wilderness": Emigration and the Decline of the Austrian School', *History of Political Economy*, 38(4): 617–64.
Klein, P. G. (ed.) (1992) *The Fortune of Liberalism: Essays on Austrian Economics and the Ideal of Freedom*, Chicago: The University of Chicago Press.
Knight, F. H. (1932a) 'Das Wertproblem in der Wirtschaftstheorie', in H. Mayer (ed.), *Die Wirtschaftstheorie der Gegenwart*, 2:52–72.
Knight, F. H. (1932b) 'Interest', *Encyclopedia of the Social Science*, 8, edited by R. A. Seligman and A. Johnson, New York: MacMillan.
Knight, F. H. (1933) 'Capitalistic Production, Time and the Rate of Return', *Economic Essays in Honor of Gustav Cassel*, London: George Allen & Unwin Ltd.
Knight, F. H. (1934) 'Capital, Time and the Interest Rate', *Economica*, n.s., 1 (August), 257–86.
Knight, F. H. 'Correspondence with Oskar Morgenstern', *Oskar Morgenstern Papers*. (Box 3, Box 6).
Leonard, R. J. (1995) 'From Parlor Games to Social Science: von Neumann, Morgenstern, and the Creation of Game Theory 1928–1944', *Journal of Economic Literature*, XXXIII(June): 730–61.
Leonard, R. J. (2004) "'Between worlds", or an imagined Reminiscence by Oskar Morgenstern about Equilibrium and Mathematics in the 1920s', *Journal of the History of Economic Thought*, 26(3): 285–310.
Liefmann, R. (1932) 'Zur Diskussion über die Kosten- und Ertragstheorie', *Zeitschrift für Nationalökonomie*, 3(3): 368–83.
Malkiel, B. G. (1973/2003) *A Random-walk Down Wall Street: the time-tested strategy for successful investing*, New York, London: W. W. Norton & Company.
Mayer, H. (ed.) (1927) *Gesamtbild der Forschung in den einzelnen Ländern*, (Der erste Band von *Die Wirtschaftstheorie der Gegenwart*), Vienna: Verlag von Julius Springer.
Menger, K. (1934/1979) 'The Role of Uncertainty in Economics', *Selected Papers in Logic and Foundations, Didactics, Economics*, Dordrecht, Boston, London: D. Reidel Publishing Company: 259–78. ('Das Unsicherheitsmoment in der Wertlehre', *Zeitschrift für Nationalökonomie*, 5(4): 459–85.)
Menger, K. (1936/1979) 'Remarks on the Law of Diminishing Returns: A Study in Meta-Economics', *Selected Papers in Logic and Foundations, Didactics, Economics*, Dordrecht, Boston, London: D. Reidel Publishing Company: 279–302. ('Bemerkungen zu den Ertragsgesetzen', *Zeitschrift für Nationalökonomie*, 7(1): 25–56.)
Morgenstern, O. (1927) 'International vergleichende Konjunkturforschung', *Zeitschrift für die gesamte Staatswissenschaft*, 83(2): 261–90.

Morgenstern, O. (1928a) *Wirtschaftsprognose: Eine Untersuchung ihrer Voraussetzungen und Möglichkeiten*, Vienna: Julius Springer.

Morgenstern, O. (1928b) 'Qualitative und quantitative Konjunkturforschung', *Zeitschrift fur die gesamte Staatswissenschaften*, 85(1): 54–88.

Morgenstern, O. (1931) 'Offene Probleme der Kosten- und Ertragstheorie', *Zeitschrift für Nationalökonomie*, 2(4): 481–522.

Morgenstern, O. (1934a/1976) 'The Time Moment in Value Theory', in Morgenstern, Schotter and Nadiri (1976): 151–67. ('Das Zeitmoment in der Wertlehre', *Zeitschrift für Nationalökonomie*, 5(4): 433–58.)

Morgenstern, O. (1934b) *Die Grenzen der Wirtschaftspolitik*, Vienna: Julius Springer.

Morgenstern, O. (1935a/1976) 'Perfect Foresight and Economic Equilibrium', in Morgenstern, Schotter and Nadiri (1976): 169–83.

Morgenstern, O. (1935b) 'Zur Theorie der Produktionsperiode', *Zeitschrift für Nationalökonomie*, 6(2): 196–208.

Morgenstern, O. (1936/1976) 'Logistics and the social sciences', in Morgenstern, Schotter and Nadiri (1976) *Selected Economic Writings of Oskar Morgenstern*, New York: New York University Press,: 389–404. (Originally in German, *Zeitschrift für Nationalökonomie*, 7(1): 1–24.)

Morgenstern, O. (1943) 'On the international spread of business cycles', *The Journal of Political Economy*, LI(4): 287–309.

Morgenstern, O. (1951/1976) 'Joseph A. Schumpeter, 1883–1950', in Morgenstern, Schotter and Nadiri (eds) *Selected Economic Writings of Oskar Morgenstern*, New York: New York University Press, 489–97. (Originally in *Economic Journal*, 61(241): 197–202.)

Morgenstern, O. (1976) 'The Collaboration Between Oskar Morgenstern and John von Neumann on the Theory of Games', *Journal of Economic Literature*, 14(3): 805–16.

Morgenstern, O. Papers [= OMP]. Special Collections Library. Duke University.

Morgenstern, O., Schotter, A. and Nadiri, M. I. (eds) (1976), *Selected Economic Writings of Oskar Morgenstern*, New York: New York University Press.

Morgenstern, O. and Granger, C. W. T. (1970), *Predictability in the Stock Market Prices*.

Nakayama, C. (1997) 'The Process of Collaboration between Oskar Morgenstern and John von Neumann', *History of Economics Review*, 39(26): 40–50.

Pavanelli, G. and Nakayama, C. (2008) 'A Lifelong Friendship: The Correspondence between Oskar Morgenstern and Luigi Einaudi', *Storia Del Pensiero Economico*, n. s., Ann. 5, n. 1, 95–120.

Rellstab, U. (1992) *Ökonomie und Spiele. Die Entstehungsgeschichte der Spieltheorie aus dem Blickwinkel des Ökonomen Oskar Morgenstern*, Chur: Rüegger.

Rockefeller Foundation (1933) 'Social science fellowships of the Rockefeller Foundation, 1924–1932 (voted prior to October 1, 1932)', Rockefeller Foundation European Office.

Rothbard, M. N. (1977) 'Introduction', in Fetter (ed.) (1977).

Schlesinger, K. von (1936) 'Ein Beitrag zu Mengers "Bemerkungen zu den Ertragsgesetzen" ', *Zeitschrift für Nationalökonomie*, 7(3): 398–400.

Schmidt, C. (1996) 'Risk and Uncertainty: A Knightian distinction revisited', in C. Schmidt (ed.), *Uncertainty in Economic Thought*, Cheltenham and Brookfield: Edward Elgar.

Schumpeter, J. A. (1910) 'Die neuere Wirtschaftstheorie in den Vereinigten Staaten', *Jahrbuch für Gesetzgebung, Verwaltung und Volkswirtschaft,* 34(3): 1–51.
Schumpeter, J. A. (1926/1954) 'Gustav v. Schmoller und die Probleme von Heute', *Dogmenhistorische und Biographische Aufsätze,* Tübingen: J. C. B. Mohr.
Schumpeter, J. A. (1927) 'Deutschland', in H. Mayer (ed.), *Gesamtbild der Forschung in den einzelnen Ländern, Die Wirtschaftstheorie der Gegenwart,* 1: 1–30.
Skousen, M. (2005) *Vienna & Chicago Friends or Foes?: A Tale of Two Schools of Free-Market Economics,* Lanham: Capital Press.

Part V

Transition of the Austrian School

13
On Menger, Hayek and on the Concept of *'Verstehen'*

Kurt R. Leube

> Soweit es sich um menschliche Handlungen handelt, *sind* die Dinge das, was die Menschen glauben, dass sie sind.
>
> (Hayek, 1979: 31)

1. Introduction

On 3 July 1866 the Prussian army won a decisive victory over the Austrians at the battle of Königgrätz. Ill-equipped with outdated muzzle-loading rifles and under the blundering leadership of Ludwig von Benedek, the Austrian army suffered a crushing and devastating defeat (see among others Craig, 1964 or Herre, 1978). Not even the brilliant and much celebrated military victories at Custozza by Archduke Albrecht and at Lissa by Admiral Wilhelm von Tegettoff could offset this lasting humiliation. This stigma conspicuously contributed to the fact that the label 'Austrian' had acquired a somewhat condescending implication in the German Reich. Especially the academic community in the Austro-Hungarian Empire[1] was frequently looked down upon and most of their publications were often ranked inferior.[2]

In Imperial Germany at the time, Gustav von Schmoller (1838–1917) was widely acknowledged as a leading social scientist. Under his mostly undisputed leadership, the so-called 'younger German Historical School' soon became the dominant force within the social sciences in the German Reich. This status allowed Schmoller and his fellow traveller Friedrich Althoff[3] to develop a system by which they managed not only to occupy the most important academic positions. The *'System Althoff'* as it became known, also pushed the natural sciences in Prussia to new heights by seriously compromising the ideal of academic freedom that Wilhelm von Humboldt had proclaimed at the University of Berlin in the early nineteenth century. While such 'guiding supervision' may be seen as less contentious within the realm of the natural sciences, the brazen interference by Althoff and von Schmoller proved especially ominous in the politically more sensitive subjects of the social sciences. Under the 'System Althoff' there was almost no room left for new theories or approaches to be developed in the social sciences, let alone to advance new insights and findings. Thus, well into the last century it was almost impossible for a scholar in the tradition of the 'Austrian School of Economics' to attain a meaningful position at any decent German university.[4] According to Ludwig von Mises, one of the most famous Prussian scientists of the time, Emile du Bois-Reymond once even 'boasted that the University of Berlin was 'the intellectual bodyguard of the House of Hohenzollern' (Mises, 1969: 26).

In 1873, Gustav von Schmoller and his followers also founded the 'Verein für Sozialpolitik', which soon developed into an academically important and politically effective association. Mainly due to their strong leaning towards a kind of 'evolutionary' socialism, many members of this society became known as '*Kathedersozialisten*' and soon dominated economic research at the German universities (see Schefold, 1987).

The common methodology of the 'younger German Historical School' focused increasingly on economic history with the conscious rejection of pure theory in the social sciences. Schmoller and most of his disciples discarded the abstract, axiomatic-deductive approach and considered theoretical analysis to be of minor importance or even 'useless'.[5] Its applicability was limited to artificially isolated fragments of the social realm, which they wanted to perceive in all its many facets. Unlike the 'older German Historical School' and despite the fact that von Schmoller publicly discredited Auguste Comte (1798–1857) and his 'Positivism' conceivably on grounds of the latter's agnosticism and French origin, most of his followers nevertheless seem to have embraced Comte's positivistic ideas.[6]

It may be useful here to briefly summarize the essence of Comte's methodological position. Although not the founder of positivism, he is widely considered the originator of the term 'sociology', the new branch of the social sciences with which he replaced the traditional methods of dealing with human action. In broad and general terms, Comte thought that social wholes were better known than the elements of which they consist and social theory, therefore, ought to start from our knowledge of the directly perceived social wholes. Comte even claimed that the entire society was the real thing, and individuals were only an abstraction. Thus, his countless followers turned toward a method that

The concepts and terms *'understanding'* or *'verstehen'* as well as *'conceptualizing'* or *'begreifen'* which are characteristic for the Austrian approach to interpret typical courses of actions in economic theory have often been belittled and even ridiculed. According to Ludwig von Mises's classic statement we learn that, '*Understanding* is the grasping of the sense which human actors associate with their aims [...] *Understanding* is to begin with identification of the irrational fact and then attempt to feel with the senses and feelings which have led the human actors to their evaluation of these irrational facts.'[9] In other words, Mises's *'verstehen'* is aimed at grasping the meaning of actions that only pursue ends and search for goals without being concerned about the nature of these ends or goals. It is the process of comprehending the meaning that the acting human beings see in their goals. For Mises the term *'verstehen'* comes into the discussion where the subjectivity of values, judgments or of any assessment begins. Rephrasing Mises, this process searches for meaning by trying to recreate, reconstruct or mentally relive an entire situation. For example, we choose our words in order to invite our listeners to follow us by attempting a 'mental reproduction' of the event we are talking about, and at times parts of our audience may even be able to 'solidarize' with it. Nevertheless, whether the individuals will and can follow us is exclusively determined by their previously received sensations and by their particular knowledge of similar events. *Understanding* is the method that the historical sciences employ in dealing with the non-repeatable. Yet, through intuitions and opinions we cannot obtain indisputable knowledge: Of course, *verstehen* is always subjective (see Mises, 1940: 51–63).

Verstehen as a theoretical method enables its user to interpret the meaning of typical action series by using characteristic schemata or designs of thought because we ourselves are acting human beings. Our daily routine chores, a certain household plan, or shopping patterns developed over time might serve here as examples.

One can only individually *verstehen* the meaning of our goals, as *verstehen* is primarily the realization of the rational or irrational state of affairs. *Verstehen* can assist in the attempt to empathize with the sensations and feelings of others. The process of *verstehen* that we use to move about in society is not different in its essence from the term *verstehen* in psychology or in history, as 'we "understand" the way in which the results we observe can be produced, although we possibly might never be in a position to observe the whole process or to predict its precise course or the exact result' (see Hayek, 1979: 52; author's translation). The praxeological approach also does not really differ from the logic and process that individuals use in everyday life. In general terms, following Mises, one could even say that *verstehen* as a method has had fruitful applications in the clarification of any text, be it more generally in history or more specifically in the domains of law, theology or philosophy.

In Austrian methodology, the method of *verstehen* is complemented by the equally important term '*begreifen*' or '*conceptualizing*' or '*praxeological cognition*' which paraphrases the attempt to comprehend meaning through a somewhat 'rambling' thinking or '*diskursives Denken*' (see Mises, 1940: 51). Whereas *verstehen* always refers to the knowledge of the immediate experiencing of the values, emotions and essences, the term *begreifen* suggests a conceptualization of our recognition of objects outside of our realm. In other words, *begreifen* is the holistic interpretation of experiences. However, this distinct approach is by no means restricted to economics, rather it is applicable to all social sciences as it transcends economics and allows us to '*verstehen*' and to '*begreifen*' the ultimate development and formation of spontaneous social orders.

Thus, the concept of *begreifen* is always subjected to firm logic and can be validated or refuted. Furthermore, within its context the subject can also be discussed in terms of true or false. All that we gain through the application of *begreifen* ought to be acknowledged as either proven or erroneous, and thus cannot be circumnavigated or ignored. *Begreifen,* in other words, only relates to the readiness and the ability to think logically and apply consistently any previously received sensations or information. The *praxeological cognition* grasps the meaning of action through *begreifen*. In all our actions, we follow the 'economic calculus' or 'pure logic of choice' (see Hayek, 1937), which depends on our individual knowledge of the specific circumstances of time and place. This means, then, that every economically or socially relevant action must depend on the expectations of the other individual market participants. This approach is fully justified by the fact that all human actions are oriented around individual plans and are purposefully undertaken with the expectation of being better off than if one had acted otherwise. The *begreifen* of a particular event always means to find the relation to other events through which the form and existence of this particular event is determined.[10]

However, we cannot grasp logically the reasons or motives of the relative valuation of the exchanged goods or services through *begreifen*. The goal, that is, the end-purpose, and its respective evaluation cannot be comprehended praxeologically, nor can these mental subjects be explained with the methods of historicism: Their meaning and their valuation can only be *understood*. Every human action is undertaken because of physical and biological insights and experiences that are not always transparent in all their consequences and which differ from science only because of their lack of a systematic classification. We will never be able to understand the process as a whole or predict its exact bearings, yet we can properly *understand* 'the way in which the results we observe can be produced' (Hayek, 1979: 52; author's translation). *Begreifen* is the logical precedent of *verstehen*. We interpret the meaning of typical action series with the support of thought patterns that are at our disposal through experience and thus the 'pure logic of choice'. What matters here is of course the state of knowledge as the origin of human action and the process of its changes over time. As stated above, within the social sciences this means that all human actions depend on the actions or expectations of other participants in the market place. Because of the pre-existing fact that we have goals, purposes or desires and always act to attain them, we are able to interpret the meaning of another person's actions. In other words, we know *a priori* that all human actions are purposefully undertaken with the rational expectation of being better off than one would be otherwise. '*Begreifen*' thus is thinking, and '*verstehen*' is watching (see Mises, 1940: 56).

By assuming that all circumstances remain unchanged, the properties of rocks or of water can be correctly analyzed and the reactions can be measured, and at least in principle even predicted. Applied to human beings, however, this approach must consistently abandon reason or concepts related to personal purposes, goals or individual preferences. We even would have to turn away from any ideas usually associated with studying or learning as, according to this view, only physical events can be described.

But the question remains, as to why the methods associated with the exact sciences are still so widely used in theoretical economics? Why is it that the vast majority of professional social scientists today seem to firmly believe that only the utilization of 'objective' mathematics can warrant a clear and consistent methodology to be used within the social sciences? This phenomenon is probably as old as the theoretical thinking about the subject and regretfully follows the '*Zeitgeist*' of popular superstitions, intellectual trends and of cultural developments.

Positivists have always assumed that our sensory experiences can be understood as the result of a process by which fixed classifications of common knowledge are imposed on our chaotic and disorderly world. The methods of the natural sciences thus ought to be used in order to measure, evaluate or compare human activities, because only the physical sciences experiments allow us to verify or falsify hypotheses. These hypotheses thus are framed in order to explain and distinguish certain classes of behaviour or groups of motions, and various propositions are deduced for either *verification* or *falsification* of the theories by empirical checks of these observable uniform or homogenous events. In order to draw conclusions from experiences, serious research in the social sciences ought to collect figures, draw charts, compare countries or diligently compute averages. Only with such data available the researcher may be able, to deal with uniform or homogenous events that can be examined for quantitative regularities and constants. If we were not able to investigate the dependence or independence of the elements of any natural phenomenon through the variation of one or more elements in the experiment, then we probably will not be able to *understand* the relations that govern nature through empirical laws.

It is precisely here where the cognitive aim and the direction of thought of the Austrian methodology come forth. As mentioned above, Carl Menger's important insight, that human beings and their actions must be investigated and analyzed with a methodology that sharply differs from the methods used in the natural sciences is truly fundamental and influenced all proponents of the school. This is the thoroughly misunderstood and sometimes ridiculed 'praxeological approach' of the Austrian School of economics that played a dominant role in Carl Menger's first book[11] and which found in Hayek's crucial, yet widely neglected work on *The Sensory Order* (1952)[12] its most elaborate explanation to date.

4. Compositive methods in the social sciences: The importance of Hayek's *The Sensory Order*

Following Menger, Friedrich A. Hayek recommended identifying the methods used in the social sciences as *compositive*[13] in order to clearly distinguish them from the *analytical* methods of the natural sciences. In other words, after linking our individual observations to their properties which are already known to us in a systematic way, and after having mentally reconstructed these individual elements into unique new perceptions, we learn to isolate a single social phenomenon from the totality of all observed events. Although our minds develop vastly different goals, they react to the unknown and ever so rapidly changing circumstances of time and place always according to our previously received sensations. This is the difficult field of the 'sensory order' which is not built up from 'a basis in raw sense impressions', as most positivists seem to have suggested.

According to Ernst Mach, individuals combine sense data into complexes under the influence of others, especially the ones who taught him to speak, then his teachers and so on. The individual is thus always influenced by language and the information communicated to him.[14] In contrast to Mach, Hayek drew a distinction between the phenomenal and the physical order and concluded that the contrast between the two orders rests on the differences of events in their effects upon each other and on us. Following Hayek,[15] our mind rather learns in an evolutionary process to put together a system of links, which records the recurrence with which different bundles of internal and external stimulants have acted together upon our organism. Each 'individual impulse or group of impulses will on its occurrence evoke other impulses which correspond to the other stimuli which in the past have usually accompanied its occurrence' (Hayek, 1963: 42–66). Through its acquired connections the primary stimulus will then set up several secondary impulses, always subsequent to the principal impulse, and ceaselessly so on. It is for these reasons, that Hayek thinks 'it will be the total or partial identity of this following of the primary impulse which makes them members of the same class' (ibid.: 64). All sensory perception must be viewed as an act of classification, and what we *understand* are never unique properties of individual objects, but always only properties which these recognized objects might have in common with other objects. As a result, our perception must always be viewed as an interpretation, in other words as the placing of something into one or several classes of objects. All sensory perceptions are necessarily abstract, and subjectively always select certain aspects or particular features of a given situation. The characteristic 'attributes of sensory qualities', or the classes into which these different events are eventually placed in the process of perception, consist then entirely of the differentiating responses of the organism by which the order of these events is created. Accordingly, this classification is based on the connection created in the nervous system by past 'linkages', as Hayek labelled these connections.

This means however, that this organizing function of our mind must be prior to the perception of particular things, since all information we get about the external world (for instance, the social and physical environment in which we are living), has gone through this kind of sorting and filtering process. In addition, this process itself will develop as the mind keeps recognizing new links or new distinctions between our past experiences or sensations. Therefore, every single sensation must be regarded as an interpretation of an event in the light of an individual's past experiences, because for Hayek all our experiences operate on physiological events and arrange them into an order that becomes the basis of their mental significance. The distinction between the sensory qualities, in terms of which alone our conscious mind can learn about all things in our social environment, must therefore be seen as the result of a so-called 'pre-sensory' experience.

Every sensory experience of an event is therefore likely to possess unique attributes (in Hayek's words) to which no other similar attribute or property corresponds. These attributes are the significance, which the organism has learned to assign to a class of events based on the past associations of events of this category with certain other classes of events. So far as a conscious sensory experience is concerned, it thus cannot be true that everything we know is due to such experience. Experience of this kind would only become possible after an experience in the sense of a linkage that has created the order of sensory qualities. For Hayek, the fact that there can be nothing in our 'mind' which is not the result of onto – or phylogenetically established linkages, is not meant to exclude a process of a re-classification.

The term 'mind' used in the sense of an organism which reproduces the image of the external world is defined here by Hayek as 'a particular order of a set of events taking place in some organism and in some manner related to, but not identical with, the physical order of events in the environment' (ibid.: 16). This means then that the same kind of regularities which we have learnt throughout our life to discover in our surrounding world, are in principle also capable of building up an order that is quite similar to our mind. For Hayek however, there exists an absolute limit to what the human brain can ever accomplish by way of explanation, due to the nature of the explanation itself. The distinct character of mental entities and of their mode of operation is determined by their relation to or their position in the system of all other mental entities. This simple fact renders it impossible to ever complete a particular process.

From all that it follows, then, that no one of them can ever be explained without at the same time explaining the others or the entire structure of the relationship determining their character. Any attempt to explain particular mental processes must contain references to other mental processes and therefore prevent us from an ability to fully describe things in physical terms. 'Such a completion of the task of science, which would place us in a position to explain in detail the manner in which our sensory picture of the external world represents relations existing between the parts of this world, would mean that this reproduction of the world would have to include a reproduction of that reproduction...and so on *ad infinitum*' (ibid.: 194). Although, we shall never be able to provide a full explanation of mental phenomena, Hayek contends that we can still use our 'introspective' knowledge of mental events in order to *verstehen* (understand) and in some measure even to predict (pattern predictions) the result mental processes will lead to in certain conditions.

This is, in summary, Hayek's characteristic approach that is geared towards the interpretation of cultural facts. Its aim is always directed not only towards the discovery of quantitative relationships among socio-economic phenomena, but also towards an understanding of the meaning of human actions. The experience that praxeology deals with is inevitably always part of history. Yet, all history from the most precise historical description to the most updated statistical data, remains confined to the historicist method (see Collingwood, 1946: 221). Historical events are not homogenous in any sense of the word, rather they are complex, unique consequences of countless causal-genetic factors and therefore can neither be used for a positivistic test, nor combined with other events in the form of statistical correlation thereby achieving any meaningful results. The aggregation of data will not lead to a gain of theoretical insights, since we can only see empirical observations as complex phenomena that are the result of a joint influence of an unknown number of unknown components. To demand that history should become a theoretical science or, worse, theory should ever be historical is in fact a contradiction in terms. It was already pointed out by Carl Menger that because of the problem of free will, 'empirical laws of absolute strictness are out of the question in the realm of phenomena of human activity' (see Menger, 1985: 214–15). In the social sciences we are neither able to experiment nor to verify or falsify empirically our hypotheses and cannot arrive at any empirical laws.

It is of interest here to mention that while reading Ernst Mach's book *Erkenntnis und Irrtum* (1905, 2nd ed. 1906) in October 1906, Carl Menger wrote to Mach that he was not able so far 'to get rid of all objections against your point of view. In any case you are, my right honorable colleague, the most empirical contemporary philosopher, who in a certain sense is most independent of hypotheses.'[16]

5. Menger's objection to the use of mathematical methods

In his published work, Carl Menger never made a direct reference to mathematics and statistics as useful research methods. By looking at his correspondence with Walras and a few annotations that he scribbled into his own books, we can assume that he did not have a particularly strong mathematical or statistical bent.[17] His son Karl, himself a noted mathematician, in 1983 claimed that his father's distaste for mathematics and its methods, had its origin in the poor, if not inadequate mathematical training he had received in the 'Gymnasium' (high school) of his home town, Neu Sandez in rural Galizien during the 1850s.[18] Yet, even if this statement were true, his methodological objections against the use of mathematics and statistics as research tools are based on the result of his insights discussed above. Mention should also be made to the somewhat curious fact that Joseph A. Schumpeter not only attended Carl Menger's lectures at the University of Vienna but also was an active participant in the famous seminar that Eugen von Böhm-Bawerk conducted there.[19] Yet, he saw in the methods of his own teachers only a more or less imperfect preliminary to the theories of Walras and his group that later developed into the 'Lausanne School'. Schumpeter even claimed that the 'defective technique only prevented them [that is, the Austrians] from climbing to the top of it' (Schumpeter, 1954: 918).

Although the correspondence between Menger and Leon Walras consists of only four letters (Walras, 1965), Menger's part should here be sufficient to show the core of his objection to the use of mathematics as a *research* tool for economic analysis. From his atomistic point of view, Menger made it clear to Walras that 'we do not simply study quantitative relationships but also the *nature* (*das Wesen*) of economic phenomena. How can we attain to the knowledge of this latter (e.g., the nature of value, rent, profit, the division of labour, bimetallism, etc.) by mathematical methods?' He described the task of economics to Walras further as ' [...] the tracing back of the complex phenomena of the economy to their true causes, to their constitutive elements, and the investigation of the laws according to which these build themselves up into complex phenomena of the economy' (ibid.: 126). In other words, Menger's real objection to mathematics was that it simply amounted to not much more than a supplementary tool of exposition which cannot enhance the social scientist's ability to explain human action.

In stark contrast to Menger, L. Walras and W. St. Jevons appreciated the use of mathematics because it enabled them, among other things, to demonstrate the conditions for an equilibrium in a given market situation where exchanges usually take place. Yet, the economic analysis derived from their work took on an essentially static quality that must be viewed as an attempt to determine only the necessary prerequisites for a market equilibrium (see among other works, Jaffé, 1976). However, equilibrium theory can be meaningful only in a framework of a real time dimension as all transactions are dynamically undertaken in the course of time and involve individual plans. This problem cannot be resolved by splitting actions into several successive equilibriums as these render sense only if they are used for the analysis of the actions of an individual. It was Walras who emphasized that any passage of time before the equilibrium is achieved must undermine that very equilibrium, because all data-changing events that might happen on the way to the equilibrium necessarily will contribute to determine that state of affairs. All transaction undertaken in the course of achieving the equilibrium, thus, must be revoked.

Menger's approach, on the other hand, in comparison had important dynamic qualities that set it apart from any other school of thought. As the role of time is absolutely essential for Carl Menger's approach, an equilibrium was considered purely as a useful limiting case that portrayed the circumstances under which no further motivations for exchange among traders would exist. The importance of marginal utility for Menger was precisely its value in enabling an analysis of the exchange process itself, regardless of the concrete manifestation of any eventual equilibrium outcome. Menger clarified his position further in his essay, 'Grundzüge einer Klassifikation der Wirtschaftswissenschaften' (Menger, 1889). Moreover, he elaborated on it especially in his critical review of *Untersuchungen über die Theorie des Preises* (1889) by the two Viennese authors, Rudolf Auspitz und Richard Lieben.[20] Although, these authors were overall quite sympathetic to Menger's approach, his review of it carried a somewhat testy undertone. He ended it with the sarcastic observation that, although the authors have presented their essentially wrong messages in a graphically correct way, they nonetheless failed to overcome the ultimate deficiency of their suppositions. In a few notes that Menger scribbled into the German translation of John St. Mill's *Grundsätze der politischen Ökonomie* (1864) he also rejected the theory of equilibrium. He demonstrated here that his causal-genetic method is simply incompatible with Walras's position due to the latter's assumption that different elements of the economic processes were interrelated and must be linked by static functional relations (see Kauder, 1965: 99 and the literature there).

6. On the use of knowledge in society

Human actions can only be interpreted as being in an equilibrium if they are part of an individual plan. Only if all human actions were to take place at the same time and under identical circumstances could we ever substantiate our claim about the links of which we reach a conclusion from our assumption of the knowledge and the subjective preferences of an individual's action. All data, which lead to an individual's action are in their totality necessarily only known to the actor and, thus, can never be assumed as objective facts that are equally *understandable* to all. Because for any social interaction or transfer to take place, the information on which an individual grounds his or her plans, inevitably must represent the expectation that others will act in a certain way. In other words, it is a necessary precondition for the compatibility of individual plans that the intended actions of one individual contain the data for the formation of another person's plan or strategy. Such an assumption, however, seems highly impossible and the attempt to circumnavigate this flaw by assuming that all participating individuals possess the same bits and pieces of information at the same time does not contribute to resolving it.[21] If the analysis of one individual's equilibrium is applied to the entire society, the definition of the equilibrium necessarily must acquire a different meaning. On the one hand, every change concerning the relevant knowledge of an individual will undermine the state of equilibrium that existed in all actions the individual has undertaken either prior or after the change of knowledge took place and, thus, could only exist at the time when the so-called rational expectations proved to be correct. On the other hand, the time factor becomes essential as an equilibrium ought to be defined as a relationship between at least two actions that necessarily take place successively. However, if the time factor is neglected, the explanatory value of the equilibrium theory quickly dwindles to zero.

7. Conclusions

Although it is obvious that 'data' are always known, we never know who knows what and who controls them. Is it assumed that those studying individual transactions possess this knowledge or do we suggest that the individual whose actions are studied has this information? As the categories of the 'logic of choice' (the economic calculus) are subjectively known means and ends, we must accept that the relevant 'data' leading to a particular human action can only be known to the acting person. In other words, it is misleading to believe that all data that are relevant for individual decision-making processes are objectively the same for all and as such are also equally relevant and available for all at the time of making a choice.

No data analysis can identify a certain thing or a physical good, nor can it render anything substantial about the behaviour of prices of different goods or services. The only insight we gain is that acting people have formed a certain opinion about the way they are going to use this information. In other words, prices or data serve only as a signal and can only be fully explained through the *verstehen* and *begreifen* of the acting people's opinions, which lead to certain actions.

After all, 'as far as human actions are concerned, things are what people believe that they are' (Hayek, 1979: 31; author's translation).

Notes

1. After the '*Ausgleich*' of December 1867, Hungary was recognized as a co-ordinate part of the Habsburg Empire which became the '*Österreichisch-Ungarische Monarchie*' (kuk).
2. See Schmoller (1883) or Hutchison (1962). See also, Sombart (1930): Sombart succeeded in radically changing his methodological and political positions at least three times, always according to the prevailing '*Zeitgeist*'. It should be mentioned here that although Menger dedicated his *Grundsätze der Volkswirthschaftslehre* (1871) to the eminent German scholar and royal Saxonian councillor Wilhelm Roscher (who praised it), this book was suspiciously ignored or misunderstood in the German Reich. Of the four professional journals that existed at that time, only three of them published short reviews, but generally missing the central idea of Menger's book. One exception should perhaps be made for Hack (1872) who at least appreciated Menger's scholarship. For an almost complete record of these book reviews, see Howey (1960).
3. Friedrich Althoff (1839–1908) was one of Germany's three most influential academic administrators between W. von Humboldt and C.H. Becker. From 1882–1907 Althoff 'manipulated' and controlled all professorial appointments in Imperial Germany. See the interesting study by B. vom Brocke (1988).
4. Since Schumpeter's methodological position followed naturally from his view that Walras's accomplishments represented the true height of economic thought, he cannot be counted as a 'pure' Austrian. The appointment of F. A. Hayek at the University of Freiburg in 1962 must therefore be regarded as the sole exception to date.
5. See F. A. Hayek's Introduction to Menger's *Principles* (Menger, 1981: 23).
6. From 1817–1824, Comte was a disciple of the influential Henri de Saint Simon (1760–1826). See especially Hayek (1979: 265–88). Also of interest here are Fuchs-Heinritz (1998), Kaesler (2000) and Eucken (1938).
7. It seems important to note here, that Menger (1985: 142) considered Comte's theories as *wahnwitzig* (insane): 'when A. Comte conceives of "societies" as real organisms and to be sure as organisms of a more complicated nature that the natural one and designates their theoretical interpretation as the incomparably more complicated and more difficult scientific problem, he exposes himself forthwith to a serious error. His theory would be correct

only as against sociologists who might get the idea, which is really *insane* in the light of the present state of the theoretical natural sciences, of wanting to interpret social phenomena not in a specifically sociological way, but in the atomistic way of the natural sciences'.

8. Ludwig von Mises claimed that this term was misleading, as 'the issue was not to discover the most appropriate procedure for the treatment of the problems commonly considered as economic problems. The matter in dispute was essentially whether there could be a thing as a science, other than history, dealing with aspects of human action', see Mises (1969).
9. See Mises (1940: 52–4). Mises distinguished clearly between '*verstehen*' and '*begreifen*' in this opus magnum. Due to the time and the location of its publication, this treatise regretfully did not reach the German reader anymore; but in my opinion it is by far superior to its English version, *Human Action* (Mises, 1949). An exhaustive and important analysis of the concept of 'Verstehen' was given by the Austrian philosopher Gomperz (1929). According to Steffy Browne, Gomperz (1873–1942) sporadically visited the Mises-Seminar in Vienna during the late 1920s. In the 1930s he emigrated to the USA and taught at USC in Los Angeles.
10. See especially Englis (1930: 15; 1927). One of the regretfully less known members of the third generation, Englis was Minister of Finance of Czechoslovakia in the interwar period. Another eminent Czech scholar was Franz Cuhel, a member of Böhm-Bawerk's Seminar at the University of Vienna. For his *Theorie der Bedürfnisse* (Cuhel, 1907), see Leube (1995). Also of interest is Riedl (1978).
11. See Menger (1981: 116): 'Just as a penetrating investigation of mental processes makes the cognition of external things appear to be merely our consciousness of the impressions made by external things upon our persons, and thus, in the final analysis, merely the cognition of states of our own persons, so too, in the final analysis, is the importance that we attribute to things of the external world only an outflow of the importance to us of our continued development (life and well-being)'.
12. See Hayek (1963). I should add here that Hayek, barely 20 years old, had already drafted a psychological essay in German when he was a student at the University of Zürich. He completed his 'Beiträge zur Theorie der Entwicklung des Bewusstseins' in early September 1920 while he spent a few short weeks in Norway to get relief from his malaria. This 'youthful effort' (Hayek) of about 40 pages nevertheless became the nucleus of his *The Sensory Order*, originally published in 1952.
13. It was F.A. Hayek who discovered that Menger scribbled the term 'compositive' as a substitute above the word 'deductive'. For details see, Hayek (1979: 301). Hayek appreciates here also the use of this term by Cassirer (1932), a member of the Vienna Circle. Cassirer used the term in order to suggest that because the elements in the social sciences are directly and immediately known to us we thus can only start our inquiries with this method. This comes close to the meaning of Mises's 'praxeological a priori'.
14. See Karl Menger's (son) introduction to Mach's *The Science of Mechanics* (1960: 7–18).
15. As I attempt here to briefly sketch and summarize Hayek's important, yet complex, theory of a 'sensory order', I follow to an extent the phrasing

of his book *The Sensory Order* (Hayek, 1963). This work is crucial for any understanding of Hayek's thought.

16. Letter from Carl Menger to Ernst Mach, 'Hayek Papers', Box 116 at the Hoover Archives, Stanford University; author's translation.
17. Of course, Menger made use of some statistics in order to emphasize certain points. For instance, in his contribution to *Die österreichisch-ungarische Monarchie in Wort und Bild*, the so-called 'Kronprinzenwerk' of 1884–1902, he mentioned the beer consumption of the population of Salzburg, where 59 breweries produced 277,584 hecto litres of beer in 1885. According to Menger 'with an overall population of 165.000 the annual per capita production of beer then amounts to roughly 170 litres', which seems almost impossible or at least, disputable. *Aus dem Kronprinzenwerk des Erzherzog Rudolf, ausgewählt von Christiane Zintzen*, Section Industry and Trade [Industrie und Handel Salzburg], pp. 90–5. Menger was appointed to be the economic editor ('Redacteur des volkswirtschaftlichen Teiles') of the 'Kronprinzenwerk' and received for his service 'the thanks of his Majesty, the Emperor' on 10 February 1902.
18. Karl Menger, junior made this humorous comment at a luncheon which I organized in the restaurant 'Ancora Verde' in Vienna in 1983 to celebrate the centenary of Ludwig von Mises's birthday. It was in this small downtown restaurant that the participants of the Mises Seminar used to meet after their sessions during the 1920s and early 1930s. In addition to K. Menger, Steffy Browne, G. von Haberler, F. A. Hayek and his wife, Margit von Mises, Max von Thurn, my wife and I were present. The tape is in my possession.
19. Eugen von Böhm-Bawerk and his brother-in-law, Friedrich von Wieser, were the leading representatives of the second generation of the Austrian School of Economics. Schumpeter, is by many considered a leading member of the third.
20. See Menger's article in the *Wiener Zeitung*, 8/9 March 1889: 'Neuere nationalökonomische Literatur', I and II. See also Leube (1993).
21. See Hayek (1976). His 'The Use of Knowledge in Society' (reprinted in Nishiyama and Leube, 1984) is probably the best known and most quoted essay on this topic.

References

Blaug, M. (1986) *Great Economists before Keynes: An Introduction to the Lives and Works of One Hundred Great Economists of the Past*, Brighton: Wheatsheaf.

Brocke, B. vom (1988) 'Von der Wissenschaftsverwaltung zur Wissenschaftspolitik. Friedrich Althoff 1839–1908', *Berichte zur Wissenschaftsgeschichte*, 11(1).

Cassirer, E. (1932) *Philosophie der Aufklärung*, Tübingen: Mohr.

Collingwood, R. G. (1946) *The Idea of History*, Oxford: Clarendon Press.

Craig, G. A. (1964) *The Battle of Königgrätz*, Palo Alto: Stanford University Press.

Cuhel, F. (1907) *Theorie der Bedürfnisse,* Innsbruck: Wagner'sche Universitäts-Buchhandlung.

Englis, K. (1927) *Handbuch der Nationalökonomie*, Brünn: Rudolf M. Rohrer.

Englis, K. (1930) *Begründung der Teleologie als Form des empirischen Erkennens*, Brünn: Rudolf M. Rohrer.

Eucken, W. (1938) 'Die Überwindung des Historismus', *Schmollers Jahrbuch*, 62(2): 63–86.
Fuchs-Heinritz, W. (1998) *Auguste Comte*, Munich: VS Verlag für Sozialwissenschaften.
Gomperz, H. (1929) *Über Sinn und Sinngebilde. Verstehen und Erklären*, Tübingen: J.C.B. Mohr.
Hack, N. (1872) 'Review of Grundsätze der Volkswirthschaftslehre', *Zeitschrift für die gesamte Staatswissenschaft*, 28(1): 183–4.
Hayek, F. A. (1937) 'Economics and Knowledge', *Economica*, 4(13): 33–54.
Hayek, F. A. (1963) *The Sensory Order*, Chicago: University of Chicago Press.
Hayek, F. A. (1976) *Preise und Produktion*, 2nd edition, edited by K. R. Leube, Vienna: Springer.
Hayek, F. A. (1979) *Missbrauch und Verfall der Vernunft*, 2nd edition, edited by K. R. Leube, Munich: Philosophia Verlag.
Herre, F. (1978) *Kaiser Franz Joseph von Österreich*, Cologne: Kiepenheuer & Witsch.
Howey, R. S. (1960) *The Rise of the Marginal Utility School 1870–1889*, Lawrence: University of Kansas Press.
Hutchison, T. W. (1962) *A Review of Economic Doctrines*, Oxford: Clarendon Press.
Jaffé, W. (1976) 'Menger, Jevons and Walras De-Homogenized', *Economic Inquiry*, 14(4): 511–24.
Kaesler, D. (ed.) (2000) *Klassiker der Soziologie, Vol 1: Von A. Comte bis N. Elias*, Munich: Beck Verlag.
Kauder, E. (1965) *A History of Marginal Utility Theory*, Princeton: Princeton University Press.
Leube, K. R. (1993) 'Einige Bemerkungen zu den Untersuchungen über die Theorie des Preises aus der Sicht der Österreichischen Schule der Nationalökonomie', in B. Schefold (ed.), *Vademecum zu einem Klassiker der Preistheorie*, Düsseldorf: Verlag Wirtschaft und Finanzen.
Leube, K. R. (ed.) (1995) *Die Österreichische Schule. Von Menger bis Mises*, Frankfurt am Main: FAZ Verlag.
Mach, E, (1960) *The Science of Mechanics: A Critical and Historical Account of Its Development*, 6th edition, translated by T. J. McCormack, Chicago: Open Court.
Menger, C. (1871) *Grundsätze der Volkswirthschaftslehre*, Vienna: Braumüller.
Menger, C. (1889) 'Grundzüge einer Klassifikation der Wirtschaftswissenschaften', *Jahrbücher für Nationalökonomie und Statistik*, 19(3): 465–96.
Menger, C. (1981) *Principles of Economics*, New York: New York University Press.
Menger, C. (1883/1985) *Investigations into the Method of the Social Sciences with Special Reference to Economics*, New York: New York University Press.
Mill, J. St. (1864), *Grundsätze der Politischen Ökonomie*, 2nd edition, Hamburg: Perthes-Besser und Mauke 1852.
Mises, L. von (1940/1981) *Nationalökonomie. Theorie des Handelns und Wirtschaftens*, 2nd edition, Geneva: Editions Union, Munich: Philosophia Verlag.
Mises, L. von (1949/1959) *Human Action: A Treatise on Economics*, 6th edition, New Haven: Yale University Press.
Mises, L. von (1969) *The Historical Setting of the Austrian School of Economics*, New York: Arlington House.
Nishiyama, C. and Leube, K. R. (eds) (1984) *The Essence of Hayek*, Stanford: Hoover Institution Press.

Riedl, M. (1978) *Verstehen oder Erklären*, Stuttgart: Klett-Cotta.
Schefold, B. (1987) 'Schmoller, Gustav von (1838–1917)', in J. Eatwell, M. Milgate and P. Newman (eds), *The New Palgrave: A Dictionary of Economics*, Vol. 4, London: Macmillan.
Schmoller, G. von (1883) 'Zur Methodologie der Staats- und Sozialwissenschaften', *Schmollers Jahrbuch*, 7(3): 975–94.
Schumpeter (1954) *History of Economic Analysis*, New York: Oxford University Press.
Sombart, W. (1930) *Die drei Nationalökonomien*, Leipzig and Munich: Duncker & Humblot.
Spiegel, H. W. (1983) *The Growth of Economic Thought*, Durham: Duke University Press.
Screpanti, E. and Zamagni, S. (1995) *An Outline of the History of Economic Thought*, translated by D. Field, Oxford: Clarendon Press.
Walras, L. (1965) *Correspondence of Leon Walras and Related Papers*, edited by W. Jaffé, 2 vols, Amsterdam: North-Holland Publishing.

14
Hayek's Cognitive Psychology

Susumu Egashira

The Sensory Order published in 1952 is unique among Hayek's works. Although many economists and political scientists acknowledge its significance, they have seldom studied it because it requires the reader to have some knowledge of cognitive psychology.[1] Despite this, many researchers have regarded it as the beginning of Hayek's knowledge theory and have suggested the necessity of a detailed investigation. Kurt Leube, the author of Chapter 13 of this volume worked as Hayek's assistant for many years and pointed out the significance of *The Sensory Order*. This chapter is supplementary to Leube's chapter.

According to Hayek's retrospect, as an undergraduate, he was unsure of whether to choose economics or psychology as a career option. In an article written by him in September 1920, 'Beiträge zur Theorie der Entwicklung des Bewusstseins' (The Contribution to Theory of Development of Consciousness), he criticized the contemporary trends in psychology; he was disappointed that while sense consciousness was discovered to be related to the firing of a neuron, the problem of the relationship between an external stimulus and consciousness remained unsolved.[2] In this context, Hayek's theme in this article is similar to that in *The Sensory Order*, save for the fact that in the article, he adopted Ernst Mach's concept of 'sensory elements', a theme that he abandoned in *The Sensory Order*.

In this chapter, we will review the foundation of Hayek's theory of knowledge from the viewpoint of his theory of cognitive psychology as presented in *The Sensory Order*. In addition, we will discuss how basic arguments and conclusions can change if his concepts were introduced into modern economics. The introduction of the viewpoint of cognitive psychology will clarify the relationship between information and knowledge and may fundamentally change the concepts of information and rationality of economic agents in economics. Here we will consider the concept of knowledge to consist of the foundation of Hayek's theory of social evolution.

1. Review of *The Sensory Order*

Hayek's aim in *The Sensory Order* is to propose a hypothesis on the mechanism of 'classification' in our minds. He investigates why similar or different physical stimuli from outside make similar sense on one occasion and mean something else on another. Hayek criticized the behaviourist school of thought, which argues against the direct and mechanical connection between the process of sense stimuli and the response of a particular part of the nervous system, and emphasized the interposition of 'consciousness' in the process.

In the same vein, he criticized Gestalt psychologists such as Wolfgang Köhler. Hayek has also mentioned the names of some psychologists whose works had influenced him, such as H. von Helmholtz, W. Wundt, W. James and G. E. Müller, and E. Mach. It is obvious that although Hayek was initially influenced by functionalism and behaviourism, it seemed as though he was influenced by the Gestalt School and the new movement of psychology in 1940s–1950s when he published *The Sensory Order*.

As mentioned earlier, *The Sensory Order* consists of four parts.

(1) The setting of the problem. The problem of psychology at the time was an issue to be considered.
(2) A Neurophysiologic explanation of the classification of senses.
(3) The psychological structure of cognition.
(4) A philosophical inquiry into the sensory order.

Although Hayek's psychology is relatively older than the modern perspective, it can be regarded as the forerunner of the modern connectionist theory in terms of the parallelism between the physical structure of sensory classification, which is explained from the viewpoint of neurophysiology and the formation of consciousness. In fact, at present, it is still worth reading due to its discussion of the role of consciousness in the process of the classification of the senses.

In this section, we consider only the arguments in (1), (2) and (3) since that presented in (4) is more or less covered in (2) and (3).

1.1. The setting of the problem

The Sensory Order, as discussed by Hayek, consists of two different categories into which we arrange or classify the objects of the world around us – the phenomenal order, that is, 'the order of our sense experiences in which events are classified according to their sensory properties such as colors, sounds, odors, feelings of touch, etc.' and the physical order, that is, 'an order which includes both these same and other events but which treats them as similar or different accordingly, as, in conjunction with other events, they produce similar or different external events' (Hayek, 1952a: 3).

The physical order is a pattern of the combination of the impulses that classify individual stimuli in the nervous system. However, Hayek did not propose a one-to-one relation between particular stimuli and a particular stream of impulses. In fact, they are related at many levels, and he asserted that this feature of the nervous system provides a solution to the question of why we perceive similar stimuli to be similar or different on one occasion and different stimuli to be similar or different on another.

On the other hand, the phenomenal order forms the mental qualities. We perceive our environmental order as stimuli through our sense organs. Although the mental order such as consciousness is dependent on the external environment, it does not immediately reflect the environment. In other words, although our environment affects the formation of our recognition of the world, a decision or a selection of a particular behaviour is not made according to the external order itself but on the basis of the internal and phenomenal order formed in mind. The point that he emphasized here was the relationship between these orders, that is, 'to show how it is possible to build from the known elements of the nervous processes a structure of intermediate link between the physical stimuli and the overt responses, [... ...]' (ibid.: 18).

It is obvious that this awareness was based on the controversy between the Behaviourist and Gestalt schools. Critics of behaviourism avoided naïve physicalism and empiricism by dividing the sensory order into a physical layer and a mental layer and by emphasizing the importance of consciousness.

We can observe the influence of Ernst Mach who particularly inspired Hayek in the latter's unpublished article in 1920, where he perceived an aspect of the mental phenomenon as a physical 'relationship'. However, Hayek criticized Mach because Mach exclusively insisted that naïve empiricism and Mach's concept of 'sensory elements' were unnecessary. Although Mach's psychological works affected the birth of Gestalt psychology and aroused Hayek's interest in this field, the psychology that Hayek has mentioned in his book was aimed at establishing a mental, theoretical model according to the experiments conducted between the 1920s and the 1940s. As a result, there is nothing left of Mach's concepts in *The Sensory Order*.

However, Hayek's paraphernalia was relatively out of date even at his time and the influence of Karl Popper is not clear in his work. This fact suggests that although he quoted other's works published around the 1940s, the main part of his book had been written much earlier. It is necessary to understand that Hayek's original contribution was not his argument on neurophysiology but rather his work on the mental model on phenomenal aspects – the primitive model of a neural network that was eventually proposed at that time.

1.2. The neurophysiologic explanation of sense classification

The first part of *The Sensory Order* begins with an explanation of Hayek's hypothesis on the sense classification. Although his method of research did not depend on his own experiment, he constructed a theoretical model inductively on the basis of the results of experiments conducted in the field. First, his explanation confirms the anatomical and neurophysiologic structure of the brain, which includes neurons and synapses – the knowledge of which had already been established at that time. However, Hayek did not focus on the physical structure of the connection between neurons. Instead, he examined the stream of impulses in the nervous system. To make his argument clear, we must emphasize that his argument was different from other similar arguments. In other words, Hayek did not assume that any (for example, a particular neuron and physical network of neurons) particular component of the nervous system physically corresponded to a particular stimulus. He considered that similar stimuli are not necessarily transferred similar impulses on the synaptic network. Therefore, Hayek's argument is distinct from other arguments on processes such as the increase in the blood stream or the firing of neurons in a specific part of the brain. This feature of his argument focuses not on individual impulses but on a combination of impulses, namely, a 'class'. The difference in the intensity and quality of stimuli not only changes the intensity of the impulse but also structure of classes. A classification of stimuli is not made on the basis of a class, but some classes are combined and each forms a class of a higher dimension corresponding to a stimulus and a particular situation. Hayek named this process a 'linkage'; a linkage constitutes the 'quality of a sense'. It consists of electrical streams, and according to Hayek, the logical combination is more important than the physical characteristics. Hayek's model of cognition did not assume the existence of the physical and fixed counterparts of stimuli. Moreover, it is different from Mach's argument that a priori assumed several primitive sensory elements such as painful, pleasant, unpleasant, offensive sensations and the united sense recognized as a combination of them. Mach understood the sense in terms of functional relations and avoided referring to it as a 'thing in itself' (*Ding an sich*). This concept may exist out of the scope of human cognition, but Hayek did not accept it on the basis of the senses.

The advantage of this concept is that senses can be classified almost infinitely because the combination of impulses does not necessarily depend on that of synapses. Moreover, by ignoring the primitive elements of the senses, we can consider the more delicate and complex cognitions. In addition to this, Hayek understood the formation of classes and their linkage in the process of empirical learning. Therefore, the classification of senses is not only the recognition of external stimuli but also the establishment of a stable and complicated linkage between classes. It is a mechanism of a recurrent learning in modern terminology, and this linkage is stable but not fixed and includes the possibility of change as the result of an accumulation of experiences.

However, Hayek did not propose any concrete model for the classification and the combination, and this is why his argument compares unfavourably with contemporary psychologists. Hayek's argument was barely included in the history of psychology because his methods and concepts at that time were already out of date. For example, McCulloch and Pitts published a mathematical model of the neural network of hypothetical neurons in 1943, and Rosenblatt proposed a perception model that provided a mechanism of learning in 1957. Moreover, a model of recurrent learning discussed by Hayek had already been proposed at that time (Abraham, 2002). Therefore, his own contribution to the theory of the physical mechanism of cognition did not stand out.

1.3. Mental structure of cognition

The Sensory Order is important in the study of Hayek's argument due to its highly suggestive nature in the consideration of Hayek's concept of knowledge. For Hayek, knowledge possessed by individuals is a dynamic concept that is acquired through daily activities and continues to change gradually in correspondence with a change in circumstances.

Moreover, personal knowledge forms the framework of cognition when individuals interpret the signals that they perceive in their circumstances. *The Sensory Order* puts forward Hayek's idea of the relationship between cognition and consciousness, the process of learning and the process of development in his theory of knowledge.

Hayek introduced the two phenomenal concepts of a 'map' and a 'model' in the mind to explain the development of the order of the mind parallel to the formation of the order of the central nerves. A map is an overview of the routes of impulses; it is gradually formed during a long process and is relatively stable. On the other hand, a model is a temporal mental image of a circumstance in which an individual is located but it does not necessarily reflect everything around him. For example, if the individual concentrates on a particular object, the model is definitive.

Hayek explained the relationship between the map and the model.

> The relation which exists between our 'model' and 'map' may also be concerned in some respects to the relation existing between some complex geometrical structure and the system of co-ordinates with reference to which it can be defined. [...] What is significant about the structure of our 'model' is not the actual relations in space between the impulse, but solely their relations to the structure of connections, relations which correspond to those expressed by the equation by which a given structure is defined in analytical geometry. (Hayek, 1952a: 117)

As mentioned above, a particular class of impulses does not have a one-to-one relationship with a particular quality of the mind. Although mental qualities are gradually combined and form the conscious, they do not immediately correspond to a physiological linkage and are therefore, formed as 'the resultant of the interaction of a multiplicity of streams of impulses'. (Hayek, 1952a: 119)

This was not the same as old psychology that considers a mental image or a conception to be an association of other conceptions. An individuals' adaptive behaviour is explained as a result of interaction of the model formed in the context of the situation in which a person is located and its arrangement on the map. That is, the reason why individuals are able to survive biologically and socially is that they have cognitive adaptive mechanisms that collate the model in the order of past experiences.

Hayek explained that this structure of the model and map relates to the prediction of the future.

> In general, if the conditions required for the persistence of any more complex structure are not likely always to prevail at the place where it happens to be, it will continue to exist only of (and we shall encounter such substructures, except as temporary phenomena, only in so far as) they can respond appropriately to certain events, and even in some measure anticipate their occurrence, i.e. perform the appropriate response as soon as certain other events occur which indicate the imminence of the harmful one.
>
> (Hayek, 1952a: 129)

Moreover, this structure becomes more stable if it memorizes the relationship between an event and a precursory event and learns the method of responding appropriately to it.

This is the process of human consciousness, but Hayek did not consider that it does not necessarily require intention and intentional learning. Hayek emphasized the parallelism of a physiological and mental structure and maintained that an unconscious behaviour or learning also forms a class of impulses – lower-level classes are combined to form a higher-level class and this in turn prepares a response to external events. Such preparations will work only when a similar type of event takes place again.[3]

In *The Sensory Order*, Hayek basically explained the process of classification of external stimuli, and he regarded other mental activities such as differentiation, generalization, abstraction and conceptual thinking as a variation of this classification. In addition to this, he suggested that the argument of the formation of a sensory order can explain not only a classification of simple stimuli but also higher-level mental activities that are dependent on various factors that are more complicated, such as the economic calculation in a market. Hayek recollected that '…its out lines have gradually developed, and it has often proved helpful in dealing with the problems of the methods of the social sciences' (Hayek, 1952a: v).[4] In the next section, we will consider the relationship between Hayek's cognitive psychology and his theory of knowledge that had been proposed in the controversy of collectivist economic planning over the 1930s and 1940s.

2. The sensory order and the spontaneous social order

Hayek accepted that the sensory order developed evolutionarily in the sense of both ontogeny and phylogeny. Some scholars point out the similarity between *The Sensory Order* and the theory of spontaneous order.

However, even if we discuss the surface similarity of the mechanism, it means nothing more than the fact that the relationship between the two theories is an analogy. If we consider the consistency between them, we have to consider an immediate and theoretical common ground.

Social orders explained by Hayek are patterns that emerged as the result of interactions in the behaviour of individuals. When a number of people live together, an individual gradually accumulates experience from watching how others behave. Subsequently, he or she can gradually predict the behaviour and thoughts of the others on the basis of previous experience. The reason that an individual can make optimistic predictions is the character of interdependency in individual behaviours. That is, the stability of the spontaneous order depends on the degree of conviction by the individual that unless he or she changes his or her behaviour, others will not change their behaviour. This is the origin of habits and customs, and these tacit understandings of the rules and behaviours of individuals are institutionalized.

It is noteworthy that such a conviction that forms the spontaneous order is merely a kind of 'assumption'. In other words, individuals deductively predict the patterns of others according to their past experiences with them (Hayek, 1955). We cannot predict the future accurately. The only thing we can do is to 'expect' that the near future is an extension of the past. If reality defies a prediction, individuals revise their understanding on the patterns. According to *The Sensory Order*, humans equip themselves with mechanisms such as prediction and a revision as functions of a brain (Hayek, 1979: 30).

Thus, we may say that the concept that characterizes Hayek's knowledge is 'the knowledge of the particular circumstances of time and place' (Hayek, 1936: 80). He asserted that in our society, knowledge, while largely unorganized and local, is not theoretical and technical. Hayek proposed this concept during the controversy of collectivist economic planning. We can use the latter in a market but the central authority of a socialist nation cannot utilize it. This concept is well-known because it does not only point out the fatal problem of a socialist nation but also the nature of the market economy.

The knowledge is context-dependent in the specific circumstances of time and place. It can psychologically be explained in that the formation of a linkage corresponds to external stimuli and a map. For example, consider a fisherman's knowledge with which he is able to recognize a tidal current. The map in his knowledge reflects his repeated experience with a specific area of the sea. Then, a model of a condition in a specific time and area is formed and located in the map. Considering this process, it is obvious that 'the knowledge of the particular circumstances of time and place' is the sensory order on the map and proficiency that signifies the formation of a more detailed map through repeated experiences.

> There exists a great deal of evidence that the capacities for sensory discrimination can be greatly developed by practice. The sensory greatly heightened capacities for tactual, auditory and olfactory discrimination....
>
> (Hayek, 1952a: 152–3)

The concept of 'the knowledge of the circumstances of time and place' was developed in Hayek's studies in the 1960s and became the core of an evolutionary social theory of *The Fatal Conceit* in 1988, which was the last book written by him. The unorganized and local knowledge is situated between reason and instinct, and the theory of knowledge is a basis of human behaviour supported by the foundation of Hayek's liberalism.

If knowledge corresponds to the specific circumstances of time and place, the sensory order must psychologically reflect the external order in a sense. In particular, a map that immediately relates the unorganized and local knowledge is the stable order that is dependent on experiences of the past and does not reflect each stimulus. However, a map is something organized – an intermittent, consistent stream of stimuli in some form even if it is not an exact mapping; and if this is the case, then the map is revised and partly abandoned. This means that the process, which includes the experiences of the stimuli, the formation of the sensory order, judgment, behaviour, and the formation of a social order, has bidirectional dependence. The social order as well as the human internal order is statistically stable. For this reason, humans attempt to predict the future according to a pattern and the interdependence between the sensory order and the social order forms a society.

3. Economics based on Hayekian cognitive science

Hayek's cognitive psychology in *The Sensory Order* lacks the concept of a 'thing in itself' (*Ding an sich*). Hayek did not adopt the setting where a person is able to recognize the thing in itself; instead, he considered that all consciousness is an activity of the brain, in other words, the relationship between impulses. Therefore, any epistemological problems are reduced to a problem of the classification of a sense and a cognitive mechanism of the brain. Although Mach had a similar concept, Hayek understood his own concept to be more abstract in the sense that he abandoned the concepts of sensory elements that Mach had assumed.

This thought process is absolutely different from the viewpoint of modern economics that understands human knowledge and cognitive abilities in terms of the perfect and imperfect. From Hayek's viewpoint, if we regard cognition and knowledge as a subjective function of the brain, it is absurd to suppose the existence of a perfect entity outside a person. In other words, a person is not able to correctly recognize something outside him or her, not because of the restrictive ability of humans, but because cognition is an internal activity and personal consciousness is isolated from the outside. It is fundamentally impossible to know whether what we talk about exists or not. Therefore, the thought of modern economics that assumes a criterion of perfectness or objectivity and defines the concept of imperfectness of ability, knowledge and information as discounted from perfectness is completely different from that of Hayek. It is frequently said that Hayek's works after the controversy of the collectivist economic planning had inspired the argument of bounded rationality in modern economics without accurate evidence. However, if we understand the argument presented in *The Sensory Order*, it will be obvious that the backgrounds of both concepts are largely different.

We should now discuss how economics changes with the introduction of the concept of an agent, as suggested in Hayek's cognitive psychology. The history of modern economics has been the history of the development of an assumption on a subjective economic agent. Jevons, Menger, Walras and Edgeworth's utility theories; von Neumann-Morgenstern's expected utility; liquidity preference; rational expectation; and subjective probability are some of the theories that had been formulated throughout the development of economics. The difference between each theory is dependent on the difference in the assumptions about the subjectivity of agents.

However, the assumed subjectivity of an agent in modern economics is unique. As mentioned above, not only the concept of the rational economic man but also bounded rationality necessitates an assumption of the perfection of human ability. Modern economics usually supposes that some assumption of information and an agent who can use it at full value are necessary to arrive at equilibrium. Then, it assumes the heterogeneous abilities of the interpretation of information or imperfect information. Since the condition of perfect information is strictly defined, that of imperfect information and ability can also be clearly defined. Although this definition of perfectness-imperfectness is convenient in terms of manipulation, we must say that it is arbitrary because an assumption involves a result. Behavioural economics – that introduces irrationality such as emotion and some limit of ability into economics but does not abandon the assumption of a unique utility function – stays within the framework of modern economics.

However, the result of Hayek's cognitive psychology has a feature that is not consistent with such assumptions of neoclassical economics (and for a period of time, even with Hayek's own argument). According to him, a personal decision is always made by an individual as an interaction between a model and a map in his or her mind. That is, when a person has to, consciously or unconsciously, choose something in society, it does not mean that he or she responds to signals from his or her circumstances or situations immediately but that the signals are utilized as information after they are interpreted through a cognitive framework. Although such a framework is dependent on experience, experiences possessed by individuals are not necessarily the same – it is impossible to confirm it in principle. As a result, there is a possibility that a different person may respond to a similar or different situation similarly or differently. According to Hayek's cognitive psychology, it is natural to assume a heterogeneous agent in economics, and if we assume a homogeneous agent, we should give an additional explanation as to the appropriateness of such an assumption.

As noted in section one, Hayek's argument in psychology is a kind of cognitive model proposed during the period of the birth of neural network models. If we accurately introduce his argument into economics, it requires a model of a continuous game with multiple agents that are equipped with a learning mechanism. The model has to assume not only an interaction among the agents but also an evolutionary system of the agents' cognitive framework expressed by a neural network. We have to redefine the concept of information. It is impossible to consider information without knowledge because the concept of interpretation through a cognitive framework is built within the model. Therefore, to consider a role or effect of information requires an observation of the condition of the individuals' knowledge in a particular time period. Hayek regarded the market price as critical information in economic activities. This is not because it leads economic agents to exhibit the same behaviour simultaneously but because it increases the variety of the individuals' behaviours, as a result, potentially enhancing the possibility of the survival of the market as a whole.

Moreover, it is obvious that the concept of information is largely a dynamic one. For example, consider that a person obtains information *A* that relates to the prediction of *a* events in the future. What he or she has to do is to obtain additional information *B* in order to confirm the reliability of information *A*. However, they also have to obtain information *C* to confirm the reliability of *B*. Thus, in the subjective world, a pursuit of the confirmation of information is infinitely continuous and information is fundamentally imperfect in this sense. However, we do not actually suffer from infinite information-seeking. In many cases, although we give up gathering information, we seldom encounter a serious problem in our daily lives. This information-seeking process is mainly the result of the stylized behaviours of people and institutions. The introduction of the concept of subjective information makes it possible for us to understand the importance of society from the viewpoint of an institution. Moreover, while on the one hand, the subjective activity of a person is the cause of a social change, on the other hand, an institution brings stability to our society. In this sense, economics that assumes subjective information is dynamic in terms of essentially including both the factor of a change and stability.

As we have discussed above, if we introduce Hayek's psychological argument into economics, it will lead to radical changes, particularly in microeconomics. The concept of radical, subjective agents who possess an evolutionary cognitive framework and fundamentally imperfect information may not be consistent with the theory of equilibrium. It is not equilibrium-based economics but knowledge-based economics that focuses on the pattern of peoples' actions and thoughts and describes the phenomenon of economics as a micro-macro loop between agents and society.

4. Conclusion

In this chapter, we survey Hayek's psychology in *The Sensory Order* and consider what changes would take place in the event we introduce into economics the concept that Hayek considered in his psychology. However, some methodological problems have to be solved if we are to consider this approach. Although computer simulation may be a powerful method, a multi-agent model with a learning mechanism by a neural network frequently shows a very complicated performance, and the result is very difficult to interpret. On the one hand, we have to develop the statistical method to understand such complicated results, and on the other hand, it is necessary to observe that a direct introduction of the result of psychology may not enrich economics.

Nevertheless, the studies in *The Sensory Order* and the possibility of the application of their arguments to economics have recently emerged. The fact that the book has been frequently picked up after much neglect suggests a change in economics. The development of several instruments in psychology and neurophysiology has gradually brought about the realization of cooperation between economics and psychology; something which had rarely taken place in the past. With regard to this, we can say that Hayek had provided a way for the future of economics more than half a century ago.

Notes

1. For example, in Japan, only Shimazu's *Jiseiteki Chitsujo* (*The Spontaneous Order*) addressed *The Sensory Order* directly. In Europe and America, the number of papers that deal with Hayekian psychology has gradually increased with the publication of works such as de Vries (1994), Smith (1997) and Reisman (1997).
2. Hayek also wrote another unpublished article, 'Das Wesen des Geistigen', which has no date but was probably written around 1923. This article seems to be the prototype of *The Sensory Order* because its argument is similar to that given in the former. However, it seems to be an unfinished work.
3. Hayek (1952a: 135) explained that there is an intermediate level between consciousness and unconsciousness and that the border between them is ambiguous. Conscious behaviour is to (a) be able to 'give an account' of what he is or has been doing, (b) be able 'to take account' simultaneously in his actions and (c) to be a guide to a large extent not only by his current perceptions but also by image and by the reproduction of circumstances, which might be evoked by an existing situation.
4. However, Hayek differentiated between the sphere that economics deals with and that which psychology deals with; he denied that an economist considers the mentality of economic agents in *The Counter-revolution of Science,* which was published in the same year as *The Sensory Order*, and discussed the methodology of economics.

References

Abraham, T. H. (2002) '(Physio) logical Circuits: The Intellectual Origins of the McCulloch-Pitts Neural Networks', *Journal of the History of the Behavioral Sciences*, 38(1): 3–25.

de Vries, R. P. (1994) 'The Place of Hayek's Theory of Mind and Perception in the History of Philosophy and Psychology', in J. Birner and R. V. Zijp (eds), *Hayek, Co-ordination and Evolution*, London: Routledge.

Frowen, S. F. (ed.) (1997) *Hayek: Economist and Social Philosopher*, New York: St. Martin's Press.

Hayek, F. A. (1920) 'Beiträge zur Theorie der Entwicklung des Bewusstseins', BOX104, no. 23 at the Hoover Archives, Stanford University.
Hayek, F. A. (n.d. around 1920?) 'Das Wesen des Geistigen', BOX104, no. 20 at the Hoover Archives, Stanford University.
Hayek, F. A. (1936 [1948]) 'The Use of Knowledge in Society', in: *Individualism and Economic Order*, Chicago: University of Chicago Press.
Hayek, F. A. (1952a) *The Sensory Order*, Chicago: Chicago University Press.
Hayek, F. A. (1952b) *The counter-revolution of Science: studies on the abuse of reason*, Illinois: Free Press.
Hayek, F. A. (1955 [1967]) 'The Theory of Complex Phenomena', in: *Studies in Philosophy, Politics and Economics*.
Hayek, F. A. (1979) *Law, Legislation and Liberty*, vol. III, London: Routledge.
Hayek, F. A. (1988) *The Fatal Conceit*, London: Routledge.
McCulloch, W. S. and Pitts, W. (1943) 'A Logical Calculus of the Ideas Immanent in Nervous Activity', *Bulletin of Mathematical Biophysics*, 5(1): 115–33.
Reisman, D. A. (1997) 'Discussant's Comments: The Connectionist as a Conservative,' in Frowen (1997).
Shimazu, I. (1985) *Jiseiteki Chitsujo*, Tokyo: Bokutakusha.
Smith, B. (1997) 'The Connectionist Mind: A Study of Hayekian Psychology', in Frowen (1997).

15
Hayek's Transformation of Market-Images in the 1930–40s

Makoto Nishibe

1. What is Hayek's transformation problem?

It is often admitted that great philosophers and economists tend to show very drastic turns in the evolution of their ideas or theories. For example, we may quote, on the one hand, Kant and Wittgenstein for such philosophers, and on the other, Keynes and Marx for such economists. Hayek will certainly be included in this list.

Since Hutchison (1981) divided Hayek between Misesian a priorist 'Hayek I' and Popperian falsificationist 'Hayek II' and Caldwell (1988) set out to discuss the nature of 'Hayek's Transformation' in view of the concept of equilibrium, many have joined on the argument of this theme and generally accepted that Hayek transformed his theoretical and methodological positions in the 1930s, and that his seminal essay 'Economics and knowledge' in 1937 is the breakpoint. It is also acknowledged that this view is endorsed by Hayek's own remark:

> Though at one time a very pure and narrow economic theorist, I was led from technical economics into all kinds of questions usually regarded as philosophical. When I look back, it seems to have all begun, nearly thirty years ago, with an essay on 'Economics and Knowledge' in which I examined what seemed to me some of the central difficulties of pure economic theory.
>
> (Hayek, 1967: 91)

But there is still much disagreement on the nature and extent of Hayek's transformation. First, is it a 'once and for all' clean break that was seemingly implied at least in the initial question raised by Caldwell, or, is it 'continuous' until he became an interdisciplinary socio-economist of a spontaneous order with transcendental realist ontology in later years (Lawson, 1994), or 'gradual' since he was a technical economist on monetary business cycle (Foss, 1995)? Second, is it mainly caused or strongly influenced by such exogenous factors as Hayek's involvement in the Socialist Calculation Debate (SCD) as Caldwell (1988, 1994, 2004) suggested, or by such endogenous effects as a methodological turn seen in his essays 'Scientism and the study of society' in 1942–44 (Lawson, 1994; Fleetwood, 1995), or, as an inner development within technical economics in his subsequent responses to criticisms by Myrdal, Hicks, Sraffa and Morgenstern to Hayek's early work on inter-temporal equilibrium under perfect foresight (Foss, 1995)? Third, is it once or more? Fleetwood (1995), for instance, insists Hayek has experienced transformations 'twice' and divides Hayek into three periods: Hayek I (–1937), Hayek II (1937–1960) and Hayek III (1960–) in view of his philosophy of ontology, not epistemology.

In this chapter, I contend that Hayek transformed in terms of not only the concepts of equilibrium but also his vision of the market in the 1930s and 1940s as he had become involved in SCD, and that a more crucial breakpoint lies in 1946, rather than in 1937 as is commonly assumed.[1] The reason why I suppose so is as follows.

Hayek, in his 1937 essay, was still haunted by the idea that use of the notion of equilibrium is necessary for a positivist scientific explanation and tried to introduce subjective/objective knowledge based on the concepts of equilibrium. However, Hayek, in his 1940 article, drastically changed his attitude towards general equilibrium theory (GET) and counterattacked market socialism (MS). GET depicts the vision of the market centrally operated by an auctioneer and provides theoretical backing for 'a trail and error method' executed by a central planner in order to determine the shadow prices of production goods. Accordingly, MS can be thus given endorsement by GET on the ground that the former is no less feasible and desirable than the latter. Hayek was then urged to rethink the validity and reality of variant concepts of static equilibrium that he held as a technical economist on his recognition that Walrasian *tâtonnement*, groping method to find equilibrium prices that match supply and demand for all goods, can be utilized for MS. Eventually, he realized that it is necessary, in order to run through a logical defensive line of MS, to criticize the 'hardcore' concepts of equilibrium and competition underpinning GET.

Hayek, in his 1946 paper, first acknowledged the true meaning of 'competition' utterly different from 'perfect competition' in GET, or 'rivalry' in Lavoie's (1985) term, as a main driving force to make the market process dynamic and non-equilibrium. This signifies a clean break with GET, but it is not a birth of a new theory. Here neither his economic theory nor his explicit methodology, but the vision of the market, which is tacitly and subjectively held 'pre-analytical framework' (Schumpeter, 1954) for substantive economics,[2] has changed and developed. So the dividing line between Hayek I and Hayek II should be drawn in 1946, not in 1937. There is certainly a huge gap between his view of the market as 'the telecommunications system' before 1946 and that as 'rivalry and discovery process for knowledge' after 1946. Putting both together in Hayek II would lead us to overlook such important issues as I have just explained.

2. From a critique of socialist economic planning to a critique of general equilibrium theory

Now I shall demonstrate, from a detailed study on Hayek's articles in SCD and thereafter, that a key concept for Hayek to be able to break through the concept of equilibrium particularly embodied in GET is rival-like competition as discovery process that first emerged in 1946, not subjective and dispersive knowledge in 1937.

Hayek participated in SCD by editing the English translation of Mises's 1920 German paper and others as *Collectivist Economic Planning* in 1935.[3] In order to consider the nature and cause of Hayek's transformation concerning his vision of the market, I shall focus on his transition from a critique of socialist planning to a critique of GET.

The decisive change from his 1935 book to his 1940 paper 'Socialist calculation III: the competitive "solution"' lies in the fact that, while Hayek criticized the competitive solution of MS, he has come to view GET more critically, although he has then constructed an inter-temporal equilibrium model for monetary business cycles using GE. He criticizes Lange and Dickinson (Lange, 1936–37; Dickinson, 1939) as:

> [...] it is difficult to suppress the suspicion that this particular proposal has been born out of an excessive preoccupation with problems of the pure theory of stationary equilibrium
>
> (Hayek, [1940] 1948: 188)

Hayek investigates the problems that Lange and Dickinson applied GET to a socialist economy in the static sense. Obviously, he is aware of defects of static equilibrium, but he has not reached a point where he can represent any alternative theory to it. So he cannot help but point out the gap between the dynamic nature of a real market and the static nature of a market theory: 'With given and constant data such a state of equilibrium could indeed be approached by the method of trial and error. But this is far from being the situation in the real world, where constant change is the rule' (Hayek, [1940] 1948: 188). Hayek also exposed his criticism to MS.

> Or, to change the metaphor, the difference between such a system of regimented prices and a system of prices determined by the market seems to be about the same as that between an attacking army in which every unit and every man could move only by special command and by the exact distance ordered by headquarters and an army in which every unit and every man can take advantage of every opportunity offered to them.
>
> (Ibid.: 187)

This metaphor well grasps the difference between a concentrated market-image contained in MS model and a dispersive market-image that he feels for a real market. It is not difficult to see that Hayek's critique of MS in this paper is convertible to that of GET. However, Hayek had not yet firmly formed the criticism of such 'hard core' assumptions of GET as 'the parametric function of prices', (Lange, [1936–37] 1938: 70) equivalent to the 'price-taker' or 'perfect competition' assumption. This is why Hayek must depend on his image of a real market on his criticism against Lange and Dickinson.

Hayek's criticism towards GE originated from his unique market-image that was not articulated yet as a market theory, but was only realized as 'tacit knowledge' (Polanyi, 1967). It depends on his actual experiences and observations, but is not directly induced from them. The central planner who executes a trial and error method utilizing 'the parametric function of prices' was just imitating a price-adjusting auctioneer in Walrasian *tâtonnement* process for finding a GE solution. So if Hayek condemned Lange for being wrong, he would give Walras the same judgment. Hayek's metaphor suggests that the market depicted in GET is actually centralized and well-organized and the real market is decentralized and autonomous.

3. Compromise to general equilibrium: division of knowledge is insufficient to overturn it

In order to see how his critical position towards GET moves, we must turn to Hayek's arguments developed away from such controversial scenes. Hayek's criticism of GE first appeared in the famous paper in 1937, 'Economics and knowledge', in which Hayek focused on the problem of knowledge in economics and critically examined the presuppositions of GET.

Although he attempted to describe his own market-image by the 'division of knowledge' (Hayek, 1937 [1948]: 50) with subjective and dispersive character of individual knowledge, he gave some concessions to GET. For example, he said that tautologies in a formal equilibrium analysis could survive as the logic to explain a social process if they were reinforced by some empirical hypotheses. This makes his position towards GET blurred. He takes the problem regarding the boundaries of equilibrium analysis as the tautological 'Pure Logic of Choice' (ibid.: 35).

> I have long felt that the concept of equilibrium itself and the methods which we employ in pure analysis have a clear meaning only when confined to the analysis of the action of a single person and that we are really passing into a different sphere and silently introducing a new element of altogether different character when we apply it to the explanation of the interactions of a number of different individuals.
> (Ibid.: 34–5)

This question can easily be understood if we remember the distinction between 'economic problems' and 'technological problems' in his lead paper of his edited book (Hayek, [1935b] 1948: 121–2).[4] Then we can interpret that Hayek proposed that GET should be applied only to technological problems. Nonetheless, Hayek never went on abandoning the whole concepts of equilibrium. According to Hayek, the problem of 'Pure Logic of Choice' does not lie in too much formalization of a theory, but insufficiency of it. If it were formalized sufficiently so that this particular field of theory of logic could completely be isolated from the substance of economics, it would become possible to use formal economic theory as a tool in the same way as mathematics (Hayek, [1937] 1948: 35). Hayek seemed to think here that the application of GET could be limited strictly to technological problems by its complete formalization, or, in other words, that GET is valid and applicable as an abstract theory only if it is as a purely tautological formal system as mathematics even though it does not have its corresponding real objects in society.[5]

It is apparent from this that Hayek criticizes Lange for his applying GET to economic problems in a socialist planned economy. But, if the application of GET to a planned economy is an error, its application to a market economy must be also an error because both economies must face economic problems. If so, Hayek's claim that only a market economy is feasible cannot be maintained regardless of his endorsement of GET.

It thus follows that Hayek needs to show what kind of market economy was presumed, in order to present the ground for his criticism against economic planning, and that he must start to criticize GET as a market theory. It remained as Hayek's task to examine why GET cannot be applied to economic problems, show the limits of GET as a market theory and, finally, represent his original market-image in contrast with that of GET.

Hayek's criticism of Lange should have been accomplished by showing clearly that a 'real market' is virtually the opposite of the perfectly competitive and concentrated market depicted by GET. Hayek's market-image is 'rivalrous and dispersive' that is completely different from GET.

The term 'rivalrous' refers to the state of affairs in which, under a circumstance where the ends and purposes of multiple economic agents conflict with each other, all economic agents struggle to attain their own plans. 'Economic rivalry is', as Lavoie put it, 'the clash of human purposes' (Lavoie, 1985: 22), that is, 'some plans are necessarily disappointed by the carrying out of rival plans by others' (ibid.: 23). This concept of competition is meaningful in a dynamic market process and completely different from that of the neo-classical 'perfect competition' that is presupposed as defining the end state attained through competition. On the other hand, the term 'dispersive' indicates the nature of a reticulated network where each agent, being mediated by neither an auctioneer nor a central planner, is in direct connection with his or her neighbours.[6]

According to this terminology, the 'concentrated' market indicates the 'well-organized market' assumed in GET where an auctioneer exists and money functions solely as *numeraire* or means of exchange; and the 'dispersive' market indicates the market where money can be hoarded so that buying and selling can take place independently without coordination. 'Say's law' does not hold well, and 'the parametric function of prices' does not work properly in the 'dispersive' market.

Let us get back to the original topic. Hayek, furthermore, tried to show the theoretical importance of the concept of equilibrium, making the distinction between 'subjective equilibrium' and 'objective equilibrium'. If the conditions for subjective equilibrium hold, and if the individual sets of subjective data exactly correspond to the objective data, the development of the objective data is completely foreseen and causes no exogenous disturbance. The situation is now called 'objective equilibrium'. While subjective equilibrium means the compatibility of expectations and plans of different individuals, objective equilibrium means the correspondence of the expectations and plans to external events, or, the correspondence of subjective data to objective data. Since the correspondence of subjective data to objective data is simply assumed in 'Pure Logic of Choice', it does not pay attention to how its correspondence would be reached. In other words, both subjective and objective equilibriums are presupposed in the beginning. This shows why a pure analysis of equilibrium is called the tautological system.

From such viewpoint, Hayek criticizes GET as 'Pure Logic of Choice' for its assumption of 'perfect information' or, in Hayek's term, 'perfect knowledge' (ibid.: 49). Hayek claims that we cannot presuppose perfect knowledge as long as knowledge of each economic agent is limited and there exists the 'division of knowledge'(ibid.: 50), and that the aim of equilibrium theory should be to explain how individuals obtain knowledge, and how subjective data thus correspond to objective data. But even if we remove the assumption of perfect information and take into consideration the formation of expectations under imperfect information, GET can still survive as we can now see it as 'the economics of information'.[7] Then it has become clear that the assumption of perfect information is not necessarily the 'hardcore' assumption for the concentrated market-image of GE. It is, rather, more important to note that subjective disequilibria are ordinary states in a 'real' market, and that the rivalry in which 'any development of the external facts might bear out somebody's expectations and disappoint those of others' is universal.

Notably, Hayek's claim that 'Pure Logic of Choice' is a tautological system of equilibrium leads to criticism against the mathematical method in which equilibrium prices are obtained by solving simultaneous equations with respect to demand and supply of capital goods. Hayek's criticism against the applicability of GE prices to a socialist economy is therefore valid for Barone-type mathematical method for solutions even though Barone himself was already sceptical about the calculation of equilibrium prices on the desk (Barone, 1908).

But the same criticism does not hold good to Walras's *tâtonnement* and Lange's trial and error method, where each economic agent (consumer or productive manager) does not necessarily need to possess complete objective data nor knowledge concerning other agents' states and plans, but has only to make decisions in accordance with its maximizing (or minimizing) rule given a set of prices under its own subjective data: preferences as to consumer goods and leisure; and conditions for productive techniques. The initial errors of the central planner can be corrected as a result of the trial and error process. What was stated here similarly holds to Walras's *tâtonnement* process.[8] Noteworthy is that such analysis of subjective equilibrium is not self-evident tautology because, differently from a mathematical solution, it analyzes a 'dynamic' process that starts from subjective equilibrium and finally reaches objective equilibrium even though it confined itself to the analysis of static state.

What rather seems to be problematic in Lange's trial and error method is that the parametric function of prices is a requisite for it. This also holds for GET. The postulate or rule that each economic agent takes maximizing behaviour with given prices under its own constraints shows the condition under which each economic agent can independently make its own decision without using the knowledge of the economy as a whole and of other agents' plans and behaviours. If the influence of each agent's behaviour is negligibly small, prices can be conceived as public information commonly known to each agent, in other words, parameters that each agent may take as given. In such a situation each economic agent need to neither expect other agents' behaviours nor put their influence into its own data so that it may never cause economic agents' plans to contradict each other nor to be incompatible. For the parametric function of prices logically excludes the possibility of this kind of contradiction and every economic agent is supposedly ensured in subjective equilibrium.[9]

It is hence apparent that the assumption of perfect information is not a 'hardcore' postulate for GET, and that a perfectly competitive market eventually corresponds to a concentrated market-image consisted of the well-organized market and its auctioneer (or a price-adjusting central planner). Hayek's dispersive market-image that gradually becomes clearer is in contrast to such a concentrated market-image. Although Hayek intended to call into question the situation of subjective disequilibrium where plans of different individuals are incompatible with each other, there was no such situation with the parametric function of prices working. Since Hayek criticized GET without questioning the point, regardless of presenting a new view on division of knowledge, he finally returned to a concentrated market-image.

Hayek, taking it for granted from empirical observations that there exists 'a tendency toward equilibrium', only questioned the mechanism how objective equilibrium is arrived through spontaneous interplay of individuals. Though Hayek in the former part of this paper indicated the difficulty of application of GET to a social process, the problem that he proposes at this stage shows his regression to only an extended version of GET dealing with subjectively held and dispersive knowledge.

Why does Hayek's ambivalence to the concept of equilibrium arise? In 1936 when Hayek delivered his presidential address before the London Club, he remained sceptical of GET as capable to become an empirically useful science in spite of his position in favour of Popperian falsificationism. Hayek seems to unknowingly accept the parametric function of prices and, as a result of it, a concentrated market-image because he *a priori* believes in Adam Smith's harmonious view of the market where pursuits of personal interests based on individual self-love would be finally coordinated through a market process regardless of conflicts and competitions.

4. Breakthrough from general equilibrium: rivalrous competition as a discovery procedure is crucial to take it off

Two papers in the mid-1940s showed a sharp contrast in terms of the subtle but crucial theoretical difference between Hayek's division of knowledge and GET.

In 'The use of knowledge in society' in 1945, Hayek proposes to 'look at the price system mechanism as such a mechanism for communication information' (Hayek, [1945] 1948: 86):

> [F]undamentally, in a system in which the knowledge of the relevant facts is dispersed among many people, prices can act to co-ordinate the separate actions of different people in the same way as subjective values help the individual to co-ordinate the parts of his plan.
>
> (Ibid.: 85)

At first, Hayek insisted that the problems which 'economic calculus' (or the Pure Logic of Choice) 'are solving are *not* the economic problems which society faces' (ibid.: 77). This is because we have to consider that the knowledge which we can use 'never exists in concentrated or integrated form but solely as the dispersed bits of incomplete and frequently contradictory knowledge which all the separate individuals possess' (ibid.). Nevertheless, when Hayek thereafter explains 'economic problems' as follows it is no doubt that economic problems are reduced to technological ones as to efficient utilization of dispersive knowledge.

> The economic problem of society is thus not merely a problem of how to allocate 'given' resources [...] It is rather a problem of how to

> secure the best use of resources known to any of the members of society, for ends whose relative importance only these individuals know. Or, to put it briefly, it is a problem of the utilization of knowledge which is not given to anyone in its totality.
>
> (Ibid.: 77–8)

The main subject for Hayek to explain here is how fragmentary knowledge is as efficiently utilized in a market as in the conscious planning by the single authority. Hayek, in order to criticize constructivist economic planning, emphasizes that a market mechanism is not the product of human design, and that its efficiency is accomplished as an unintended result. This line of discussion, however, can be interpreted to mean that he gave particular importance to the merit of a 'result' from coordination of different motives and ends of multiple economic agents by an 'invisible hand' in a market.

The view that dispersive knowledge is socially best utilized in the market does not go beyond the framework of GET. It is a mere analogous definition of equilibrium as the state in which dispersive knowledge is most efficiently utilized in a market, while equilibrium in the conventional sense is the state where scarce resources are most efficiently allocated. In other words, the market-image of 'a system of telecommunications' is still not essentially different from that of GET.

> It is more than a metaphor to describe the price system as a kind of machinery for registering change, or a system of telecommunications which enables individual producers to watch merely the movement of a few pointers, as an engineer might watch the hands of a few dials, in order to adjust their activities to changes of which they may never know more than is reflected in the price movement.
>
> (Ibid.: 87)

Hayek's market-image seen here is in fact similar to Lange's in which a market is regarded as a servomechanism given by nature for calculating equilibrium prices.

In contrast with this, the essay 'The meaning of competition' in 1946 is indeed crucial as Hayek started to struggle against 'perfect competition' to take off from the paradigm of GET. He, in the light of the economic problem, elaborates the meaning of competition in the dynamic market process.

> If the state of affairs assumed by the theory of perfect competition ever existed, it would not only deprive of their scope all the activities which the verb 'to compete' describes but would make them virtually impossible [...] Advertising, undercutting, and improving ('differentiating') the goods or services produced are all excluded by definition – 'perfect' competition means indeed the absence of all competitive activities.
>
> (Hayek, [1946] 1948: 92, 96)

The concept of perfect competition implies a stationary state where all economic activities are completely adjusted and nothing takes place without exogenous disturbances. But in a state where multiple economic agents are trying to realize independent plans, their subjective data are mutually incompatible and changes constantly occur in their subjective data. This is caused by various causal factors 'in the form of the acquisition of new knowledge by the different individuals or of changes in their data brought about by the contacts between them' (ibid.: 94). Since 'competition is by its nature a dynamic process whose essential characteristics are assumed away by the assumptions underlying static analysis' (ibid.), it is certain that Hayek's concept of competition is meaningful only in the analysis of dynamic process.

> The solution of the economic problem of society is in this respect always a voyage of exploration into the unknown, an attempt to discover new ways of doing things better than they have been done before. This must always remain so as long as there are any economic problems to be solved at all, because all economic problems are created by unforeseen changes which require adaptation.
>
> (Ibid.: 101)

It was not until this stage that Hayek had illuminated the idea of a discovery process of knowledge: in the 'competitive' market where ends and purposes of different individuals conflict and contradict each other and, moreover, data are constantly changing, competition encourages incessant discovery of new knowledge. Such a process is 'a voyage of exploration into the unknown, an attempt to discover new ways of doing things better than they have been done before'. Both Eatwell and Milgate (1994) and Lavoie (1995) emphasize, Hayek's concept of dynamic competition or rivalry, which, both of them suggest, in turn resembles Marx's concept of competition rather than neo-classical perfect competition, plays a crucial role in such a theory of market.

The substantial difference from the previous standpoint is what Hayek's main concern had shifted from an *end state* with efficient use of subjective and dispersive knowledge to a competitive or rivalrous *process* through which discovery of the unknown is encouraged. Hayek had *ipso facto* taken a step out of GET by examining the subjective and objective disequilibrium process. He here set up as the object of a theoretical investigation a basically different entity from a concentrated market: the *dispersive and rivalrous* market where the parametric function of prices is not in operation. The difference between these two articles in terms of both the problematic domains and the investigative objects is so subtle that it has been frequently overlooked. But this change was decisive for Hayek who hereafter deepened his criticism of GET and began to regard the market as a social institution.

The criticism of GET was further extended in the essay 'Competition as a discovery procedure' based on some lectures held in 1968. Hayek has now come to recognize this subject in a clearer form than before. Thus, his criticism of GET appeared to become unambiguous and irreversible.

Hayek, in this essay, elucidated the idea of 'competition as a discovery procedure':

> [...] *wherever* the use of competition can be rationally justified, it is on the ground that we do *not* know in advance the facts that determine the actions of competitors [...] I propose to consider competition as a procedure for the discovery of such facts as, without resort to it, would not be known to anyone, or at least would not be utilized.
>
> (Hayek, 1978: 179)

> Economic theory sometimes appears at the outset to bar its way to a true appreciation of the character of the process of competition, because it starts from the assumption of a 'given' supply of scarce goods. But which goods are scarce goods, or which things are goods, and how scarce or valuable they are – these are precisely the things which competition has to discover. Provisional results from the market process at each stage alone tell individuals what to look for. Utilization of knowledge widely dispersed in a society with extensive division of labour cannot rest on individuals knowing all the particular uses to which well-known things in their individual environment might be put. Prices direct their attention to what is worth finding out about market offers for various things and services. This means that the, in some respects always unique, combinations of individual

> knowledge and skills, which the market enables them to use, will not merely, or even in the first instance, be such knowledge of facts as they could list and communicate if some authority asked them to do so. The knowledge of which I speak consists rather of a capacity to find out particular circumstances, which becomes effective only if possessors of this knowledge are informed by the market which kinds of things or services are wanted, and how urgently they are wanted.
>
> (Ibid.: 181–2)

As far as the knowledge to be discovered through competition in the market depends on individual's 'capacity to find out particular circumstances', it cannot be regarded as 'given data', for it is obvious that the unused knowledge without being discovered by competition continuously exists. Hayek here no longer takes the view that a market economy accomplishes efficiency as the result of competition.

> The results of a discovery procedure are in their nature unpredictable; and all we can expect from the adoption of an effective discovery procedure is to improve the chances for unknown people. The only common aim which we can pursue by the choice of this technique of ordering social affairs is the general kind of pattern, or the abstract character, of the order that will form itself.
>
> (Ibid.: 184)

Hayek maintains here that what we expect from competition as a discovery procedure is neither the attainment of optimal allocation of resources nor efficient utilization of knowledge in a state of equilibrium, after all, but merely 'the general kind of pattern, or the abstract character, of the order that will form itself'. In short, competition does not bring about 'equilibrium', but merely certain 'pattern of order' that corresponds to Hayek's spontaneous order that is the concept more relevant in economics and economic policy.

Hence I may conclude that Hayek could finally renounce the market-image of GET at this stage owing to an alternative concept of competition. This does not mean that he has presented any alternative 'market theory' to GET. But, notably, he has introduced the concept of 'order' instead of 'equilibrium' as describing the main character of a new market-image.

5. Hayek's transformation of market-images in 1930–40s: vision, theory and methodology

Regarding the initial questions on the nature and extent of Hayek's transformation, I would like to draw my conclusion. Hayek's transformation is not once and for all, but twice with discontinuous breaking points in 1946 and 1960. The transformation involves not only methodology or theory but also vision, in particular the vision of the market, which can work as a catalyst to help create a new theory and methodology. The key concept for Hayek to break with GE and reach a new market-image is rivalrous and discovery competition since 1946, not subjective and dispersive knowledge since 1937, and that this break is mainly caused by his SCD battle with Lange's trial and error method in 1936–37 that makes GE endorse MS to be feasible.

Finally, I will explain the implications of such theses for the relation between vision and theory or methodology, making my comments on the previous interpretations of Hayek's transformation. Caldwell, while withholding direct attribution of the cause of Hayek's transformation to his participation in SCD, emphasized a strong influence of the debate on it.[10] He thereafter toned down his insistence regarding this issue.[11] Then he has reached his updated interpretation on the matter, '[i]n my opinion, the calculation debate did not *cause* Hayek to come up with a specific idea; rather, it was what helped him *put together* the ideas mentioned above in the specific way that he did' (Caldwell, 2004: 214).

I tried to reconstruct the argument to contend that the main *cause* for Hayek's transformation is, regardless of Caldwell's withholding, 'his battle with the market socialists'. I basically agree with Caldwell's last interpretation but would like to clarify what the distinction between 'to come up with a specific idea' and to '*put together* the ideas' implies in the present context. In my account, 'to come up with a specific idea' is such analytic act in science as to define, deduce or induce, and to '*put together* the ideas' is preanalytic integrative act in science to grasp the reality, that might be regarded as 'abduction' in Peirce's term[12] or 'vision' in Schumpeter's term. In this article, I claim, using the concept 'vision' or 'image' as preanalytic cognitive framework prior to any analytic activity that functions as a catalyst to create a new concept or theory of science, that Hayek's vision of the 'market' that 'Hayek I' had been engaged in was turned over by his encounter to the market socialists's defensive argument of socialism by using GET. Subsequently, the uneasiness that occurred in his mind must have made

Hayek notice that subjectively held and dispersive knowledge as well as a discovery of tacit and new knowledge that he had so far neglected play important roles in a rivalrous and dispersive market process of a real world. This triggered Hayek's transformation in which static and fictitious images of the market were gradually replaced by dynamic and real ones.

Kirzner, on the other, seems to support my thesis that Hayek transformed his vision of the market though SCD when he emphatically states in his article on SCD:

> Not only was the debate an important episode, of course, for its own sake. It was, in addition, I shall claim, important as a catalyst in the development and articulation of the modern Austrian view of the market as a competitive-entrepreneurial process of discovery.
>
> (Kirzner, 1988: 1)

He appreciated SCD as essential lessons for Austrians, contrary to Lavoie's interpretation of the debate inclined towards self-justification of Austrian (Lavoie, 1985), because it is a self-discovery or self-awareness process in which what Mises and Hayek tacitly understood but could not explicitly demonstrate in terms of their unique vision of the market has become more articulated through exchanges of opinions with different positions in SCD. 'My contention is that what Austrians learnt was more than a technique of exposition; they learnt to appreciate more sensitively how their own tradition understood the market process' (Kirzner, 1988: 3). I agree with Kirzner in this respect and would like to further add regarding social 'welfare' that any scientific debate as well as the market is a discovery process in which scientists of different parties can at least gain the benefit of articulating their own positions and differences between opinions, apart from a problem of winning or losing.

Both Lawson (1994) and Fleetwood (1995) regard Hayek's transformation as the one in methodology, in which Hayek, via positivism and subjectivism, reached in his late career a final ontological position, quasi- transcendental or critical realism. Fleetwood's elaborate study is successful in describing Hayek as becoming an interdisciplinary social theorist who based on the general theory of socio-economics by redirecting seemingly subjective knowledge and rules as scientific objects allocated in a deep domain. Obviously, his main focus is on Hayek III's quasi-transcendental realism, and he has not therefore fully investigated the aspects of his economic research in Hayek I and II. I rather try to show an implication for the relationships of vision, theory and methodology in economics by examining how Hayek's transformation has taken place.

I contend that Hayek's socio-economics results not only from his philosophical and methodological turns particularly observed in his Scientism essays in 1942–44, as Lawson and Fleetwood indicate, but also from the change of his vision of the market that is a complex of some basic concepts in theory. Hayek had experienced his philosophical turns through I–III as Fleetwood showed, however, the transformation in methodology had not taken place by itself. Once Hayek forms a particular market-image that works not only for utilization of dispersive knowledge but also for discovery and creation of new knowledge through rivalry, he was then first able to criticize GE by it, not a theory. Such particular 'hardcore' concepts (in Lakatos's term) as equilibrium, competition and knowledge have changed and, finally, at some threshold point, the vision of the market changed. The vision of the market is a complex constituted by those concepts to support a total structure of a theory, so its change or replacement is potentially able to overturn the economic theory as a whole. Methodological shifts followed these changes in order to build the foundations.

Now I presume, by abductive inference, that Hayek's transformation, or, generally speaking, anyone's transformation occurs in a sequence of (1) vision, (2) theory, (3) methodology, not in the reverse order. Vision gradually turns into theory. Once theory is established, methodology is abstracted from theory as meta-theory and it fundamentally determines the basic nature and structure of theory. But methodology does not create or transform a theory. It is often observed that a shift in methodology is not the cause, but the result of change of theoretical endeavour as substantive scientific activities grappling with reality.

Vision in substantive economics is no less important than methodology, particularly in order to discover a new finding, create a new framework and improve scientific knowledge of reality. Vision offers a metaphor, an analogy or an image to activate *abduction* different from deduction and induction, which consists in a cognitive movement from surface phenomena to some deeper mechanisms, structures, rules, power or relations. So it is recognized that vision is necessary for scientific hypothetical reasoning which enables creation of new theories or concepts. Once vision transforms, it requires a change of methodology in order to present an integrative and consistent basis of a new theory so that it can formally systemize itself. The vision of a theory as the frame of reference to key concepts in economics, even though they cannot be expressed in explicit manner in the first place, are not less important than methodology in order for economics to explore the unknown reality of our socio-economic world.

So I believe that the rivalrous and dispersive market-image for discovery of knowledge should be a vision for establishing a new theory of the market as a self-organizing complex system or a 'spontaneous order' that is the basic idea of Hayek III, whilst Hayek himself had not accomplished it.

Notes

1. This article is based on part of chapter 4 of my Japanese book (Nishibe, 1996). The basic theses contained herein remain the same but for minor amendments, but arguments are made clearer and references are amplified.
2. 'Obviously, in order to be able to posit to ourselves any problems at all, we should first have to visualize a distinct set of coherent phenomena as a worth-while object of our analytic efforts. In other words, analytic effort is of necessity preceded by a preanalytic cognitive act that supplies the raw material for the analytic effort. In this book, this preanalytic cognitive act will be called Vision. It is interesting to note that vision of this kind not only must precede historically the emergence of analytic effort in any field but also may re-enter the history of every established science each time somebody teaches us to *see* things in a light of which the source is not to be found in the facts, methods, and results of the pre-existing state of science' (Schumpeter, 1954: 41).
3. Two years before, Hayek (1933) had first criticized socialist planning whose origin is regarded in Historical School, in 'The trend of economic thinking', but he hadn't begun his criticism to MS and the concept of equilibrium yet.
4. While 'economic problems' relate to a socio-economic situation where different ends and motives of multiple individuals conflict with one another, 'technological problems' relate to a situation where a single economic agent just like Robinson Crusoe has to make a proper decision on alternative opportunities subject to certain constraints.
5. I would like to point out that Hayek's idea of what is to be called 'formal economic theory as a tool' is nearly approaching Schumpeter's idea of 'economic analysis' (Schumpeter, 1954) assumed as formal techniques and tools in economics. Since Schumpeter believed in the reality of 'economic analysis' as a supra-historic standard or rule applicable to every kind of economy, he endorsed Lange's application of GET to a socialist economy at least in the scope of static problems. On the contrary, Hayek could never find any corresponding reality to formal economic theory other than Robinson Crusoe's economy with a single agent and therefore insisted that its application to a socialist economy is impossible. This is truly a big difference, but Hayek's 'formal economic theory as a tool' is almost identical to Schumpeter's 'economic analysis' in the sense that both of them neglect that such formalization of theory involves a particular method of abstraction from reality and of discrimination from other theories, and that both of their

arguments are attempting, as a result, to defend GET. Hayek had foreseen the rapid upswing of the axiomatic formalization and mathematical generalization in GET since the 1950s, however, contrary to Hayek's proposal, GET has kept being applied not only to a single person's technological problem but also to a society's economic problem. This would mean, regardless of Hayek's criticism, that GET has been misconceived until now as the theory of a 'real' market, not as 'Pure Logic of Choice'.

6. This might be regarded as similar to the concept of 'decentralized' that is often used in the literature of economics. But I will here introduce the term 'dispersive' instead of 'decentralized' since the latter is in many cases misleading as, for instance, the following discussions illustrate. The pair of terms 'decentralized' and 'centralized' expresses the degree of concentration of decision-making power, whether it is either political or economic, say, in a society and a firm. However, the dichotomy between a centralized planned economy and a decentralized market economy frequently gives us a preconception that planned economy is always 'centralized' and a market economy is always 'decentralized,' and then tends to lead us to neglect a possibility of the existence of a 'centralized' market and 'decentralized' planning. Since there is, at the same time, a modern neo-classical usage of those terms for classification of market structures where an oligopolistic or a monopolistic market is 'centralized', and a competitive market is 'decentralized', we are likely to confuse their meanings in political and economic decision making in the former case and those in the market structure in the latter case. I therefore propose that we should reserve 'centralized' and 'decentralized' exclusively for *the economic and political decision-making* sense, and prepare another pair of terms 'concentrated' and 'dispersive' for *the market structure* sense.
7. Caldwell (1997) has examined such newly emerged problems as incentive compatibility and asymmetry of information that were embedded in MS of SCD and have recently become well noticed in the economics of information. Caldwell made his conclusion on the economics: 'he [Hayek] might warn against an excessive preoccupation with question of information' (Caldwell, 1997: 1886). Such a warning about the economics of information is shared by Nishibe (1996) and the present chapter. And this must affect what interpretation of Hayek's transformation is relevant.
8. It was theoretically believed so at the time, even though it was made clear that excess demand function of all goods must satisfy certain conditions for convergence towards equilibrium and such stability conditions are considerably restricted.
9. Such parametric function (or signalling function) of prices requires satisfaction of such conditions for perfect competition as: (1) one-price to one-good law holds because prices in a market are transmitted instantly and with no cost to each economic agent; (2) each economic agent behaves as a price taker because a large number of small sized agents are assumed; (3) there is freedom for firms of entry to and exit from industries and no institutional obstacles for that; and (4) all goods are homogeneous in quality.
10. He initially stated, 'I will argue that it was his participation in the socialist calculation debate which helped lead Hayek to realize the centrality of the question of coordination, and of its links with specific assumptions

concerning knowledge [...] Though I will not claim that his participation in the debate *caused* Hayek's transformation, a knowledge of his role will be helpful in understanding why events unfolded as they did' (Caldwell, 1988: 515–6).

11. He put, 'I stand by my intention of the nature of Hayek's transformation. I would like to qualify, however, my discussion of the causes of his change [...] I still think that it is correct to say that, if one looks at the episode in retrospect, the causal factor that eventually emerged as most important was his battle with the market socialists [...] But this is different from saying that his battle with the socialists was the main cause at the time that Hayek's transformation was actually taking place. No single cause stands out' (Caldwell, 1994: 121–2).
12. 'All the ideas of science come to it by the way of Abduction. Abduction consists in studying facts and devising a theory to explain them. Its only justification is that if we are ever to understand things at all, it must be in that way' ('Harvard Lectures on Pragmatism', Peirce, 1903; 1931–58: vol. 5, 145).

References

Barone, E. (1908) 'Ministry of production in the collectivist State', in Hayek (ed.) (1935a).

Caldwell, B. (1988) 'Hayek's transformation', *History of Political Economy*, 20(4): 513–41.

Caldwell, B. (1994) 'Four theses on Hayek', in Colonna, Hagemann and Hamouda (eds) (1994).

Caldwell, B. (1997) 'Hayek and Socialism' *Journal of Economic Literature*, 35(4): 1856–90.

Caldwell, B. (2004) *Hayek's Challenge: An Intellectual Biography of F.A. Hayek*, Chicago: University of Chicago Press.

Colonna, M. and Hagemann, H. (1994) *The Economics of F.A. Hayek, Vol. I: Money and Business Cycles*, Cheltenham: Edward Elgar.

Colonna, M., Hagemann, H. and Hamouda, O. F. (1994) *The Economics of F.A. Hayek, Vol. II: Capitalism, Socialism and Knowledge*, Cheltenham: Edward Elgar.

Dickinson, H. D. (1939) *Economics of Socialism*, Oxford: Oxford University Press.

Eatwell, J. and Milgate, M. (1994) 'Competition, prices and market order', in Colonna and Hagemann (eds) (1994).

Fleetwood, S. (1995) *Hayek's Political Economy*, London: Routledge.

Foss, N. J. (1995) 'More on "Hayek's Transformation"', *History of Political Economy*, 27(2): 345–64.

Hayek, F. A. (1933) 'The trend of economic thinking', *Economica*, 13: 121–37.

Hayek, F. A. (1935a) *Collectivist Economic Planning*, London: George Routledge & Sons.

Hayek, F. A. (1935b) 'Socialist calculation I: The nature and history of the problem', in Hayek (ed.) (1935a), Hayek (1948).

Hayek, F. A. (1935c) 'Socialist calculation II: The state of the debate', in Hayek (ed.) (1935a), Hayek (ed.) (1948).

Hayek, F. A. (1936) 'Economics and knowledge', *Economica*, 6: 33–54, in Hayek (ed.) (1948).

Hayek, F. A. (1940) 'Socialist calculation III: The competitive "solution"', *Economica*, 7: 125–49, in Hayek (ed.) (1948).
Hayek, F. A. (1943) 'The facts of the social sciences'; in Hayek (ed.) (1948).
Hayek, F. A. (1945) 'The use of knowledge in society', *The American Economic Review*, 35(4): 519–29, in Hayek (ed.) (1948).
Hayek, F. A. (1946) 'The meaning of competition', in Hayek (ed.) (1948).
Hayek, F. A. (1947) 'Free enterprise and competitive order,' in Hayek (ed.) (1948).
Hayek, F. A. (1948) *Individualism and The Economic Order*, Chicago: University of Chicago Press.
Hayek, F. A. (1964) 'Kinds of rationalism', in Hayek (ed.) (1967).
Hayek, F. A. (1967) *Studies in Philosophy, Politics and Economics*, Chicago: University of Chicago Press.
Hayek, F. A. (1968) 'Competition as a discovery procedure', in Hayek (ed.) (1978).
Hayek, F. A. (1978) *New Studies in Philosophy, Politics and Economics*, Chicago: University of Chicago Press.
Hutchison, T. W. (1981) *The Politics and Philosophy of Economics*, Oxford: Basil Blackwell.
Kirzner, I. M. (1988) 'The economic calculation debate: lessons for Austrians', *The Review of Austrian Economics*, 2: 1–18.
Lange, O. (1936–37) 'On the economic theory and socialism', *Review of Economic Studies*, 4, in B. E. Lippincott (ed.): *On the Economic Theory of Socialism*, 1938, Minneapolis: Minnesota University Press.
Lavoie, D. (1985) *Rivalry and Central Planning – The Socialist Calculation Debate Reconsidered*, Cambridge: Cambridge University Press.
Lawson, T. (1994) 'Realism and Hayek: a case of continuous transformation', in Colonna and Hagemann (ed.) (1994).
Nishibe, M. (1996) *Shijo-zo no Keifugaku* (A Genealogy of Market-images), Toyo Keizai Shinpo Sya.
Peirce, C. S. (1931–35) *Collected papers of Charles Sanders Peirce*, Vols. 1–6, edited by C. Hartshorne and P. Weiss, Cambridge, MA: Harvard University Press.
Polanyi, M. (1967) *The Tacit Dimension*, London: Routledge & Kegan Paul.
Schumpeter, J. A. (1954) *History of Economic Analysis*, Oxford: Oxford University Press.

16
Carl Menger and the Later Austrian School of Economics: An Analysis of their Methodological Relationship

Tsutomu Hashimoto

1. Introduction

Would it be a normative imperative that the methodology of social science should be neutral in respect to any ideological value? Or would it be an illusion that the methodology is exclusively useful for scientific procedures?

When we look at the history of the '*Methodenstreit*' and thereafter, we find an extra role of the methodology in ideological debate. From the late nineteenth century to the middle of the twentieth century, an expected role of methodology was to provide a scientific solution for the problem of institutional choice between socialism and capitalism. Many social scientists tried to explain how and why the one system is scientifically better than the other. However, since there was no immediate consensus on the concept of 'science' or 'scientific', they first needed to articulate the definition of the science. This situation would explain why many social scientists were involved in the study of methodology. Methodology was important, not only in scientific investigation per se, but also in matters of institutional choice, which are intertwined with ideological values.

I will argue that the methodological investigation was the last resort for the ideological controversy between socialism and capitalism. Participants in this controversy tried to use vocabularies of scientific methodology for their external effect on ideological values. Methodology could function to carry some ideological implications. Let us call this effect the 'thought-ladenness of methodology',[1] where 'thought' means ideology or an element of ideology. I use the term 'thought' instead of 'ideology' because the latter is usually used in criticizing the opponent's view and not in defending the proponent's own view. The 'thought-ladenness of methodology' is observed in the debate between proponents and opponents of capitalism (liberalism), notably in the first half of the twentieth century.

In this chapter, I shall examine Menger's methodology in the light of its thought-ladenness and reconstruct the history of methodological developments from Menger to Mises and Hayek from this perspective. Since Menger's two disciples, Mises and Hayek, were involved in the debate on capitalism versus socialism, tracing the development of the 'Austrian' methodology back to Menger may help to understand the nature of the relation between methodology and ideology. Mises and Hayek developed Menger's methodology in their own ways, but it is not well investigated how and why they did so. This chapter examines the development of the methodology of Austrian economics from Menger to Mises and Hayek in the light of 'the thought-ladenness of methodology'.

2. Menger versus Schmoller

A standard interpretation of the '*Methodenstreit*' between Menger and Schmoller is provided by Joseph Schumpeter (1914, 1926, 1954). Roughly speaking, Schumpeter describes how (a) Schmoller was wrong in his epistemological explanation, but (b) that this debate can be reconciled or regarded as 'even' between them when we emphasize Schmoller's original contribution to methodology. However, this interpretation seems to be inappropriate. Therefore, I first re-examine Menger's methodology and the Methodenstreit (2.1). Then, I examine Schumpeter's standard interpretation of the debate (2.2), and present my own alternative (2.3).

2.1. Methodenstreit

When Menger's *Principles* were published in 1871, they did not exert great influence in Germany where the Historical School was the mainstream paradigm of economics at that time. Menger must have been discontent with his reception in Germany since one of his aims was to contribute to the development of German economics.[2] In order to attract more attention to his masterpiece, Menger wrote another book, *Investigations into the Method of Social Sciences: with special reference to economics* (1883) ('Methods of Economics'). In this book, Menger aims to provide scientific legitimacy concerning methodology for his theory of value, namely the marginal utility theory of prices.

Against the German Historical School's claim that a science of economics should be methodologically unified in its investigation, Menger first divided the research programs of social science into two categories: a science of history and a science of theory. He also made clear that the science of theory contains two sub-categories: a realistic-empirical approach, and an exact one. Then Menger tried to provide a scientific status (legitimacy) for the 'exact approach in the science of theory'.

In his classification of social sciences, Menger then adds a third category of science called 'practical science or technology (economic and fiscal policy of national economy)'. However, he did not explain this one extensively. He just noted a few remarks and did not assign an extra chapter for their explanation. However, from the perspective of 'the thought-ladenness of methodology', it is important to consider how Menger's 'practical science' is related to other categories of science. But first, let us examine Menger's distinction between the science of history and the science of theory.

Menger's immediate aim was to criticize the scientific status of the Historical School and to defend his 'exact-empirical approach'. In order to do so, Menger put forward the following three arguments.

First, Menger defends a methodological monism of natural and social sciences against the methodological dualism that is favoured by the Historical School. While the Historical School presupposes that it is impossible to attain exact laws in social sciences due to their material complexity, Menger recognizes neither conflict nor contrast between natural and social sciences. According to Menger, the different objects of research in natural and social sciences do not imply any difference of methodologies (1883: 39; see also ibid.: appendix V, n. 145). He finds that both a realistic-empirical and an exact approach can be useful in natural and social sciences alike. Thus, Menger justifies his exact approach in the social sciences. Moreover, as we will see in the next section, he justifies his methodology by referring to realism[3] and pragmatism.[4]

Second, Menger criticized the self-image of the Historical School regarding its methodology. Although the Historical School claims that it would only use the inductive method, Menger points out that it is a logical misunderstanding of what they really do. For example, the statement that phenomenon C generally occurs in situations A and B even if A and B are not observable, or the statement that phenomenon C generally accompanies situations A and B, is beyond our experience and therefore beyond the method of the strict realistic approach (1883: 35; 1986: 44). The inductive method is not enough to establish a general law (or regularity) in the study of history. We need to appeal to an abstract procedure to establish general laws. Thus, Menger insists that even the realistic approach of the Historical School must already have been beyond a naïve realism.

Third, Menger points out that the Historical School mixes up the natures of theoretical and historical understanding. While the latter refers to recognizing a generative process of a particular phenomenon, the former relates to a particular phenomenon as an illustration of a successive regularity (1883: 17). Some might think that Menger's view on the 'theoretical understanding' is properly placed in the context of the traditional German *Geisteswissenschaft*. However, Menger did not give us any positive justification for it. He did not think that the method of 'understanding', both historical and theoretical, was unique to the social sciences.[5] He just pointed out that there are two approaches, both a realistic and an exact one, and he does not present any positive argument to justify the latter approach.

Hence, Menger's criticism of the Historical School is not crucial. It would be reasonable to say that Menger gave an appropriate category to the Historical School in terms of methodology. However, the Historical School might have been aware of the importance of 'law' in its investigations.[6] If this were the case, disagreements between Menger and the Historical School in the *Methodenstreit* would converge to a certain epistemological agreement. Then, what would really be at stake is the question of whether or not Menger's exact approach is justifiable.

According to Menger, the only cognitive principle for a theoretical truth, which constitutes the exact approach, is the following requirement: the event that occurred once needs to be repeated under the same condition (1883: 40). In order to fulfil this requirement, we must first reduce a given phenomenon to its simplest constituent and compose a theory or a law from it. For Menger's theoretical concern, the most basic constituent of his theory is 'desire', the pursuit of the perfect satisfaction. 'The exact approach of the theoretical study [...] must teach us not the whole life of the human being but the law from which the complex phenomena of human relations develop' (1883: 45). Here, Menger regards his exact science of economics as the theory that 'has a task of presenting a set of understanding in the economic aspect which is special to and the most important in our life'.

However, although Menger presents a clear methodological procedure and a scope for his research, his exact approach serves the function of criticizing the insufficiency of the realistic approach of the Historical School. Three remarks should be made on Menger's negative justification for his methodology.

First, according to Menger, the Historical School believed that, since human will is led by numerous motives which are reciprocally conflicting and contradicting, an exact law of human action, especially of economic action, is not attainable (1883: 73). Since the Historical School denies the hypothesis of 'self-interested economic man' or 'atomism', this view may lead us to misunderstanding the substantiation of a collective agency such as 'nation' which itself desires, economizes, works or consumes (1883: 86). Menger, on the other hand, regards a national economy as a complex of single economies. He therefore justifies a method of abstracting a single economy in an atomistic way as a tool of the cognitive construction of our society.

Second, while the Historical School rejects 'eternalism' – that is, the view that claims theory to be valid throughout history – Menger does not think that history influences the formal character of any exact theory (1883: 117). For Menger, denying 'eternalism' is not sufficient to negate the possibility of an exact theory.

Third, according to Menger, it is insufficient for the Historical School to point out differences in phenomena among local communities or districts in order to show the invalidity of universalism. Since such a difference occurs within the same local area, the implication of the emphasis on local difference is not only to deny universalism but also to deny localism (1883: 113).

Thus, those three arguments would reinforce Menger's exact approach negatively: it is necessary only because the methodological cognition of the Historical School is insufficient.[7]

2.2. Schumpeter's interpretation of the *Methodenstreit*

Were Menger's aforementioned arguments on methodology successful? In the standard interpretation of the *Methodenstreit*, Schumpeter gives the impression that Menger has never won over his opponents.[8] Schumpeter reconciles Menger's methodology with Schmoller's by emphasizing the latter's contribution. According to Schumpeter, there is no crucial issue in the controversy because neither party made the opponent's methodology fundamentally dubious. Both parties just struggled over the priority or the primacy of their methodologies. If they could put the opponent's position in a proper place in the system of social sciences, the conflict would be reconciled (Schumpeter, 1954:

814–15).[9] For Schumpeter, the issue of the controversy was not about the justification of the methodological procedure, but rather about the scope and the status of their respective research fields.

Thus, Schumpeter sees the controversy from the perspectives of each research program and hence evaluates the fruitfulness of Schmoller's project.[10] Schumpeter thinks highly of Schmoller's program, because it opens a new possibility for a synthetic economic sociology with certain perspectives and norms in its methodology.[11] Although Schumpeter seems to exaggerate Schmoller's contribution, his evaluation of the Historical School is right in emphasizing the fruitfulness of its research program.

2.3. Thought-ladenness of methodology in the *Methodenstreit*

Schumpeter presented his interpretation from a non-vindicating view of the scientific methodology. However, I would like to raise another perspective with reference to its ideological effects. While Schumpeter sees the role of methodology within the scope of scientific activities, I would like to examine its implication for ideological controversies. As stated above, since the methodology of social sciences sometimes takes on a role of settling ideological issues, it would be important to explain how Menger and Schmoller opposed each other ideologically. I examine the issue of methodological justification from a perspective of the 'thought-ladenness of methodology', irrespective of its fruitfulness as a research program.

To be precise, Schumpeter was not insensitive to the problem of the 'thought-ladenness' of methodology when he emphasized Schmoller's contribution to the study of methodology. He also appraised Schmoller's ideological implication (Schumpeter, 1926) and described it as follows: rationalization, standardization, automation and democratization, all of which participate in the culture of capitalism, making it easier to unify people's desires. A future epoch is now gradually approaching, where people's desires are unified so that we can set social goals by means of science. It is already possible to command by using the categories of 'right' and 'wrong' without great costs in many fields, especially in the fields of monetary and credit policies. This is what Schmoller means when he makes a value judgment and sets a target for his research. It has already been possible to make such a command in his case study at his time. It was just a 'skill' to command at his time, which would become 'technology' in due course. What Schmoller essentially desired was to create the national economics that serves technology and makes use of verification and demonstration (Schumpeter, 1926, 1972: 441–3).

As for Schmoller's thought-ladenness of methodology, Schumpeter notes some normative background of Schmoller's concern in his *History of Economic Analysis*. Schumpeter points out that Schmoller was against both economic liberalism and the Classical School of economics in Britain, which defends self-interest on behalf of 'private profit' (Schumpeter, 1954: 811–12). This view would explain why Schmoller regarded his school as 'historical-ethical' and why he was opposed to Menger's assumption of the 'self-interested economic man'.[12] In fact, the only problematic issue that Schmoller raised clearly in the controversy is the very abstraction of a self-interested economic man. However, the conjecture that Menger's exact approach has a particular 'thought-ladenness' for recommending a policy of economic liberalism is not correct. Since a rational man can pursue altruistic purposes rationally, Menger's methodology needs to be understood separately from the ethical value of egoism and altruism.

Of course, Menger's methodology is not completely independent of ethical or ideological values. He did not make any clear distinction between methodology and ideology in his 'Method of Science' or the later works. In fact, Menger shows his 'thought-ladenness of methodology' indirectly by criticizing the opponent's ideology on its methodological implications. My concern here is to examine the elements of his liberal ideology in his methodological works.[13]

First, there is the issue of the effects for the practical sciences the exact approach of social sciences has. Menger insists that both the investigation in social sciences and the practices in politics need to acquire general knowledge or regularity from concrete events in order to make a conclusive judgment on future events. This proposal, according to Hayek (1973: 278–9), implies the impossibility of a constructivist control of the economy: Menger was completely conscious about the limits of his theory regarding predictions, and he was content with it. According to Hayek, the attitude to make use of all available statistical information in order to predict future events is generated from a desire to control the economy (1973: 281). In the light of this issue, the thought-ladenness of Menger's methodology lies in criticizing the constructivism. Menger emphasized the methodological status of his exact approach in order to depreciate Schmoller's political implications of constructivism.

Second, Menger criticizes Schmoller's concern for constructivism by showing the methodological disconnection between the Historical School of economics and the old Historical School of E. Burke and

F. K. von Savigny. According to Menger, the German economists of the Historical School mistook the revolutionary ideas of the Historical School of law: it is not appropriate that they have a self-recognition of succeeding the tradition of the Historical School of law. Menger argues that the Historical School of law aimed to provide a historical understanding of a particular law: it tried to prove the fact that a particular law is a result of the unreflective process of its organic development (1883: 222). In the response to Schmoller's criticism to Menger in his affirming of Savigny's contribution, Menger points out that the purpose is to understand the present social institutions in general, especially those generated in an organic manner, and therefore to preserve the institution which has remained through harsh tests against the reformist propensity and its one-sided rational understanding of the national economy. It is partly necessary to protect the organically generated economy from destruction by pragmatism, which obliges us to move on to socialism against the proponents' will (1883: 208). In other words, Menger believes that understanding the spontaneous development of law would be connected with the practice to protect it from radical reform. Thus, Menger gave rebirth to the methodological insights of the old historical school of law in the field of economics. It is clear why Menger insisted that the historical school's 'organic understanding' was not enough and that the 'mechanistic conception' and the 'pragmatic interpretation' was necessary for understanding social institutions.[14]

These two arguments examined above show Menger's thought-ladenness of methodology: one is a criticism of constructivism, and the other one of the understanding of law that has a political orientation of the socialist pragmatism. Here we can see a phase of the ideological conflict between constructivism and spontaneous order.[15] It would be correct that most parts of Menger's methodology are neutral to any thought. However, I insist that the *Methodenstreit*'s central issue lies in the problem of the thought-ladenness of methodology. This view would also explain why Mises and Hayek took over the investigation of methodology in Menger's heritage. If we take the Schumpeterian view on the controversy, we cannot fully evaluate the significance of Mises's and Hayek's methodologies.

3. From Menger to Mises and Hayek

Mises and Hayek, as leading representatives of the third generation of Austrian Economists, took Menger's methodology seriously and developed their views under Menger's influence. Roughly speaking, Mises took over Menger's methodology in its totality, whereas Hayek chose to develop it in terms of its ideological aspects. Here I investigate how they developed their methodologies from Menger's. First, I examine Menger's methodology and describe the problem which Mises and Hayek faced. Second, I compare their methodologies with Menger's one.

3.1. Beyond Menger's methodology

Although Menger is said to have found the ultimate foundation of his methodology in Aristotle's realism (see Smith, 1990) he did not explicitly provide us with such an ultimate justification. He tried to construct a fundamental for 'scientific' methodology by means of separating his methodology from its metaphysical foundations. What Menger tried to make clear is that the exact approach is possible in social sciences. In other words, for Menger the issue at stake was to give a scientific foundation for his research program without appealing to any metaphysical premises. If this interpretation of Menger's methodology is correct, we need to examine his methodology from the following four premises.

First, there is an argument that denies any possibility of deriving a general law through the exact approach in social sciences. It locates social sciences including economics in the tradition of *Geisteswissenschaft* (Dilthey), a science of history (Windelband) or a science of culture (Rickert), all of which are contrasted with the natural sciences which are capable of setting general laws. Opponents of categorical statements in economics argue that our recognition of regularities in a society always assumes a particular social order and we cannot recognize such laws without reference to it. On the other hand, proponents of a general law in economics argue that our recognition of that law in a society, just like the same observation in nature, does not depend on any particular order. However, these proponents provide no evidence for deriving a general regularity in economics. As Oppler (1930) observes, the question we need to ask would be the possibility to assume a general law rather than its existence or its verification. It must be a primary task to search a set of logical conditions under which economic laws can require their general validity. Mises's praxeology took over this task from Menger's methodological investigation.

Second, even if the exact approach enabled us to formulate a general law, there is another remaining question whether it can be a productive heuristic as a scientific research program. According to Max Alter, Menger presents arguments on methodological justification, but fails to provide a scientific research program in the light of the growth of knowledge (Alter, 1990b: 327–8). On the other hand, Milford (1990: 235) evaluates Menger's methodology, arguing that it serves as the foundation for the research program of Austrian Economics. It's a controversial issue to ask whether or not Menger's exact approach is fruitful as a scientific research program. Menger's exact approach seems to be placed as the core of his research program rather than being a positive heuristic for developing an applied economic science. Therefore, his methodology would not be properly evaluated in terms of its fruitfulness as a heuristic method.

Third, there is the problem of falsifiability of any exact theory (Birner, 1990: 249; Hutchison, 1973). Menger was well aware of this problem and had already expected the ensuing criticism from the German Historical School: an exact theory needs to be modified by the realistic-empirical study, which is in turn subject to an empirical test. Menger's response to this issue was that it is illogical and misinterpreting, regarding the foundation of the exact approach, to assume that an exact theory can be corroborated by pure experience (1883: 54). Menger is right in pointing out that an exact theory cannot be subject to any direct testing through experience, because the constructed assumptions of the theory are too abstract to find their correspondence in reality. It might be said that to deny the possibility of testing would not satisfy the criterion of falsifiability, proposed by Karl Popper, which distinguishes science from metaphysics. However, falsification as a criterion of science has become dubious in recent decades, especially in the fields of social sciences. There is another view suggesting that Karl Popper was not a perfect falsificationist when it comes to social sciences (Redman, 1991). Hence, the criticism of Menger's methodology from a Popperian perspective, as Hutchison did, from any point of view is not crucial. Menger's argument on the impossibility of testing theories has not yet been logically discarded.

Fourth, there is a question of how we make a clear distinction between exact theory and empirical-realistic theory. Menger admits that the elements of the first would be established partly through empirical-realistic analysis (Menger, 1883: 41). And he observes that while exact laws describe the increase of the price through the increase of desire under certain assumptions in terms of their quantity, the realistic law describes it in terms of their ratio (1883: 58). However, it seems to be a question of self-reflective interpretation of a theory rather than of its internal logic whether a theory should be categorized as exact or empirical-realistic. The difference seems to be just a question of degree, of quantitative precision or the resolution of the predictive power. Thus, it seems to be difficult to find a clear demarcation between the exact and the realistic theories. At this point, Menger seems to misunderstand the nature of 'law'.[16] If the difference between the exact and the empirical-realistic laws were just a matter of degree of precision, one of the main issues of the controversy would be reconciled: they would find their own places in a variety of approaches in social sciences in terms of the degree of abstractness, the degree of generality of law and the degree of forms and scopes of testing.[17] However, if we admit this reconciliation of the controversy, we would also come to admit that Menger's criticism of the German Historical School did not have a decisive impact. Is this a correct evaluation for the history of economic methodology? At least, we need to consider why both Mises and Hayek developed their methodological investigations from Menger. The place of Menger's contribution to methodology would be properly situated when we trace the forgoing process and how successors developed Menger's heritage.

3.2. Mises

As a representative of Austrian Economics, Mises undertook the task of providing a strong justification for the exact theory that Menger manifested. For Mises, justifying the status of exact theory (general law) seemed to corroborate the validity of the following proposition: it is logically impossible to assume that the law of the market economy could be transformed into the law of the socialist economy. Thus the argument on the justification of methodology for Mises is connected with a basic theory of ideology through the function of 'the thought-ladenness of methodology'. Let us examine how Mises developed Menger's methodology.

As stated in the last section, Menger's methodology did not give us any positive justification for exact theory. Although it is sometimes said that Menger founded his methodology on the Aristotelian philosophy of realism, it is not well grounded: considering this statement, Azuma (1985) argues as follows.

While Aristotle regarded natural science as exact knowledge, he regarded the science of the state (social science) as the contingent knowledge due to its fluid character of the object. Menger, on the other hand, made a categorical distinction between natural and social sciences not by means of their characters of the respective objects, but by means of their epistemological characters. And he insisted that exact knowledge is possible even in the investigation of social sciences when the exact method is effective. This transformation of the methodological perspective would be successful when we assume that (1) the cognition of the theory is subjectively universal and independent of the contingent character of reality, or (2) the reality of the social phenomena is not fluid in its substance. If we accept the first interpretation, Menger's methodology would be properly placed in the Kantian tradition of epistemology rather than in the Aristotelian tradition, in its emphasis on the universal subjectivity of the cognition. If we take the second interpretation, his methodology would be located in the Aristotelian tradition, though its foundation seems to be contingent. Whether or not the exact approach is effective depends on how social scientists form their cognition of reality: when they regard social reality as stable, then the exact approach would be justifiable. When they regard social reality as fluid, the approach would not be justifiable.

In order to overcome the epistemological ambivalence in Menger's methodology, Mises tried to develop a system of logical deductions named 'praxeology' from an a priori true proposition; 'human being acts'. Mises aimed to give a final solution to Menger's problem of founding the methodology of exact theory in social sciences. He presented a firm foundation for the deduction of universal laws without appealing to any positivistic criteria of testability. Mises's idea also gives us a successful demarcation between exact and empirical theories by reference to the criterion of the deduction from an a priori true proposition.[18]

Mises's praxeology has been criticized and almost neglected due to the dominance of positivism throughout the twentieth century: for positivists, Mises's apriorism seems to have been attributed to the realm of metaphysics because it is not subjected to any test by experiences. However, as our understanding of the nature of 'science' becomes more elaborate, Mises's methodology becomes more considerable: It gave us a criticism for the self-understanding of a positivistic conception of science.

The other thing Mises adopted from Menger's methodology was the transformation of the concept of 'apriorism'. Mises developed Menger's methodology in the direction of the Kantian epistemology. Barry Smith calls Menger's apriorism 'reflectionist apriorism', because it assumes that (1) a true proposition is attainable when the truth reflects reality and (2) that proposition does not need to be exposed to a test of confirmation. On the other hand, Smith labels Mises's methodology 'impositionist apriorism', since it assumes that human beings need to impose the categories of their minds in order to attain a priori knowledge, for otherwise we would see the state of affairs in a kaleidoscopic change (Mises, 1949: 32; Smith, 1990: 280). This impositionist view assumes that there is a true category of our mind prior to our experience. In fact, this view was shared among new Kantians (including Max Weber) at his time. Among them, Mises took a particular position that takes basic categories of human action as a priori true. The development of the methodological prescriptions from Menger to Mises would be described as a transformation from 'reflectionist apriorism' to 'impositionist apriorism'. It is in this transformation that Mises overcame the difficulties in Menger's methodology: for Mises, the impositionist apriorism gives a special foundation for exact theories in assuming that there is an a priori true structure of human mind. Of course, it would be necessary to examine to what degree Mises's solution is successful for developing Menger's methodology. However, we can find a historical succession of Menger's project of founding methodology in a firm epistemology in Mises's work.[19]

3.3. Hayek

Next, let us examine the development of methodology from Menger to Hayek. As I have stated above, Hayek evaluates Menger's methodology emphasizing his arguments on the limits of science. Menger's appraisal of the methodology of the old historical school of law is based on the conception of the spontaneity of a social order and this insight comes to develop Hayek's theory of spontaneous order. However, although Hayek succeeded Menger's methodology in its ideological aspect, he seems to have discarded a large part of it. The following examination will show how Hayek partly took over and also discarded Menger's legacy.

Hayek regards the following question by Menger as a central task in which social scientists need to engage: how are institutions which serve our common welfare generated without our common will for their creation (1952: 146–7)?

In order to investigate this problem, Hayek models methodological individualism, a constitutive method in which he succeeds Menger's heritage (1973; Hashimoto, 1991: 172–4). However, what Hayek really did in his study of social order was not to address this question directly but to explain the spontaneous character of the order through the study of history of ideas. He uses neither methodological individualism nor the constitutive method coherently. The discourse of methodological individualism in Hayek's work seems to be a transient strategy to persuade his opponents in the context of 'the thought-ladenness of methodology'.[20]

On the other hand, Hayek regards the issue of justification in Menger's methodology as irrelevant to his investigation. Unlike Mises, Hayek does not think that giving a scientific foundation for general laws in social sciences serves to support the superiority of the market economy. For Hayek, it is more important to criticize harmful effects of 'scientism', which has no understanding for the limits of science. In place of scientism, Hayek tried to restore the tradition of 'moral science' or '*Geisteswissenschaft*'. Here he was critical towards Menger's methodology, which places too much emphasis on the exactness of the theory and the similarity between natural and social sciences. Hayek states that it is easy to see how Menger was greatly concerned about the natural sciences and there is a strong bias as to their method in Menger's work (Hayek, 1934: 396). In contrast to Menger's scientistic attitude, Hayek emphasizes the fact that a law in social sciences describes 'a belief of human being' and is based on the methodology of subjectivism. While Menger conceives that the knowledge both in common sense and in science is a copy ('*Abbild*') of the phenomena in mind, Hayek conceives that the valid knowledge in social sciences is the 'understanding of the subjective ideas of human being'. According to Hayek, the data in social sciences are subjective and include agents' interpretations. In addition, the conclusions drawn from that data are not what state 'the objective facts' but remain as 'the constitutive'.[21] When Hayek criticizes Menger's methodology in its scientific proclivity, Hayek seems to be alert of the issue of the connection between socialism and constructivism: Hayek seems to find an ideological hazard in Menger's exact approach.

Suppose that we conceive the relations between theories (laws) and realities as fixed. And suppose next that we can make no distinction between natural and social sciences in terms of methodology. Then, what we would get is a justification for a project of constructivism: the constructivist controllability of the object in natural sciences gives us the implication that the very same controllability in policy making is possible and scientifically valid. The whole society would seem to be controllable. This is the thought-ladenness of methodology derived from our supposition of the methodological monism. Hayek was critical of this implication of Menger's methodology.

One may point out that there is a similarity of Menger's and Hayek's methodologies in their reluctance to admit the testability or the falsifiability of theories.[22] However, this similarity does not imply the resemblance of their concern. Hayek proposes a method of 'pattern prediction' as a research program in social sciences and this methodology is quite contrary to Menger's exact approach (Hayek, 1973: 278). Concerning marginal utility theory, Hayek sees its validity derived from a method of pattern prediction, namely from its rough predictive power, whereas Menger sees its validity stemming from its exactness under certain ceteris paribus clauses.

To sum up: while Mises developed Menger's methodology of justificationism through his praxeological conception of universal truth, Hayek succeeded Menger's methodology on the issue of the limits of science and its implication for the ideology. On the other hand, Hayek also criticized Menger's methodology in terms of its inclination to the scientism and he discarded Menger's exact approach. From a perspective of the historical transformation from justificationism to non-justificationism, Hayek's methodology would be more successful than Mises's in developing Menger's legacy. However, in the subsequent development of the methodology from non-justificationism to anarchism of science, which denies any advantageous status of 'the science', Mises's research program could be estimated pragmatically as one of the fruitful heuristics as well as Hayek's: the world of methodological anarchism gives room for Mises's position.

4. Conclusion

In this chapter, I have raised three points: (a) a new interpretation of the *Methodenstreit*, (b) a critical examination of Carl Menger's methodology of economics and (c) an interpretation of the continuity and change of methodology within the Austrian School of economics, from Menger to Mises and Hayek.

(a) The *Methodenstreit* was a controversy between Carl Menger, the founder of the Austrian School of Economics, and Gustav von Schmoller, the leading representative of the younger German Historical School of economics. The debate was mainly about methodological issues, especially on economics. Joseph Schumpeter notably gave a standard interpretation of the controversy, from an internal perspective of scientific research programs. However, I have presented another interpretation from a wider perspective of methodology in terms of its ladenness of extra-scientific ideas. I claim that some aspects of Menger's methodology can be explained by his ideological commitment to the idea of spontaneous order and of anti-constructivism. Menger is characterized not only as a social scientist but also as a thinker of liberal ideology in terms of his methodology.

(b) It is without doubt that Menger's methodology made a great contribution to the advancement of social sciences, but I have raised some criticism especially on (1) the justifiability of his 'exact theories', (2) the productivity of his research program, (3) the falsifiability of his methodology and (4) the criterion of demarcation between the 'exact' and the empirical theories.

(c) By examining Menger's methodology and his ideological commitment, I have shed new light on the theoretical development of the Austrian School of economics from Menger to Mises and Hayek. I have examined how and why Mises and Hayek processed Menger's methodology in the development of ideological controversy between capitalism and socialism.

Notes

1. See Hashimoto (1994) for the details of the functional analysis of methodology.
2. See Hayek's comment on the reception of Menger's work (Hayek, 1973: 279).
3. Aristotelian Realism appears in Menger (1883: 161–2). See also Kauder (1965), Azuma (1985) and Smith (1990: 264–70).
4. Menger (1884) states that a historian as a 'retrospective predictor' cannot be an exclusive authority in the realm of practical economics.
5. On this point, compare my interpretation with that of Alter (1990a, 1990b). My interpretation is different from Alter's in the following two ways: first, Menger's concept of 'understanding' is not limited to the realm of social sciences; second, Menger's method of 'understanding' does not have a strong connection with his methodological individualism.
6. See Schumpeter's (1926) view on Schmoller's methodology.
7. Some might say that Aristotle's realism could serve as a positive basis for Menger's methodology. However, we will argue that it is not in the following section.
8. Schumpeter (1914, 1954) defends Schmoller's research program and wrote a long essay, titled 'Gustav Schmoller and the Problems of Today' (Schumpeter, 1926), where he put forward his evaluation of Schmoller's methodology. Although Schumpeter's evaluation of Schmoller's methodology was very unique at that time, his interpretation has become standard today. Yoshida (1986: 396) also points out that Schmoller was right in criticizing Menger's proclivity to a scholastic philosophy. See also Tamanoi (1975).
9. See also Yoshida (1986) and Smith (1990: 274) on the later historical school's reception and incorporation of Menger's methodology.
10. The basic and original provision of the methodological belief of the Historical School lies in the idea that the components of scientific economics should consist of both conclusions and generalizations attained from historical monographs (Schumpeter, 1954: 809). The provisions of the Historical School are: (1) to approach materials with a minimal burden of an a priori cognition, (2) to conceive various relations, (3) to increase an a priori recognition as to future events, (4) to attain new views on various materials and

(5) to proceed the investigation through a continual interaction between examining and processing materials (Schumpeter, 1926).

11. See Schumpeter (1914, 1926).
12. See Schmoller (1883).
13. It is known that Menger was a liberal who supported interventionism. See Böhm's (1985) study on Menger's collected works. In contrast, Streissler's (1990) study on Menger's Lecture to Crown Prince Rudolf shows that Menger was more libertarian than Adam Smith. See also Kirzner (1990). In any event, these studies on Menger are not related to the study on his methodology.
14. See Menger's (1883: 162) comment on a pragmatic explanation of his methodological individualism on the origins and spontaneous processes of social phenomena.
15. Hayek's theoretical framework of constructivism versus spontaneous order is developed from Menger's argument. Here we owe Hayek's framework for articulating Menger's thought-ladenness of methodology.
16. See Kaufmann (1933). Kaufmann describes Menger's methodological position as 'analytical school'. Menger's terminology of 'exact' approach has been changed; from 'analytic', 'analytic-synthetic', 'analytic-compositive' to 'exact', and subsequently it changed to 'resolute-compositive' and 'compositive'. Hayek prefers to use 'compositive', See Alter (1990b: 329).
17. On this point, see Birner's (1990: 248) proposal for the demarcation between exact and empirical theory.
18. I place Mises's methodology in a Kantian tradition. However, there is another interpretation, which places Mises in the Aristotelian tradition. See Smith (1986, 1990) and Rothbard (1957, 1976).
19. Mises's justificationism of methodology had a significant role during the ideological debate in the last century. See Hashimoto (1994) for the examination of the problem on the thought-ladenness of methodology in Mises.
20. See Hashimoto (1991). On the similarity of thought between Menger and Hayek, see Shearmur (1986, 1990).
21. See Hayek (1952: 61–4). Hayek's usage of the constitutive method is different from Menger's: While Menger sees reality as composed of its constituents, and theories therefore can be the image of a reality, Hayek regards reality as more chaotic and the constitutive character is primarily applied to theories and constitutions, hence his emphasis on human minds and the results of human actions.
22. See Hashimoto (1991) on the transition of Hayek's attitude on the falsifiability of theories.

References

Alter, M. (1990a) *Carl Menger and the Origins of Austrian Economics*, Oxford: Westview Press.

Alter, M. (1990b) 'What do we know about Menger?', in Caldwell (ed.) (1990).

Azuma, S. (1985) 'Methodological Characters of Menger's Economics', *Ningenkagakukenkyukiyo*, 2, Edogawagakuen (in Japanese).

Böhm, S. (1985) 'The political solution to a fundamental problem in Menger's methodology and beyond', in Caldwell (ed.) (1990).

Caldwell, B. J. (ed.) (1990) *Carl Menger and His Legacy in Economics*, Durham, NC: Duke University Press.

Grassl, W. and Smith, B. (eds) (1986) *Austrian Economics: Historical and Philosophical Background*, London: Croom Helm.

Hashimoto, T. (1991) 'Hayek's labyrinth: on his methodological transformations', *Gendai-shiso*, 19(12) (in Japanese).

Hashimoto, T. (1994) *Logic of Liberty: Mises, Popper and Hayek*, Tokyo: Sobunsha (in Japanese).

Hayek, F. A. (1934) 'Carl Menger', in *The Collected Works of Carl Menger* (1871–1915), 4 volumes with an Introduction by F.A. Hayek, London: The London School of Economics and Political Science, 1934–1936.

Hayek, F. A. (1952) *The Counter-Revolution of Science: Studies on the Abuse of Reason*, Glencoe: The Free Press.

Hayek, F. A. (1973) 'The Place of Menger's *Grundsätze* in the History of Economic Thought', in Hicks and Weber (eds) (1973).

Hicks, J. R. and Weber, W., (eds) (1973) *Carl Menger and the Austrian School of Economics*, Oxford: Clarendon Press.

Hutchison, T. W. (1973) 'Some Themes from Investigations into Method', in Hicks and Weber (eds) (1973).

Hutchison, T. W. (1981) *The Politics and Philosophy of Economics: Marxians, Keynesians and Austrians*, Oxford: Basil Blackwell.

Kauder, E. (1965) *A History of Marginal Utility Theory*, Princeton: Princeton University Press.

Kaufmann, F. (1933) 'On the subject-matter and method of economic science', *Economica*, O.S., 42: 381–401.

Kirzner, I. M. (1990) 'Menger, Classical Liberalism, and the Austrian School of Economics', in Caldwell (ed.) (1990).

Menger, C. [1883] (1969) 'Untersuchungen über die Methode der Sozialwissenschaften, und der politischen Ökonomie insbesondere', in *Gesammelte Werke*, Band II, Tübingen: J.C.B. Mohr.

Menger, C. [1884] (1969) 'Die Irrtümer des Historismus in der deutschen Nationalökonomie', in *Gesammelte Werke*, Band II, Tübingen: J.C.B. Mohr.

Milford, K. (1990) 'Menger's methodology', in Caldwell (ed.) (1990).

Mises, L. von (1949) *Human Action: A Treatise on Economics*, New Haven: Yale University Press.

Oppler, E. (1930) *Der Begriff des Wirtschaftsgesetzes in der Volkswirtschaftslehre: Eine problemgeschichtliche Untersuchung*, Münster: Helios.

Redman, D. A. (1991) *Economics and the Philosophy of Science*, Oxford: Oxford University Press.

Rothbard, M. N. (1957) 'In defense of extreme apriorism', *Southern Economic Journal*, 23(3): 315–20.

Rothbard, M. N. (1976) 'Praxeology: The method of Austrian Economics', in E. G. Dolan (ed.) *The Foundations of Austrian Economics*, Kansas City: Sheed and Ward.

Schmoller, G. von (1883) 'Zur Methodologie der Staats- und Sozialwissenschaften', *Schmollers Jahrbuch für Gesetzgebung, Verwaltung und Volkswirtschaft*, N.F., 7: 975–94.

Schumpeter, J. A. (1914) *Epochen der Dogmen- und Methodengeschichte: Grundriß der Sozialökonomik*, 1. Aufl., Tübingen.

Schumpeter, J. A. (1926) 'Gustav v. Schmoller und die Probleme von Heute', *Schmollers Jahrbuch für Gesetzgebung, Verwaltung und Volkswirtschaft*, 50: 337–88.

Schumpeter, J. A. (1954) History of Economic Analysis, New York: Oxford University Press.

Shearmur, J. (1986) 'The Austrian Connection: Hayek's Liberalism and the Thought of Carl Menger', in Grassl and Smith (eds) (1986).

Shearmur, J. (1990) 'From Hayek to Menger: Biology, Subjectivism and Welfare', in Caldwell (ed.) (1990).

Smith, B. (1986) 'Austrian Economics and Austrian Philosophy', in Grassl and Smith (eds) (1986).

Smith, B. (1990) 'Aristotle, Menger, Mises: An essay in the metaphysics of economics', in Caldwell (ed.)(1990).

Streissler, E. W. (1990) 'Carl Menger on economic policy: The Lectures to Crown Prince Rudolf', in Caldwell (ed.) (1990).

Tamanoi, Y. (1975) 'Menger versus Schmoller on methodological debate', in *Tenkan-suru-keizaigaku*, Tokyo: Tokyo University Press (in Japanese).

Yoshida, S. (1986) 'Translator's introduction', *in Keizaigaku-no-Houhou*, Tokyo: Nihon-hyouronsha, the Japanese translation of Menger (1883; 1884 =1986) (in Japanese).

Name Index

Subject Index